Social Foundations for Becoming a Teacher

Forrest W. Parkay
Washington State University

PEARSON

Boston ○ New York ○ San Francisco
Mexico City ○ Montreal ○ Toronto ○ London ○ Madrid ○ Munich ○ Paris
Hong Kong ○ Singapore ○ Tokyo ○ Cape Town ○ Sydney

Executive Editor and Publisher: Stephen D. Dragin
Editorial Assistant: Meaghan Minnick
Marketing Manager: Tara Kelly
Production Editor: Annette Joseph
Editorial Production Service: Modern Graphics, Inc.
Composition Buyer: Linda Cox
Manufacturing Buyer: Andrew Turso
Electronic Composition: Modern Graphics, Inc.
Interior Design: Glenna Collett
Photo Researcher: Po Yee Oster
Cover Administrator: Kristina Mose-Libon

For related titles and support materials, visit our online catalog at www.ablongman.com.

Between the time website information is gathered and then published, it is not unusual for some sites to have closed. Also, the transcription of URLs can result in typographical errors. The publisher would appreciate notification where these errors occur so that they may be corrected in subsequent editions.

Library of Congress Cataloging-in-Publication Data
Parkay, Forrest W.
  Social foundations for becoming a teacher / Forrest W. Parkay.—1. ed.
    p. cm.
  Includes bibliographical references and index.
  ISBN 0-205-42422-8
    1. Education—Social aspects—United States. 2. Teaching—Social aspects—United States.
3. Teachers—Professional relationships—United States. I. Title.

  LC191.4.P39 2006
  306.43—dc22

                                                                    2005050906

Printed in the United States of America

Photo Credits: Page 2, Tim Boyle/Getty Images; 20, Rachel Epstein/The Image Works; 23, Marc Asnin/CORBIS SABA; 31, Rhoda Sidney/The Image Works; 42, Michael Newman/PhotoEdit; 52, Ariel Skelley/CORBIS; 63, Mary Kate Denny/PhotoEdit; 73, Jim Cummins/Getty Images; 84, Bettmann/CORBIS; 88, 90, 92, 96, North Wind Picture Archives; 97, 99, Library of Congress; 101, 102, North Wind Picture Archives; 104, The Granger Collection, New York; 105, Bettmann/CORBIS; 106, Courtesy of the State Historical Society of Wisconsin, image number WHi (x3) 48032; 107, 108, Lyrl Ahern; 109, Bettmann/CORBIS; 110, Lyrl Ahern; 124, Zephyr Picture/IndexStock Imagery; 137, Library of Congress; 141, Robert E. Daemmrich/Getty Images; 146, Rick Gerharter/Impact Visuals; 149, AP/Wide World Photos; 170, Tony Freeman/PhotoEdit; 185, Will Hart/PhotoEdit; 190, Stephen Ferry/Liaison/Getty Images; 193, Will Faller; 201, Michael Newman/ PhotoEdit; 212, Cindy Charles/PhotoEdit; 221, Lindfors Photography; 225, Elena Rooraid/ PhotoEdit; 238, Mark Richards/PhotoEdit; 244, Jim Cummins/CORBIS.

Brief Contents

Contents

3   History of Education in the United States   84

Diversity in U.S. Education   124

**5 Social Realities and Today's
    Schools   170**

**6 Teacher Leaders and the
    Professionalization of
    Teaching   212**

Preface

Teaching is one of the world's most important professions—and one of the most challenging. With continuing calls for higher standards, greater teacher accountability, and legislation such as the No Child Left Behind Act of 2001, becoming a teacher requires more professionalism and expertise than ever. To facilitate your journey toward becoming a successful teacher, *Social Foundations for Becoming a Teacher* will provide you with an understanding of the societal influences on our nation's schools. The book explains the trends, issues, and forces that influence teachers in today's high-stakes environment of education. The book illustrates how social forces—parental concerns, popular culture, gender, ideologies, beliefs about race and ethnicity, and historical events, to name a few—come together to determine teachers' daily experiences in the classroom.

The book also presents a realistic description of teachers' working conditions, so you can make a critical decision about becoming a teacher. Several features of the book are designed to give you an accurate picture of the world of teaching and to prepare you to take advantage of teachers' expanding leadership roles.

A Teachers' Voices feature in each chapter presents a short, first-person article written by a teacher to illustrate how teachers apply chapter content to actual classroom situations. The features will provide you with firsthand insights into real-world challenges teachers face and practical solutions for meeting those challenges.

To help you get the most out of your teacher education program, each chapter of this book includes a feature titled Relevant Standards. This feature illustrates how chapter content relates to standards developed by four professional associations: the Interstate New Teacher Assessment and Support Consortium (INTASC), the National Council for Accreditation of Teacher Education (NCATE), the Praxis Series: Professional Assessments for Beginning Teachers, and the National Board for Professional Teaching Standards (NBPTS).

Each chapter also includes a Case for Reflection designed to give you an opportunity to reflect on the contemporary issues teachers must deal with on a daily basis. The cases focus on controversial trends and issues that have aroused public opinion and have attracted media attention.

A Technology in Teaching feature in each chapter illustrates how educational technology is related to chapter content. This feature also provides current examples of how educational technologies are influencing schools and the profession of teaching.

Social Foundations for Becoming a Teacher also includes many learning aids to help you prepare for a rewarding future in teaching. Guiding Questions at the beginning of each chapter present the questions posed in the main headings within each chapter. Realistic opening scenarios present decision-making or problem-solving situations teachers frequently confront. At the end of each chapter, Reflective Application Activities (Discussion Questions, Professional Journal, Online Assignments, and Observations and Interviews) present further opportunities to apply chapter content.

The book also includes a Professional Portfolio feature that will enable you to document your professional growth over time. These features present guidelines for creating portfolio entries that you can use when you begin teaching, or you may wish to use selected portfolio entries during the process of applying for your first teaching position. As a further study aid, Key Terms and Concepts are boldfaced in the text and listed with page cross-references at the ends of chapters. A Glossary at the end of the book can help you quickly locate the definitions of key terms and concepts and the text pages on which they appear.

Acknowledgments

Many members of the Allyn and Bacon team provided the author with expert guidance and support during the writing of *Social Foundations for Becoming a Teacher*. The author benefited from the consistent encouragement and excellent suggestions provided by Steve Dragin, Executive Editor and Publisher. His extensive understanding of textbook publishing was invaluable in conceptualizing the book. In addition, Meaghan Minnick, Editorial Assistant, provided helpful feedback on the manuscript and steadfast support and encouragement.

The author wishes to thank the following reviewers, who provided concise, helpful feedback on draft manuscripts of the book: Don W. Collins (Western Kentucky University), James J. Rivard (Oakland University & Marygrove College), and Elizabeth M. Werre (Pensacola Junior College).

The author also appreciates the support of his friends and colleagues while writing this book. In particular, Phyllis Erdman, Chair of the Department of Educational Leadership and Counseling Psychology at Washington State University; Gail Furman, Coordinator of the Educational Leadership Program Area; Len Foster, Coordinator of the Higher Education Program Area; and Eric J. Anctil, Assistant Professor of Educational Leadership, provided invaluable ideas and much-appreciated encouragement and support.

In addition, the author gives a sincere thanks to students (many of them now teachers and school administrators) in the classes he has taught at Washington State University. Conversations with them over the years have been thought provoking and professionally rewarding. And, for demonstrating the power of professional inquiry, he owes a profound debt to a great teacher, mentor, and friend, Herbert A. Thelen, Professor Emeritus, University of Chicago.

Lastly, the author would like to thank Wu Mei for her friendship, spiritual support, and encouragement during the writing of this book. Ni shi diyige, ye shi zuihou yige, wade yiqie.

Forrest W. Parkay

Social Foundations
for Becoming
a Teacher

1 Societal Influences on Education

We would be naïve if we did not realize that there are factors in our culture that can have negative effects on teachers and their students.

—Carl Glickman, Stephen Gordon, and Jovita Ross-Gordon
SuperVision and Instructional Leadership, 2004

Ann is a fifteen-year-old African American who lives in a poor area of a large city. She is the oldest child in a family of six children. Three years ago, her father left the family because he was unable to find a job. He knew his family would receive more financial support from the government if he left the family. Since her mother works during the evening, Ann must take care of the apartment and her younger brother and two younger sisters when she gets home from school. The apartment has only three rooms and is continually infested with cockroaches. It has poor plumbing, and occasionally hot water is not available. During the winter months, the children must wear heavy sweaters or jackets to stay warm. The children usually go to school without breakfast, and they frequently go to bed hungry.

Frank is a fifteen-year-old white boy who lives in a middle-class suburb of the same city. He has a seventeen-year-old sister. Frank's father is a physician who works at a hospital downtown and commutes daily, often arriving home late in the evening. Lately, his father has been staying overnight at the hospital two or three times a month. Frank's mother is socially active, and she has a serious drinking problem. His parents often have loud arguments and have begun to talk about divorce. Frank's sister uses cocaine, and she often spends the weekend with her boyfriend. Frank is well fed, lives in a large home, and receives a generous monthly allowance.

Harold is a fifteen-year-old white boy who lives near a factory at the edge of the same city. He has an older brother and older sister. Harold's father works at the nearby factory on the assembly line. Harold lives in a small, but comfortable, three-bedroom home. The family doesn't have money for "extras," but the family's basic needs are well satisfied. Harold's parents are deeply religious, and he attends church every Sunday and again on Wednesday evening. His father, a Vietnam veteran and member of the local VFW, often shows visitors three medals in a framed display case hanging on a living-room wall. Harold's parents spend much time with their children. Often, they overhear their parents talking about how "liberals" and minority groups are "taking over the country."

Guiding Questions

1. What are the social foundations of education?
2. What are society's goals for schools?
3. What are the characteristics of schools in our society?
4. As social institutions, what are schools like?
5. What are the characteristics of "successful" schools?
6. What can we learn from the foundations of education in other countries?

All three of the youth in the above scenario attend the same high school and many of the same classes. Harold walks four blocks to school, and both Ann and Frank ride the bus. Obviously, Ann, Frank, and Harold are unique with regard to the social backgrounds from which they come. Their teachers, however, must deal with the differences they bring from diverse social backgrounds. On the other hand, their teachers must understand the similarities among these and other students and provide them all with appropriate learning experiences.

What Are the Social Foundations of Education?

To effectively teach students like Ann, Frank, and Harold, teachers must have a unique array of knowledge, skills, attitudes, and values. They must have knowledge of themselves, their subjects, their students, and educational theories and research, for example. Successful teaching also requires knowledge of the **social foundations of education**—the trends, issues, and forces that shape public and private education in the United States. The foundations of education influence the effectiveness of schools and the development of youth and children across the country. The ability of schools to address issues such as poverty, school violence, drug use, and homelessness has profound consequences for students and their teachers.

To facilitate your journey toward becoming a successful teacher, *Social Foundations for Becoming a Teacher* will provide you with an understanding of the societal influences on our nation's schools. The book will explain how social forces such as parental concerns, popular culture, gender ideologies, beliefs about race and ethnicity, and historical events influence the profession of teaching. A companion volume to this book, *Political Foundations for Becoming a Teacher*, examines four additional foundations of education—political, legal, philosophical, and economic—and how these foundations are related to continuing calls from various groups for educational reform and teacher accountability.

Today's Influences on Tomorrow's Schools

Schooling in the United States is shaped not only by the *past* and the *present*; it is shaped by the *future* as well. Society is continuously changing, not static. As a result, teachers must continually modify their understanding of how society influences schools. Success as a teacher requires continuous reevaluation of the past, the present, and the future.

Though no one can predict the future, it has a profound effect on teaching. As Alvin Toffler (1970, 363) stated decades ago in his best-selling book, *Future Shock*, "All education springs from some image of the future. If the image of the future held by a society is grossly inaccurate, its educational system will betray its youth." Among the factors that will influence schools in the future are social, economic, and political forces and technological developments (see Figure 1.1).

Social Forces   Soaring numbers of runaway children and cases of child abuse suggest that the family is in trouble. Tomorrow's teachers will find that more and more

Figure 1.1   Significant forces shaping the future of education in the United States.

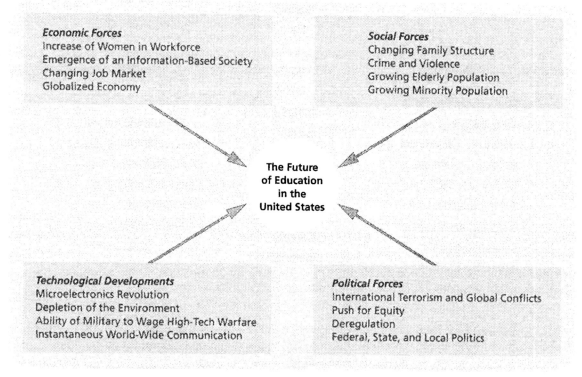

of their students are from families that are smaller, have working mothers, have a single parent present, or have unrelated adults living in the home.

While crime and delinquency may have declined recently, they will continue to impact tomorrow's schools. Much of the crime that occurs in and around schools is related to students' use of drugs. Violence and vandalism in some schools have already reached epidemic proportions. What was originally characterized as an urban problem has now spread to the suburbs and rural areas. Certainly, the reduction of school crime and violence is one of the critical challenges tomorrow's teachers will face.

The United States of the future will be even more culturally diverse than it is today. African Americans, Latino and Hispanic Americans, Asian Americans and Pacific Islanders, Native Americans and Alaskan Natives, and others will come to represent an ever-increasing proportion of the total population. Teachers of the future will be responsible for developing curricula and instructional methods that cultivate the potentialities of students from a wide variety of backgrounds.

With computer-age advances in health care, the life span of Americans is steadily being extended. The 85-plus group is the fastest-growing demographic segment in the United States, and the number of people 100 and older has exploded as well.

The U.S. Census Bureau projects that the number of people age 85 and older could increase from 4 million in 2000 to 19 million by 2050. And the number of people age 100 and older is projected to more than quadruple from 65,000 in 2000 to 381,000 in 2030. In addition, older Americans of the future will be better educated and more physically, intellectually, and politically active than their predecessors. Tomorrow's elderly will recognize education as one of the keys for a satisfying, productive old age.

Economic Forces   The jobs we are trained for today may not exist tomorrow. During the last half decade, for example, very few kinds of work have been unaltered by the onrushing developments in computer technology. Today's worker must be able to learn to operate an ever-increasing array of technological devices. Workers who excel are measured not by how much they can produce but by how quickly and well they can learn new skills.

The composition of the workforce is also changing. As a result of gains made by the women's movement, for example, more and more women are not only moving out into the workforce, they are moving up. Women are obtaining increasing numbers of executive-level positions in the professions, business, and education. Slowly, the workplace is changing to accommodate the career patterns of women. Business and industry, for example, are receiving pressure from women's groups to provide preschool and day care programs as part of their fringe-benefit packages.

Another major economic force in the United States is the continuing shift from a product-oriented to an information-based, service-oriented economy. Moreover, this "new" economy is not the isolated, self-contained economy of one nation; it is a global economy. Our participation, cooperation, and competition in this global economy depends on rapid communication of information around the world. Information is steadily becoming the critical resource of our age and the ability to learn it and to use it the chief aim of education.

Political Forces   Education in the future will certainly be strongly influenced by political forces at the local, state, and federal levels. As a result of continuing deregulation of business and industry, the way has been paved for the corporate sector to become more involved in education. Comments made by Frank Shrontz, Chairman and CEO of the Boeing Company, at Washington State University's College of Education typify the willingness of business to participate in improving American education:

> Providing our children with a world class education is not just desirable—it's a matter of our national survival. The challenge is too big for one sector of society to tackle alone. That leaves us no real alternative but to foster a true partnership of effort from individuals and groups in both the private and public sector.

Companies such as Boeing, IBM, Coca-Cola, RJR Nabisco, and General Electric, recognizing the stake they have in improving education, are making unprecedented grants to encourage educators to restructure schools.

Another dominant political force will be continued demands for equity in all sectors of American life. For example, the constitutionality of school funding laws will be challenged where inequities are perceived, and tax reform measures will be adopted to promote equitable school funding.

Technological Developments   The microelectronics revolution has had a great impact on education. Computers, video equipment, and high-speed telecommunications equipment are having profound effects on our lifestyles. These technological advances are changing not only how we learn, and what we learn but are also forcing us to realize that the future will require all of us to be continuous, lifelong learners.

Fiber-optic cables and communication via satellite have made possible instantaneous, worldwide communication. Research in computer-based artificial intelligence has produced systems that can recognize speech, read characters, and diagnose illnesses. Prototypes already exist of "teachable," "thinking" machines that can learn from experience and perform both inductive and deductive reasoning. This research may make possible new models of human intelligence with significant applications to teaching and learning.

The "Pillars" of Education in the United States

The social foundations can be compared to the pillars upon which a building rests. *Social Foundations for Becoming a Teacher* addresses six of these "pillars," as illustrated in Figure 1.2: (1) the role of schooling in society, (2) teachers' working conditions, (3) historical events that have influenced the development of education, (4) social issues and problems that impact schools, (5) increasing diversity and cultural pluralism, and (6) teacher leaders and the "professionalization" of teaching. This book will provide you with an understanding of how these six social founda-

Figure 1.2   Social foundations or "pillars" of education in the United States.

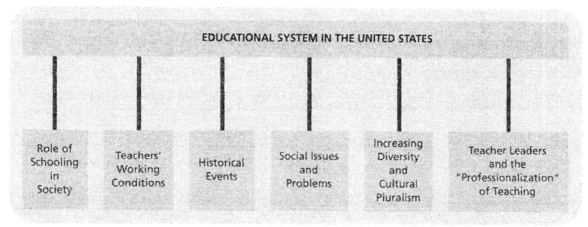

tions of education will influence your career as a teacher. The remainder of this chapter examines the first of these social foundations—the role of schooling in U.S. society.

What Are Society's Goals for Schools?

The United States, like other nations of the world, has established schools and educational programs to induct children and youth into society and to maintain, and improve, its culture and way of life. Throughout the United States, people agree that the purpose of schools is to educate. Unlike other societal institutions—family, mass media, work/career, the law, and healthcare, for example—the primary function of schools is teaching and learning. However, the public is not always in agreement about what the outcomes of this teaching and learning should be. Our disagreement about what it means to be an educated person illustrates this lack of consensus. Does having a college degree mean that one is educated? Or, is meeting life's challenges with integrity and humility the mark of an educated person? Might a hermit who lives a serene life at the base of a remote mountain be more educated than the corporate executive who received a degree from a prestigious university? Or, what is the definition of *education* used by the increasing number of colleges and universities that give course credit for "life experiences"?

Debate about the role of schooling in society is not new. In the fourth century B.C., philosopher Aristotle framed the debate this way: "The existing practice [of education] is perplexing; no one knows on what principle we should proceed—should the useful in life, or should virtue, or should the higher knowledge, be the aim of our training; all three opinions have been entertained" (1941, 1306). Aristotle's questions cannot be answered once and for all; instead, each generation must develop its own set of principles that apply to the role of schooling in society. While different groups in our society—educators, parents, students, and politicians, for example—have conflicting views on the specific goals of education, there is greater agreement on a broader, more general level. Currently, our nation's schools are focused on six broad goals: academic achievement, teaching values, socialization of children and youth, personal growth, social change, and expanding equality of opportunity for all groups in the United States.

Achievement of Academic Goals

Among the different perspectives on the role of schooling in society, the achievement of academic goals is the most universally agreed upon. Most people believe the primary purpose of schools is to provide students with academic knowledge and skills needed for schooling beyond high school or for the world of work. Political, religious, and cultural beliefs and ideologies aside, people believe that schools should teach academic content.

America's Education Goals   In 1994, President Clinton signed into law the **Goals 2000: Educate America Act**, to help schools achieve eight national academic goals. Six of these goals were developed at a 1989 educational summit meeting convened by the first President Bush for fifty state governors. The goals placed a high priority on increasing student achievement in English, mathematics, science, history, and geography; creating more effective learning environments in the nation's schools; providing for teachers' professional development; and increasing parental involvement.

In February 1999, the National Education Goals Panel acknowledged that the goals would not be met and passed a resolution to rename the National Education Goals as "America's Education Goals" and to continue striving to meet the eight goals "beyond the year 2000 without a specific deadline for their achievement." Although some states reached some goals by 2000, none achieved all eight. Schools in North Carolina, South Carolina, California, Colorado, and Texas showed the most signs of improvement during the 1990s. Though the goals were not met, the panel pointed out that America's Education Goals made significant contributions in the following areas: launching and supporting the academic standards movement, legitimizing "benchmarking" and state and international comparisons, increasing the attention paid to early childhood education, and focusing and sustaining educational reform (National Education Goals Panel 1999).

No Child Left Behind   In 2002, after almost 12 years of operation, the National Education Goals Panel was disbanded when the second President Bush signed the **No Child Left Behind (NCLB) Act**. Rather than emphasize academic goals per se, the NCLB reform bill mandated statewide testing in reading and mathematics each year in grades 3–8, and schools would be held accountable for students' performance on state proficiency tests. Key features of NCLB follow:

- States create their own standards for what a child should know and learn for all grades. Standards must be developed in math and reading immediately. Standards must also be developed for science by the 2005–06 school year.

- With standards in place, states must test every student's progress toward those standards by using tests that are aligned with the standards. Beginning in the 2002–03 school year, schools must administer tests in each of three grade spans: grades 3–5, grades 6–9, and grades 10–12 in all schools. Beginning in the 2005–06 school year, tests must be administered every year in grades 3 through 8 in math and reading. Beginning in the 2007–08 school year, science achievement must also be tested.

- Each state, school district, and school will be expected to make **Adequate Yearly Progress (AYP)** toward meeting state standards. This progress will be measured for all students by sorting test results for students who are economically disadvantaged, are from racial or ethnic minority groups, have disabilities, or have limited English proficiency.

- School and district performance will be publicly reported in district and state report cards. Individual school results will be on the district report cards.

- If the district or school continually fails to make adequate yearly progress toward the standards, then they will be held accountable (U.S. Department of Education 2002a).

While NCLB allows each of the fifty states to select the test it wishes to use, a Gallup poll of the public's attitudes toward the public schools revealed that 68 percent of respondents favor requiring all fifty states to use a nationally standardized test (Rose and Gallup 2002).

Education and Values

While debate continues about which academic goals schools should address, the public agrees that schools should teach values such as honesty, patriotism, fairness, and civility. The well-being of any society requires support of such values; they enable people from diverse backgrounds to live together peacefully. One poll of the public, for example, revealed that 90 percent or more believed that the following values should be taught in public schools: honesty, democracy, acceptance of people of different races and ethnic backgrounds, caring for friends and family, moral courage, and patriotism/love of country (Rose and Gallup 1999).

Support for prosocial values reflects the public's belief that the schools should play a key role in promoting the democratic ideal of equality for all. As President George Bush stated when he signed NCLB into law, "[I have a] deep belief in our public schools and their mission to build the mind and character of every child, from every background, in every part of America."

As teachers and other educators respond to social issues and changing values in the wider society, they are influenced by their own educational philosophies and by prevailing educational theories. As a result, current social concerns find their way into instructional practices, textbooks, teaching aids, and lesson plans. Often, curricular and instructional changes are made in the hope that changing what students learn will help solve social problems or achieve local, statewide, or national goals.

Divergent Values   Because the United States is so culturally diverse, proposed changes in education also reflect divergent values. This divergence can lead to controversies over curricular and instructional practices and conflicting calls for reform. For example, from time to time legal issues are raised in response to the demands of some groups that Christian teachings and observances be included in public school curricula or that materials regarded as objectionable on religious grounds be censored or banned. Similarly, legal issues have been raised in several states that have passed English-only laws (23 states had such laws as of 2003 [Crawford 2003]), and controversy erupted in California in late 1996 around the teaching of "ebonics" or "black English."

Additional controversies have arisen over calls to eliminate activities or symbols related to organized religion, including even secularized or commercialized ones such as Halloween and the Easter bunny. Moreover, instructional and curricular changes to promote greater social integration or equity among racial or ethnic groups may draw complaints of irrelevancy or reverse discrimination. For example, "traditionalists" may object to curriculum changes that reflect feminist views.

Teachers and administrators are not the only ones influenced by diverse values found in the larger society; curriculum planners, textbook authors, and publishers are influenced by trends in education and by social issues. In response to criticism, for example, textbook publishers are now careful to avoid bias in terms of gender, religion, class, race, and culture. However, because the goal of business is profit, publishers are most responsive to market trends and customer preferences. Publishers often are reluctant to risk losing sales by including subjects that are controversial or that may be offensive to their bigger customers. They also may modify textbooks to appeal to decision makers in populous states that make statewide adoptions of textbooks, such as California and Texas. About half the states have statewide adoption policies that school districts must follow in selecting textbooks.

As you can imagine, consensus on many educational reform issues and the values embedded in those issues is never achieved. However, because of their public accountability, schools must be prepared to respond to those issues. For example, one survey revealed that during a one-year period, half the school districts in Florida received complaints about curriculum content. Included were complaints claiming that the schools were undermining family values, overemphasizing globalism, underemphasizing patriotism, permitting profanity and obscenity, and teaching taboo subjects such as satanism and sex (Sheuerer and Parkay 1992). In the end, the creative and evaluative tasks involved in teaching are a source of both empowerment and frustration for teachers. Budget constraints, social and legal issues, and state and local curriculum mandates often determine instructional and curricular choices.

Emphasizing Our Nation's Successes   Two years after the terrorist attacks on the World Trade Center on September 11, 2001, the nonpartisan Albert Shanker Institute (named after the former head of the American Federation of Teachers, the nation's second largest teachers' union) released a report urging schools to place more emphasis on America's successes and less on America's "darker moments." The report, *Education for Democracy*, maintained that America's failings—Vietnam, Watergate, the impeachment hearings, and cynicism about politics in America, for example—are overemphasized in schools. The report called for greater emphasis in social studies courses on nondemocratic societies. "Sanitized accounts" of real-life horrors in these countries fail to show the "genius" of America's democratic system, according to the report. The report cited signs of apathy and low patriotism—for example, children touring Washington, D.C., said that Memorial Day is "the day the pools open" (Feller, September 10, 2003).

Socialization of Children and Youth

Through their experiences in schools, children and youth become socialized—they learn to participate responsibly in our nation's society. At the local level, this purpose is evident in countless schools whose mission statements focus on preparing students for responsible citizenship, further learning, and productive employment in our nation's economy. In effect, schools reflect or "mirror" society; they reproduce the knowledge, skills, values, and attitudes that society has identified as essential.

Education is the primary means of producing enlightened citizens. Without such a citizenry to hold it together, a society, especially a democratic society, is at risk. The need for each nation to socialize its children and youth was recognized by Emile Durkheim (1858–1917), the great French sociologist and philosopher, when he stated in *Education and Sociology* that "society can survive only if there exists among its members a significant degree of homogeneity; education perpetuates and reinforces this homogeneity by fixing in the child, from the beginning, the essential similarities collective life demands" (Durkheim 1956, 70).

Additionally, schools, more than any other institution in our society, assimilate persons from different ethnic, racial, religious, and cultural backgrounds and pass on the values and customs of the majority. For example, California schools must serve children from more than 80 different language groups and cultures (Groves, August 15, 2000). Through the schools, children and youth from such diverse backgrounds learn English and learn about the importance of American holidays such as the Fourth of July or Memorial Day; about the contributions of Thomas Jefferson, Abraham Lincoln, or Dr. Martin Luther King Jr.; and about the importance of citizenship in a democracy.

Education and Personal Growth

Since U.S. society places great value on the dignity and worth of the individual, schools are to help the young to become all that they are capable of becoming. Unlike socialization or academic achievement, the emphasis on personal growth puts the individual first, society second. According to this view, the desired outcomes of education go beyond achievement to include the development of a positive self-concept and interpersonal skills, or what psychologist Daniel Goleman has termed **emotional intelligence**.

According to Goleman (1997, 1998), schools should emphasize five dimensions of emotional intelligence: self-awareness, handling emotions, motivation, empathy, and social skills. Emotional intelligence is essential for achievement in school, job success, marital happiness, and physical health; it enables students to live independently and to seek out the "good" life according to their own values, needs, and wants. The knowledge and skills students acquire at school enable them to achieve personal growth and self-actualization. This perspective on schools places the child, not the subject matter, at the center of the curriculum. Schooling is to prepare children for the tests of life, not merely a life of tests (Elias 2001). Thus, "emotional intelligence . . . has a rightful place alongside IQ in conceptualizing what it means to be smart" (Elias, Arnold, and Hussey 2003, ix).

Education for Social Change

Schools also provide students with the knowledge and skills to improve society and to adapt to rapid social change. Thus, "education and social change [are] inextricably tied to one another" (Rury 2002, ix). Naturally, there exists a wide range of opinion about how society might be improved. Some teachers believe that one purpose of schooling is to address social problems such as violence in society; while other teachers believe schools should teach academic content, not try to change society.

Service Learning   Less controversial have been efforts to prepare students to serve others through volunteerism and to participate actively in the political life of the nation. To help students see that they are not only autonomous individuals but also members of a larger community to which they are accountable, some high schools now require that students complete a service requirement. Other schools have introduced service-learning activities into their curricula.

Service learning provides students with opportunities to deliver service to their communities while studying and reflecting on the meaning of those experiences. Service learning brings young people into contact with the elderly, the sick, the poor, and the homeless, as well as acquaints them with neighborhood and governmental issues. Service learning can lead to changes in educational attitudes and improved school performance (Center for Human Resources 1999). Research on school-based service learning has identified several benefits for society:

- Students who engage in service learning are more likely to treat one another kindly, help one another, and care about doing their best.
- Male middle-schoolers report increased self-esteem and fewer behavioral problems after engaging in service learning.
- High school and middle school students involved in service learning are less likely to engage in behaviors that lead to pregnancy or arrest.
- High school students who participate in high-quality service-learning programs are more likely to develop bonds with more adults, to agree that they can learn from and work with the elderly and disabled, and to feel that they trust others besides parents and teachers to whom they could turn for help (Billig 2000).

One example of service learning involves Huntingdon Area Middle School in rural Pennsylvania. A team of math, science, social studies, and language arts teachers uses the problem of stormwater runoff from a nearby wetland to develop a flexible interdisciplinary curriculum. Classroom and field experiences range from learning about erosion, monitoring water quality, and involving the community to writing reports, interpreting statistics, using computer databases to construct charts and graphs, and reporting findings to the community (Institute for Educational Leadership 2002).

Education for Equal Educational Opportunity

Ample evidence exists that certain groups in U.S. society are denied equality of opportunity economically, socially, and educationally. For example, the percentage of children three to four years old who participate in early childhood programs such as Head Start, nursery school, and prekindergarten reveals that children from lower-income families are less likely to have such opportunities (National Center for Education Statistics 2003a). Also, Latino children are less likely to be enrolled than white or African American children. Such experiences help children from less advantaged backgrounds start elementary school on an equal footing with other children. In addition, there is a positive relationship between parents' educational attainment and their children's enrollment in early childhood programs.

Extensive programs at the federal, state, and local levels have been developed to provide equity for all people—regardless of race, ethnicity, language, gender, or religion. The United States has always derived strength from the diversity of its people, and all students should receive a quality education so that they may make their unique contributions to society. As Durkheim (1956, 68) asserted, ". . . the education of our children should not depend upon the chance of their having been born here or there, of some parents rather than others."

The goal of providing equal educational opportunity for all has long distinguished education in the United States from that found in most other countries. Since the 1850s, schools in the United States have been particularly concerned with providing children from diverse backgrounds the education they need to succeed in our society. As James Banks (1999, 4) suggests,

> Education within a pluralistic society should affirm and help students understand their home and community cultures. [To] create and maintain a civic community that works for the common good, education in a democratic society should help students acquire the knowledge, attitudes, and skills needed to participate in civic action to make society more equitable and just.

Society expects a lot of its schools and those who teach its children and youth. Our nation's most precious resource is our children and youth; they represent our hope for the future. To ensure that all students are taught by competent, effective teachers, several professional associations and state departments of education have developed standards that reflect the knowledge, skills, and dispositions that society expects teachers to possess. Most likely, the teacher education program you are enrolled in will use one or more of these sets of standards to evaluate your progress toward becoming an effective teacher. The professional standards that have had the greatest impact on teacher education programs nationally (as well as on teachers' ongoing professional growth and development) are those developed by the **Interstate New Teacher Assessment and Support Consortium (INTASC)**, the **National Council for Accreditation of Teacher Education (NCATE)**, the **Praxis Series: Professional Assessments for Beginning Teachers**, and the **National Board for Professional Teaching Standards (NBPTS)**.

To help you get the most out of your teacher education program, each chapter of this book includes a feature titled Relevant Standards that illustrates how a professional standard developed by each of these four groups is related to chapter content. Figure 1.3 presents an overview of standards developed by each group. Which of these sets of standards have influenced the teacher education program in which you are enrolled? Does your state have a set of professional standards that also applies to your teacher education program?

Figure 1.5   Professional standards society expects teachers to possess.

INTASC Standards

A consortium of more than thirty states that has developed standards and an assessment process for initial teacher certification. INTASC model core standards are based on ten principles evident in effective teaching regardless of subject or grade level. The principles are based on the realization that effective teachers integrate *content knowledge* with *pedagogical understanding* to assure that all students learn (INTASC 1993).

1. Knowledge of Subject Matter
2. Knowledge of Human Development and Learning
3. Adapting Instruction for Individual Needs
4. Multiple Instructional Strategies
5. Classroom Motivation and Management
6. Communication Skills
7. Instructional Planning Skills
8. Assessment of Student Learning
9. Professional Commitment and Responsibility
10. Partnerships

NCATE Standards

Standards for the accreditation of colleges and universities with teacher preparation programs. Currently, fewer than half of the 1,300 institutions that prepare teachers are accredited by NCATE. Although NCATE standards primarily apply to teacher education programs, not to teacher education students per se, NCATE believes that "the new professional teacher who graduates from a professional accredited school, college, or department of education should be able to" do the following (NCATE 2002):

- Help all prekindergarten through twelfth grade (P–12) students learn
- Teach to P–12 student standards set by specialized professional associations and the states
- Explain instructional choices based on research-derived knowledge and best practice
- Apply effective methods of teaching students who are at different developmental stages, have different learning styles, and come from diverse backgrounds
- Reflect on practice, act on feedback, and integrate technology into instruction effectively

What knowledge, skills, and dispositions does society expect teachers to possess?

NBPTS Standards

A board that issues professional certificates to teachers who possess extensive professional knowledge and the ability to perform at a high level. Certification candidates submit a portfolio including videotapes of classroom interactions and samples of student work plus the teacher's reflective comments. Trained NBPTS evaluators who teach in the same field as the candidate judge all elements of the assessments. NBPTS has developed five "core propositions" on which voluntary national teacher certification is based (NBPTS 1994):

1. Teachers are committed to students and their learning.
2. Teachers know the subjects they teach and how to teach those subjects to students.
3. Teachers are responsible for managing and monitoring student learning.
4. Teachers think systematically about their practice and learn from experience.
5. Teachers are members of learning communities.

Praxis Series

Based on knowledge and skills states commonly require of beginning teachers, the Praxis Series assesses individual development as it corresponds to three steps in becoming a teacher. These three areas of assessment are Academic Skills Assessments: entering a teacher education program (Praxis I); Subject Assessments: licensure for entering the profession (Praxis II); and Classroom Performance Assessments: the first year of teaching (Praxis III). Praxis III involves the assessment of actual teaching skills in four areas (Danielson 1996):

1. *Planning and Preparation*
- Demonstrating knowledge of content and pedagogy
- Demonstrating knowledge of students
- Selecting instructional goals
- Demonstrating knowledge of resources
- Designing coherent instruction

2. *The Classroom Environment*
- Creating an environment of respect and rapport
- Establishing a culture for learning
- Managing classroom procedures
- Managing student behavior
- Organizing physical space

3. *Instruction*
- Communicating clearly and accurately
- Using questioning and discussion techniques
- Engaging students in learning
- Providing feedback to students
- Demonstrating flexibility and responsiveness

4. *Professional Responsibilities*
- Reflecting on teaching
- Maintaining accurate records
- Communicating with families
- Contributing to the school and district
- Growing and developing professionally

What Are the Characteristics of Schools in Our Society?

Given the extensive differences among schools in the United States, many approaches can be used to describe the distinguishing characteristics of schools. Schools can be described according to the focus of their curricula; for example, high schools may be college prep, vocational, or comprehensive. Another approach is to describe schools according to their organizational structure; for example, alternative schools, schools-within-schools, or magnet schools. An **alternative school** is a small, highly individualized school separate from the regular school. A **school-within-a-school** is an alternative school (within a regular school) designed to meet the needs of students at risk. A school organized as a **magnet school** allows students, regardless of where they live within a community, to attend the school if its specialized program meets their needs. For instance, some magnet schools are organized around academic disciplines such as science, mathematics, or the basic skills; others focus on the performing and visual arts, health professions, information technology, or international studies and languages.

Metaphorical Views of Schools

One way to understand the characteristics of schools in the United States is to use metaphors; that is, to compare them to well-known features of contemporary life. For example, schools have been compared to factories; students are "raw material" that enter the school (or "factory"), move through the curriculum (or "assembly line") in a structured manner, and then exit the school as finished "products." Arthur Powell, Eleanor Farrar, and David Cohen (1985) suggest that high schools are like shopping malls; there is something for everyone, and students are "consumers" looking for the best value. Terrence Deal and Kent Peterson (1999, 21) offer a more positive metaphor for schools; exemplary schools, they contend, "become like tribes or clans, with deep ties among people and with values and traditions that give meaning to everyday life." Still others have suggested that schools can be compared to banks, gardens, prisons, mental hospitals, homes, churches, families, and teams.

According to the school-as-family metaphor, for example, an effective school is like a caring community of adults who attend to the academic, emotional, and social needs of the children and youth who are members of the "family."

Social Class-Based Views of Schools

While few people deny that schools should promote positive social change and equal opportunity, some people maintain that schools also function to "reproduce" the existing society and its inequities. According to this view, schools present different curricula and educational experiences to students from different socioeconomic classes. As a result, schools ultimately influence social stratification, social mobility, and adult socioeconomic success in the United States. For example, students at a school in an affluent suburb of a large city may study physics in a well-equipped lab and take a field trip to a high-tech industry to see the latest application of research on shock wave physics, while students at a school in an impoverished neighborhood in the same city may study physics in outdated texts, have no lab in which to conduct experiments, and take no field trips because the school district has limited funds.

Schools, in effect, preserve the stratification within society and maintain the differences between the "haves" and the "have-nots." As Joel Spring puts it: "the affluent members of U.S. society can protect the educational advantages and, consequently, economic advantages, of their children by living in affluent school districts or by using private schools. [T]heir children will attend the elite institutions of higher education, and their privileged educational background will make it easy for them to follow in the footsteps of their parent's financial success" (Spring 1999, 290–291).

Four Types of Schools   A useful way to talk about the relationship between schooling and social class in the United States is suggested by the four categories of schools Jean Anyon (1996) found in her study of several elementary schools in urban and suburban New Jersey. Anyon maintains that schools "reproduce" the existing society by presenting different curricula and educational experiences to students from different socioeconomic classes. As a result of their experiences at school, students are prepared for particular roles in the dominant society.

The first kind of school she calls the *working-class school*. In this school, the primary emphasis is on having students follow directions as they work at rote, mechanical activities such as completing dittoed worksheets. Students are given little opportunity to exercise their initiative or to make choices. Teachers may make negative, disparaging comments about students' abilities and, through subtle and not-so-subtle means, convey low expectations to students. Additionally, teachers at working-class schools may spend much of their time focusing on classroom management, dealing with absenteeism, and keeping extensive records.

The *middle-class school* is the second type identified by Anyon. Here, teachers emphasize to students the importance of getting right answers, usually in the form of words, sentences, numbers, or facts and dates. Students have slightly more opportunity to make decisions, but not much. Most lessons are textbook based. Anyon points out that "while the teachers spend a lot of time explaining and expanding on what the textbooks say, there is little attempt to analyze how or why things happen. . . . On the occasions when creativity or self-expression is requested, it is peripheral to the main activity or it is 'enrichment' or 'for fun' " (Anyon 1996, 191).

The *affluent professional school*, unlike the previous two types of schools, gives students the opportunity to express their individuality and to make a variety of choices. Fewer rules govern the behavior of students in affluent professional schools, and teacher and student are likely to negotiate about the work the students will do.

Anyon provides the following definition of the fourth type of school she identified, the *executive elite school*:

> In the executive elite school, work is developing one's analytical intellectual powers.
> Children are continually asked to reason through a problem, to produce intellectual
> products that are both logically sound and of top academic quality (Anyon 1996,
> 196).

In the affluent professional and executive elite schools, teacher–student relationships are more positive than those in the working-class and middle-class schools.
Teachers are polite to their students, seldom give direct orders, and almost never
make sarcastic or nasty remarks.

In applying Anyon's categories to schools in the United States, keep in mind
that few schools are one type exclusively, and few schools actually fit the categories
in all ways. Instead, most schools probably contain individual classrooms that represent all four types. Also, it is possible for one type of school to exist within a
school of another type—for example, an advanced placement program (essentially,
an affluent professional or executive elite school) within an urban working-class
school.

Also, keep in mind that Anyon studied a small group of schools in one metropolitan area, and her criteria are linked almost exclusively to socioeconomic status.
There are many schools in poor urban areas, for example, whose culture is more
like the affluent professional school Anyon describes than the working-class school,
and vice versa. Nevertheless, regardless of how schools in the United States are categorized, it seems they do reflect the socioeconomic status of the communities
they serve.

As Social Institutions, What Are Schools Like?

Schools are social institutions. An **institution** is an organization established by
society to maintain and improve its way of life. Our society has established schools
for the purpose of educating the young. For the last 200 years, schools in the
United States have developed complex structures, policies, and curricula to accomplish this mission.

Schools as a "Mirror" of Society

Schools do not exist in a vacuum. They must continually respond to changing
expectations of students, parents, teachers, communities, and the public at large.
As pointed out earlier, schools "mirror" the national culture and the surrounding
local culture and other special interests. Private, parochial, and religious schools,
for example, are often maintained by groups that see the school as a means of
perpetuating their preferred way of life. Schools reflect contemporary priorities of
life in the United States as evidenced by the growing number of public schools
located in shopping malls and other "alternative" settings. Reflecting on the
advantages of attending a school located in the Landmark Shopping Mall in Northern Virginia, one student expresses the goal of countless students around the coun-

Case for Reflection

Community Influences on the School

You are working at a school located in a poor, high-crime section of a big city. Twenty years ago the neighborhood that surrounds the school was made up of well-kept homes belonging to middle-income families. Today, the neighborhood reveals the scars of urban blight and decay. Most homes in the neighborhood are in disrepair. Yards overgrown with weeds, wrecked cars in driveways and on the streets, and graffiti on fences, buildings, and street signs reflect the decline that has overtaken the area.

The school, four stories tall and built at the end of World War II, also shows signs of neglect and abuse. The school's yellow brick walls have been the target of graffiti artists. Several window panes at the street level are boarded over.

About one-fifth of the students who attend the school are from families where English is not the first language. More than 60 percent of the students are from families on some form of public assistance. Students at the school have a reputation throughout the city for below-average achievement, absenteeism, and chronic misbehavior.

It is early in the school year, and you are standing at an overhead projector in front of your students, ready to begin a new unit of instruction. Your students, evenly divided between boys and girls, are seated in five parallel rows. Projected on the screen behind you are four "guiding questions" that will help students organize the material you will present that year.

Students seated near the front of the room appear to be involved and ready to learn. They are either looking directly at you or writing down the four questions on the transparency. Several students seated in the back half of the room, however, squirm restlessly and are involved in various off-task behaviors. One girl matter-of-factly braids the hair of the girl sitting in front of her. A boy seated to the right of her yawns and then places his head on his desk. Two boys look out the window at four youths who are seated on the steps leading into a run-down apartment building across the street. One girl leaves her desk without permission and walks across the room to deliver a note to a friend.

Questions

1. How might students' home environments influence their motivation to learn and to behave in a self-disciplined way?
2. How should you deal with students' lack of attention?
3. Why do you suppose some students appear as though they do not want to learn? In spite of their off-task behaviors, might they *really* want to learn?
4. How might you involve the home and parents of inattentive students to increase their motivation and learning?

try: "As well as getting an education, I get a job" (Spring 1997, 4). Nevertheless, as Mary Henry (1993, 29) points out, "Schools are . . . not simply puppets of the dominant mainstream society. They have their own unique concerns and their own 'poetry' of people and events. Whether public or private, all schools are not the same."

Schools in Rural, Suburban, and Urban Settings   Schools also reflect their location. As Durkheim (1956, 68) pointed out: "do we not see education vary with . . . locality? That of the city is not that of the country." Schools in rural, urban, and suburban settings often have significantly different cultures. Rural schools are often the focal point for community life and reflect values and beliefs that tend to be more conservative than those associated with urban and suburban schools. While the small size of a rural school may contribute to the development of a family-like culture, its small size may also make it difficult to provide students with an array of curricular experiences equal to that found at larger schools in more populated areas. In contrast, large suburban or urban schools may provide students with more varied learning experiences, but these schools may lack the cohesiveness and community focus of rural schools.

Schools and Their Surrounding Neighborhoods   The differences among the neighborhoods that surround schools can be enormous. Urban schools found in or near decaying centers of large cities often reflect the social problems of the surrounding area, such as drug abuse, crime, and poverty. One of the most serious problems confronting education in the United States is the quality of such schools. Across the country—in Chicago, New York, Los Angeles, St. Louis, Detroit, and Cleveland—middle-class families that can afford to move away from urban centers or place their children in private schools do so. As a result, students in urban school districts are increasingly from low-income backgrounds.

In what ways do schools reflect their communities and the wider U.S. society? How might the surrounding neighborhood influence this school? The students who attend it? The teachers who work there?

In *Savage Inequalities*, Jonathan Kozol documents the startling contrast between the neighborhoods that surround impoverished inner-city schools and those that surround affluent suburban schools. In comparing New Trier High School in affluent Winnetka, Illinois, and Chicago's DuSable High School, an inner-city school at which the author taught for eight years, Kozol points out that New Trier is in a neighborhood of "circular driveways, chirping birds and white-columned homes" (1991, 62). In contrast, DuSable's surroundings on Chicago's South Side are "almost indescribably despairing"; across the street from the school is "a line of uniform and ugly 16-story buildings, the Robert Taylor Homes, which constitute . . . the city's second-poorest neighborhood" (1991, 68, 71). Similarly, the author of this book offers a grim description of the school and its surrounding environment when he began his teaching career at the school:

> *The Robert Taylor Housing Project, the largest housing project in the world, overshadowed DuSable High School both physically and spiritually. Outside the school, hundreds of broken, boarded-up windows on all three floors were in evidence. Heavy chain-link meshing over the first floor windows appeared to have minimized the street level damage.*
>
> *On the walls were countless spray-painted messages. Each message, I thought, perhaps a cry against a school system that seemed to teach only frustration and failure and a society that recognized ghetto students only as statistical entries in the categories of race, poverty, and crime. Most of the graffiti seemed done not only out of boredom and spite but also for identification, distinction. Here I am, and here is my mark. This now has my character and is part of my personality, my property (Parkay 1983, 4).*

Though the extreme poverty found in some communities may impact their schools in undesirable ways, effective teachers at such schools communicate to students that they are "rich" in ways that go beyond material wealth—as one adult wrote to her second-grade teacher (Paul and Smith 2000, 53):

> *Dear Mrs. Smith,*
>
> *This letter is to thank you for your kindness and support when I was in your second grade class. . . . My family was receiving public assistance and people were always coming to the school to check my shoes or my coat to see if I qualified for new ones. . . . You never drew attention to me when I needed to go into the hall to see one of the public assistance workers and you were always adding little things to my lunches. You even did a lesson about having real wealth and I knew that you were talking to me. You were a wonderful, caring teacher and I will never forget you.*
>
> *THANK YOU! Jenny*

Jenny was fortunate that her teacher saw her not merely as a child living in an impoverished neighborhood, but as a child needing validation and support to realize her full potential. This chapter's Relevant Standards feature attests to the importance of understanding the neighborhoods that surround schools.

Relevant Standards

Connections Between Students' Lives and the Curriculum

As the following standards indicate, teachers must understand how their students' experiences within their neighborhoods influence their learning at school. Successful teachers are able to make connections between the subjects they teach and their students' life experiences.

- "[Teacher candidates] consider school, family, and community contexts in connecting concepts to students' prior experience and applying the ideas to real-world problems." (National Council for Accreditation of Teacher Education [NCATE], 2002, 15. Standard 1: Candidate Knowledge, Skills, and Dispositions, "target" level of knowledge.)

- "Teachers . . . cultivate knowledge about the character of the community and its effects on the school and students. They develop an appreciation of ethnic and linguistic differences, of cultural influences on students' aspirations and expectations, and of the effects of poverty and affluence. [The] cultural diversity represented in many communities can serve as a powerful resource in teaching. [Accomplished] teachers seek to capitalize on these opportunities and to respond productively to students' diverse backgrounds." (National Board for Professional Teaching Standards [NBPTS], 2002, 20. "Supporting statement" for Proposition #1:

"Teachers are committed to students and their learning.")

- "The teacher knows how to take contextual considerations (instructional materials, individual student interests, needs, and aptitudes, and community resources) into account in planning instruction that creates an effective bridge between curriculum goals and students' experiences." (Interstate New Teacher Assessment and Support Consortium [INTASC], 1992, 27. "Knowledge" statement for Principle #7: "The teacher plans instruction based upon knowledge of subject matter, students, the community, and curriculum goals.")

- "Teacher's efforts to engage families in the instructional program are frequent and successful. Students contribute ideas for projects that will be enhanced by family participation." (Praxis Series, "distinguished" level of performance for Domain 4: Professional Responsibilities, Component 4c: Communicating with Families.) (From Danielson 1996, 112)

School Culture

Although schools are very much alike, each school is unique. Each has a culture of its own—a network of beliefs, values and traditions, and ways of thinking and behaving that distinguishes it from other schools.

Much like a community, a school has a distinctive culture—a collective way of life. Terms that have been used to describe **school culture** include *climate, ethos, atmosphere,* and *character.* Some schools may be characterized as community-like places where there is a shared sense of purpose and commitment to providing the best education possible for all students. Other schools lack a unified sense of purpose and drift, rudderless, from year to year. Still others are characterized by internal conflict and divisiveness and may even reflect what Deal and Peterson (1999) term a "toxic" school culture; students, teachers, administrators, and parents may feel that the school is not sufficiently meeting their needs. The following excerpt from the mission statement of an award-winning school in the high desert of Northern Arizona illustrates several qualities of a school culture that nurtures students:

> The Ganado Primary School's mission is to provide opportunities for children to make sense of their world, to respect themselves and others, to respect their environment, and to appreciate and understand their cultural and linguistic heritage. [Our] mission is to help everyone [children, teachers, and administrators] negotiate their experiences with the content of the classroom, instructional style, and the social, emotional, physical and professional interactions of school life. We believe that a relaxed atmosphere [characterized by] surprise, challenge, hard work, celebration, humor, satisfaction, and collegiality is the natural order of the day for all (Deal and Peterson 1999, 17).

To understand school culture more fully, Table 1.1 presents several elements that contribute to a school's culture. Reflect on a school with which you are familiar; to what extent does each factor in Table 1.1 characterize the school? What additional elements would be useful in characterizing the culture of that school?

These children are participating in the culture of their school. What other behaviors, formal practices, and school traditions are probably part of their school's culture?

Table 1.1 Elements of school culture	
Dress. How are the children dressed? Comment on neatness and apparent affluence. Also note differences in dress among groups of children.	Consider dress, language, race, interests, how physical, materialistic, and so on. How rigid is group definition? That is, are some students members of more than one group? Or do some members of groups at least mix with members of other groups? Are there loners? What are their characteristics?
Language. What is their out-of-class language like? How is it different from their in-class language? What sorts of emotions do they express with their language? Do they use abusive language? Note differences in languages among groups of children.	**Territory.** Does each of the groups have its own "territory"? Which one has the most territory? The least territory? How closely guarded is each group's territory?
Interests. If you are unobtrusive, you will be able to overhear fragments of conversations. What do the children talk about? Teachers? Sports and cars? Grades? The opposite sex? Clothes? Current events? Tests? Note differences in topics of conversation for different groups.	**Conflict.** What sorts of conflict do you observe? Are the protagonists members of different groups? What is the source of the conflict (e.g., physical or verbal abuse, invasion of one group's territory by another)? How is the conflict settled (if at all) and by whom?
Groups. What groups can you identify? (Groups are particularly noticeable in secondary schools.) Some groups you might notice are "jocks," "druggies," "skaters," "snobs," "nerds," "preps," and students of various racial and ethnic backgrounds. How would you characterize each group?	**Dominance and Power.** Do any of the groups appear to be dominant? Which are the most and the least powerful groups? What is the source of each group's power (e.g., academic skills, athletic skill, muscle, "street knowledge")? Do any of the groups depend on adult approval for their power?

Source: George J. Posner, *Field Experience: A Guide to Reflective Teaching,* 6th ed. Boston: Allyn and Bacon, 2005, p. 95.

The Physical Environment The physical environment of the school both reflects and helps to create the school's overall culture. As Winston Churchill said, "We shape our buildings and they shape us."

Some schools are dreary places or, at best, aesthetically bland. The tile floors, concrete block walls, long, straight corridors, and rows of fluorescent lights often found in these schools contribute little to their inhabitants' sense of beauty, concern for others, or personal comfort.

Other schools are much more attractive. They are clean, pleasant, and inviting; and teachers and students take pride in their building. Overall, the physical environment has a positive impact on those who spend time in the school; it encourages learning and a spirit of cohesiveness.

A synthesis of research on the design process for building new schools revealed that excellent school designs involved the following steps:

- Plan schools as community spaces (e.g., schools share space with community centers, libraries, or recreational facilities).
- Involve all stakeholders in the design and building process.
- Design spaces to be flexible.
- Design a safe, comfortable school.
- Accommodate the needs of all learners.
- Incorporate technology planning from the beginning of the process.

- Strive for smaller designs of both buildings and classrooms.
- Decentralize the facility both administratively and architecturally.
- Locate early childhood education in the school.
- Separate children and pedestrians from vehicles and service entrances (Lackney 2000).

School "Regularities"   Schools in the United States share a common set of programmatic or structural "regularities." For example, classes consist of about 25 pupils; students are grouped heterogeneously or homogeneously; class periods run about 50–60 minutes; and special programs may be available for students with disabilities, gifted and talented students, or students with other special needs. **School "regularities"** such as these influence how schools are organized and staffed, and they are "regular" features of most schools.

The regularities of schools are well known to anyone who has been educated in U.S. schools. With few exceptions, students attend school from six years of age through sixteen at least, and usually to eighteen, Monday through Friday, September through May, for twelve years. For the most part, students are assigned to grade level on the basis of age rather than ability or interest. Assignment to individual classes or teachers at a given grade level, however, may be made on the basis of ability or interest.

Teachers and students are grouped in several ways in the elementary school and in one dominant pattern in junior and senior high school. At the elementary school level, the **self-contained classroom** is the most traditional and prevalent arrangement. In this type of classroom, one teacher teaches all or nearly all subjects to a group of about twenty-five children, with the teacher and students remaining in the same classroom for the entire day. Often art, music, physical education, and computer skills are taught in other parts of the school, so students may leave the classroom for scheduled periods. Individual students may also attend special classes for remedial or advanced instruction, speech therapy, or instrumental music and band lessons.

In **open-space schools**, students are free to move among various activities and learning centers. Instead of self-contained classrooms, open-space schools have large instructional areas with movable walls and furniture that can be rearranged easily. Grouping for instruction is much more fluid and varied. Students do much of their work independently, with a number of teachers providing individual guidance as needed.

In middle schools and junior and senior high schools, students typically study four or five academic subjects taught by teachers who specialize in them. In this organizational arrangement, called **departmentalization**, students move from classroom to classroom for their lessons. High school teachers often share their classrooms with other teachers and use their rooms only during scheduled class periods.

School Traditions   The traditions of a school are those elements of a school's culture that are handed down from year to year. **School traditions** reflect what students, teachers, administrators, parents, and the surrounding community believe is important and valuable about the school. One school, for example, may have developed a tradition of excellence in academic programs; another school's traditions may emphasize the performing arts; and yet another may focus on athletic programs. Whatever a school's traditions, they are usually a source of pride for members of the school community.

Ideally, traditions are the "glue" that holds together the diverse elements of a school's culture. They combine to create a sense of community, identity, and trust among people affiliated with a school. Traditions are maintained through stories that are handed down, rituals and ceremonial activities, student productions, and trophies and artifacts that have been collected over the years. For example, Joan Vydra, principal of Briar Glen Elementary School in Wheaton, Illinois, initiated Care Week as part of the fall tradition at her former school, Hawthorne Elementary. Vydra believed that a tradition of care would nurture student success. On the first day of Care Week, students learned the importance of caring for themselves; on Tuesdays, caring for their families; on Wednesdays, caring for each other; on Thursdays, caring for the school; and on Fridays, caring for those served by local charities (Deal and Peterson 1999).

Classroom Culture

Just as schools develop their unique cultures, each classroom develops its own culture or way of life. The culture of a classroom is determined in large measure by the manner in which teacher and students participate in common activities. In addition, "the environment of the classroom and the inhabitants of that environment—students and teachers—are constantly interacting. Each aspect of the system affects all others" (Woolfolk 2001, 434).

The quality of teacher–student interactions is influenced by the physical characteristics of the setting (classroom, use of space, materials, resources, etc.) and the social dimensions of the group (norms, rules, expectations, cohesiveness, distribution of power and influence). These elements interact to shape **classroom culture.** Teachers who appreciate the importance of these salient elements of classroom culture are more likely to create environments that they and their students find satisfying and growth promoting. For example, during the second month of student teaching in the second grade, "Miss Martin" reflects on her efforts to create a classroom culture characterized by positive teacher–student interactions:

> I started off with a big mistake. I tried to be their friend. I tried joining with them in all the jokes and laughter that cut into instruction time. When this didn't work, I overcompensated by yelling at them when I needed them to quiet down and get to work. I wasn't comfortable with this situation. I did not think it was like me to raise my voice at a child. I knew I needed to consider how they felt. I realized that if I were them, I'd hate me, I really would. In desperation, I turned to my education textbooks for advice.
>
> This was a huge help to me, but a book can only guide you. It can't establish a personality for you or even manage your classroom for you. You have to do that yourself and as lovingly and effectively as possible. But I had so much trouble finding a middle

ground: love them, guide them, talk to them, manage them, but don't control them (Rand and Shelton-Colangelo 1999, 8–9).

Similarly, students believe that effective teachers develop positive, task-oriented classroom cultures, while ineffective teachers develop negative cultures. At one inner-city school, for example,

> [Sixth-grade] students saw their social studies/language arts teacher as someone they could learn from and relate to well, while they seemed to constantly do battle with their math and science teacher. Students portrayed [the math and science teacher] as overdemanding, impatient, and insensitive; [the social studies/language arts teacher] seemed to be just the opposite. [The math and science teacher], according to one student, "has an attitude problem. She wants us to be so good the first time. She wants us to always be perfect. She has us walk in a line in the hallway. We are the only class in the school to do that. . . . She is the only [teacher] who won't go over things. She never comes in with a smile; she is always evil. By not going over it, we got a bad attitude. I haven't learned nothing in her class" (Wilson and Corbett 2001, 54–55).

Clearly, the math and science teacher has developed an adversarial, counter-productive relationship with students. The social studies/language arts teacher, on the other hand, recognizes the importance of developing positive relationships with students and understands how such relationships pave the way for student learning.

What Are the Characteristics of "Successful" Schools?

Like Miss Martin, you may be uncertain of your ability to develop a positive class-room climate when you become a teacher. Moreover, the many social problems and issues that impact schools may seem daunting at this point in your professional education. However, a great many schools in all settings and with all kinds of students are highly successful, including inner-city and isolated rural schools and schools that serve pupils of all socioeconomic, racial, and ethnic backgrounds. What are the characteristics of these schools? Do they have commonalities that account for their success?

Perspectives on Successful Schools

First, we must define what we mean by *a successful school*. One measure of success, naturally, is that students at these schools achieve at a high level and complete requirements for graduation. Whether reflected in scores on standardized tests or other documentation of academic learning gains, students at these schools are learning. They are achieving literacy in reading, writing, computation, and computer skills. They are learning to solve problems, think creatively and analytically, and, most importantly, they are learning to learn.

Another valid measure of success for a school is that it achieves results that sur-pass those expected from comparable schools in comparable settings. The achieve-ment of students goes beyond what one would expect. In spite of surrounding social, economic, and political forces that impede the educative process at other schools, these schools are achieving results.

Finally, successful schools are those that are improving, rather than getting worse. School improvement is a slow process, and schools that are improving—moving in a positive direction rather than declining—are also successful.

School Effectiveness Research

During the 1980s and early 1990s, much research was conducted to identify the characteristics of successful (or effective) schools. The characteristics of successful schools were described in different ways in several research projects. The research indicates that effective schools are created through the combined effort of many individuals—students, teachers, administrators, parents, and community members. The effective school is student centered, vibrant, and growing. Since each school has a unique culture, the qualities of an effective school cannot be standardized; however, research has identified the following seven characteristics, each of which makes a contribution toward maximizing the learning of all students.

1. *Strong leadership*—Successful schools have strong leaders—individuals who value education and see themselves as educational leaders, not just as managers or bureaucrats. They monitor the performance of everyone at the school—teachers staff, students, and themselves. These leaders have a clear, compelling vision of the school as a more effective learning environment, and they take decisive steps to bring that about. Daily bulletins, memos, letters to parents, and so on indicate that the administrative team values learning. School leaders describe their school in terms that are overwhelmingly positive, and they are visible throughout the building and at school events.

2. *High expectations*—Teachers at successful schools have high expectations of students. These teachers believe that all students, rich or poor, can learn, and they communicate this to students through realistic, yet high, expectations. When talking about their students, teachers convey belief in their students' ability to learn. Students' comments indicate that they are expected to reach specific academic goals when they come to school.

3. *Emphasis on basic skills*—Teachers at successful schools emphasize student achievement in the basic skills of reading, writing, and mathematical computation. Evidence of students' progress in basic skills is readily available. Appropriate remediation is provided to students who have not demonstrated mastery of skills.

4. *Orderly school environment*—The environment of a successful school is orderly, safe, and conducive to learning. Discipline problems are at a minimum, and teachers are able to devote greater amounts of time to teaching. Classes begin and end on time. The building is clean and well maintained; the behavior of students on the school grounds, in entranceways, and in hallways just before school begins and ends is appropriate.

5. *Frequent, systematic evaluation of student learning*—The learning of students in successful schools is monitored closely. When difficulties are noticed, appropriate remediation is provided quickly. Samples of student work are on display in hallways and in classrooms.

Teachers' Voices Putting Research and Theory into Practice

We Are Friends When We Have Memories Together

Merle Weiss Scharmann

"We are friends when we have memories together." As you walk through the halls and classrooms of Greeley School, you may see this memory statement in various forms and places. This beautiful refrain is usually accompanied by pieces of collaborative work generated by our children. These works cause one to pause—amazed by the power, elaborate use of material, and obvious level of knowledge expressed.

[During the] year several of my colleagues began to share experiences from their study of the Reggio Emilia early childhood programs in Italy. That summer several of the Reggio educators came to share their knowledge with Winnetka, Illinois, teachers. Learning about the philosophy and approach of the Reggio program was exciting, but it was the discussion of giving children the opportunity and time to revisit prior learning that caught my attention.

[At] Greeley we continually look for ways to encourage children to be reflective about their own learning and growth. . . . The classrooms at Greeley are busy places, alive with interesting experiences for all of our children. The excitement and joy one feels during holidays is evident in our schoolhouse all the year round.

Questions

1. In what ways does Greeley School show evidence of the four characteristics of successful schools presented on page 30?
2. What adjectives best describe the culture at Greeley School?
3. To what degree is the Greeley School culture similar to (or different from) the school cultures you have experienced?
4. In the subject area and at the level for which you are preparing to teach, how might you "look for ways to encourage [students] to be reflective about their own learning and growth"?

Merle Weiss Scharmann teaches junior and senior kindergarten at the Greeley School in Winnetka, Illinois, and serves as chair of her district's kindergarten grade level. The preceding is excerpted from her article in *Young Children* 53, 3 (March 1998), pp. 27–29.

6. *Sense of purpose*—Those who teach and those who learn at successful schools have a strong sense of purpose. From the principal to the students, everyone at the school is guided by a vision of excellence. Students, teachers, administrators, staff, and community members describe the school in terms that are positive.

7. *Collegiality and a sense of community*—Teachers, administrators, and staff at successful schools work well together. They are dedicated to creating an environment that promotes not only student learning but also their own professional growth and development. In the teachers' lunchroom and lounge, conversations among teachers include sharing professional ideas and strategies for increasing students' learning. Teachers do not work exclusively in isolated classrooms; they frequently collaborate and help one another.

Research has also focused on strategies for making schools more effective. Since the early 1990s, school districts across the nation have been participating in school restructuring that changes the way students are grouped, uses of classroom time and space, instructional methods, and decision making. A synthesis of research (Newmann and Wehlage 1995) conducted between 1990 and 1995 on restructuring schools identified four characteristics of successful schools:

1. *Focus on student learning*—Planning, implementation, and evaluation focus on enhancing the intellectual quality of student learning. All students are expected to achieve academic excellence.

2. *Emphasis on authentic pedagogy*—Students are required to think, to develop in-depth understanding, and to apply academic learning to important, realistic problems. Students might, for example, conduct a survey on an issue of local concern, analyze the results, and then present their findings at a town council meeting.

3. *Greater school organizational capacity*—The ability of the school to strive for continuous improvement through professional collaboration is enhanced. For example, teachers exchange ideas to improve their teaching, they seek feedback from students, parents, and community members, and they attend conferences and workshops to acquire new materials and strategies.

4. *Greater external support*—The school receives critical financial, technical, and political support from outside sources.

In short, the cultures of effective schools encourage teachers to grow and develop in the practice of their profession. The Teachers' Voices feature on page 29 illustrates how one teacher collaborated with her colleagues to create an effective school culture.

What Can We Learn from the Foundations of Education in Other Countries?

The world has truly become smaller and more interconnected as telecommunications, cyberspace, and travel by jet bring diverse people and countries together. Moreover, as a report titled *Beyond September 11: A Comprehensive National Policy on International Education* stated, "The tragic events of September 11, 2001, crystallized in a single, terrible moment the challenges of globalization and the importance of international research and education to our national security. Like it or not, Americans are connected with people the world over" (American Council on Education 2002, 7).

Clearly, education is crucial to the well-being of every country and to the world as a whole. "[Americans] instinctively know the value of building global competence, [and] recent surveys show that the American public sees international education as essential to success in the job market and daily life" (American Council on Education 2002, 8).

For teachers, on whom the quality of education ultimately depends, the challenges and opportunities related to improving education are remarkably similar worldwide. There is much the United States can learn from other countries about how societal problems influence schools and how schools can best promote the ability of teachers and students to solve those problems. For example, an editorial in the *Bangkok Post* on the need to prepare Thai youth for a changing world echoes calls for educational reform in the United States: "The country's policy planners [s]hould seriously review and revamp the national education system to effectively prepare our youths [for] the future" (Sricharatchanya 1996, 15). Similarly, a community leader's comments about educating young substance abusers in Bangkok's Ban Don Muslim community could apply to youth in scores of American communities: "We are in an age of cultural instability. Children are exposed to both good and bad things. [I]t's hard to resist the influences and attitudes from the outside world that are pulling at the children's feelings" (Rithdee 1996, 11).

U.S. educators also can learn from their counterparts in Japan. For example, the curriculum goals at Shiose Junior High School in Nishinomiya, Japan, which are based on Japan's fifteenth Council for Education, would "fit" American junior high schools as well. Principal Ako Inoue (1996, 1) presented one of his school's goals when the Nishinomiya Board of Education visited the College of Education at Washington State University: "Students will acquire the ability to survive in a changing society, that is, students will study, think and make judgments on their own initiative. It is also important that we provide a proper balance of knowledge, morality, and physical health, and that we nurture humanity and physical strength for that purpose." As a result of universal goals such as these, educators are entering an era of increasing crossnational exchanges that focus on sharing resources, ideas, and expertise for the improvement of education worldwide.

What societal trends and issues might influence events in this classroom? How would these trends and issues be similar to those that influence classrooms in the United States? How would they be different?

Technology in Teaching

The importance of information technology in the school curriculum: An international comparison

Today's students, both in the United States and around the world, will compete for jobs in a global economy that is powerfully influenced by information technology. The "coin of the realm" for the global economy of the twenty-first century is neither raw materials nor labor but information. As a result, the place of information technology in the school curriculum is critical.

Figure 1.4 shows the percentage of the public in eleven countries who gave information technology and technical studies a rating of either "essential" or "very important" in the school curriculum. Information technology (e.g., computing and database management) was viewed as more important than technical studies (e.g., metal shop and drafting) in all countries except Spain, where they were viewed as nearly the same. Notice that the U.S. public, more than the public in the other countries, views information technology as especially important. Do you believe the actual emphasis on information technology in school curricula reflects the importance the U.S. public attaches to this area of the curriculum? As a teacher, how can you ensure that your students acquire the information technology skills they will need for their future in a global economy?

Comparative Education

As the nations of the world continue to become more interdependent, policies for educational reform in the United States will be influenced increasingly by **comparative education**, the study of educational practices in other countries. Comparative education studies show how school systems in other countries work and how American students compare with students in other countries on certain measures of schooling and achievement. In addition, research in comparative education enables professionals to share information about successful innovations internationally. Teachers can collaborate on global education projects, test change models that have proved successful in other countries, and compare curricular goals and instructional strategies across countries. For example, the above Technology in Teaching feature examines how the United States compares to other countries regarding the importance of information technology in the school curriculum.

International Comparisons of Achievement   The first International Assessment of Educational Progress (IAEP) in 1991 revealed that the achievement levels of U.S. students were often below those of students from other countries. Subsequent IAEP comparisons have shown some improvement in the rankings of American students in mathematics and science. Figure 1.5(a) on page 34, for example, based on the **Third International Mathematics and Science Study (TIMSS)** (International Association for the Evaluation of Educational Achievement, 1997a, 1997b) compares the mathematics and science achievement of fourth-grade U.S. students with students from

Figure 1.4 The importance of information technology and technical studies: An international perspective.

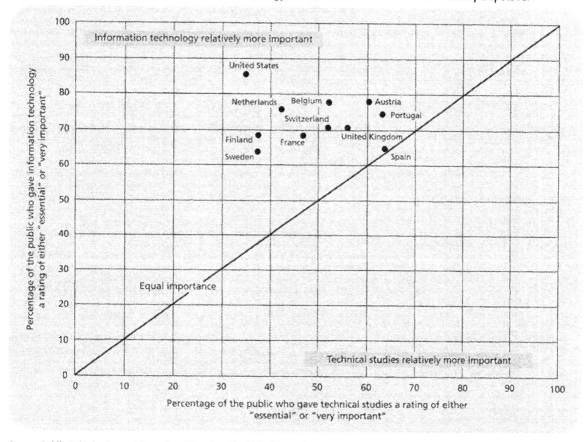

Source: Public Attitudes Toward Secondary Education: The United States in an International Context. Washington, DC: U.S. Department of Education, 1997.

several other countries. However, as Figure 1.5(b) shows, the relative standing of U.S. students in these subject areas was significantly lower by the final year of secondary school. Gains in literacy, however, have been more significant. For example, *A First Look—Findings from the National Assessment of Educational Progress* reported that U.S. fourth-graders ranked second in 1995 on a thirty-two-nation survey of reading skills.

Since the publication of *A Nation at Risk* (National Commission on Excellence in Education 1983), a national report critical of U.S. education, there has been an unbroken trend for the media and some observers of U.S. education to decry the perceived poor performance of U.S. students on international comparisons of achievement. A closer examination of international comparisons, however, reveals the seldom-reported fact that the United States' position in country-by-country rankings is based on *aggregate* achievement scores—in other words, achievement

Figure 1.5   Nation's average mathematics and science performance compared with the United States.

Nations' Average Mathematics and Science Performance Compared with the United States—Grade 4

MATHEMATICS		SCIENCE	
Nation	Average	Nation	Average
Singapore	625	▲ Korea	597
Korea	611		
▲ Japan	597	Japan	574
Hong Kong	587	United States	565
(Netherlands)	577	= (Austria)	565
(Czech Republic)	567	(Australia)	562
(Austria)	559	(Netherlands)	557
		Czech Republic	557
(Slovenia)	552		
Ireland	550	England	551
(Hungary)	548	Canada	549
= (Australia)	546	Singapore	547
United States	545	(Slovenia)	546
Canada	532	Ireland	539
(Israel)	531	Scotland	536
		Hong Kong	533
(Latvia LSS)	525	▼ (Hungary)	532
Scotland	520	New Zealand	531
England	513	Norway	530
Cyprus	502	(Latvia LSS)	512
Norway	502	(Israel)	505
▼ New Zealand	499	Iceland	505
Greece	492	Greece	497
(Thailand)	490	Portugal	480
Portugal	475	Cyprus	475
Iceland	474	(Thailand)	473
Iran, Islamic Republic	429	Iran, Islamic Republic	416
(Kuwait)	400	(Kuwait)	401
International Average = 529		International Average = 524	

(a)

Nations' Average Mathematics and Science General Knowledge Performance Compared with the United States—Final Year of Secondary School

MATHEMATICS		SCIENCE	
Nation	Average	Nation	Average
(Netherlands)	560	▲ Sweden	559
Sweden	552	(Netherlands)	558
(Denmark)	547	(Iceland)	549
Switzerland	540	(Norway)	544
(Iceland)	534	(Canada)	532
(Norway)	528	New Zealand	529
▲ (France)	523	(Australia)	527
New Zealand	522	Switzerland	523
(Australia)	522	(Austria)	520
(Canada)	519	(Slovenia)	517
(Austria)	518	(Denmark)	509
(Slovenia)	512		
(Germany)	495		
Hungary	483	(Germany)	497
		(France)	487
(Italy)	476	Czech Republic	487
(Russian Fed)	471	= (Russian Fed)	481
= (Lithuania)	469	(United States)	480
Czech Republic	466	(Italy)	475
(United States)	461	Hungary	471
		(Lithuania)	461
▼ (Cyprus)	446		
▼ (South Africa)	356		
		▼ (Cyprus)	448
		(South Africa)	349
International Average = 500		International Average = 500	

(b)

Notes:
1) Nations not meeting international guidelines are shown in parentheses.
2) The international average is the average of the national averages of the 21 nations.

▲ Nations with average scores significantly higher than the U.S.

= Nations with average scores not significantly different from the U.S.

▼ Nations with average scores significantly lower than the U.S.

Source: National Center for Education Statistics. *Pursuing Excellence: A Study of U.S. Fourth-Grade Mathematics and Science Achievement in International Context,* Figures 1 & 2. Washington, DC, NCES, 1997.

scores of all students are used to make the comparisons. Not taken into account is the United States' commitment to educating all students (not just the academically able or those from home environments that encourage education), the varying quality of U.S. schools, and differences in students' *opportunity to learn* the content covered in achievement tests.

When only the top students of each country are compared, the rankings of U.S. students improve dramatically. As David Berliner and Bruce Biddle point out in *The Manufactured Crisis: Myths, Fraud, and the Attack on America's Public Schools* (1995, 52), "If one actually looks at and thinks about the comparative evidence, [o]ne discovers that it does not confirm the myth of American educational failure. Indeed, it suggests that in many ways American education stands head and shoulders above education in other countries."

Berliner and Biddle summarize an analysis of data (Westbury 1992) from the Second International Mathematics Study, which purported to show U.S. eighth-graders significantly behind their Japanese peers in mathematics achievement. The analysis revealed that Japanese eighth-grade students were *required* to take courses that covered algebra, while U.S. students typically take such courses a year or two later. When the achievement of U.S. and Japanese students who had taken prealgebra and algebra was compared, the achievement of U.S. students matched or exceeded that of Japanese students.

Berliner and Biddle (1995, 63) go on to offer these cautions about interpreting crossnational studies of educational achievement.

- Few of those studies have yet focused on the unique values and strengths of American education.
- Many of the studies' results have obviously been affected by sampling biases and inconsistent methods for gathering data.
- Many, perhaps most, of the studies' results were generated by differences in curricula—in opportunities to learn—in the countries studied.
- Aggregate results for American schools are misleading because of the huge range of school quality in this country—ranging from marvelous to terrible.
- The press has managed to ignore most comparative studies in which the United States has done well.

A National Curriculum?   Decisions about the operation of schools in the United States are made largely at the district or individual school level. However, in some countries (Japan, Korea, and England, for example) education is centralized and teachers follow a standardized national curriculum. Since the first International Assessment of Educational Progress (IAEP) in 1991 revealed that the achievement levels of U.S. students are often below that of students from other countries (many of which have national curricula), some have proposed a **national curriculum** for the United States. Proposals for a national curriculum are also supported by the public. The 2002 Gallup poll of the public's attitudes toward the public schools revealed that 66 percent would "favor" a standardized national curriculum, and 31 percent would "oppose" such a curriculum (Rose and Gallup 2002).

Although there is widespread support for national examinations and a national curriculum similar to those found in other countries, there is also significant opposition to such a system. For example, in his comparative study of U.S. and Japanese education, Harry Wray (1999, 137) concluded that Japan's system of national examinations "reinforce[s] excessive conformity, passivity, standardization, anxiety, group consciousness, and controlled education." Furthermore, Wray goes on to say, "Excessive emphasis on passing entrance examinations plays a contributing role in killing most students' interest in studying and scholarship after entering a university, especially for those outside the science, engineering, and medical areas. Students exhausted by the dehumanizing methodology lose motivation and curiosity" (Wray 1999, 138).

National examinations have also been criticized because they encourage students to take a narrow view of learning and they tend to emphasize lower-order thinking skills. As one Japanese university student confided to Wray:

> In elementary school we had many occasions to give our opinions; however, after we entered junior high school, we did not get such opportunities because all the studies are for high school entrance examinations, and all the studies in high school are for university entrance examinations. One who is considered "intelligent" is one who can get good grades, not those who have their own opinions (Wray 1999, 137).

Lessons from Other Countries

The previous comments about Japanese education aside, U.S. educators can learn a great deal from their colleagues around the world regarding what works and what doesn't work in other countries. When considering the possibility of adopting practices from other countries, however, it is important to remember that educational practices reflect the surrounding culture. When one country tries to adopt a method used elsewhere, a lack of support from the larger society may doom the new practice to failure. In addition, it is important to realize that the successes of another country's educational system may require sacrifices that are unacceptable to our way of life. Nevertheless, there are many practices in other countries that American educators and policymakers should consider.

Support for Teachers and Teaching   In many other countries, teachers and the profession of teaching receive a level of societal support that surpasses that experienced by U.S. teachers. For example, teachers in many countries are accorded greater respect than their U.S. counterparts. Moreover, the annual salary of experienced teachers relative to per capita gross domestic product for teachers in several other countries is significantly greater than it is for U.S. teachers (Organization for Economic Cooperation and Development 2000).

In addition, most U.S. teachers have about one hour or less per day for planning, and U.S. high school teachers teach about thirty classes a week, compared with twenty by teachers in Germany and fewer than twenty by Japanese teachers (U.S. Department of Education and International Institute on Education 1996). "[T]his leaves them [U.S. teachers] with almost no regular time to consult together or learn about new teaching strategies, unlike their peers in many European and Asian countries where teachers spend between 15 and 20 hours per week working jointly on refining lessons, coaching one another, and learning about new methods" (National Commission on Teaching and America's Future 1996, 14).

The National Commission on Teaching and America's Future (1996) also found that other countries invest their resources in hiring more teachers, who constitute about 60 to 80 percent of total staff compared to only 43 percent in the United States. The Commission noted (1996, 15) that in U.S. schools "too many people and resources are allocated to activities outside of classrooms, sitting on the sidelines rather than the front lines of teaching and learning." Many other countries also invest more resources in staff development and beginning teacher support programs than U.S. schools. New teachers in other countries receive more support than their U.S. counterparts, according to a joint report by the U.S. Department of Education and the Education Forum of APEC (Asia-Pacific Economic Cooperation). In other nations

1. New teachers are viewed as professionals on a continuum, with increasing levels of experience and responsibility; novice teachers are not expected to do the same job as experienced teachers without significant support.

2. New teachers are nurtured and not left to "flounder on their own"; interaction with other teachers is maximized.

3. Teacher induction is a purposeful and valued activity.

4. Schools possess a culture of shared responsibility and support, in which all or most of the school's staff contributes to the development and nurturing of the new teacher.

5. Assessment of new teachers is downplayed (U.S. Department of Education 1997).

Parental Involvement   The powerful influence of parental involvement on students' achievement is well documented (Booth and Dunn 1996; Buzzell 1996; Epstein, 2001; Hiatt-Michael, 2001). Parental involvement promotes better student attendance, higher graduation rates from high school, fewer retentions in the same grade, increased levels of parent and student satisfaction with school, more accurate diagnosis of students for educational placement in classes, reduced number of negative behavior reports, and, most notably, higher achievement scores on reading and math tests.

Japan probably leads the world when it comes to parental involvement in education. Japanese mothers frequently go to great lengths to assure that their children get the most out of the school's curriculum. The *kyoiku mama* (literally, *education mother*) will tutor her child, wait for hours in lines to register her child for periodic national exams, prepare healthy snacks for the child to eat while studying, forego television so her child can study in quiet, and ensure that her child arrives on time for calligraphy, piano, swimming, or martial arts lessons. Though few U.S. parents might wish to assume the role of the *kyoiku parent*, it seems clear that U.S. students would benefit from greater parental involvement.

Pressure to Excel   There have been many calls to make U.S. schooling more rigorous—a longer school calendar, longer school days, more homework, and harder examinations, for example, have all been proposed. These changes, it is assumed, would increase student achievement and find favor with the majority of the public that wants greater academic rigor in the schools. More often than not, Japan, Korea, and other Asian countries are held up as models for the direction U.S. education should take.

But should U.S. schools be patterned after schools in these countries? Several of those who have studied and experienced Asian schools are beginning to think not. For example, Paul George (1995), who studied the Japanese public school his son attended for two years, reports in *The Japanese Secondary School: A Closer Look* that large numbers of students, deprived of sleep from having attended *jukus* (cram schools) to do well on college entrance exams, waste time in school, having been told by their *juku* instructors not to pay attention to their teachers. Additionally, a teacher of English in rural Japan reports that 70 percent of students at her school attend *jukus* and frequently are awake past midnight (Bracey 1996). According to Gerald Bracey (1996, 128), if U.S. parents want their children to achieve at the level of Asian students, which is often only a few percentage points higher on standardized examinations, they must understand the sacrifices made by Asian students and their parents and be prepared to adhere to these guidelines:

1. [W]hen their children come home from public school, they should feed them and then ship them off to a private school or tutor until 10 P.M.; most youngsters, both elementary and secondary, will need to go to school all day on Sunday, too.

2. [They should] spend 20 to 30 percent of their income on [a]fter-school schools.

3. [W]hen their children turn four, they should take them on their knees and tell them, "You are big boys and girls now, so you need to start practicing for college entrance examinations" (Bracey 1996, 128).

In addition, U.S. students would need to realize that "if they sleep four hours a night, they will get into college, but if they sleep five hours a night, they won't; they must study instead" (Bracey 1996, 128).

Summary

What Are the Social Foundations of Education?

- Students' varied social backgrounds influence schools and teachers; teachers must consider these backgrounds as they develop appropriate learning experiences for all students.

- Social foundations of education are the societal trends, issues, and forces that have shaped (and continue to

shape) public and private education in the United States.

- Among the factors that will influence schools in the future are social, economic, and political forces and technological developments.

- Six major social foundations, or "pillars," of education in the United States are: (1) the role of schooling in society;

(2) teachers' working conditions; (3) historical events that have influenced the development of education; (4) social issues and problems that impact schools; (5) increasing diversity and cultural pluralism; and (6) teacher leaders and the "professionalization" of teaching.

What Are Societal Goals for Schooling in the United States?

- Agreement exists regarding six broad goals for education in the United States: academic achievement, teaching values, socialization of children and youth, personal growth, social change, and expanding equality of opportunity for all groups in the United States.

- Society's goals for education are reflected in the No Child Left Behind (NCLB) Act of 2002. The Act mandates statewide testing in reading and mathematics each year in grades 3–8 and holding schools accountable for students' performance on state proficiency tests.

What Are the Characteristics of Schools in Our Society?

- Schools can be categorized according to the focus of their curricula and according to their organizational structures.

- Metaphors for schools have suggested that schools are like families, tribes or clans, banks, gardens, prisons, and so on, with the school-as-family metaphor often describing schools that are successful.

- Some people believe that schools reproduce the existing social class structure, that they maintain differences between the "haves" and "have-nots." For example, Jean Anyon's four categories of schools—working-class schools, middle-class schools, affluent professional schools, and executive elite schools—illustrate the relationship between schooling and social class.

As Social Institutions, What Are Schools Like?

- As social institutions that contribute to the maintenance and improvement of society, schools mirror the national U.S. culture and the surrounding local milieu.

- Several professional associations and state departments of education have developed standards that reflect the knowledge, skills, and dispositions that society expects teachers to possess. Four associations

have a significant impact on teacher education programs on teachers' professional development: Interstate New Teacher Assessment and Support Consortium (INTASC), National Council for Accreditation of Teacher Education (NCATE), Praxis Series: Professional Assessments for Beginning Teachers, and National Board for Professional Teaching Standards (NBPTS).

- Schools develop their own unique cultures, and the surrounding neighborhood environment can impact a school's culture positively or negatively.

- All schools share a common set of programmatic or structural "regularities,"—similar class sizes, arrangements for grouping students, length of class periods, or special programs, for example.

- Elements of a school's physical environment such as self-contained classrooms, open-space arrangements, and departmentalization contribute to a school's character and culture. Similarly, each classroom develops its own culture, which is influenced by the physical setting and the social dimensions of the group.

What Are the Characteristics of "Successful" Schools?

- Three views of "successful" schools have been suggested: (1) their students manifest a high level of learning; (2) their results surpass those for comparable schools; and (3) they are improving rather than getting worse.

- Research has identified seven characteristics of effective schools: strong leadership, high expectations, emphasis on basic skills, orderly school environment, frequent and systematic evaluation of student learning, sense of purpose, and collegiality and a sense of community.

- Research indicates that successfully restructured schools emphasize student learning, authentic pedagogy, building organizational capacity, and external support.

What Can We Learn from the Foundations of Education in Other Countries?

- The challenges and opportunities for teachers are remarkably similar worldwide, and teachers in different countries can learn much from one another. Comparative education, the study of educational practices in other countries, enables educators to collaborate internationally.

- The International Assessment of Educational Progress (IAEP) has revealed that the achievement levels of U.S. students are lower than those of students in other countries; however, these results reflect the United States' commitment to educating all students and differences in opportunity to learn among countries.

- The Third International Mathematics and Science Study (TIMSS), like the IAEP, has revealed that the achievement levels of U.S. students are often lower than those of students in other countries.

- Education in many other countries is centralized and teachers follow a national curriculum. While a majority of the public supports a national curriculum and national examinations for the U.S. educational system, there are several disadvantages to such a system.

- Many other countries tend to provide greater support for teachers and teaching and have greater parental involvement, two practices that would benefit U.S. education. However, pressure for students in other countries to excel is often extreme.

Key Terms and Concepts

Adequate Yearly Progress (AYP), 9
alternative school, 16
classroom culture, 26
comparative education, 32
departmentalization, 25
emotional intelligence, 12
Goals 2000: Educate America
    Act, 8
institution, 18
Interstate New Teacher Assessment
    and Support Consortium
    (INTASC), 14

magnet school, 16
National Board for Professional
    Teaching Standards (NBPTS), 14
National Council for Accreditation of
    Teacher Education (NCATE), 14
national curriculum, 35
No Child Left Behind (NCLB)
    Act, 9
open-space schools, 25
Praxis Series: Professional
    Assessments for Beginning
    Teachers, 14

school culture, 22
school "regularities," 25
school traditions, 25
school-within-a-school, 16
self-contained classroom, 25
service learning, 13
social foundations of
    education, 4
Third International Mathematics and
    Science Study (TIMSS), 32

Reflective Application Activities

Discussion Questions

1. What evidence suggests that schools reproduce the existing class and social structure in the United States? What evidence suggests that students from the lower socioeconomic classes are not really being prepared for upward social mobility?

2. Using Anyon's four categories of schools (working-class, middle-class, affluent professional, and executive elite),

describe the types of schools you have attended. In what ways have those schools contributed to (or detracted from) your own upward mobility within U.S. society?

Professional Journal

1. Identify four or five goals that you consider most important for education. What do these goals say about your view of the central purpose(s) of schooling? What additional goals should schools emphasize?

2. Reflect on the seven characteristics of effective schools (see pages 28–29). Are you surprised that one (or more) of the characteristics is included on the list? What additional characteristics might have been included?

Online Assignments

1. Visit the website for one of the following: New Teacher Assessment and Support Consortium (INTASC), National Council for Accreditation of Teacher Education (NCATE), Praxis Series: Professional Assessments for Beginning Teachers, and National Board for Professional Teaching Standards (NBPTS). At that site, identify at least one standards statement on which you will place particular emphasis as you continue preparing to become a teacher. What will be your strategy for acquiring the knowledge, skills, and dispositions of that standard?

2. Visit the website for the Third International Mathematics and Science Study (TIMSS) or the International Assessment of Educational Progress (IAEP). At that site and with reference to the grade level and subject area with which you are most interested, gather recent data comparing the achievement of U.S. students with students in other countries.

Observations and Interviews

1. Visit a school in your community recognized as effective or successful. During your visit, take descriptive field notes on one of the characteristics of effective schools as discussed in this chapter. Also, if possible, interview a few students, teachers, staff, and members of the administrative team. During your interviews, which should be brief, informal, and nonevaluative, pose questions based on the characteristic of effective schools you selected. Lastly, transcribe your notes into a brief narrative report and pool your findings with those of your classmates. Based on the accumulated evidence, what additional observations can you make about the characteristics of effective schools?

2. Visit a local school and then develop a case study of that school's culture. Organize your case in terms of the following: (1) Environment: Describe the school facility in regard to material and human resources. Describe the climate of the school. To what extent is the surrounding social milieu reflected in the school? (2) School "regularities": What grades are included at the school? What are the goals of the school's curriculum? (3) Traditions: What events, activities, and rituals are important to students, teachers, administrators, and parents? How do community members describe the school?

Professional Portfolio

To help you in your journey toward becoming a teacher, each chapter of this book includes an entry for your professional portfolio. If you make these entries, at the end of this course you will be well on your way toward developing a portfolio that contains evidence of the professional knowledge and skills you have acquired. As you take additional courses in your teacher education program, your professors may ask you to continue adding to your portfolio. On completion of your program, then, you would have a portfolio that reflects the richness and complexity of teaching and documents your growth and development over time.

Your portfolio should represent your *best work* and give you an opportunity to become an advocate of *who you are* as a teacher. Because a primary purpose of the professional portfolio is to stimulate reflection and dialogue, you may wish to discuss what entries to make in your portfolio with your instructor or other teacher education students.

What will your portfolio contain? Written materials might include: lesson plans and curriculum materials, reflections on your development as a teacher, journal entries, writing assignments made by your instructor, sample tests you have prepared, critiques of textbooks, evaluations of students' work at the level for which you are preparing to teach, sample letters to parents, and a resume. Nonprint materials might include video- and audiotapes featuring you in simulated teaching and role-playing activities, audiovisual materials (transparencies, charts, etc.), photographs of bulletin boards, charts depicting room arrangements for cooperative learning or other instructional strategies, sample grade book, certificates of membership in professional organizations, and awards.

For your first portfolio entry, prepare a journal entry (or videotaped version) describing what has drawn you to teaching. Describe or list your reasons for deciding to become a teacher. What will the rewards of teaching be for you? What aspects of teaching will you find satisfying?

2 Teachers' Working Conditions

*T*he reward of teaching is knowing that your life makes a difference.

—William Ayers
To Teach: The Journey of a Teacher, 2001

experience the tension between the rolled-up-sleeves feeling of teaching in action and the higher philosophical aims I formulate about what I do. It's as if there are two opposing worlds for education, one seething with organic activity, the other a pristine latticework of ideas and beliefs. When I started my internship at Twain (Middle School), experienced teachers laughed knowingly as I told them about the theories we were studying in our night classes. "All that philosophical thinking about education is interesting," they would say, "but you'll find it isn't worth squat in the classroom. That's teaching."

Meanwhile, in the seminar rooms at (the university), I was being told to challenge that opinion. I needed to bring my philosophical beliefs into the classroom and act upon them as I taught. "That's professionalism," my professors said.

"Okay," I thought, being a smart-aleck just out of college and full of ideas. "I'll try it."

Very quickly I found out for myself that action and reflection in teaching can be worlds apart. The smell of a middle school, the whirlwind appearance of the classroom, the things there that have been touched, chewed, stepped on by adolescents—these things drive clean, well-crafted, long-prepared ideas from the building screaming in terror. Oh, you could probably heavily Scotchgard the ideals and smuggle them in, but don't expect miracles. "Be pessimistic," I hear teachers say in their hesitant suggestions about my grand ideas. "That way, you won't be disappointed when they don't work."

Do I dare put my emotional and intellectual foundations on the line every day by attempting to reflect on my deepest beliefs in the daily tempest of middle school? Is self-preservation a good enough excuse to answer no?

I don't think I'm ready. . . . But don't count me out yet. I still take great pleasure in returning to the safety of my home, where I can face the things I believe at the bottom of my heart. . . . I tell myself, "I am a teacher." My ideals intact . . . I sit and reflect upon the day that, once the laughter and the tears have been wiped away, becomes a tool with which I may better myself. For now, it's the most professional thing I can do (Henry et al. 1995, 106–107).

Guiding Questions

1. How does society view teachers and teaching?
2. What has drawn you to teaching?

3. **What challenges confront teachers?**

4. **What is it like to be a teacher?**

5. **What reform trends are changing the profession of teaching?**

I n the preceding excerpt from *To Be a Teacher: Voices from the Classroom,* Jeff Huntley reflects upon his introduction to the conditions under which teachers work. Now a sixth-, seventh-, and eighth-grade reading teacher, Huntley recognized early in his career that teachers' working conditions are characterized by uncertainties. He also realized quickly that applying what he learned in education classes would not be easy, "that action and reflection in teaching can be worlds apart." Much to his credit, though, he was quick to learn that the hallmark of a professional teacher is the ability to reflect upon one's experiences in the classroom. He learned that teaching is a complex act—one that requires thoughtfulness, insight into the motivations of others, and good judgment.

Among the factors that enabled Huntley to have a constructive, meaningful internship were his ability to draw from what he learned in a fifth-year M.A.T. (Master of Arts in Teaching) program and the support, guidance, and encouragement he received from a mentor teacher at the school. Thus, by the end of his internship, Huntley was well on his way to developing an understanding of the teacher's complex role in our society.

How Does Society View Teachers and Teaching?

In some respects, the public is ambivalent regarding its view of teachers. On the one hand, teachers are seen as members of a "noble," critically important profession; on the other, they are given salaries and a level of respect which suggest that they are "only teachers." Dan Lortie (1975, 10) points out in his classic book, *Schoolteacher*, that "The services performed by teachers have usually been seen as above the run of everyday work, and the occupation has had the aura of a special mission honored by society. But social ambiguity has stalked those who undertook the mission, for the real regard shown those who taught has never matched the professed regard."

Some members of the public even believe that teachers are not as smart as other professionals and that teaching does not require a high degree of skill and intelligence. However, evidence suggests that the talents and abilities of teacher education students equal those of students in other majors at our nation's universities. In fact, David Berliner (2000) presents compelling evidence that teachers are as bright as lawyers, managers, and business executives.

Mistaken perceptions of teachers' intelligence and the level of skill needed to teach effectively probably had their origins at the beginning of the twentieth century when there was a dramatic increase in the need for teachers. At that time, an increasing number of women entered teaching field, beginning a trend often referred to as the "feminization of teaching." Female teachers were given less respect from the community than their male predecessors, though they were still more highly regarded than women who worked in factories or as domestics. In addition, they were expected to be of high moral character. They were subjected to a level of public scrutiny hard to imagine today, as illustrated by a 1927 public school contract teachers were required to sign (see Table 2.1).

The public's perceptions of teaching today are much different than they were at the beginning of the previous century. One view of the status accorded today's teachers comes from the NEA 2002 Teacher Day online ballot. Seventy-nine percent of respondents reported that they would consider a teaching career, and 68 percent would recommend teaching as a career choice to their children (National Education Association 2002a). Similarly, when asked which of eight professions "provides the most important benefit to society," 67 percent of the public chose teaching and only 17 percent chose physicians (Recruiting New Teachers 2001). However, perhaps the most accurate view of the status accorded teachers comes from the teachers themselves. In 1984, 47 percent of the 1,981 teachers responding to *The Metropolitan Life Survey of the American Teacher* agreed with the statement, "As a teacher, I feel respected in today's society." According to the 1995 survey of 1,011 teachers, the number of teachers agreeing with the statement had increased to 53 percent (Louis Harris and Associates 1995, 16). (Since the 1995 survey, the question has not been asked).

Table 2.1   Teacher contract from 1927

I promise to take vital interest in all phases of Sunday-school work, donating of my time, service, and money without stint for the uplift and benefit of the community.

I promise to abstain from all dancing, immodest dressing, and any other conduct unbecoming a teacher and a lady.

I promise not to go out with any young men except in so far as it may be necessary to stimulate Sunday-school work.

I promise not to fall in love, to become engaged or secretly married.

I promise not to encourage or tolerate the least familiarity on the part of any of my boy pupils.

I promise to sleep at least eight hours a night, to eat carefully, and to take every precaution to keep in the best of health and spirits, in order that I may be better able to render efficient service to my pupils.

I promise to remember that I owe a duty to the townspeople who are paying me my wages, that I owe respect to the school board and the superintendent that hired me, and that I shall consider myself at all times the willing servant of the school board and the townspeople.

Source: Willard Waller, *The Sociology of Teaching*, New York: John Wiley, 1932, p. 43. Copyright © 1932 by John Wiley.

The Public Trust

Clearly, teachers are seen as public servants accountable to the people. As a result, society has high expectations of teachers—some would say too high. Entrusted with our nation's most precious resource, its children, today's teachers are expected to have advanced knowledge and skills and high academic and ethical standards. Although promoting students' academic progress has always been their primary responsibility, teachers are also expected to further students' social, emotional, and moral development and to safeguard students' health and well-being. Increasingly, the public calls on teachers and schools to address social problems and risk factors that affect student success.

Teaching is subject to a high degree of public scrutiny and control. The level of trust that the public extends to teachers as professionals varies greatly. The public appears to have great confidence in the work that teachers do. Because of its faith in the teaching profession, the public invests teachers with considerable power over its children. For the most part, parents willingly allow their children to be influenced by teachers and expect their children to obey and respect teachers. However, the public trust increases and decreases in response to social and political changes that lead to waves of educational reform.

In the 1970s, for example, teachers were often portrayed as incompetent, unprofessional, unintelligent, and generally unable to live up to the public's expectations. Calls for higher standards, minimum competency testing, and "teacher-proof" curricula reflected the diminished public trust. During the 1980s, the image of teachers was eroded by alarming national reports, a press intent on highlighting the inadequacies of U.S. education, and public outcry for better schools. National reports, such as *A Nation at Risk* (National Commission on Excellence and Education 1983), declared that U.S. education was inadequate, perhaps even a failure. Three years after the release of *A Nation at Risk*, Recruiting New Teachers (RNT), Inc., a national nonprofit organization, was launched to raise esteem for teaching, expand the pool of prospective teachers, and improve the nation's teacher recruitment and development policies and practices.

In the 1990s, further deliberate efforts were made to elevate the status of the profession of teaching. To highlight the important work of teachers, public and commercial television stations aired programs with titles such as "Learning in America: Schools That Work," "America's Toughest Assignment: Solving the Education Crisis," "The Truth about Teachers," "Why Do These Kids Love School?," "Liberating America's Schools," and "America's Education Revolution: A Report from the Front." The Learning Channel began to air *Teacher TV*, a news-style program that explores education trends and issues and features teachers, schools, and communities around the country. Many national corporations initiated award programs to recognize excellence among teachers. Disney Studios, for example, initiated Disney's American Teacher Awards in 1991. As a tribute to countless outstanding teachers, a major media campaign to recruit new teachers in the early 1990s was formed around the slogan, "Be a Teacher. Be a Hero." Table 2.2 shows

Table 2.2   Ratings given the local public schools (in percent)

	2004	2003	2002	2001	1999	1998	1995	1993	1991	1989	1987	1985	1983
A&B	47	48	47	51	49	46	41	47	42	43	43	43	31
A	13	11	10	11	11	10	8	10	10	8	12	9	6
B	34	37	37	40	38	36	33	37	32	35	31	34	25
C	33	31	34	30	31	31	37	31	33	33	30	30	32
D	10	10	10	8	9	9	12	11	10	11	9	10	13
Fail	4	5	3	5	5	5	5	4	5	4	4	4	7
Don't know	6	6	6	6	6	9	5	7	10	9	14	13	17

Sources: Alec M. Gallup, Lowell C. Rose, and Stanley M. Elan, "The 24th Annual Gallup Poll of the Public's Attitudes toward the Public Schools," *Phi Delta Kappan*, September 1992, p. 32; Stanley M. Elam and Lowell C. Rose, "The 27th Annual Phi Delta Kappa/Gallup Poll of the Public's Attitudes toward the Public Schools," *Phi Delta Kappan*, September 1995, p. 42; Lowell C. Rose and Alec M. Gallup, "The 30th Annual Phi Delta Kappa/Gallup Poll of the Public's Attitudes toward the Public Schools," *Phi Delta Kappan*, September 1999, p. 45; Lowell C. Rose and Alec M. Gallup, "The 34th Annual Phi Delta Kappa/Gallup Poll of the Public's Attitudes toward the Public Schools," *Phi Delta Kappan*, September 2002, p. 43 (www.pdkintl.org/kappan/k0209pol.htm#1a); Lowell C. Rose and Alec M. Gallup, "The 35th Annual Phi Delta Kappa/Gallup Poll of the Public's Attitudes toward the Public Schools," *Phi Delta Kappan*, September 2003, p. 44; Lowell C. Rose and Alec M. Gallup, "The 36th Annual Phi Delta Kappa/Gallup Poll of the Public's Attitudes toward the Public Schools," *Phi Delta Kappan*, September 2004, p. 44.

how people rated their public schools in selected years between 1983, just after the release of *A Nation at Risk*, and 2004.

Teachers' Knowledge and Skills

Society believes that competent, effective teachers are important keys to a strong system of education. Accordingly, teachers are expected to be proficient in the use of instructional strategies, curriculum materials, advanced educational technologies, and classroom management techniques. They also are expected to have a thorough understanding of the developmental levels of their students and a solid grasp of the content they teach. To maintain and extend this high level of skill, teachers are expected to be informed about exemplary, research-based practices and to demonstrate a desire for continuing professional development.

Teacher competency and effectiveness includes the responsibility to help all learners succeed. Though today's students come from a diverse array of backgrounds, society expects teachers to hold strong beliefs about the potential for all children. Regardless of their students' ethnicity, language, gender, socioeconomic status, family backgrounds and living conditions, abilities, or disabilities, teachers have a responsibility to ensure that all students develop to their fullest potential. To accomplish this, teachers are expected to have a repertoire of instructional strategies and resources to create meaningful learning experiences that promote

Technology in Teaching

Will I be prepared to teach in a digital age?

Today, thousands of teachers and students routinely use desktop, laptop, and handheld computers with built-in modems, faxes, CD-ROM/DVD players, camcorders, optical scanners, speech and music synthesizers, laser printers, digital cameras, wireless phones capable of Web browsing, e-mail, handwriting recognition, and LCD projection panels. In addition, they use sophisticated software for e-mail, word processing, desktop publishing, presentation graphics, spreadsheets, databases, statistical analyses, and multimedia applications.

To prepare teachers to use these new technologies, many teacher education programs and state departments of education have developed technology competency guidelines for classroom teachers. The following competencies are among those that teachers are using in today's classrooms. How many of these competencies do you possess? What steps can you take to acquire those you do not have?

- Use video media such as videotape recorders, laser disc players, and DVDs
- Use drawing, authoring, spreadsheet, and presentation software
- Develop and use linear and nonlinear multimedia presentations
- Use scanners, digital cameras, and video cameras linked to computers and software
- Download and print resource material from the World Wide Web.
- Send and receive e-mail messages and attached files
- Create and use listservs for e-mail
- Set up chat rooms for students to have synchronous, asynchronous, and threaded discussions
- Conduct video teleconferences
- Set up and maintain databases

students' growth and development. In short, teachers demonstrate their commitment to students and their learning by meeting standards such as those presented in this chapter's Relevant Standards feature.

Accountability for Student Learning

Teachers must "be mindful of the social ethic—their public duties and obligations—embodied in the practice of teaching" (Hansen 1995, 143). Society agrees that teachers are primarily responsible for promoting students' learning, though it is not always in agreement about what students should learn. In any case, society expects teachers to understand how factors such as student backgrounds, attitudes, and learning styles can affect achievement, and it expects that teachers will create safe and effective learning environments. Society also believes that teachers and schools should be accountable for equalizing educational opportunity and maintaining high professional standards.

Since the mid 1990s, there has been an increased emphasis in the United States on holding teachers accountable for students' learning. This increased emphasis on

Relevant Standards

Commitment to Students and Their Learning

The following professional standards stress the need for teachers to have a strong commitment to *all* students and their learning. Moreover, to meet the needs of today's increasingly diverse student populations, successful teachers are committed to their own continuous professional growth, and they actively seek new methods and materials.

- "[Teacher candidates] demonstrate their commitment to students, skills to manage and monitor student learning, capacity to think systematically about their practice, ability to learn from experience, and involvement as members of learning communities." (National Council for Accreditation of Teacher Education [NCATE], 2002, 20. Standard 1: Candidate Knowledge, Skills, and Dispositions.)

- "Teachers are committed to students and their learning. (Core Proposition #1). Accomplished teachers are dedicated to making knowledge accessible to all students. They act on the belief that all students can learn. They treat students equitably, recognizing the individual differences that distinguish one student from another and taking account of these differences in their practice." (National Board for Professional Teaching Standards [NBPTS], 2002, 3.)

- "The teacher is committed to the continuous development of individual students' abilities and considers how different motivational strategies are likely to encourage this development for each student." (Interstate New Teacher Assessment and Support Consortium [INTASC], 1992, 23. "Disposition" statement for Principle #5: "The teacher uses an understanding of individual and group motivation and behavior to create a learning environment that encourages positive social interaction, active engagement in learning, and self-motivation.")

- "Teacher persists in seeking effective approaches for students who need help, using an extensive repertoire of strategies and soliciting additional resources from the school." (Praxis Series, "distinguished" level of performance for Domain 3: Instruction, Component 3e: Demonstrating Flexibility and Responsiveness.) (From Danielson 1996, 112)

accountability is a result of recent studies indicating that teacher quality is one of the most important factors affecting student achievement (Brown 2002). A few states and school districts in the United States hold teachers accountable for student achievement. In Kentucky and North Carolina, for example, salary bonuses for teachers are linked to increases in student achievement. Some states that have union contracts with teachers are examining proposals that would give teachers salary-based bonuses for students' gains on standardized tests.

Unlike teachers in the United States, teachers in other industrialized countries experience less public pressure to be held accountable for student achievement. Instead, greater emphasis is placed on "teacher qualifications, with rigorous requirements for years of study, content knowledge and certification" (Council for Basic Education and Milken Family Foundation 2002, 6). For example, teacher candidates in Germany must complete two years of student teaching and pass two rigorous national certification exams. The first exam focuses on content-area academics and includes a written thesis. The second focuses on teaching ability and classroom performance. Similarly, teachers in France and Japan must pass highly competitive qualifying examinations.

Teacher accountability also means meeting high standards of conduct. Teachers are no longer required to sign contracts with statements such as those contained in the teacher contract presented in Table 2.1. Nevertheless, society does expect teachers to hold high standards of professional ethics and personal morality and to model behaviors that match those standards.

What Has Drawn You to Teaching?

People are drawn to teaching for many reasons. For some, the desire to teach emerges early and is nurtured by positive experiences with teachers during the formative years of childhood. For others, teaching is seen as a way of making a significant contribution to the world and experiencing the joy of helping others grow and develop. And for others, life as a teacher is attractive because it is exciting, varied, and stimulating. Figure 2.1 shows the top reasons teachers feel satisfied with their jobs.

Desire to Work with Children and Youth

The desire to work with children and youth is the most frequently cited reason teachers give for choosing their profession, according to the National Education Association (NEA) research report, *Status of the American Public School Teacher* (2003). Though the conditions under which teachers work may be challenging, their salaries moderate, and some parents and segments of their communities unsupportive, they teach because they care about students. Good teachers derive greatest satisfaction when they are effective in promoting students' learning—when they "make a difference" in students' lives.

As a result of their day-to-day interactions in the classroom, teachers and students develop strong bonds. Daily interactions also enable teachers to become familiar with the personal and academic needs of students, and their commitment to students' well-being and growth helps teachers to cope with the difficulties and frustrations of teaching. As the following quotations from highly accomplished individuals illustrate, the teacher's potential to make a difference in students' lives can be profound:

The dream begins, most of the time, with a teacher who believes in you, who tugs and pushes and leads you on to the next plateau, sometimes poking you with a sharp stick called truth.

—Dan Rather, national news commentator

Compassionate teachers fill a void left by working parents who aren't able to devote enough attention to their children. Teachers don't just teach; they can be vital per-

Figure 2.1 Why teachers are satisfied with their jobs.

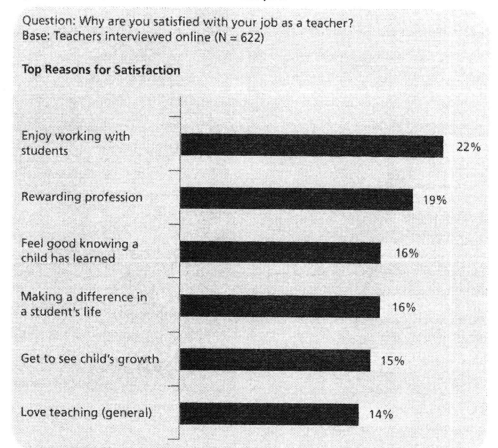

Question: Why are you satisfied with your job as a teacher?
Base: Teachers interviewed online (N = 622)

Top Reasons for Satisfaction

Enjoy working with students — 22%

Rewarding profession — 19%

Feel good knowing a child has learned — 16%

Making a difference in a student's life — 16%

Get to see child's growth — 15%

Love teaching (general) — 14%

Source: The MetLife Survey of the American Teacher: Key Elements of Quality Schools. New York: Harris Interactive, Inc. 2001, p. 111.

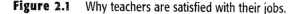

sonalities who help young people to mature, to understand the world and to understand themselves.

—Charles Platt, science fiction novelist

One looks back with appreciation to the brilliant teachers who touched our human feelings. The curriculum is so much necessary raw material, but warmth is the vital element for the growing plant and for the soul of the child.

—Carl Jung, psychoanalyst

Most teachers appreciate the unique qualities of children and youth. They enjoy the openness, curiosity, and trust of young children or the independence and idealism of adolescents. Like the following teacher, they want to be connected to their students: "I now know that I teach so I can be involved in my students' lives, in their real life stories" (Henry et al. 1995, 69).

Teachers can play a critical role in shaping the future of young people. What positive effects might this teacher have on her students?

Teachers also derive significant rewards from meeting the needs of diverse learners. Although students from the United States' more than one hundred racial and ethnic groups and students with special needs are increasing in number, effective teachers recognize that their classrooms are enriched by the varied backgrounds of students. To enable you to experience the satisfaction of helping all students learn, Chapter 4 of this book is devoted to differences among students in regard to gender, race, ethnicity, culture, and socioeconomic status. An appreciation for **student diversity**, then, will help you to experience the rewards that come from enabling each student to make his or her unique contribution to classroom life.

As the following comments from the 2001 *Metropolitan Life Survey of the American Teacher: Key Elements of Quality Schools* suggest, the privilege of working with children and youth, regardless of their stage of development or their life circumstances, is a primary reason people are drawn to teaching and remain in the profession throughout their careers:

> *Where else can you regularly get hugged, get smeared with finger paints, receive hand made cards, wipe tears, share smiles, wiggle loose teeth, share awful cafeteria food, read silly stories, and know that you are changing the world? . . .*

The rewards are great, when you see a child suddenly grasp a concept or write that poem that he/she thought they couldn't, these are the moments that let me know that I am in the right profession! (Harris Interactive 2001, 118).

Passion for Teaching

The 2001 *Metropolitan Life Survey* reported that 79 percent of teachers "strongly agree" that they are passionate about teaching (Harris Interactive 2001). Elementary and secondary teachers, as well as new and experienced teachers, were equally likely to describe themselves as passionate about teaching. Why do teachers find teaching so satisfying? What does it mean to be *passionate* about teaching?

Passion for the Subject   Some teachers who report that they are passionate about teaching may mean that they are passionate about teaching in their subject area. As an inner-city teacher who responded to the 2001 *Metropolitan Life Survey* put it: "Teaching is my purpose in life. I am very passionate about learning and think that I was placed here on this earth to teach. I feel good about being a teacher. I have enthusiasm, knowledge, and love to teach the children" (Harris Interactive 2001, 26).

Passion for the Life of a Teacher   Not surprisingly, many teachers enjoyed their own school experiences. For them, the life of a teacher is appealing—to belong to a profession that places education and the life of the mind in high regard, and to have daily opportunities to see students become excited about learning. Albert Einstein, for example, regretted that he did not devote his career to teaching:

Believe it or not, one of my deepest regrets [is that I didn't teach]. I regret this because I would have liked to have had more contact with children. There has always been something about the innocence and freshness of young children that appeals to me and brings me great enjoyment to be with them. And they are so open to knowledge. I have never really found it difficult to explain basic laws of nature to children. When you reach them at their level, you can read in their eyes their genuine interest and appreciation (quoted in Bucky 1992, 99).

Passion for the Teaching–Learning Process   To be passionate about teaching can also mean to be passionate about the process of teaching and students' subsequent learning. Many teachers focus on the teaching–learning process as much as they focus on the subject and their students. Such teachers relish the spontaneity of teaching and are invigorated by the need to "think on their feet" and to make the most of teachable moments. "[T]hey possess a variety of schemata for seeing what is important, [and they] have a broad repertoire of moves with which to quickly and gracefully act on the situation that they see" (Eisner 1998, 200).

Influence of Teachers

The journey toward becoming a teacher often begins early in life. While few people are "born teachers," their early life experiences often encourage them to enter the teaching profession. With the exception of their parents or guardians, the adults who have the greatest influence on children are often their teachers. Having a positive relationship with a teacher is often the catalyst for deciding to become a teacher. For example, of the respondents to the NEA 2002 Teacher Day online ballot who reported that they would consider becoming a teacher (eight out of ten), 22 percent identified the influence of a teacher in elementary or secondary school as the principal reason for considering a teaching career (National Education Association 2002a).

Evidence also suggests that those who become teachers were often more influenced by their teachers as people than as subject-matter experts. "It is the human dimension that gives all teachers . . . their power as professional influences" (Zehm and Kottler 1993, 2). Behind the decision to become a teacher is often the inspirational memory of earlier teachers to whom one continues to feel connected in a way that goes beyond the subjects they taught.

Desire to Serve

Many choose to teach because they want to serve others; they want their life's work to have meaning beyond providing support for themselves and their families. Some people select another major in college or they leave teaching after a few years to earn more money elsewhere; however, they often return to teaching, recognizing that the other major or career lacked the meaning and significance of teaching. To be of service to others is the primary reason they become teachers.

Most who decide to become teachers do so for altruistic reasons. Altruism is at the heart of their motivation to teach. As the authors of *On Being a Teacher* observe:

> Very few people go into education in the first place to become rich or famous. On some level, every teacher gets a special thrill out of helping others. . . . The teachers who flourish, those who are loved by their students and revered by their colleagues, are those who feel tremendous dedication and concern for others—not just because they are paid to do so, but because it is their nature and their ethical responsibility *(Zehm and Kottler 1993, 8–9).*

For many teachers, the decision to serve through teaching was influenced by their experiences as volunteers. Nearly half of the teachers surveyed by the New York City School Volunteer Program, for example, reported that they had served as volunteers in an educational setting before deciding to become a teacher, and 70 percent of these teachers reported that this experience contributed to their decision to become a teacher (Educational Testing Service 1995). As one New York teacher said, "I always wanted to be a teacher, and all of my volunteer experiences contributed to this career choice" (8).

After the terrorist attacks of September 11, 2001, many people reported that the uncertainty caused by the attacks led them to consider teaching as a career. According to school officials, the national wave of soul-searching after the attacks swelled the number of people seeking jobs as teachers. Clearly, they saw teaching as a way to serve.

The desire to serve others and give something back to society is a key attraction of the **Teach for America** program developed in 1989 by Wendy Kopp as an outgrowth of her senior thesis at Princeton University. Teach for America volunteers, recent graduates from some of the United States' best colleges and universities, are assigned to teach for a minimum of two years in urban and rural school districts with severe shortages of science, math, and language arts teachers. Volunteers complete five weeks of intensive training at the Teach for America Institute in Houston. After two years of teaching, being monitored by state and school authorities, and taking professional development courses, Teach for America teachers can earn regular certification. Upon completion of their two-year assignment, volunteers then return to their chosen careers in other fields, though more than half remain in education as teachers, principals, and educational administrators. Teach for America placed 3,200 members in urban and rural areas across the country in 2003 (Teach for America 2003).

To explore your reasons for becoming a teacher, consider the following list of characteristics and experiences that may indicate your probable satisfaction with teaching as a career. Rate each item on a 1–5 scale (1 = very applicable; 5 = not at all applicable) for how well it describes you. Then, calculate your total score; highest score = 60; the lowest = 12. Interpret the results of your self-assessment with caution. A high score does not necessarily mean that you will be dissatisfied as a teacher, nor does a low score mean that you will be highly satisfied.

1. A passion for learning
2. Success as a student
3. Good sense of humor
4. Positive attitude toward students
5. Tolerance toward others
6. Patience
7. Good verbal and writing skills
8. Appreciation for the arts
9. Experiences working with children (camp, church, tutoring, etc.)
10. Other teachers in family
11. Encouragement from family to enter teaching
12. Desire to serve

Practical Advantages of Teaching

The practical advantages of teaching also draw people to the profession. Teachers' hours and vacations are among the well-known advantages. While the hours most teachers devote to their jobs go far beyond the number of hours they actually spend at school, their schedules are more flexible than those of other professionals. Teachers with young children can often be at home when their children are not in school, and nearly all teachers, regardless of their years of experience, have numerous holidays and a long summer vacation. On the other hand, with the continued growth of year-round schools—3,181 schools in forty-six states were on year-round schedules in 2002–2003—many teachers have three or four "mini vacations" throughout the year and welcome the flexibility of being able to take vacations during off-peak seasons (National Association for Year-Round Education 2003).

Salaries and Benefits Although intangible rewards represent a significant attraction to teaching, teachers are demanding that the public acknowledge the value and professional standing of teaching by supporting higher salaries. According to a 2002 poll, *A National Priority: Americans Speak on Teacher Quality* (Hart and Teeter 2002), 83 percent of the public favors increased salaries for teachers, even if it means paying higher taxes. As a result, teacher salaries have increased steadily since the 1990s. The average salaries of all teachers in 1990 was $31,367; by 2007, it is estimated that teachers' average salaries will be $52,146 (National Center for Education Statistics 2003). Table 2.3 shows a state-by-state ranking of salaries for public school teachers for 2003–2004.

While there is a widespread belief that today's teachers are underpaid, teacher salaries are becoming more competitive with other occupations; in fact, salaries are becoming one of the attractions for the profession. For example, based on the fact that 884 teachers were paid more than $70,000 during 1997–1998 in New Jersey, John Challenger, a job placement specialist and CEO, predicted that New Jersey would soon see its first $100,000 teacher. According to Challenger, occupations typically stereotyped as moderate-to-low paying will experience a "windfall" in the twenty-first century. As private businesses invest in public schools to help develop tomorrow's skilled workforce, teachers will be "able to contract their skills and wares to the highest corporate bidder, yet remain on the payroll at their school" (United Press International 1998).

When comparing teacher salaries state by state, it is important to remember that higher salaries are frequently linked to a higher cost of living, a more experienced teaching force, and a more desirable location. In addition, many districts have developed salary policies to attract high-quality graduates of teacher education programs, to encourage the best teachers to remain in the classroom, or to draw teachers into subjects and geographic areas in which there are shortages. These policies can increase a teacher's salary by thousands of dollars; for example, the Southern Regional Education Board reported that states in the region offered annual quality-based incentives that ranged from $1,000 to $7,500 during 2000 (Grimes 2000). Some states and school districts also offer new teachers scholarships and loan-forgiveness programs, cash bonus incentives, housing assistance, free graduate courses, and other incentives.

Teachers' salaries are typically determined by years of experience and advanced training as evidenced by graduate credit hours or advanced degrees. Additional duties, such as coaching an athletic team, producing the yearbook and school newspaper, sponsoring clubs, or directing the band, can boost teachers' salaries. Most districts offer at least limited summer employment for teachers who wish to teach summer school or develop curriculum materials. Earning a master's degree or certification by the National Board for Professional Teaching Standards (NBPTS) often results in a raise in pay, as does acting as a mentor teacher. Additionally, about one-fourth of the nation's three million public school teachers "**moonlight**" (i.e., hold a second job) to increase their earnings.

Teachers also receive various **fringe benefits**, such as medical insurance and retirement plans, which are usually given in addition to base salary. These benefits

Table 2.3 Average salaries of public school teachers, 2003–04

Rank 2002–03	Rank 2003–04	State	2003–04	% change from 2003	2002–03
1.	1.	CALIFORNIA	58,287*	3.6	56,283*
2.	2.	CONNECTICUT	57,337	3.6	55,367
3.	4.	NEW JERSEY	55,592	2.6	54,166
4.	5.	MICHIGAN	54,806*	2.3	53,563*
5.	6.	NEW YORK	54,054*	2.0	53,017
6.	7.	MASSACHUSETTS	53,076*	2.5	51,803
7.	8.	ILLINOIS	52,950	2.9	51,475
8.	10.	PENNSYLVANIA	52,200	1.5	51,428
9.	9.	RHODE ISLAND	52,261*	2.3	51,076*
10.	3.	DISTRICT OF COLUMBIA	57,009	12.3	50,763
11.	11.	ALASKA	51,736	4.1	49,685
12.	12.	MARYLAND	50,261	1.2	49,677
13.	13.	DELAWARE	49,366	1.2	48,791
14.	14.	OREGON	59,169*	3.3	47,600
15.	16.	GEORGIA	45,938	0.9	45,533
16.	15.	OHIO	46,572*	2.4	45,490
17.	17.	INDIANA	45,791	1.8	44,966
18.	19.	WASHINGTON	45,439	1.1	44,958
19.	20.	MINNESOTA	45,375	1.4	44,745
20.	18.	HAWAII	45,479	2.3	44,464
21.	22.	WISCONSIN	43,382*	1.4	42,775
22.	23.	COLORADO	43,319	1.5	42,680
23.	21.	VIRGINIA	43,417*	2.3	42,432
24.	24.	NORTH CAROLINA	43,211	1.9	42,411
25.	25.	NEW HAMPSHIRE	42,689	1.9	41,909
26.	26.	NEVADA	42,254	1.1	41,795*
27.	27.	VERMONT	42,007	1.2	41,491
28.	28.	ARIZONA	41,843*	2.3	40,894*
29.	29.	SOUTH CAROLINA	41,162	2.0	40,362
30.	31.	FLORIDA	40,604	0.8	40,281
31.	30.	IDAHO	41,080*	2.3	40,148
32.	32.	TEXAS	40,494	1.3	39,974
33.	33.	TENNESSEE	40,318	2.9	39,186
34.	38.	IOWA	39,432	1.0	39,059
35.	34.	KENTUCKY	40,240	3.2	38,981
36.	37.	WYOMING	39,532	1.8	38,840
37.	35.	MAINE	39,864	3.5	38,518
38.	42.	WEST VIRGINIA	38,461	−0.1	38,481
39.	40.	UTAH	38,976	1.9	38,268
40.	39.	ARKANSAS	39,314*	3.0	38,167
41.	36.	NEBRASKA	39,635	4.6	37,896
42.	41.	KANSAS	38,883	2.9	37,795
43.	44.	MISSOURI	38,006	0.9	37,655
44.	43.	LOUISIANA	38,300	3.1	37,166
45.	45.	NEW MEXICO	37,877	2.5	36,965
46.	46.	MONTANA	36,689*	2.6	35,754
47.	49.	ALABAMA	35,168	0.0	35,152
48.	50.	OKLAHOMA	35,061	0.5	34,877
49.	47.	MISSISSIPPI	35,684*	3.3	34,555*
50.	48.	NORTH DAKOTA	35,441	4.6	33,869
51.	51.	SOUTH DAKOTA	33,236	2.5	32,416
		U.S. AND D.C.	**46,726***	**2.0**	**45,810***

*Compiled from NEA Research, Estimates Databank. The figures are based on reports through August 2004.

Source: National Education Association, 2004. *Rankings & Estimates Update: A Report of School Statistics*. National Education Association. Washington, DC, p. 3.

vary from district to district and are determined during collective bargaining sessions. When considering a school district for your first position, carefully examine the fringe benefits package as well as the salary schedule and opportunities for extra pay.

Job Security and Job Outlook   Periods of economic recession and a need to cut costs to remain competitive in a global economy often result in layoffs for workers in other sectors of U.S. society; however, teachers tend to enjoy a higher level of job security during such times. Not surprisingly, 77 percent of teachers surveyed in 1995 rated job security as better in teaching than in other occupations they had considered (Louis Harris and Associates 1995). In addition, the widespread practice of **tenure** (job security granted to teachers after satisfactory performance for a specified period, usually two to five years) contributes to job security for teachers.

Clearly, there will be many job opportunities for teachers in the near future. As a result of what researchers call a demographic "echo" of the baby boom, the school-age population in the United States is expected to reach 48 million by 2012. In addition, the combined effects of enrollment increases, retirements, and attrition rates between 20 and 30 percent for teachers with three to five years of experience indicate that an estimated 2.2 million teachers will be needed in the next decade (Protheroe, Lewis, and Paik 2002).

Job opportunities for teachers over the next 10 years should be excellent. Currently, many school districts are luring teachers from other states and districts with bonuses and higher pay. In addition, increasing enrollments of students from minority groups, and a shortage of teachers from minority groups, is leading to increased efforts to recruit minority teachers. Also, the number of non-English-speaking students has grown dramatically, especially in California and Florida, creating a demand for bilingual teachers and teachers of English as a second language.

In response to a current shortage of teachers in some locations and anticipated teacher retirements, many states are implementing policies that will encourage more students to become teachers. Some give large signing bonuses that are distributed over the teacher's first few years of teaching. Some are increasing state scholarships, issuing loans for moving expenses, and implementing loan-forgiveness programs (U.S. Department of Labor 2003).

The supply of teachers also is expected to increase in response to reports of improved job prospects, more teacher involvement in school governance, and greater public interest in education. The improved job outlook for teachers is reflected in the steadily increasing number of bachelor's and master's degrees granted in education. Also, more people are entering the profession from other careers.

Opportunities for Teachers from Diverse Groups

During the first part of the twenty-first century, there will be exceptional job opportunities for teachers from diverse racial and ethnic backgrounds and for teachers with disabilities. Clearly, students from diverse racial, ethnic, and cultural backgrounds and students with disabilities benefit from having role models with whom they can easily identify. In addition, teachers from diverse groups and teachers with disabilities may have, in some instances, an enhanced understanding of student diversity that they can share with other teachers.

Teachers of Color   Data released in 2001 by the National Center for Education Statistics indicate that 38 percent of public school students were considered part of a minority group during 1999, an increase of 16 percent from 1972. African American and Hispanic students accounted for 16.5 and 16.2 percent of the public school enrollment, an increase of 2 and 10 percent, respectively, from 1972. The percentage of students from other racial or ethnic groups also increased from 1 percent in 1972 to 6 percent (National Center for Education Statistics 2002a).

When contrasted with the diverse mosaic of student enrollments, the backgrounds of today's teachers reveal less diversity. Teachers of color represent about 10 percent of public school teachers in the United States (National Education Association 2003). During the coming years, that percentage is expected to drop to less than 5 percent (Jorgenson 2001). This shortage is due, in part, to the fact that minority students frequently attend our nation's most impoverished schools. At such schools, students receive little motivation to become teachers. Moreover, if their school experiences are negative, they would have little incentive to pursue a career in teaching. To attract more minority candidates to teaching, Jorgenson (2001) suggests that districts

- Prioritize the recruitment of ethnic educators
- Consider nontraditional sources of teacher recruitment
- Expedite the application materials of ethnic applicants
- Discuss the possibility of offering hiring bonuses for ethnic candidates
- Develop a paraprofessional-to-teacher program
- Understand how ethnically diverse employees perceive the district
- Create a support network for educators of color

The typical undergraduate candidate preparing to teach is a young, white female who recently graduated from high school and is attending college full-time. Post-baccalaureate-level individuals preparing to teach tend to be older, to include slightly more people of color and more males, to be transitioning into teaching from an occupation outside the field of education, to have prior teaching-related experience, and to be attending college part-time (Feistritzer 1999). Figure 2.2 on page 60 illustrates the differences between the racial and ethnic composition of students enrolled in U.S. public schools and that of teacher preparation students in undergraduate and graduate programs.

Teachers with Disabilities   Research indicates that people with disabilities can be effective educators (Anderson, Keller, and Karp 1998; Karp and Keller 1998). "They

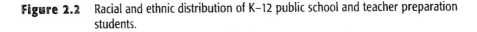

Figure 2.2 Racial and ethnic distribution of K–12 public school and teacher preparation students.

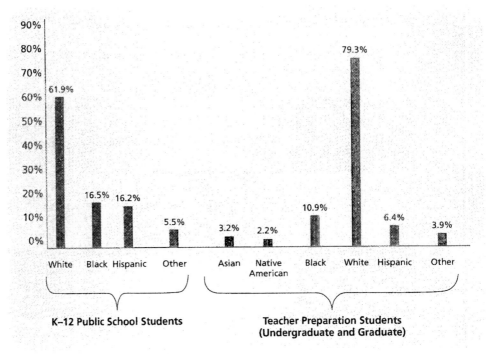

Sources: Based on data from (1) U.S. Department of Education, National Center for Education Statistics, *The Condition of Education 2001.* Washington, DC: National Center for Education Statistics, 2001. (2) C. Emily Feistritzer, *A Report on Teacher Preparation in the U.S.* Washington, DC: National Center for Education Information, 1999.

hold positions in a variety of educational professions, such as all types of teaching, counseling, administration, and speech therapy, and have a variety of disabilities, such as learning disabilities, physical disabilities, visual impairments, deafness and hearing loss, medical conditions, and brain injuries" (Keller, Anderson, and Karp 1998, 8).

The percentage of children with disabilities receiving special education in public preK–12 schools is approximately 10 percent (Hardman, Drew, and Egan 2002), and the current critical need for special education teachers is expected to continue well into the twenty-first century. Nevertheless, there is an apparent lack of information on the number of educators with disabilities—a situation that leads Keller, Anderson, and Karp (1998, 8) to suggest that our need to "approach the question of how many educators have disabilities so tentatively and circumspectly is perhaps telling."

What Challenges Confront Teachers?

Like all professions, teaching has undesirable or difficult aspects. As a high school social studies teacher put it: "Teaching is not terrible. It's great. I love it. It just feels terrible sometimes" (Henry et al. 1995, 119). Similarly, Ayers (2001, 6) points out that "The complexity of teaching can be excruciating, and for some that may be a sufficient reason not to teach (for others, it is one of teaching's most compelling allures)." In spite of the challenges that confront teachers, their overall satisfaction with their careers has increased since 1984. In 1984, 40 percent of teachers reported that they were "very satisfied" with teaching; in 2001, this figure had increased to 52 percent (Harris Interactive 2001).

Prospective teachers should consider the challenges as well as the satisfaction they are likely to encounter. Being informed about what to expect will enable you to make the most of your teacher education program. Awareness of the realities of teaching will enable you to be more effective at developing your personal philosophy of education, developing a repertoire of teaching strategies, strengthening your leadership skills, and acquiring a knowledge base of research and theory to guide your actions. In this manner, you can become a true professional—free to enjoy the many satisfactions of teaching and confident of your ability to deal with its challenges. Table 2.4 on page 62 shows that teachers must deal with a variety of problems in the schools.

Classroom Management and Increasing School Violence

Not surprisingly, discipline and increased crime and violence among youth are strong concerns among education majors. Before teachers can teach they must manage their classrooms effectively. If parents and the school community are supportive and problems are relatively minor, dealing with discipline can still be disturbing and emotionally draining. Twenty-two percent of teachers surveyed in the *Metropolitan Life Survey of the American Teacher 2001* identified "students with discipline problems" as a "big problem" (Harris Interactive 2001). Similarly, a significant percentage of teachers surveyed in the 2002 *Survey* reported that students "are disruptive" "very often" (5 percent) or "often" (14 percent), or "irritable or in bad moods" "very often" (4 percent) or "often" (15 percent) (Harris Interactive 2002).

Though acts of violence in schools are rare, the possibility of experiencing such events can cause additional job-related stress for teachers. Students, too, can experience stress regarding their safety at school; for example, 22 percent of more than 2,300 students surveyed in the *Metropolitan Life Survey of the American Teacher 2002* reported that they worry "a great deal" about "being safe at school" (Harris Interactive 2002). The last few years of the 1990s were marked by frequent reports of random, horrific violence in and around schools. Several communities previously immune to such tragedies were thrust into the national spotlight as a result of violent incidents: Littleton, Colorado; Paducah, Kentucky; Moses Lake, Washington; Springfield, Oregon; and Jonesboro, Arkansas, to name a few.

Table 2.4   What do you think are the biggest problems with which the public schools of this community must deal?

	1999 Teachers %	1996 Teachers %	1989 Teachers %	1984 Teachers %
Parents' lack of support/interest	18	22(1T)	34(1)	31(1)
Pupils' lack of interest/attitudes/truancy	13	16(3)	26(3)	20(3)
Lack of financial support/funding/money	9	22(1T)	27(2)	21(2)
Lack of discipline/more control	7	20(2)	25(4T)	19(4)
Lack of family structure/problems of home life	6	15(4)	8(8)	4(13)
Overcrowded school	4	7(5T)	7(9T)	4(10)
Use of drugs/dope	2	7(5T)	13(7)	5(7)
Fighting/violence/gangs	1	7(5T)	–	–
Moral standards/dress code/sex/pregnancy	*	7	4(15T)	2(22)

*Less than 1 percent.

Note: Figures add to more than 100 percent because of multiple answers, except 1999 figures, which add to less than 100 percent because all answers are not reported. Parenthetical figures indicate rankings. *T* indicates a response tied for a given rank.

Source: From Carol A. Langdon, "Sixth Poll of Teachers' Attitudes toward the Public Schools: Selected Questions and Responses," Bloomington, IN: Phi Delta Kappa Center for Education, Development, and Research, *Research Bulletin,* April 2000, No. 26 (www.pdkintl.org/edres/resbul26.htm).

In addition, many schools have high **teacher–student ratios**, which can make classroom management more difficult. As a result of overcrowding and the constant struggle of trying to meet the needs of all students, some teachers can experience high levels of occupational stress (Gmelch and Parkay 1995). The problem of high teacher–student ratios becomes even more acute if the school has a high **student-mobility rate**—a high proportion of students that move during an academic year. With large numbers of students transferring in (or out) throughout the year, teachers may have trouble understanding their unique learning needs. Fortunately, most teachers develop effective strategies for classroom management and learn to savor the joys and satisfactions of helping students grow and develop. During your teacher education program, you will learn how to develop a leadership plan, create a positive learning environment, and enhance your communication skills; thus, you will be well prepared to meet the challenges of classroom management.

Social Problems that Impact Students

Various social problems affect the lives and learning of many children and youth, such as poverty, substance abuse, teen pregnancy, homelessness, child abuse and neglect, violence and crime, suicide, and health problems such as HIV/AIDS and fetal alcohol syndrome. Twenty-one percent of teachers surveyed in the *Metropolitan Life Survey of the American Teacher 2001* reported that "problems such as hunger, poverty or troubled family lives" were a "big problem" in their schools. These problems were reported more frequently by urban teachers (29 percent) than by teachers in suburban/rural schools (18 percent) (Harris Interactive 2001).

The social problems that place students at risk of school failure are not always easy to detect. Students' low productivity, learning difficulties, and attitude problems demand teacher attention; yet teachers may be unaware of the source of those difficulties. Even when teachers do recognize the source of a problem, they may lack the resources or expertise to offer help. Teachers feel frustrated by the wasted potential they observe in their students. In addition, when the public calls for schools to curb or correct social problems, that expectation can increase the stress teachers experience.

Inadequate Family and Community Support

Support from parents and the community can make a significant difference in the teacher's effectiveness in the classroom. Increasingly, there has been a realization that school, parents, and community must work together so that children and youth develop to their maximum potential academically, socially, emotionally, and physically. For example, 53 percent of the student leaders who attended the 1999 U.S. Senate Youth Program said "parental support" was the biggest factor in their

Teachers frequently become politically active to get more public support for education. How politically active do you think teachers should be?

Figure 2.3   Teachers' views on parental involvement.
How many of your students have parents who need to be more involved in what their children are learning in school—all, most, some, very few, or none at all?

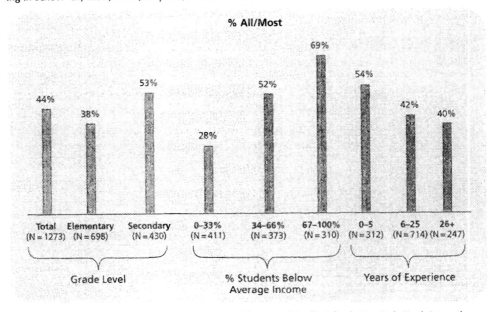

Source: The MetLife Survey of the American Teacher: Key Elements of Quality Schools. New York: Harris Interactive, Inc., 2001, p. 105.

success at high school (William Randolph Hearst Foundation 1999). Parents who talk with their children, help with homework, read to them, monitor their television viewing, and attend meetings of the Parent Teacher Organization (PTO) and school open houses can enhance their children's ability to succeed in school (Fuligni and Stevenson 1995; Henry 1996; Moore 1992). Similarly, communities can support schools by providing essential social, vocational, recreational, and health support services to students and their families. As Figure 2.3 shows, teachers included in the *Metropolitan Life Survey of the American Teacher 2001* believe that, on average, 44 percent of their students have parents who need to be more involved in their children's education. In schools with more than two-thirds of students from families with below-average income, this figure increases to 69 percent (Harris Interactive 2001).

Long Hours and Job Stress

The length of a teacher's work day may appear attractive, but teachers' actual working hours are another matter. Teachers' contracts do not include additional hours for lesson planning and evaluating students' work, nor do they include noninstructional assignments found at all levels of teaching—from recess duty to club sponsorship and coaching. On average, teachers devote 50 hours a week to their jobs, with approximately 37 hours devoted to required duties, and 12 hours devoted to uncompensated teaching tasks. Moreover, teachers, on average, spend about $443 per year of their own money on instructional materials for students (National Education Association 2003).

The need to keep accurate, detailed records of students' academic progress, absences, and tardies, as well as other forms of paperwork, is one of the teacher's most time-consuming tasks. On average, teachers spend ten hours per week on school-related responsibilities not directly related to teaching (Louis Harris and Associates 1995, 68). Other nonteaching responsibilities include supervising students on the playground, at extracurricular events, and in hallways, study halls, and lunchrooms; attending faculty meetings, parent conferences, and open houses; and taking tickets or selling at concessions for athletic events. While nonteaching responsibilities may be enjoyable and they provide good opportunities to interact informally with students, they can lessen the amount of time and energy teachers have available for teaching-related tasks.

In addition to long working hours, factors such as students' lack of interest, conflicts with administrators, public criticism, overcrowded classrooms, lack of resources, and isolation from other adults cause some teachers to experience high levels of stress. Unchecked, acute levels of stress can lead to job dissatisfaction, emotional and physical exhaustion, and an inability to cope effectively—all classic symptoms of teacher burnout. To cope with stress and avoid burnout, teachers report that activities in seven areas are beneficial: social support, physical fitness, intellectual stimulation, entertainment, personal hobbies, self-management, and supportive attitudes (Gmelch and Parkay 1995).

Gaining Professional Empowerment

Without a doubt, if people feel empowered within an organization they have higher morale. If they participate in decisions about job-related policies and if their expertise is acknowledged, they are more invested in their work.

In an interview with journalist Bill Moyers, noted Harvard educator Sara Lawrence Lightfoot eloquently describes why teachers desire **professional empowerment**:

> [Teachers are] saying, "I haven't had the opportunity to participate fully in this enterprise." Some teachers are speaking about the politics of teachers' voice. They're saying, "We want more control over our lives in this school." Some of them are making an even more subtle point—they're talking about voice as knowledge. "We know things about this enterprise that researchers and policy makers can never know. We have engaged in this intimate experience, and we have things to tell you if you'd only learn how to ask, and if you'd only learn how to listen" (Moyers 1989, 161).

Although some teachers may experience frustration in their efforts to gain professional empowerment, efforts to empower teachers and to "professionalize" teaching are leading to unprecedented opportunities for today's teachers to extend their leadership roles beyond the classroom. In fact, "Teachers in the U.S. today are developing leadership skills to a degree not needed in the past. . . . [T]he continuing professional development of teaching as a profession requires that teachers exercise greater leadership at the school level and beyond" (Parkay et al. 1999, 20–21).

What Is It Like to Be a Teacher?

At first, the question posed above may appear easy to answer. Based on your own experiences as a student, you know that teachers assign learning tasks. They ask questions and evaluate students' responses. They lecture and, on occasion, demonstrate what students are to do. They assign chapters to read in the text and then conduct recitations or give quizzes on that material. They praise some students for right answers or good work, and they prod, chastise, and, at times, embarrass others in the hope that their work will improve. And, near the end of the term or semester, they decide who has passed and who has failed.

But, is teaching the sum total of the behaviors that you have observed in your teachers? Clearly not. Teaching is much more complex. As you move ahead in your journey toward becoming a teacher, you will discover that teaching involves more than performing certain behaviors in front of a group of students. "What makes someone a good teacher is not methodology, or even ideology. [Teaching] requires engagement with identity, the way individuals conceive of themselves so that teaching is a state of being, not merely ways of acting or behaving" (Danielewicz 2001, 3). A significant portion of the teacher's work is mental and involves an inner dialogue about purposes and appropriate actions.

Teaching is a creative endeavor in which teachers are continually shaping and reshaping lessons, events, and the experiences of their students. In *To Teach: The Journey of a Teacher*, William Ayers describes the creative dimensions of teaching this way: "The work of a teacher—exhausting, complex, idiosyncratic, never twice the same—is, at its heart, an intellectual and ethical enterprise. Teaching is the vocation of vocations, a calling that shepherds a multitude of other callings. It is an activity that is intensely practical and yet transcendent, brutally matter-of-fact, and yet fundamentally a creative act. Teaching begins in challenge and is never far from mystery" (Ayers 2001, 24).

With careful attention to the details of classroom life, effective teachers artistically develop educative relationships with their students; they "read" the myriad events that emerge while teaching and respond appropriately. Consider how four teachers, identified as highly successful by their principals, view their work. Each was asked to describe those moments when they knew they were teaching effectively. As you read their words, notice how they try to describe something that is beyond easy observation and measurement. And note, too, how they convey the idea that teaching is not entirely a logical, sequential process.

Teacher 1:
Sometimes you see this little light . . . especially in math. You're explaining something, and you see all these puzzled looks on their faces. And you think, "Oh, gosh, they don't under-

stand any of this." And then all of a sudden it hits them and I think, "Aha, I got it!" And they really do! . . . When you see that expression . . . most of the time it's an expression.

Teacher 2:

I don't really know how to determine when I'm definitely reaching kids. That's what makes this job so difficult. But it's when they respond. . . . It's not any-thing. . . . I don't know how to measure it exactly. It's just a feeling. I just feel like I have the kids with me.

Teacher 3:

Well, sometimes it's lightbulb clear. Boom . . . it's there, and you can see it. The kids real-ly responding, actually learning. I don't know how you see it, but you know it.

Teacher 4:

I have to grab the kids that don't want to do math at all and somehow make them want to do this work. I'm not sure how I do it, but kids just want to do well in my class. For some mysterious reason, and I don't care why, they want to do well.

The comments of these teachers suggest the difficulty in answering the question What is it like to be a teacher? Words alone cannot capture all that a teacher does (or doesn't do) in order to teach. Just as the attraction between two persons may be the result of a mysterious "chemistry," the relationships between teachers and their students are charged with a difficult-to-describe emotional energy. Nevertheless, effective teachers direct this energy toward learning.

Though your teachers reflected different personalities and methods, your expe-riences as a student are similar to the experiences of other students. Our recollec-tions about teachers who were good or bad, easy or hard, interesting or dull are drawn from a commonly shared set of experiences. The universality of these expe-riences, then, leads us to conclude that we know "the way teaching is" and what teachers do. However, in an article aptly titled "The Way Teaching Is," noted educa-tional researcher Philip Jackson points out that teaching is "fleeting and ephem-eral" because of the "fragile quality of the psychological condition that is created by the teacher" (Jackson 1965, 62). Similarly, Dan Lortie (1975) suggests that "en-demic uncertainties" characterize teaching.

The following sections examine six **uncertainties of teaching** (see Figure 2.4), each of which illustrates the unpredictable, ambiguous dimensions of teaching. Each uncertainty also illustrates why teaching is so demanding and why it can be so exciting, rewarding, and uplifting. To say that teaching is demanding means more than the fact that Mr. Smith's third-period plane geometry students just can't seem to learn how to compute the area of a triangle; or that Ms. Ellis's sixth-grade composition class can't remember whether to use *there* or *their*; or even that 21 percent of the teacher respondents to the *Metropolitan Life Survey of the American Teacher 2001* reported that "all" or "most" of their students need, but are not receiving, social support services (Harris Interactive 2001). Although there are many frustrating, stressful events with which teachers must cope, the difficulty of teaching goes much further, or deeper, than these examples suggest.

Figure 2.4 Six uncertainties of teaching.

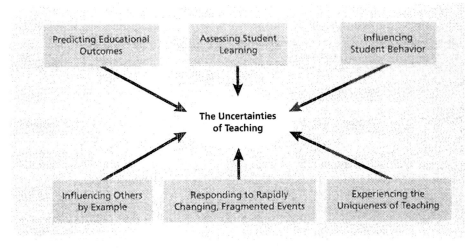

Uncertainty 1: Predicting Educational Outcomes

The outcomes of teaching, even in the best of circumstances, are neither predictable nor consistent. Any teacher, beginner or veteran, can give countless examples of how the outcomes of teaching are often unpredictable and inconsistent. Life in most classrooms usually proceeds on a fairly even keel—with teachers able to predict, fairly accurately, how their students will respond to lessons. Adherence to the best laid lesson plans, however, may be accompanied by students' blank stares, yawns of boredom, hostile acting out, or expressions of befuddlement. On the other hand, lack of preparation on the teacher's part does not necessarily rule out the possibility of a thoroughly exciting class discussion, a real breakthrough in understanding for an individual student or the entire class, or simply a good, fast-paced review of previously learned material. In short, teachers are often surprised at students' reactions to classroom activities.

Students' Responses   Contrary to the popular notion that teaching consists entirely of specific competencies or observable behaviors that have predetermined effects on students, the reactions of students to any given activity cannot be guaranteed. Furthermore, teachers, unlike other professionals, cannot control all the results of their efforts. They recognize that teaching "is full of surprises; classroom lessons that lead to unexpected questions and insights; lessons that fail despite elaborate planning; spur-of-the-moment activities that work beautifully and that may change the direction of a course; students who grow and learn; students who seem to regress or grow distant" (Hansen 1995, 12).

One example of the unpredictability of teaching is given in a teacher intern's description of setting up an independent reading program in his middle school classroom. Here we see how careful room arrangement and organization of materials do not ensure desired outcomes and how a teacher learned to adjust to one reality of teaching.

I wanted everything looking perfect. For two more hours, I placed this here and stuffed that in there. . . . There were stacks of brand-new books sitting on three odd shelves and a metal display rack. . . . I coded the books and arranged them neatly on the shelves. I displayed their glossy covers as if the room was a B. Dalton store.

A few weeks after setting up the reading program, however, this teacher observes that

The orderly environment I thought I had conceived was fraught with complications. For example, the back rows of the classroom were inaccessible regions from which paper and pencil pieces were hurled at vulnerable victims, and there were zones where, apparently, no teacher's voice could be heard. . . . The books . . . remained in chaos. Novels turned up behind shelves, on the sidewalks outside, and in the trash can. And still, at least once a week, I dutifully arranged them until I was satisfied. But something was happening. It was taking less and less for me to be satisfied. . . . [I] loosened up (Henry et al. 1995, 73–76).

Contrary to the preceding example, unpredictability in the classroom is not always bad. Another teacher intern describes her unexpected success at setting up a writing workshop at an urban middle school with a large population of at-risk students. One day she began by telling her students that

"We're going to be starting something new these six weeks. . . . We will be transforming this classroom into a writing workshop." What was I trying to do here? They're not writers. . . . Raymond stared down at Where's Waldo. Michael was engrossed in an elaborate pencil drum solo. Edwina powdered her nose and under her eyes.

"Listen to me, you guys," I said, trying not to lose it before we even started. "We're starting something completely different, something you never get a chance to do in your other classes."

A few heads turned to face me. Veronica slugged Edwina, and Edwina slid her compact into her back pocket.

"What, Miss . . . chew gum?"

In spite of her initial reservations, this teacher made the following observations the next day—the first day of the writing workshop.

Today, it's all clicking.

"Aw, man, I told you I don't understand that part. Why does that guy in your story . . . Chris . . . say that it's too early to rob the store?" David pleads. "It doesn't make sense."

Raymond tips his desk forward and smiles. "It's too early because they want to wait until the store's almost closed."

"Well, then, you've got to say that. Right, Miss?"

I lean against the door frame and try not to laugh. I listen to the conversations around me. Yes, they're loud and they're talking and they're laughing. But they're learning. My students are involved in their writing, I say to myself and shake my head (Henry et al. 1995, 54–55).

Philip Jackson describes the unpredictability of teaching in his well-known book *Life in Classrooms*:

[As] typically conducted, teaching is an opportunistic process. . . . Neither teacher nor students can predict with any certainty exactly what will happen next. Plans are forever going awry and unexpected opportunities for the attainment of educational goals are constantly emerging (Jackson 1990, 166).

Results in the Future   Teachers strive to effect changes in their students for the future as well as for the here and now. In *Life in Classrooms*, Jackson labels this the preparatory aspect of teaching. In addition to having students perform better on next Monday's unit exam or on a criterion-referenced test mandated by the state, teachers expect students to apply their newly acquired skills and knowledge at some indeterminate, usually distant, point in the future.

Just as months or years may pass before the results of teaching become clear, teachers may wait a long time before receiving positive feedback from students. The following note one teacher received from a student she had many years ago illustrates the delayed satisfaction that can characterize teaching:

> *Dear Mrs. Gilday,*
>
> *I am one of many students who fondly remembers you. I was very fortunate to have you as my fifth-grade teacher. In you we saw dignity, respect, and true caring. Your manner was gentle, your time always given freely. Your lessons were interesting and you had a sense of humor. You did not always call on the waving hands or dismiss incorrect answers or embarrass your students. Rather, you coaxed them along, enabling them to succeed.*
>
> *We were all individuals to you and were treated with respect. I never said it then, but thank you—for everything.*
>
> *Sincerely,*
> *Grace*
> *(Paul and Colucci 2000, 51)*

Uncertainty 2: Assessing Student Learning

It is difficult to assess what students learn as a result of being taught. The ultimate purpose of teaching is to lead the student to a greater understanding of the things and ideas of this world. But, as even the most casual appraisal of human nature will confirm, it is very difficult, perhaps impossible, to determine precisely what another human being does or does not understand. Although the aims or intentions of teaching may be specified with exacting detail, one of the realities of teaching, as the following junior high school teacher points out, is that some of what students learn may be indeterminate and beyond direct measurement:

> *There is no clear end result. . . . That frustrates me. I want so badly for my joy [of teaching] to be neatly tied up so that I can look at it admiringly. . . . I want so badly to see my successes—I don't know, give me certificates or badges or jelly beans. Then I can stack them up, count them, and rate myself as a teacher (Henry et al. 1995, 68–69).*

In spite of state-by-state efforts to institute standardized tests of basic skills and thereby hold teachers accountable, the conventional wisdom among teachers is that they are often uncertain about just what their students learn. We have miles of computer printouts with test data, but very little knowledge of what lies behind a child's written response, little understanding of how the child experiences the curriculum. As one educational researcher concludes: "The inaccessibility of data is similar both in science and in learning. We cannot directly 'see' subatomic particles, nor can we 'see' the inner-workings of the mind and emotions of the child. Both are inferential: both are subject to human interpretation" (Costa 1984, 202).

On the one hand, then, teachers must recognize their limited ability to determine what students actually learn; on the other, they must continuously work to become aware of the latest approaches to assessing students' learning. Figure 2.5 presents a set of guiding principles for teachers to follow in developing a student-centered approach to classroom assessment.

Uncertainty 3: Influencing Student Behavior

The teacher's ability to influence student behavior is actually quite limited. The very fact that we refer to the teaching–learning process indicates the extent to which classroom events are "jointly produced" (Doyle 1986, 395) and depend on a teacher–student partnership. According to Arthur Combs (1979, 234–35) in a book aptly titled *Myths in Education: Beliefs That Hinder Progress and Their Alternatives*:

> A teacher's influence on all but the simplest, most primitive forms of student behavior, even in that teacher's own classroom, cannot be clearly established. The older

Figure 2.5   The principles of sound assessment: a critical blend.

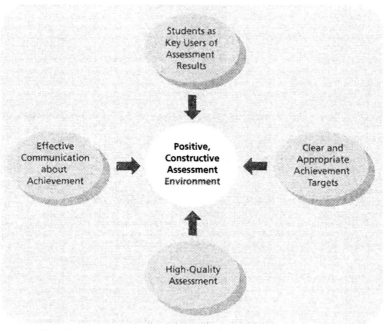

Source: Adapted from Richard J. Stiggins, *Student-Involved Classroom Assessment,* 3rd ed. Upper Saddle River, NJ: Merrill, 2000, p. 18.

children get, the less teachers can influence even those few, primitive forms of behavior. The attempt to hold teachers responsible for what students do is, for all practical purposes, well nigh impossible.

The following example, drawn from the author's experiences teaching at a high school on Chicago's South Side, illustrate how efforts to influence students' behavior can fail.

> To motivate students during a review for a test, I told them that I would distribute Halloween candy if the review went well. Since the review was well planned and the form of reinforcement (candy) was known to be important to students, I was prepared to have a "good" class.
>
> During the review, however, students were almost totally preoccupied with the candy. To my surprise, students put forth little effort during the review. Many students gave wild, preposterous answers to my review questions. Some interrupted me repeatedly to ask how many pieces of candy they would get, when they would get it, what kind it was, and would they get candy in all their classes that day.
>
> Contrary to what I knew about basic theories of reinforcement, my students appeared not to understand that behavior during the review and the reward of candy were connected—one led to the other. When I finally gave students their (unearned) reward—after weighing the pros and cons of not "rewarding" them at all—several became angry because they did not get more candy! Still others tried to steal the candy of their less aggressive classmates. The unexpected reactions of students forced me to spend the final few minutes of class, originally set aside to present new material, restoring order.

At best, a teacher tries to influence students so that they make internal decisions to behave in the desired manner—whether it be reading the first chapter of *The Pearl* by Friday or solving ten addition problems during a mathematics lesson. Teaching is a uniquely demanding profession, therefore, because the work of teachers is evaluated not in terms of what teachers do but in terms of their ability "to help the students become more effective as learners," to "become active seekers after new development" (Joyce, Weil, and Calhoun 2000, 408, 399). This reality underscores the need for a partnership between teacher and learners, including learners who are culturally diverse.

Uncertainty 4: Influencing Others by Example

With the role of teacher also comes the power to influence others by example. Educational psychologist Jeanne Ellis Ormrod (2003, 342) states that "as teachers, we 'teach' not only by what we say but also by what we do." Similarly, Sonia Nieto, an award-winning educator, points out that "[Teachers are] active agents whose words and deeds change lives and mold futures, for better or worse. Teachers can and do exert a great deal of power and influence in the lives of their students" (Nieto 2003, 19).

Clearly, students learn much by imitation, and teachers are models for students. In the primary grades, teachers are idolized by their young students. At the high school level, teachers have the potential to inspire students' emulation and establish the classroom tone by modeling expected attitudes and behaviors. In addition, as Lortie (1975, p. 70) says, "Teachers act in fishbowls; each child can normally see how others are treated."

In *Listening to Urban Kids: School Reform and the Teachers They Want* (Wilson and Corbett 2001), students express the following views about teachers' attitudes:

> *I heard teachers talking about people, saying "Those kids can't do nothing." Kids want teachers who believe in them (86).*

> *A good teacher to me is a teacher who is patient, willing to accept the fact that she might be dealing with students who have problems (87).*

> *Since this is one of his first year's teaching, I give him credit. He relates, but he also teaches. . . . He advises us. He not only tries to teach but gets involved with us (88).*

A high school teacher offers a teacher's perspective on the importance of developing positive relationships with students:

> [The] relationship between teachers and students is becoming one of the most important aspects of teaching. [In] a world of broken homes and violence, the encouragement of their teachers may be the only thing students can hold onto that makes them feel good about themselves (Henry et al. 1995, 127).

How do teachers' attitudes affect students' learning? In what ways are teachers significant role models for students?

Teachers also model attitudes toward the subjects they teach and show students through their example that learning is an ongoing, life-enriching process that does not end with diplomas and graduations. Their example confirms the often-quoted inscription above a doorway in India: "A teacher can never truly teach unless he is still learning himself. A lamp can never light another lamp unless it continues to burn its own flame." The Teachers' Voices feature on page 75 illustrates how one teacher, who moved to the United States from Haiti when she was a child, was influenced by the teachers in her life.

Uncertainty 5: Responding to Rapidly Changing, Fragmented Events

Interactive teaching is characterized by events that are rapidly changing, multidimensional, and irregular. An earlier section discussed how the outcomes of teaching are unpredictable and inconsistent. Yet the challenges of teaching go beyond this. The face-to-face interactions teachers have with students—what Jackson (1990, 152) has termed **interactive teaching**—are themselves rapidly changing, multidimensional, and irregular. "Day in and day out, teachers spend much of their lives 'on stage' before audiences that are not always receptive. . . . Teachers must orchestrate a daunting array of interpersonal interactions and build a cohesive, positive climate for learning" (Gmelch and Parkay 1995, 47).

When teachers are in the **preactive teaching** stages of their work—preparing to teach or reflecting on previous teaching—they can afford to be consistently deliberate and rational. Planning for lessons, grading papers, reflecting on the misbehavior of a student—such activities are usually done alone and lack the immediacy and sense of urgency that characterize interactive teaching. While actually working with students, however, you must be able to think on your feet and respond appropriately to complex, ever-changing situations. You must be flexible and ready to deal with the unexpected. During a discussion, for example, you must operate on at least two levels. On one level, you respond appropriately to students' comments, monitor other students for signs of confusion or comprehension, formulate the next comment or question, and be alert for signs of misbehavior. On another level, you ensure that participation is evenly distributed among students, evaluate the content and quality of students' contributions, keep the discussion focused and moving ahead, and emphasize major content areas.

During interactive teaching, the awareness that you are responsible for the forward movement of the group never lets up. Teachers are the only professionals who practice their craft almost exclusively under the direct, continuous gaze of up to thirty or forty clients. Jackson (1990, 119) sums up the experience: "The *immediacy* of classroom events is something that anyone who has ever been in charge of a roomful of students can never forget."

Uncertainty 6: Experiencing the Uniqueness of Teaching

Teaching involves a unique mode of being between teacher and student—a mode of being that can be experienced but not fully defined or described. On your journey to become a teacher, you will gradually develop your capacity to listen to students and

Teachers' *Voices* Putting Research and Theory into Practice

Education Was My Way Out

Sonie Felix

Education has been like a recurring theme in my life. The more I tried to escape it, the more it became a part of me. As I made my way through college, I began to fall in love with learning. The more I read, the freer I became. It was as if a sense of liberation swept over me and showed me the endless possibilities that were waiting for me. Through reading, I was able to free up my mind and my spirit. I read books by authors who, like myself, struggled to make it in America. They wrote about their hardships and how education helped them to overcome the obstacles that stood in their way. I read about the slaves who were denied an education and how they longed for a chance to be educated, some even risking their lives to attain it. Then I thought about my parents in my country and how they too saw the importance of learning and then it became clear to me what my purpose here on earth was. I knew right then and there what I wanted to do with my life: I wanted to teach.

Teaching to me involves more than just disseminating information to students and passing tests. It involves love, commitment, dedication, and patience. In order to teach, teachers must have faith in their students and believe in them. It cannot be just another job where you punch in at 7:00 and leave at 2:00. It is not easy being a teacher, but I believe that one has to be passionate about teaching and learning in order to teach our children.

In all of the chaos and confusion that has taken place in this system, I sometimes feel that my students and I are placed in a dark, dismal hole with a speck of light to guide us. As a teacher, it is my job to show the students that light, as dim as it may be, and let them know that bigger and better things are waiting for them on the other side. To give up now would be ludicrous. I know that my students need me now more than ever, and I need them too. All they need is a fair chance and someone to believe in them the same way my teachers believed in me. The best way that I can thank my teachers for the difference they have made in my life is by continuing the wonderful job they started. They instilled in me a love for learning and I, in turn, plan to share that with my students.

Questions

1. Felix points out that education can help people overcome obstacles in their lives. How has education helped you to overcome obstacles in your life?
2. With respect to the students whom you are preparing to teach, what obstacles in their lives might education help them overcome?
3. What does Felix mean when she says that she "needs" her students?

Sonie Felix teaches at a public school in Boston. The preceding is excerpted from Sonia Nieto's What Keeps Teachers Going? *(New York: Teachers College Press, 2003), p. 57.*

to convey an authentic sense of concern for their learning. Unfortunately, there is no precise, easy-to-follow formula for demonstrating this to students. You will have to take into account your personality and special gifts to discover your own best way for showing this concern.

One reason it is difficult to describe teaching is that an important domain of teaching, **teachers' thought processes**, including professional reflection, cannot be observed directly. Figure 2.6 shows how the unobservable domain of the teacher's "interior reflective thinking" interacts with and is influenced by the observable domain of the teacher's "exterior reflective action." Teachers' thought processes include their theories and beliefs about students and how they learn, their plans for teaching, and the decisions they make while teaching. Thought processes and actions can be constrained by the physical setting of the classroom or external factors such as the curriculum, the principal, or the community. On the other hand, teachers' thought processes and actions may be influenced by unique opportunities, such as the chance to engage in curriculum reform or school governance. The model also illustrates a further complexity of teaching—namely, that the relationships between teacher behavior, student behavior, and student achievement are reciprocal. What teachers do is influenced not only by their thought processes before, during,

Figure 2.6   A model of reflective action in teaching.

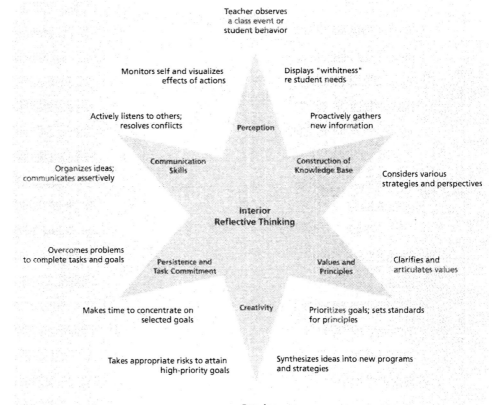

Case for
Reflection

Coping with the Uncertainties of Teaching

Lincoln School is near a busy expressway in an urban area of your state. The school has just under 1,200 pupils, of whom about 45 percent are African American, 35 percent Hispanic, 15 percent white, and 5 percent Asian. As recently as the early 1980s, the neighborhood surrounding Lincoln was predominantly middle income. Since then, however, the more upwardly mobile families began to move out of the area and into the suburbs. Today, most of the families that remain are low income.

Often, students at urban schools such as Lincoln have below-average achievement; however, the performance of Lincoln students on the annual state-mandated test of reading, writing, and mathematics skills has been just below the mean score for all schools in the state. And, compared to the other schools in the city, the achievement of Lincoln students is above average. As a result, Lincoln has a reputation throughout the city for providing students with an above-average education.

Built in the mid 1970s, Lincoln is a well-maintained two-story building. The principal, Karen Long, takes special pride in the appearance of the school and believes that it contributes to the overall morale of students and teachers.

After looking for a job for a month, you were thrilled when Karen called in early August and asked if you wanted to teach at Lincoln. Other teachers had told you how supportive Karen was of first-year teachers, and you couldn't imagine a better place to begin your teaching career.

Near the end of your first three months at Lincoln, Nancy, who is also a beginning teacher and a good friend, comes into your room after the students have left for the day.

"I'm so tired," she begins. "I don't know if I can make it until Christmas." She drops into a student's desk at the front of the room and, with a vacant look on her face, begins to watch as you continue to work at the computer on your desk. At the moment, you are scanning students' work and posting it at the Web site your students have developed.

"What's the matter?" you ask, glancing up momentarily from the computer screen. "Maybe it'll help to talk about it."

"I'm just not sure I'm cut out for teaching," Nancy says. "I like my students, and I think they like me—but I'm not sure if I'm doing a good job. It's just that . . . teaching is much more difficult than I thought it would be. I didn't think being on the other side of the teacher's desk would be so hard."

"I know what you mean," you respond.

"It seems as though I'll have days where everything goes great. The kids are motivated and really seem to learn a lot. On those days I absolutely love teaching."

"That makes it all worthwhile, doesn't it?" you comment.

"Then, other days things are really hard," Nancy continues. "The kids don't respond like I think they should, and I start putting myself down because I think I ought to be able to be that terrific teacher all the time. What do you think . . . is this what teaching is really like?"

Questions

1. How would you respond to your friend?
2. What are the uncertainties of teaching that she is beginning to discover?
3. What factors might cause students to behave differently at school from one day to the next?

and after teaching but also by student behavior and student achievement. This complexity contributes to the uniqueness of the teaching experience.

What Reform Trends Are Changing the Profession of Teaching?

Since the publication in 1983 of *A Nation at Risk: The Imperative for Educational Reform*, the United States has experienced an unprecedented push for reform in education. During that time, numerous commissions were established and scores of reports were written outlining what should be done to improve U.S. schools. Most of these reports called for changes in the education of teachers. In fact, the preparation program you are now involved in probably has been influenced by this **educational reform movement**. Calls for reform in teacher education have emphasized increased academic preparation, an expanded role for schools, and state standards boards.

Increased Academic Preparation

One call for the reform of teacher education was made by the **Holmes Group**, named after Henry W. Holmes, dean of the Harvard Graduate School of Education during the 1920s. The Holmes Group was initially made up of ninety-six major universities. In *Tomorrow's Teachers*, a 1986 report written by thirteen deans of education and one college president, the Holmes Group recommended that all teachers have a bachelor's degree in an academic field and a master's degree in education. Although the Holmes Group viewed additional academic preparation as a means of enhancing the professional status of teachers, critics maintained that students' education would be delayed and be more expensive, with no assurance that students who spent five years obtaining a teaching certificate would be paid more.

The Holmes Group held an action summit in 1993 to develop a comprehensive plan for redesigning the schools of education at Holmes Group member institutions. The plan outlined steps for creating Tomorrow's School of Education (TSE)—an institution that has put into practice the Holmes Group agenda for the reform of teacher education. In early 1995, the Holmes Group released the TSE plan, which recommended that teacher educators become more involved with schools and that students move through a five-year program in cohorts. The report also urged colleges of education to establish **professional development schools (PDSs)** that are linked to colleges or universities and operate on the same principle as teaching hospitals. Students act as intern teachers, and college faculty and school staff develop new teaching methods and collaborate on educational research projects.

In 1996, after a decade of what it described as "uneven progress" in the reform of teacher education and a realization that "the reform of professional education is so complicated and difficult that it has not yielded to any one reform group's efforts to improve it," the Holmes Group joined with other professional organizations—including the NBPTS, the National Education Association (NEA), and the

American Federation of Teachers (AFT)—to create the Holmes Partnership. The **Holmes Partnership** adopted six principal goals: high-quality professional preparation; simultaneous renewal (of public K–12 schools and pre- and in-service education); equity, diversity, and cultural competence; scholarly inquiry and programs of research; faculty development; and policy initiation (Holmes Partnership 2001).

Expanded Role for Schools

Based on his study of teacher education programs around the country, noted educator John Goodlad set forth his plan for the simultaneous renewal of schools and teacher preparation programs in his book, *Educational Renewal: Better Teachers, Better Schools.* To improve teacher preparation, Goodlad (1998) recommended the creation of Centers of Pedagogy that would operate according to a specific set of principles. These centers would take the place of current teacher education departments, and they would be staffed by a team of teacher educators, liberal arts professors, and educators from local schools. In addition, Goodlad recommended that school districts and universities create jointly operated partner schools. Selected teachers at the partner school would divide their time between teaching students at the school and supervising beginning teachers. Partner schools would thus become centers for the renewal of education as well as laboratory schools for the professional development of beginning teachers.

School-Based Teacher Education A new model of teacher preparation that provides students with extensive practical field experiences is known as school-based teacher education. In most instances, school-based programs are designed for students who have received a bachelor's degree and then wish to obtain teacher certification. Two examples are the school-based teacher education programs in Texas and the Teachers for Chicago Program.

Since 1985, completion of a school-based program has been one path to teacher certification in Texas. Candidates complete a year-long paid internship at a school, during which they undertake intensive practical study of teaching. Interns are mentored by the supervisor of the district's teacher education program, the district's curriculum specialist, the principal, the assistant principal, and, in some cases, a university supervisor. Area universities deliver courses specifically designed for the interns. At the end of the year, interns take district- and/or state-adopted tests of content and pedagogy to become eligible for standard certification.

To select, train, and retain effective teachers for Chicago's schools, a group of schools, the Chicago Teachers Union, deans of education at area universities, and the Golden Apple Foundation for Excellence in Teaching created the Teachers for Chicago Program. Candidates, selected through a rigorous interview process, enroll in a graduate education program at one of nine area colleges and universities. After a summer of coursework, they begin a two-year paid internship under the guidance of a mentor teacher. Interns fill vacant teacher positions in the schools and are responsible for the academic progress of their students. On completion of the program, interns have earned a master's degree and have met state certification requirements.

National Certification

The National Board for Professional Teaching Standards (NBPTS) was created in 1987 to develop a set of rigorous standards to provide national board certification for teachers who met the Board's high standards. In 1994–1995, the NBPTS began issuing board certification to teachers who possess extensive professional knowledge and the ability to perform at a high level. By 2002, the NBPTS had awarded national board certification to more than 16,000 teachers. The goal of the NBPTS is to have 100,000 board-certified teachers by 2006. The NBPTS is governed by a sixty-three member board of directors, the majority of whom are active class room teachers.

The NBPTS encourages school districts and states to pay its certification fee ($2,300 for 2003–2004) on behalf of teachers who seek board certification. Candidates first submit portfolios documenting their performance over several months; then they complete a series of exercises at an assessment center. Examples of NBPTS portfolio activities and assessment center activities are available at the NBPTS web site.

State Standards Boards

To regulate and improve the professional practice of teachers, administrators, and other education personnel, states have established **professional standards boards**. In some states, standards boards have the authority to implement standards; in others, they serve in an advisory capacity to educational policymakers. In Washington state, for example, the Washington Advisory Board for Professional Teaching Standards recently made a recommendation to the State Board of Education calling for a three-level teacher certification system. Candidates, on completion of an approved program, would receive a Residency Certificate. With demonstration of successful teaching and a recommendation from the employing school district, a candidate then would be eligible for a renewable, five-year Professional Certificate. Finally, persons who hold national certification from the NBPTS or who hold a combination of advanced degrees, experience, and proficiency in performance-based standards would be eligible for the optional Professional Career Certificate.

In the wake of national reports such as *What Matters Most: Teaching for America's Future* (National Commission on Teaching and America's Future 1996) and *Quality Counts 2000: Who Should Teach? (Education Week* 2000), which highlighted the common practice of teachers teaching "out-of-field," professional standards boards in many states have launched extensive reviews of their teacher certification standards. Also, some standards boards have addressed whether education students' subject-matter preparation should continue to be separate from professional preparation and whether alternative routes to certification such as school district-controlled internship programs should be encouraged.

Summary

How Does Society View Teachers and Teaching?

- The public's view of teachers and teaching is ambivalent—teaching is seen as a "noble" profession, yet the salaries and level of respect teachers receive are less than those received by members of other professions.
- Society has high expectations of the teachers to whom it entrusts its children and youth.
- The public's image of teachers and its attitudes toward schools have improved since the 1980s.
- Society expects teachers to be competent and effective, and it holds teachers accountable for student achievement, for helping all learners succeed, and for maintaining high standards of conduct.

What Has Drawn You to Teaching?

- An important reason for becoming a teacher is a desire to work with children and young people.
- Other reasons include a passion for teaching based on a passion for the subject, the teaching–learning process; the influence of teachers in one's past; and a desire to serve others and society.
- Practical benefits of teaching include on-the-job hours at school, vacations, increasing salaries and benefits, job security, and a feeling of respect in society.
- In contrast to the diversity of student enrollments, the backgrounds of today's teachers are less diverse; thus teachers from diverse racial and ethnic backgrounds and teachers with disabilities will experience exceptional job opportunities for the foreseeable future.

What Challenges Confront Teachers?

- Working conditions for teachers can be difficult and stressful; however, for most teachers satisfactions outweigh dissatisfactions.
- Though problems in schools vary according to size of community, location, and other factors, teachers face five challenges: classroom management, social problems that impact students, inadequate family and community support, long working hours and job stress, and need for professional empowerment.
- Maintaining discipline and avoiding school-based violence are major concerns among preservice teachers.
- Social problems that impact the lives of many children and youth include substance abuse, teen pregnancies, homelessness, poverty, family distress, child abuse, violence and crime, suicide, and health problems such as HIV/AIDS and fetal alcohol syndrome.
- Though hours in the teacher's work day may appear attractive, over 90 percent of teachers work more than forty hours per week and spend an average ten hours per week on work not directly related to teaching assignments.
- Though job-related factors cause some teachers to experience high levels of stress, stress-reduction activities can help teachers cope and avoid burnout.
- As a consequence of nationwide efforts to improve schools, teachers are assuming new leadership roles and experiencing higher levels of professional empowerment.

What Is It Like to Be a Teacher?

- Teaching is characterized by six uncertainties, each of which illustrates the fleeting, ephemeral quality of life in classrooms.
- The outcomes of teaching, even in the best of circumstances, are neither predictable nor consistent.
- It is difficult to assess what students learn as a result of being taught.
- The teacher's ability to influence student behavior is actually quite limited.
- With the role of teacher also comes the power to influence others by example.
- Interactive teaching is characterized by events that are rapidly changing, multidimensional, and irregular.
- Teaching involves a unique mode of being between teacher and student—a mode of being that can be experienced but not fully defined or described.

What Reform Trends Are Changing the Profession of Teaching?

- As part of the educational reform movement, the Holmes Group recommends that teachers obtain a bachelor's degree in an academic field and a master's degree in education.

- The Holmes Group recommends establishing professional development schools linked to colleges of education.

- In *Teachers for Our Nation's Schools*, John Goodlad recommends the creation of Centers of Pedagogy.

- State-level professional standards boards set criteria for the certification and professional development of education personnel in some states; in others, state standards boards are limited to advising educational policymakers.

Key Terms and Concepts

A Nation at Risk, 46
educational reform movement, 78
fringe benefits, 56
Holmes Group, 78
Holmes Partnership, 79
interactive teaching, 74
moonlight, 56

preactive teaching, 74
professional development schools (PDSs), 78
professional empowerment, 65
professional standards boards, 80
student diversity, 52
student-mobility rate, 62

Teach for America, 55
teacher accountability, 50
teacher–student ratios, 62
teachers' thought processes, 75
tenure, 58
uncertainties of teaching, 67

Reflective Application Activities

Discussion Questions

1. What attractions to teaching have not been discussed in this chapter? What challenging aspects?

2. How can society's view of teachers and teaching be improved? What strategies for changing this view do you recommend?

Professional Journal

1. Examine the teacher contract presented in Table 2.1, page 45. Write a one-paragraph description of the working conditions that characterized teaching during that period of our history. How does this description differ from the current working conditions for teachers?

2. Locate a current news article that focuses on teachers and teaching. Analyze the article in terms of whether it presents a positive, neutral, or negative view of teachers and teaching. Write a one-paragraph explanation of your conclusions.

Online Assignments

1. While on the Web, use your favorite search engine to search for information by key words or topics such as:

teachers' working conditions, teacher accountability, teacher moonlighting, teacher tenure, and professional development schools.

2. Go to the MetLife homepage at www.metlife.com. Here, you can download the complete findings of recent *Metropolitan Life Surveys of American Teachers*. Review the surveys for information related to teachers' working conditions.

Observations and Interviews

1. Visit a local school and interview several teachers for their perceptions about teachers' working conditions.

How do their perceptions compare with the information presented in this chapter?

2. Arrange to observe a teacher's class. During your observation, note evidence of the six uncertainties of teaching discussed in this chapter. After your observation, you may wish to check your perceptions with the teacher during an informal, post-observation interview.

Professional Portfolio

Create a plan for developing your portfolio. What specific outcomes or standards will you use to organize your portfolio entries? What artifacts will you use to demonstrate your professional growth and development?

3 History of Education in the United States

The true business of the schoolroom connects itself, and becomes identical, with the great interests of society.

—Horace Mann
Twelfth Report, 1848

During your first year of teaching you are talking with other teachers in the faculty lounge about the problems U.S. schools currently face. The discussion was sparked by a television special last night that most of the teachers watched about schools in the United States and how to improve them.

"I think it [the program] presented a realistic view of the challenges that confront today's teachers," one teacher says.

"Right, it was good to see a positive, honest portrayal of teachers," another offers. "The message seemed to be 'Let's get behind our teachers and support them more. The work they do is important to America.' " Two of the teachers nod their heads in agreement.

A third teacher looks up from the papers he is grading. "Exactly," he says, "I think the show helped people begin see that problems in the schools are not the fault of the schools themselves. They just reflect what's happening in society." Two of the teachers murmur their approval.

Then a teacher who plans to retire at the end of the year begins to speak. She is seated on the other end of the couch on which you're sitting. Everyone listens carefully, perhaps to communicate to her that her opinion is especially valued.

"I've been teaching for 25 years," she says, "When I started teaching we didn't have the problems we have today. We had a job to do, and that was to teach kids. We were there to teach, and the kids, believe it or not, were there to learn."

Before she continues, her attention turns to you. "Then, a few years ago the federal government started getting involved—just like they did during the sixties and seventies. Now the feds are mandating statewide tests, and thousands of kids across the country are being held back. I can't think of any real good that has come out of the federal government's involvement in education. Can you?"

What do you say?

Guiding Questions

1. What were the European antecedents of American education?

2. What were teaching and schools like in the American colonies (1620–1750)?

3. What were the goals of education during the Revolutionary Period (1750–1820)?

4. How was the struggle won for state-supported common schools (1820–1865)?

5. How did compulsory education change schools and the teaching profession (1865–1920)?

6. What were the aims of education during the Progressive Era (1920–1945)?

7. How did education change during the modern postwar era (1945–present)?

In *The Life of Reason*, George Santayana said, "Those who cannot remember the past are condemned to repeat it." Similarly, Adlai Stevenson, presidential candidate in 1952 and 1956, said, "We can chart our future clearly and wisely only when we know the path which has led us to the present." For teachers, the implication of these statements is clear—the past has an impact on teaching and schools today. Accomplished teachers learn from our nation's educational past. They know that educational practices from the past have not disappeared—they continue to evolve, and they shape the present, as well as the future. We cannot understand schools today without a look at what they were yesterday. As this chapter's Relevant Standards feature implies, today's teachers must be students of our educational past so that they may provide leadership to improve our educational future.

The current system of public and private education in the United States is an ongoing reflection of its historical foundations and of the aspirations and values brought to this country by its founders and generations of settlers. Becoming familiar with events that have shaped education in the United States is an important part of your education as a professional.

Still, you may wonder, what is the value of knowing about the history of U.S. education? Will that knowledge help you to be a better teacher? First, knowledge of the events that have influenced our schools will help you evaluate more effectively current proposals for change. You will be in a better position to evaluate changes if you understand how schools have developed and how current proposals might relate to previous change efforts. Second, awareness of events that have influenced teaching is a hallmark of professionalism in education.

This chapter begins with a brief description of some of the European influences on U.S. education. Next, the chapter presents brief overviews of six periods of education in the United States. Each section examines the social forces, events, and persons that, in the author's judgment, have had the greatest impact on education in our country.

What Were the European Antecedents of American Education?

Many practices in today's schools originated in much earlier societies throughout the world. Non-Western civilizations in ancient Egypt, China, and India, for example, emphasized the need for practical education in mathematics, astronomy, medicine, engineering, agriculture, and geography. Similarly, early Western civilizations emphasized the role of education in preparing children and youth for their roles as

Relevant Standards

Understanding How the Past Shapes the Present and Future of Education in the United States

The following professional standards stress the need for teachers to understand how the past shapes the present and future of education in the United States. Proficient teachers know that they cannot understand teaching today without appreciating our nation's educational past.

- "[Teacher candidates] understand and are able to apply knowledge related to the social, historical, and philosophical foundations of education. . . ." (National Council for Accreditation of Teacher Education [NCATE], 2002, 19. Standard 1: Candidate Knowledge, Skills, and Dispositions.)

- "As agents of the public interest in a democracy, teachers through their work contribute to the dialogue about preserving and improving society, and they initiate future citizens into this ongoing public discourse." (National Board for Professional Teaching Standards [NBPTS], 2002, 21.)

- "The teacher realizes that subject matter knowledge is not a fixed body of facts but is complex and ever-evolving." (Interstate New Teacher Assessment and Support Consortium [INTASC], 1992, 14. "Disposition" statement for Principle #1: "The teacher understands the central concepts, tools of inquiry, and structures of the discipline(s) he or she teaches and can create learning experiences that make these aspects of subject matter meaningful for students.")

- "Continuing development is the mark of a true professional, and ongoing effort that is never completed. Educators committed to attaining and remaining at the top of their profession invest much energy in staying informed. . . ." (Praxis Series, Domain 4: Professional Responsibilities, Component 4e: Growing and Developing Professionally.) (Danielson 1996, 112)

adults in society. The timeline in Figure 3.1 shows major events and individuals in Europe that had an impact on the development of education in seventeenth-century colonial America. This section presents: (1) an overview of education in Greece and Rome; (2) a brief glimpse of the kaleidoscope of European history from the fall of Rome to the start of the eighteenth century; and (3) a review of how four eighteenth-century European thinkers influenced education in colonial America.

Education in Ancient Greece

Education in ancient Greece (500–146 B.C.) has had an enduring impact on today's schools. The Greeks believed that people should use leisure time to reflect on the practical and aesthetic values of life. Based on principles of moderation and balance, the goal of Greek education was the well-rounded development of mind and body.

While the pursuit of knowledge by the ancient Greeks is worthy of imitation, other facets of this ancient civilization conflict with the values and goals of today's society. For example, the leisure enjoyed by the small middle and upper classes in

Figure 3.1   Some European influences on American education, 5000 B.C.–1900 A.D.

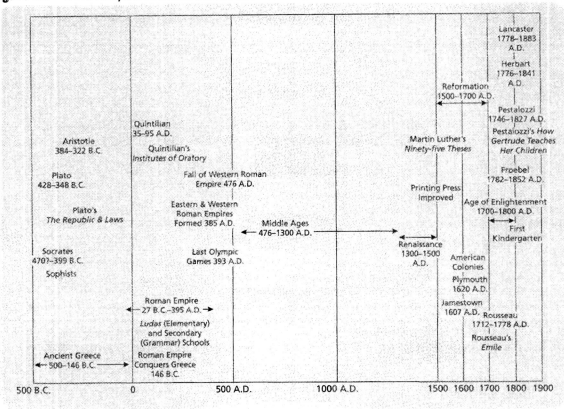

ancient Greece was made possible by a vast population of slaves, and women were not eligible to become citizens.

Several philosophers in ancient Greece shaped ideas about the relationship between education and life. Perhaps the greatest contributions were made by Socrates (ca. 470–399 B.C.), Plato (428–348 B.C.), and Aristotle (384–322 B.C.).

Socrates

Socrates   What little we know about Socrates comes to us from his portrayal in the *Dialogues* written by his student, Plato. Socrates' questioning strategies, his emphasis on discussion to promote inquiry, and his quest for virtue are reflected in today's teaching practices. Socrates questioned his pupils in a manner that led them to see errors and inconsistencies in their thinking. By using an inductive approach, Socrates believed that the truth could be discovered. **Socratic questioning**, according to contemporary educational philosopher Mortimer Adler (1982), is essential for the study of six great ideas: truth, beauty, goodness, liberty, equality, and justice. By questioning students repeatedly, Socrates led his students to these eternal truths.

Case for
Reflection

Emphasizing the Past in the Curriculum

Two weeks after the beginning of the War in Iraq, you are talking with five other teachers in the faculty lounge. The conversation is about yesterday's staff meeting, during which the principal said teachers should stress to students the importance of not isolating the approximately 30 Muslim students who attend your school.

"I think schools have a critical role in modeling principles of tolerance and understanding," says Mary.

"I agree," says Juan. "For example, I like the idea that we teach the kids about the internment of Japanese Americans during the World War II. Today, it's the same thing . . . people taking out their anger on people because they happen to be Muslim."

"Right," says Karen. "History repeats itself. For example, right after the terrorist attacks on the World Trade Center, some people suggested that Muslims be interned, just like Japanese citizens and Japanese Americans were during World War II."

Frank, who has taught at your school for fifteen years, says, "Don't get me wrong, but I don't think we as teachers should draw comparisons between the war in Iraq and events from our nation's past. I say, if discrimination happens at our school, then we deal with it—but we don't need to take time out from the curriculum to draw parallels with the past."

"I don't agree," says Nong. "Schools must play a part to assure that freedom is not denied to anyone at this critical moment in our nation's history."

"Right," says Mary. "We have an obligation to prevent discrimination, not just react to it *after* it happens. Kids need to see how understanding our past is a key to understanding ourselves and others today. If we can't get along as human beings on this planet, we're in trouble. Look at the war in Iraq, the attack on the World Trade Center, suicide bombers in Israel, the killing in Northern Ireland. Sure, we've got the Internet and all this technology, but as a species we haven't evolved at all."

"We have to learn from our past," says Karen. "That's one of the main purposes of education, to see how the great ideas—freedom, justice, equality—can help us improve things. Like I tell my students, there isn't one problem today that Shakespeare didn't have tremendous insights into four hundred years ago—war, racism, poverty."

"Well, all I know is that when I started teaching, we just taught the basics," Frank says. "It was as simple as that. We were there to teach, and the kids, believe it or not, were there to learn. Nowadays, we have to solve all of society's problems—eliminate poverty, racism, war, or whatever."

Questions

1. Do you agree or disagree with Frank's beliefs about teaching?
2. Should *all* areas of the school curriculum emphasize the past?
3. Can the past be overemphasized in the curriculum?

Plato and Aristotle   A student and disciple of Socrates, Plato believed that the individual's abilities should be developed through education for the good of society. To promote his views among Athenians, Plato founded the free, coeducational Academy, often referred to as the world's first university.

Plato believed that boys and girls should be educated from age six to eighteen, with music, mathematics, and gymnastics the main areas of study. Music was a source of "noble" emotions and included the study of literature and history. Mathematics linked the powers of reason with the processes of nature and enabled one to influence the environment. And gymnastics, which emphasized physical and mental well-being, included the study of dance, rhythm, athletics, and military arts. Taken together, the aim of this three-part curriculum was to improve the soul and enable the individual to achieve moral excellence and to realize the ultimate good.

Aristotle, Plato's most famous student, studied and taught at the Academy for twenty years. While Plato was an idealist and believed that ideas are the ultimate reality, Aristotle was a realist and believed that reality, knowledge, and value exist in the physical world independent of the mind. Goodness and virtue depend upon deeds, not knowledge.

Aristotle

Like Plato, Aristotle believed that society needed a strong system of education. Aristotle supported education for all Athenian citizens; however, the majority of Athens' inhabitants were not citizens. Women, for example, were ineligible for citizenship because it was felt they lacked the rational capacities for citizenship and wisdom.

Education in Ancient Rome

In 146 B.C., Greece was conquered by a Roman army. In 27 B.C., Augustus established the Roman Empire, which continued until A.D. 395, when it was divided into the Western Roman Empire, with the capital at Rome, and the Eastern Roman Empire, with the capital at Constantinople. In A.D. 476, the Roman Empire fell.

Roman education was heavily influenced by Greek education. The Roman school system consisted of the *ludus*, or elementary school, and a secondary or grammar school. Boys and girls aged seven to twelve attended the ludi where they learned to read, write, and compute. The education of girls seldom went beyond the ludus. Upper-class boys aged twelve to sixteen attended grammar schools where they studied Greek or Latin grammar and literature. Boys aged sixteen to twenty attended a school of rhetoric where they studied grammar, rhetoric, dialectic, music, arithmetic, geometry, and astronomy.

From the Middle Ages to the Age of Enlightenment

The period from the fall of the Roman Empire to the fourteenth century is known as the Middle Ages. During the medieval period, the Roman Catholic Church came to have the greatest influence on education in Europe. For the most part, the prevailing class structure based on feudalism was not fertile ground for the growth of schools during the Middle Ages. However, the clergy received instruction in the monasteries and at cathedral schools, and medieval universities were established in Spain, France, and England.

A rebirth of interest in Greco-Roman traditions of art, literature, and learning began in the fourteenth century and reached a peak in the fifteenth century. This period, known as the Renaissance, began in northern Europe and Italy and spread throughout Europe.

The key to improving the human condition, according to Renaissance humanists, was to transfer wealth and power from the Church to the people. In addition, humanists believed that an educational system similar to ancient Rome's should be created. They also believed that instruction should consist of the study of ancient classical literature, particularly the work of Plato and Aristotle. The ideal curriculum of the time was based on the seven liberal arts (dialectic, rhetoric, grammar, astronomy, arithmetic, geometry, and music), Greek and Latin, history, and fine arts.

Educational Thought in Eighteenth-Century Europe

The Reformation, with its questioning of religious doctrines, revived interest in the scientific understanding of nature. The eighteenth century came to be known as the Age of Enlightenment or the Age of Reason because reasoning and scientific inquiry were being used to improve society. European thinkers of the 1700s have had a lasting impact on education in the United States.

Jean-Jacques
Rousseau
(1712–1778)

Jean-Jacques Rousseau (1712–1778), considered by some to be the "father of modern child psychology" (Mayer 1973), believed that children progressed through stages of growth and development. According to Rousseau, knowledge of these stages should guide the development of instructional strategies. Rousseau also believed in the innate goodness of children—a natural goodness that society corrupts. Rousseau's child-centered educational theories influenced many educators in France and beyond. For example, John Dewey, whose educational philosophy shaped the progressive education movement in the United States from 1920–1945, was influenced by Rousseau.

Johann Heinrich Pestalozzi (1746–1827) was a Swiss educator who implemented many of Rousseau's ideas. Noted educators worldwide, including Horace Mann from the United States, traveled to Pestalozzi's experimental school in Yverdun, Switzerland, to observe his methods and learn from him. His 1826 book, *How Gertrude Teaches Her Children*, contributed greatly to the development of elementary schools.

Like Rousseau, Pestalozzi believed that the innate goodness of children was corrupted by society, and that instructional practices and curriculum materials should be selected in light of students' natural abilities and readiness to learn. Effective instruction, Pestalozzi believed, moved from concrete experiences to abstract concepts, from the simple to the complex.

Pestalozzi also recognized that children's learning was enhanced by a healthy self-esteem and feelings of emotional security. He was particularly concerned about poor children whom he believed needed to feel loved by their teachers, as Ulich (1950, 264) points out:

> In the studies of Old Swiss and German schoolmasters one could often find a reproduction of a painting of Pestalozzi, in which we see him, with a profound expression of love on his ugly and wrinkled face, embracing the children of peasants who, clad in rags, enter the simple schoolroom.

Johann Friedrich Herbart (1776–1841) was a student of Pestalozzi's and became known as the father of the science of education and of modern psychology (Schubert 1986). Herbart believed that education should focus primarily on developing moral character. His five-step systematic approach for presenting new material to students is still in use today:

1. *Preparation:* helping students make connections between what they know and what they are about to learn.
2. *Presentation:* introducing material in a manner that is appropriate for the psychological development of the student.
3. *Association:* combining new and previously learned material.
4. *Generalization:* moving from concrete examples to abstract principles.
5. *Application:* using recently acquired knowledge to learn more.

The development of schools in the eighteenth and nineteenth centuries was related to European industrialization, urbanization, and population growth. For example, in England, Joseph Lancaster (1778–1838) developed a **monitorial system** for crowded schools in which older students taught younger students. According to the Lancasterian system, one teacher instructed hundreds of pupils through

What ideas stemming from the Age of Enlightenment permanently affected the development of elementary education in the United States? How did Pestalozzi's philosophy of education reflect those ideas?

the use of student monitors—older students selected for their academic abilities. Lancaster eventually immigrated to America where monitorial schools spread rapidly in urban areas after the first school opened in New York City in 1806.

What Were Teaching and Schools Like in the American Colonies (1620–1750)?

Education in colonial America had its primary roots in English culture. The settlers of our country initially tried to develop a system of schooling that paralleled the British two-track system. If students from the lower classes attended school at all it was at the elementary level for the purpose of studying an essentialist curriculum of reading, writing, and computation and receiving religious instruction. Students from the upper classes had the opportunity to attend Latin grammar schools, where they were given a college-preparatory education that focused on perennialist subjects such as Latin and Greek classics.

Above all, the colonial curriculum stressed religious objectives. Generally, no distinction was made between secular and religious life in the colonies. The religious motives that impelled the Puritans to endure the hardships of settling in a new land were reflected in the schools' curricula. The primary objective of elementary schooling was to learn to read so that one might read the Bible and religious catechisms and thereby receive salvation.

The Status of Teachers

Colonial teachers were "special but shadowed" according to Dan Lortie (1975). Since teachers, and members of the clergy, were educated, they were "special" and expected to have high moral character. On the other hand, teachers were "shadowed" because they were subordinate to the clergy, the power elite in the community. Teachers' extra duties reflected their marginal status: "Teachers rang the church bells, . . . swept up. . . . taught Bible lessons, and occasionally substituted for the ailing pastor. Those who wished to teach had to accept stern inspection of their moral behavior" (Lortie 1975, 11).

Teaching was also shadowed by what was seen as the "real" work of the community—farming. "Farming was the vital preoccupation. And though males were preferred as teachers, in the summer months, when men were needed to work the land, women were recruited to take their places" (Lightfoot 1978, 47).

Colonial Schools

In the New England colonies (Massachusetts Bay, New Hampshire, and Connecticut), there was a general consensus that church, state, and schools were interrelated. As a result, town schools were created throughout these colonies to teach children the basics of reading and writing so they could learn the scriptures. These schools were heavily influenced by the Puritans, a group of Protestants who believed in strict religious discipline and simplified religious ceremonies.

The Puritan view of the child included the belief that people are inherently sinful. Even natural childhood play was seen as devil-inspired idleness. The path to redemption lay in learning to curb one's natural instincts and behave like an adult as quickly as possible.

To bring about this premature growth, the teacher had to correct the child constantly and try to curb his or her natural instincts. As one historian put it, "In colonial New England the whole idea of education presumed that children were miniature adults possessed of human degeneracy. The daily school routine was characterized by harshness and dogmatism. Discipline was strict, and disobedience and infractions of rules were often met with severe penalties meted out by quick-tempered, poorly qualified instructors" (Rippa 1997, 30).

The middle colonies (New York, New Jersey, Pennsylvania, and Delaware) were more diverse, and groups such as the Irish, Scots, Swedes, Danes, Dutch, and Germans established **parochial schools** based on their religious beliefs. Anglicans, Lutherans, Quakers, Jews, Catholics, Presbyterians, and Mennonites in the Middle Colonies tended to establish their own schools. In the largely Protestant southern colonies (Virginia, Maryland, Georgia, and North and South Carolina), wealthy plantation owners believed the primary purpose of education was to promote religion and to prepare their children to attend colleges and universities in Europe. The vast majority of small farmers received no formal schooling and the children of African slaves received only the training they needed to serve their masters.

No one type of schooling was common to all the colonies. The most common types, however, were the dame schools, the reading and writing schools, and the Latin grammar schools. **Dame schools** provided initial instruction for boys and, often, the only schooling for girls. These schools were run by widows or housewives in their homes and supported by modest fees from parents. Classes were usually held in the kitchen, where children learned only the barest essentials of reading, writing, and arithmetic during instruction lasting for a few weeks to one year. Females might also be taught sewing and basic homemaking skills.

Students at dame schools often began by learning the alphabet from a **horn book**. Developed in medieval Europe, the horn book was a copy of the alphabet covered by a thin transparent sheet made from a cow's horn. "The layer of horn protected the parchment from the wear and tear and smudges of little hands" (Urban and Wagoner 2004, 43). The alphabet and the horn covering were attached to a paddle-shaped piece of wood. Students often hung their hornbooks around their necks with a leather cord threaded through a hole in the paddle.

Reading and writing schools offered boys an education that went beyond what their parents could teach them at home or what they could learn at a dame school. Reading lessons were based on the Bible, various religious catechisms, and the *New England Primer*, first printed in 1690. The ***Primer*** introduced children to the letters of the alphabet through the use of illustrative woodcuts and rhymed couplets. The first couplet began with the pronouncement that

In Adam's fall

We sinned all.

And the final one noted that

Zaccheus he

Did climb the Tree

His Lord to see.

The *Primer* also presented children with large doses of stern religious warnings about the proper conduct of life.

The **Latin grammar school**, comparable to today's secondary school, was patterned after the classical schools of Europe. Boys enrolled in the Latin grammar schools at the age of seven or eight, whereupon they began to prepare to enter Harvard College (established in 1636). Following graduation from Harvard, they would assume leadership roles in the church.

The Boston Latin School, recognized as the first formal "public" secondary school in the Colonies, was founded in 1635 to provide a precollege education for the country's future leaders. At a mass meeting that April, the residents of Boston decided that "our brother Philemon Pormont shall be entreated to become schoolmaster [of the Latin School], for the teaching and nurturing of children with us" (Button and Provenzo 1983, 17).

The quality of teaching in the Latin grammar schools was higher than that found in the dame schools or reading and writing schools. Latin and Greek were the principal studies, though arithmetic was introduced in 1745. Students were required to read Latin authors and to speak Latin in poetry and prose as well as conjugate Greek verbs. The mode of instruction was rigorous:

> In most of the Latin schools, the course of study lasted for seven years. Apparently school was in session six days a week and continued throughout the winter and summer. The school day was usually from six to eleven o'clock in the morning and from one to four or five o'clock in the afternoon. The boys sat on benches for long hours. Great faith was placed in the *memoriter* method of drill and rote learning. Through repeated recitations the students were conditioned to respond with a definite answer to a particular question. Class discussions were not permitted (Rippa 1984, 43).

The Origins of Mandated Education

As today's citizens know, compulsory education laws require that parents, or those who have custody of children between certain ages, send their children to school. During the Colonial era, however, this was not the case.

Universal compulsory education had its origins in the **Massachusetts Act of 1642**, viewed by some as the first "school" law in the colonies (Urban and Wagoner 2004). Prior to this date, parents could decide whether they wished their children to be educated at home or at a school. Church and civic leaders in the colonies, however, decided that education could no longer remain voluntary. They saw that many children were receiving inadequate occupational training. Moreover, they realized that organized schools would serve to strengthen and preserve Puritan religious beliefs.

N N o A H did view
The old world & new

O Young O B A D I A S,
D A V I D, J o s I A s
All were pious.

P P E T E R deny'd
His Lord and cry'd.

Q Queen E s T H E R fues
And faves the *Jews*.

R Young pious R U T H,
Left all for Truth.

S Young S A M' L dear
The Lord did fear.

T Young T I M O T H Y
Learnt fin to fly.

U V A S T H I for Pride,
Was fet afide.

W Whales in the Sea,
GOD's Voice obey.

X X E R X E s did die,
And fo muft I.

Y While youth do cheer
Death may be near.

Z Z A c c H E U s he
Did climb the Tree
Our Lord to fee.

What do these two pages from a 1727 edition of *The New England Primer* suggest about the curriculum and aims of education in early schools in the United States?

The Puritans decided to make education a civil responsibility of the state. The Massachusetts General Court passed a law in 1642 that required each town to determine whether young people could read and write. Parents and apprentices' masters whose children were unable "to read and understand the principles of religion and the capital laws of the country" (Rippa 1997, 36) could be fined and, possibly, lose custody of their children.

Although the Act of 1642 did not mandate the establishment of schools, it did make it clear that the education of children was a direct concern of the local citizenry. In 1648, the Court revised the 1642 law, reminding town leaders that "the good education of children is of singular behoof and benefit to any commonwealth" and that some parents and masters were still "too indulgent and negligent of their duty" (Cohen 1974, 394–395). As the first educational law in this country, the Massachusetts Act of 1642 was a landmark.

The **Massachusetts Act of 1647**, often referred to as the Old Deluder Satan Act (because education was seen as the best protection against the wiles of the devil), mandated the establishment and support of schools. In particular, towns of fifty households or more were to appoint a person to instruct "all such children as shall resort to him to write and read." Teachers were to "be paid either by the parents or masters of such children, or by the inhabitants in general" (Rippa 1997, 36). This act furthermore required towns of 100 households or more to establish a Latin grammar school to prepare students for Harvard College. A town that failed to satisfy this law could be assessed a fine of five pounds.

Support for mandated education was later expanded by passage of the Northwest Ordinance in 1785 which gave federal land to the states for educational purposes. The Ordinance divided the Northwest Territories (now Illinois, Indiana, Michigan, Ohio, Wisconsin, and part of Minnesota) into thirty-six-square-mile sections, with the sixteenth square mile designated for public schools.

Education for African Americans and Native Americans

At the close of the American Revolution, nearly all of the half million African Americans were slaves who could neither read nor write (Button and Provenzo 1989). In most cases, those who were literate had been taught by their masters or through small, church-affiliated programs. Literate Native Americans and Mexican Americans usually had received their training at the hands of missionaries. One of the first schools for African Americans was started by Elias Neau in New York City in 1704. Sponsored by the Church of England, Neau's school taught African Americans and Native Americans how to read as part of the Church's efforts to convert students.

Other schools for African Americans and Native Americans were started by the Quakers, who regarded slavery as a moral evil. Though Quaker schools for African Americans existed as early as 1700, one of the best known was founded in Philadelphia in 1770 by Anthony Benezet, who believed that African Americans were "generously sensible, humane, and sociable, and that their capacity is as good, and as capable of improvement as that of white people" (Button and Provenzo 1989, 45). Schools modeled on the Philadelphia African School opened elsewhere in the Northeast.

Between the seventeenth and twentieth centuries, how did educational policies and practices reflect the American social system that had developed? How do educational policies and practices reflect the American social system today?

The Quakers also founded "Indian schools" as philanthropic enterprises. In 1819 federal funds for reservation schools were first granted through the newly created Office of Indian Affairs. Federal involvement brought little improvement in programs and enrollments, however. In 1901, for instance, only 300 of the four to five thousand school-age Navajos attended school (Button and Provenzo 1989, 276).

From the seventeenth to the late-twentieth centuries, schools were segregated by race. The first recorded official ground for school segregation dates back to a decision of the Massachusetts Supreme Court in 1850. When the Roberts family sought to send their daughter Sarah to a white school in Boston, the court ruled that "equal, but separate" schools were being provided and that the Roberts therefore could not claim an injustice (*Roberts v. City of Boston* 1850). From the beginning, however, schools were not equal, and students did not have equal educational opportunity.

As the nation moved toward civil war, positions on the institution of slavery and the education of slaves hardened. While abolitionists established schools for free and escaped blacks, some southern states made the teaching of reading and writing to slaves a crime. After emancipation and the Civil War, schools for former slaves were opened throughout the South through the **Freedman's Bureau**, but racial segregation and discrimination remained as a central feature of the American way of life.

What Were the Goals of Education during the Revolutionary Period (1750–1820)?

Education in the United States during the Revolutionary period was characterized by a general waning of European influences on schools. Though religious traditions that had their origins in Europe continued to affect the curriculum, the young country's need to develop agriculture, shipping, and commerce also exerted its influence on the curriculum. By this time, the original settlers who had emigrated from Europe had been replaced by a new generation whose most immediate roots were in the new soil of the United States. This new, exclusively American, identity was also enhanced by the rise of civil town governments, the great increase in books and newspapers that addressed life in the new country, and a turning away from Europe toward the unsettled west. The colonies' break with Europe was most potently demonstrated in the American Revolution of 1776.

Following independence, many leaders were concerned that new disturbances from within could threaten the well-being of the new nation. To preserve the freedoms that had been fought for, a system of education became essential. Through education, people would become intelligent, participating citizens of a constitutional democracy. Among these leaders were Benjamin Franklin, Sarah Pierce, Thomas Jefferson, and Noah Webster.

Benjamin Franklin's Academy

Benjamin Franklin (1706–1790) designed and promoted the Philadelphia Academy, a private secondary school, which opened in 1751. This school, which replaced the old Latin grammar school, had a curriculum that was broader and more practical and also focused on the English language rather than Latin. The academy was also a more democratically run institution than previous schools had been. Though **academies** were largely privately controlled and privately financed, they were secular and often supported by public funds. Most academies were public in that anyone who could pay tuition could attend, regardless of church affiliation (Rippa 1997, 65).

In his *Proposals Relating to the Education of Youth in Pennsylvania*, written in 1749, Franklin noted that "the good Education of youth has been esteemed by wise men in all ages, as the surest foundation of the happiness both of private families and of commonwealths" (Franklin 1931, 151).

Franklin's proposals for educating youth called for a wide range of subjects that reflected his belief that the purpose of education is to discover the universal "truths" in life: English grammar, composition, and literature; classical and modern foreign languages; science; writing and drawing; rhetoric and oratory; geography; various kinds of history; agriculture and gardening; arithmetic and accounting; and mechanics.

Sarah Pierce's Female Academy

English academies, often called people's colleges, multiplied across the country, reaching a peak of 6,185 in 1855, with an enrollment of 263,096 (Spring 1997, 22). Usually, these academies served male students only; a notable exception was Sarah Pierce's Litchfield Female Academy in Litchfield, Connecticut. Pierce (1767–1852) began her academy in the dining room of her home with two students; eventually, the academy grew to 140 female students from nearly every state and from Canada (Button and Provenzo 1989, 87).

For the most part, however, girls received little formal education in the seventeenth and eighteenth centuries and were educated for entirely different purposes than were boys. As the following mission statement for Pierce's Academy suggests, a curriculum grounded in the basic skills of reading, writing, and arithmetic was appropriate for girls:

> Our object has been, not to make learned ladies, or skillful metaphysical reasoners, or deep read scholars in physical science: there is a more useful, tho' less exalted and less brilliant station that woman must occupy, there are duties of incalculable importance that she must perform: that station is home; these duties are the alleviation of the trials of her parents; the soothing of the labours & fatigues of her partner; & the education for time and eternity of the next generation of immortal beings. . . . (Button and Provenzo 1989, 88).

Emma Willard
(1787–1870)

Some women enrolled in **female seminaries**, first established in the early nineteenth century to train women for higher education and public service outside of the home. Educational opportunities for women expanded in conjunction with social reform movements that gradually led to greater political equality for women, including the right to vote in the twentieth century. For example, Troy Seminary, founded in 1821 by educator and poet Emma Willard (1787–1870), became one of the first women's colleges in the country.

Thomas Jefferson's Philosophy

Thomas Jefferson (1743–1826), author of the Declaration of Independence, viewed the education of common people as the most effective means of preserving liberty. As historian S. Alexander Rippa put it, "Few statesmen in American history have so vigorously strived for an ideal; perhaps none has so consistently viewed public education as the indispensable cornerstone of freedom" (1997, 55).

Jefferson was born at Shadwell, Virginia, to a father who was a member of Virginia's landed gentry. Educated at the College of William and Mary, the second college to open in America, Jefferson went on to become one of this country's most influential leaders. Author of the Declaration of Independence at age 33, he also served the public as a member of the Virginia legislature, governor of Virginia, minister to France, secretary of state, vice president, and a two-term President of the United States. His life demonstrated his wholehearted dedication to education. He was fluent in Latin, Greek, and many modern languages. He was strongly influenced by the work of the English philosopher John Locke, various British ideas on constitutional law, and the writings of French educators.

Jefferson was dedicated to human freedom and repulsed by any form of tyranny or absolutism. "I have sworn," he once said, "upon the altar of God, eternal hostility against every form of tyranny over the mind of man" (Rippa 1984, 68). Toward this end, Jefferson was decidedly influential in the intellectual and educational circles of his day. He was a member of the American Academy of Arts and Sciences and president of the American Philosophical Society.

For a society to remain free, Jefferson believed, it must support a continuous system of public education. He proposed to the Virginia legislature in 1779 his Bill for the More General Diffusion of Knowledge. This plan called for state-controlled elementary schools that would teach, with no cost to parents, three years of reading, writing, and arithmetic to all white children. In addition, twenty state grammar schools would be created in which selected poor students would be taught free for a maximum period of six years. Jefferson's plan departed somewhat from the practical orientation of Franklin in that the grammar schools would teach boys a more academic curriculum: English grammar, Greek, Latin, geography, and advanced arithmetic.

Jefferson was unsuccessful in his attempt to convince the Virginia House of Burgesses of the need for a uniform system of public schools as outlined in his bill. The cost of supporting the bill and the special interests of various classes most likely led to its defeat. Jefferson was, however, able to implement many of his educational ideas through his efforts to found the University of Virginia. He devoted the last years of his life to developing the university, and he lived to see the university open with forty students in March 1824, one month before his eighty-first birthday.

While many leaders of Jefferson's time recognized the importance of an educated public, it was not until the 1830s that a tax-supported system of schools would become a reality. Though various religious groups were still wary of a state-supported system of schools that might not represent their interests, the influence of religion on education was beginning to decline. In addition, prosperous Virginians and conservative legislators who had been generally suspicious of any form of strong central government were beginning to recognize that good citizenship and a strong, free nation required an educational system that was available to all.

Noah Webster's Speller

Noah Webster
(1758–1843)

In the years following the Revolution, several textbooks were printed in the United States. Writers and publishers saw the textbook as an appropriate vehicle for promoting democratic ideals and cultural independence from England. Toward this end, U.S. textbooks were filled with patriotic and moralistic maxims. Among the most widely circulated books of this type were Noah Webster's *Elementary Spelling Book* and *The American Dictionary*, a tremendously influential work based on twenty-five years of painstaking research.

Born in Connecticut, Noah Webster (1758–1843) had successful careers as a lawyer, writer, politician, and schoolmaster. He first introduced his speller in 1783 under the cumbersome title, *A Grammatical Institute of the English Language*. Later versions were titled the *American Spelling Book* and the *Elementary Spelling Book*. Webster's speller earned the nickname "the old blue-back" because early copies of the book were covered in light blue paper and later editions covered with bright blue paper.

In the introduction to his speller, Webster declared that its purpose was to help teachers instill in students "the first rudiments of the language, some just ideas of religion, morals and domestic economy" (Button and Provenzo 1989, 65). Throughout, the little book emphasized patriotic and moralistic virtues. Short, easy-to-remember maxims taught pupils to be content with their lot in life, to work hard, and to respect the property of others. Readers were cautioned to "prefer solid sense to vain wit" and to "let no jest intrude to violate good manners." Webster also gave readers extensive instructions on how to behave in school:

> He that speaks loud in school will not learn his own book well, nor let the rest learn theirs; but those that make no noise will soon be wise, and gain much love and good will.
>   Shun the boy that tells lies, or speaks bad words; for he would soon bring thee to shame (Commager 1962, 61–63).

Webster's speller was so popular that it eventually sold over 24 million copies. Historian Henry Steele Commager said of the book, "The demand was insatiable. . . . No other secular book had ever spread so wide, penetrated so deep, lasted so long" (1958, 12). It has been estimated that more than one billion people have read Webster's book.

Webster's speller addressed so many topics that it has been called one of the first curriculum guides for the elementary grades (Johanningmeier 1980, 65). Webster was a post-Revolutionary educational leader who had a profound impact on the American language, and he "did much to help define the new nation" (Urban and Wagoner 2004, 79).

How Was the Struggle Won for State-Supported Common Schools (1820–1865)?

The first state-supported high school in the United States was the Boston English Classical School, established in 1821. The opening of this school, renamed English High School in 1824, marked the beginning of a long, slow struggle for state-supported **common schools** in this country. Those in favor of free common schools tended to be city residents and nontaxpayers, democratic leaders, philanthropists and humanitarians, members of various school societies, and working people. Those opposed were rural residents and taxpayers, members of old aristocratic and conservative groups, owners of private schools, members of conservative religious sects, Southerners, and non-English-speaking residents. By far the most eloquent and effective spokesperson for the common school was Horace Mann.

Horace Mann's Contributions

Horace Mann
(1796–1859)

Horace Mann (1796–1859) was a lawyer, Massachusetts senator, and the first secretary of a state board of education. He is best known as the champion of the common school movement, which has led to the free, public, locally controlled elementary schools we know today. Mann worked tirelessly to convince people that their interests would be well served by a system of universal free schools for all:

> [A free school system] knows no distinction of rich and poor, of bond and free, or between those, who, in the imperfect light of this world, are seeking, through different avenues, to reach the gate of heaven. Without money and without price, it throws open its doors, and spreads the table of its bounty, for all the children of the State (Mann 1868, 754).

Improving Schools   In 1837, Mann accepted the position of Secretary of the Massachusetts State Board of Education. At the time, conditions in Massachusetts schools were deplorable, and Mann immediately began to use his new post to improve the quality of schools. Through the twelve annual reports he submitted while secretary and through *The Common School Journal*, which he founded and edited, Mann's educational ideas became widely known in this country and abroad.

In his widely publicized *Fifth Report* (published in 1841), Mann told the moneyed conservative classes that support of common public schools would provide them "the cheapest means of self-protection and insurance." Where could they find, Mann asked, "any police so vigilant and effective, for the protection of all the rights of person, property and character, as such a sound and comprehensive education and training, as our system of Common Schools could be made to impart?" (Rippa 1997, 95).

In his *Seventh Report* (published 1843), Mann extolled the virtues of schools he had visited in Prussia that implemented the humanistic approaches of noted Swiss educator Johann Heinrich Pestalozzi (1746–1827). "I heard no child ridiculed, sneered at, or scolded, for making a mistake," Mann wrote (Rippa 1997, 96).

The Normal School   During the late 1830s, Mann put forth a proposal that today we take for granted. Teachers, he felt, needed more than a high school education to teach; they should be trained in professional programs. The French had established the *école normale* for preparing teachers, and Mann and other influential educators of the period, such as Catherine Beecher (1800–1878), whose sister, Harriet Beecher Stowe (1811–1896), wrote *Uncle Tom's Cabin*, believed that a similar program was needed in the United States. Through her campaign to ensure that women had access to an education equal to that of men and her drive to recruit women into the teaching profession, Beecher contributed significantly to the development of publicly funded schools for training teachers (Holmes and Weiss 1995).

The first public **normal school** in the United States opened in Lexington, Massachusetts, on July 3, 1839. The curriculum consisted of general knowledge courses plus courses in pedagogy (or teaching) and practice teaching in a model school affiliated with the normal school. In 1849, Electa Lincoln Walton (1824–1908), an 1843 graduate of the normal school, became acting head administrator and the first woman to administer a state normal school. Walton was energetic and determined to succeed, as her journal reveals:

> *Many people think women can't do much. I'd like to show them that they can keep a Normal School and keep it well too. . . . I will succeed. . . . I will never be pointed at as an example of the incompetency of woman to conduct a large establishment well"* (Holmes and Weiss 1995, 42).

When Mann resigned as secretary in 1848, his imprint on education in the United States was broad and deep. As a result of his unflagging belief that education was the "great equalizer of the conditions of men—the balance wheel of the social machinery" (Mann 1957, 87), Massachusetts had a firmly established system of common schools and led the way for other states to establish free public schools.

Reverend W. H. McGuffey's Readers

Reverend William Holmes McGuffey (1800–1873) had perhaps the greatest impact on what children learned in the new school. Far exceeding Noah Webster's speller in sales were the famous **McGuffey readers**. It has been estimated that 122 million copies of the six-volume series were sold after 1836. The six readers ranged in difficulty from the first-grade level to the sixth-grade level. Through such stories as "The Wolf," "Meddlesome Matty," and "A Kind Brother," the readers emphasized virtues such as hard work, honesty, truth, charity, and obedience.

Absent from the McGuffey readers were the dour, pessimistic views of childhood so characteristic of earlier primers. Nevertheless, they had a religious, moral, and ethical influence over millions of American readers. Through their reading of the "Dignity of Labor," "The Village Blacksmith," and "The Rich Man's Son," for example, readers learned that contentment outweighs riches in this world. In addition to providing explicit instructions on right living, the McGuffey readers also taught countless children and adults how to read and study.

McGUFFEY'S PRIMER.

LESSON LXXXVIII.

flew	knew	once
than	school	tri-ed
been	would	ta-ble
shone	wi-ser	tall-er

I once knew a boy. He was not a big boy. If he had been a big boy, he would have been wi-ser. He was a lit-tle boy, not tall-er than the ta-ble.

One fine morn-ing, he was sent to school. The sun shone, and the birds sang on the trees.

This lit-tle boy was not fond of stud-y, but he was fond of play.

This fine morn-ing, he was a long, long time on his way to school.

He met a bee, and tri-ed to get it, but the bee flew a-way.

He met a dog too, but the dog did not stop to play with him.

When the boy got to school, it was ver-y late.

Do you think a good boy will do as this boy did?

What did children learn from typical lessons in nineteenth-century textbooks such as this one from McGuffey's Third Reader?

Justin Morrill's Land-Grant Schools

The common school movement and the continuing settlement of the West stimulated the development of public higher education. In 1862, the **Morrill Land-Grant Act**, sponsored by Congressman Justin S. Morrill (1810–1898) of Vermont, provided federal land for states either to sell or to rent in order to raise funds for the establishment of colleges of agriculture and mechanical arts. Each state was given a land subsidy of 30,000 acres for each representative and senator in its congressional delegation.

Eventually, seven and one-half million dollars from the sale of over seventeen million acres was given to land-grant colleges and state universities. The Morrill Act of 1862 set a precedent for the federal government to take an active role in shaping higher education in the United States. A second Morrill Act in 1890 provided even more federal funds for land-grant colleges.

How Did Compulsory Education Change Schools and the Teaching Profession (1865–1920)?

From the end of the Civil War to the end of World War I, publicly supported common schools steadily spread westward and southward from New England and the

Middle Atlantic states. Beginning with Massachusetts in 1852, compulsory education laws were passed in thirty-two states by 1900 and in all states by 1930.

Because of compulsory attendance laws, an ever-increasing proportion of children attended school. In 1869–70, only 64.7 percent of five- to seventeen-year-olds attended public school. By 1919–20, this proportion had risen to 78.3 percent; and in 1995–1996, it was 91.7 percent (National Center for Education Statistics 1999, 50). The growth in enrollment on the high school level was exceptional. Historical data from the National Center for Education Statistics (1999) enable us to determine that between 1880 and 1920, the population in the United States increased 108 percent, and high school enrollment increased 1,900 percent!

As common schools spread, school systems began to take on organizational features associated with today's schools: centralized control; increasing authority for state, county, and city superintendencies; and a division of labor among teachers and administrators at the individual school site. Influenced by the work of Frederick W. Taylor (1856–1915), an engineer and the founder of **scientific management**, school officials undertook reforms based on management principles and techniques from big business. For example, they believed that top-down management techniques should be applied to schools as well as factories.

Higher Education for African Americans

In *Up from Slavery*, Booker T. Washington (1856–1915) recounts how he walked part of the five hundred miles from his home in West Virginia to attend the Hampton Normal and Agricultural Institute of Virginia, one of the country's first institutions of higher education for African Americans. Four years after graduating from Hampton, Washington returned to be the school's first African American instructor.

Washington had a steadfast belief that education could improve the lives of African Americans just as it had for white people: "Poverty and ignorance have affected the black man just as they affect the white man. But the day is breaking, and education will bring the complete light" (Rippa 1997, 122). In 1880, Washington helped to found the Tuskegee Institute, an industrial school for African Americans in rural Alabama. According to Washington, the Institute would play a key role in bringing about racial equality:

> The Tuskegee idea is that correct education begins at the bottom, and expands naturally as the necessities of the people expand. As the race grows in knowledge, experience, culture, taste, and wealth, its wants are bound to become more and more diverse; and to satisfy these wants there will be gradually developed within our ranks—as already has been true of the whites—a constantly increasing variety of professional and business men and women (Button and Provenzo 1989, 274).

W.E.B. DuBois
(1868–1963)

Not all African Americans shared Washington's philosophy and goals. William E. Burghardt DuBois (1868–1963), the first African American to be awarded a Ph.D. and one of the founders of the National Association for the Advancement of Colored People (NAACP), challenged Booker T. Washington's views on education. In his book *The Souls of Black Folks*, DuBois criticized educational programs that seemed to imply that African Americans should accept inferior status and develop manual skills. DuBois called for the education of the most "talented tenth" of the African American population to equip them for leadership positions in society as a whole.

The Kindergarten

Early childhood education also spread following the Civil War. Patterned after the progressive, humanistic theories of the German educator Friedrich Froebel (1782–1852), the **kindergarten**, or "garden where children grow," stressed the motor development and self-activity of children before they began formal schooling at the elementary level. Through play, games, stories, music, and language activities, a foundation beneficial to the child's later educational and social development would be laid. After founding the first kindergarten in 1837, Froebel developed child-centered curriculum materials that were used in kindergartens in the United States and throughout the world.

Margarethe
Schurz
(1832–1876)

Margarethe Schurz (1832–1876), a student of Froebel, opened the first U.S. kindergarten in her home at Watertown, Wisconsin, in 1855. Her small neighborhood class was conducted in German. In 1860, Elizabeth Palmer Peabody (1804–1891), sister-in-law of Horace Mann and the American writer Nathaniel Hawthorne, opened the country's first private English-speaking kindergarten in Boston.

Initially, kindergartens were privately supported, but in St. Louis in 1873, Susan Blow (1843–1916) established what is commonly recognized as the first successful public kindergarten in the United States. She patterned her kindergarten after one she visited while in Germany. So successful was her program that by 1879, a total of 131 teachers were working in fifty-three kindergarten classes (Button and Provenzo 1989, 169).

The U.S. Bureau of Education recorded a total of twelve kindergartens in the country in 1873, with seventy-two teachers and 1,252 students. By 1997, enrollments had mushroomed to 2,847,000 in public kindergartens and 575,000 in private kindergartens (National Center for Education Statistics 1999, 61).

The Professionalization of Teaching

During the later 1800s, professional teacher organizations began to have a great influence on the development of schools in America. The National Education Association (NEA), founded in 1857, and the American Federation of Teachers (AFT), founded in 1916, labored diligently to professionalize teaching and to increase teachers' salaries and benefits. The NEA also appointed its Committee of Ten in 1892 and its Committee of Fifteen in 1893 to make recommendations for secondary and elementary curricula, respectively. In 1913, the NEA appointed the Commission on the Reorganization of Secondary Education to reexamine the secondary curriculum in regard to students' individual differences.

Committee of Ten   During 1892–93, the directors of the National Education Association appropriated $2,500 for a **Committee of Ten** to hold nine conferences that focused on the following subjects in the high school curriculum: (1) Latin; (2) Greek; (3) English; (4) other modern languages; (5) mathematics; (6) physics, astronomy, and chemistry; (7) natural history (biology, botany, and zoology); (8) history, civil government, and political science; and (9) geography (physical geography, geology, and meteorology). The group's members decided that the primary function of high schools was to take intellectually elite students and prepare them for life. Their recommendations stressed mental discipline in the humanities, languages, and science.

Committee of Fifteen   The report of the Committee of Ten sparked such discussion that in 1893 the National Education Association appointed the **Committee of Fifteen** to examine the elementary curriculum. In keeping with the view that high schools were college preparatory institutions, the committee's report, published in 1895, called for the introduction of Latin, the modern, languages, and algebra into the elementary curriculum. In addition, the curriculum was to be organized around five basic subjects: grammar, literature, arithmetic, geography, and history.

Reorganization of Secondary Education   In 1913 the National Education Association appointed the **Commission on the Reorganization of Secondary Education**. The commission's report, *Cardinal Principles of Secondary Education*, was released in 1918 and called for a high school curriculum designed to accommodate individual differences in scholastic ability. Seven educational goals, or "cardinal principles," were to provide the focus for schooling at all levels: health, command of fundamental processes (reading, writing, and computation), worthy home membership, vocation, citizenship, worthy use of leisure time, and ethical character.

Women's Influence on Teaching   By the early 1900s, the demand for teachers had grown dramatically. Because of greater demand for teachers, greater job mobility, and more and more women becoming teachers, the character of teaching changed. Both respected and regarded with suspicion, teachers became distanced from the communities they served. In his classic book *The Sociology of Teaching*, Willard Waller (1932) refers to this distancing as an "impenetrable veil" between the teacher and the rest of the community. Even in the 1930s, "teachers were kept humble and socially isolated from the seats of power. This was more easily done because teaching, since the turn of the century, had been dominated by women, a group that had its own stigma of second-class citizenship" (Andrews, Sherman, and Webb 1983, 43).

In spite of their status in society, women became influential in shaping educational policies during the early 1900s, in part through the women's suffrage movement that led to the right to vote. Women such as Ella Flagg Young (1845–1918), superintendent of Chicago schools from 1909 to 1915, and Catherine Goggin and Margaret Haley, leaders of the Chicago Teachers Federation, played important roles in the governance of Chicago schools (Holmes and Weiss 1995; Button and Provenzo 1989). Another Chicagoan and visionary educational leader, Jane Addams (1860–1935), founded Hull House, a social and educational center for poor immi-

Margaret Haley

grants. In *Democracy and Social Ethics* (published in 1902), Addams drew from her training as a social worker and developed a philosophy of socialized education that linked schools with other social service agencies and institutions in the city. At the ceremony to present her the Nobel Peace Prize in 1931, Addams was described as "the foremost woman of her nation" (Rippa 1997, 142).

What Were the Aims of Education during the Progressive Era (1920–1945)?

From the end of World War I to the end of World War II, education in the United States was influenced significantly by the philosophy of progressivism. **Progressivism** is a philosophical orientation based on the belief that life is evolving in a positive direction, that people may be trusted to act in their own best interest, and that education should focus on children's interests and practical needs.

During the late nineteenth and early twentieth centuries, supporters of the progressive movement were intent on social reform to improve the quality of American life. In 1919, the Progressive Education Association was founded and went on to devote the next two decades to implementing progressive theories in the classroom that they believed would lead to the improvement of society.

Progressives were not united by a single educational philosophy. For the most part, they were opposed to: autocratic teaching methods; teaching styles that relied almost exclusively on textbooks, recitations, and rote memorization; the relative isolation of the classroom from the real world; and classroom discipline based on fear or physical punishment.

Teachers in progressive schools functioned as guides rather than taskmasters. They first engaged students through providing activities related to their natural interests, and then they moved students to higher levels of understanding. To teach in this manner was demanding:

> Teachers in a progressive school had to be extraordinarily talented and well educated; they needed both a perceptive understanding of children and a wide knowledge of the disciplines in order to recognize when the child was ready to move through an experience to a new understanding, be it in history or science or mathematics or the arts (Ravitch 1983, 47).

John Dewey's Laboratory School

John Dewey
(1859–1952)

Progressive educational theories were synthesized effectively and eloquently by John Dewey (1859–1952). Born in the year that Darwin's *Origin of Species* was published, Dewey graduated from the University of Vermont when he was twenty. He later earned a doctorate at Johns Hopkins University, where his thinking was strongly influenced by the psychologist William James.

From 1894 to 1904, Dewey served as head of the departments of philosophy, psychology, and pedagogy at the University of Chicago. From 1904 until he retired in 1930, Dewey was a professor of philosophy at Columbia University. Dewey's numerous writings have had a profound impact on U.S. schools. In his best-known works, *The School and Society* (1900) and *The Child and the Curriculum* (1902), Dewey states that school and society are connected and that teachers must begin with an understanding of the child's world, the psychological dimension, and then progress to the logical dimension represented by the accumulated knowledge of the human race.

While at the University of Chicago, Dewey and his wife, Alice, established a Laboratory School for testing progressive principles in the classroom. The school opened in 1896 with two instructors and sixteen students and by 1902 had grown to 140 students with twenty-three teachers and ten university graduate students as assistants. The children, four to fourteen years old, learned traditional subjects by working cooperatively in small groups of eight to ten on projects such as cooking, weaving, carpentry, sewing, and metalwork (Rippa 1997). With Dewey as director and his wife as principal, the school became a virtual laboratory for testing Dewey's ideas. The school was so unique that historian Lawrence Cremin referred to it as "the most interesting experimental venture in American education" (1961, 136).

What made Dewey's Laboratory School so unique was that it was thoroughly child centered. The curriculum was a natural outgrowth of the children's interests. The faculty was committed to following the lead set by students. In addition to giving students a meaningful, relevant education, Dewey's school had two purposes: "(1) to exhibit, test, verify, and criticize [Dewey's] theoretical statements and principles; and (2) to add to the sum of facts and principles in its special line with question marks, rather than fixed rules" (Mayhew and Edwards 1936, 3).

What hallmarks of progressive education are evident in this photograph of one of the first classrooms in the country operated according to Dewey's philosophy? How would a progressive classroom look today?

Maria
Montessori
(1870–1952)

Maria Montessori's Method

While Dewey's ideas provided the basis for the development of progressive education in the United States, progressive educators in Europe were similarly developing new approaches that would also impact American education. Chief among
these was Maria Montessori (1870–1952), an Italian physician who was influenced
by Rousseau and believed that children's mental, physical, and spiritual development could be enhanced by providing them with developmentally appropriate educational activities.

   At Montessori's school for poor preschool-age children in Rome, teachers created learning environments based on students' levels of development and readiness
to learn new material. According to the **Montessori method**, prescribed sets of
materials and physical exercises are used to develop students' knowledge and skills,
and students are allowed to use or not use the materials as they see fit. The materials arouse students' interest, and the interest motivates them to learn. Through
highly individualized instruction, students develop self-discipline and self-
confidence. Montessori's ideas spread throughout the world; by 1915, almost one
hundred Montessori schools were operating in the United States (Webb, Metha,
and Jordan 1999). Today, Montessorian materials and activities are a standard part
of the early childhood and elementary curricula in public schools throughout the
nation.

The Decline of Progressive Education

By the start of World War II, the progressive education movement, faced with rising public criticism, began a rapid decline. Many of the schools' deficiencies were
blamed on progressive approaches that were seen as soft and lacking the structure
and discipline children needed. In 1955, the Progressive Education Association
ceased operation. Patricia A. Graham (1967, 145) has observed that when the Association began in 1919 "progressive education meant all that was good in education;
35 years later nearly all the ills in American education were blamed on it."

   In spite of its short life, the progressive education movement had an unmistak-
able impact on American education. Many current practices in schools have their
origins in the experimentation of the progressive era: inquiry or discovery learning, self-paced instructional approaches, field trips, flexible scheduling, open-
concept classrooms, nongraded schools, small group activities, and school-based
counseling programs, to name a few.

Education of Immigrants and Minorities

The diversity of America's school population increased dramatically during the late
nineteenth and early twentieth centuries. Latin Americans, Eastern Europeans, and
Southern Europeans followed earlier waves of Western- and Northern-European
immigrants such as the Irish and Germans. As with Native American education,
the goal of immigrant education was rapid assimilation into an English-speaking
Anglo-European society that did not welcome racially or ethnically different
newcomers.

Teachers' Voices   Putting Research and Theory into Practice

Native American Teachers Need Support

Kristine Shotley

When I was studying to be a teacher, a white female student in the same program asked me what I thought my chances were of finding a job after graduation. I replied that because I am Native American, and a woman, I thought I would have excellent opportunities for immediate employment. "How nice," she said, "to turn two negatives into two positives!" I was taken aback. It had not occurred to me that in this day and age, I would still have to defend my identity.

In the United States, most Native American children are still taught by non-Native teachers. There are fewer than 18,000 Native American teachers working today.

To recruit more teachers, we need to develop curricula that affirm our Native American identity. For example, elementary school kids need to learn an accurate and truthful account of American history. How many times do we have to reiterate that Christopher Columbus did not "discover" America?

When I was growing up, Native American history was not taught. I endured the appalled looks of my white classmates when our teachers presented a one-sided account of American history. I felt apologetic for my ancestors who tried to defend their lands from white settlers.

The United States [must address] the lack of Native American teachers. I want my son and other Native American sons and daughters to realize they can become anything they choose because they have the educational background they need.

Questions

1. Shotley says teachers should develop curricula that "affirm" Native American identity. What are the characteristics of curricula that "affirm" the diverse identities of today's students?
2. What should a teacher do if the only instructional materials available present outdated, perhaps even distorted, interpretations of American history?

Kristine Shotley is a member of the Fond Du Lac Tribe of Ojibwe in Minnesota, and she writes for *The Circle*, a Native American news and arts paper published in Minneapolis. This article is from Progressive Media Project, January 12, 2000.

Also at stake was the preservation or loss of traditional culture. In some areas, school policies included the punishment of Cuban and Puerto Rican children, for example, for speaking Spanish in school, and some children even learned to mock their unassimilated parents. In other areas, efforts were made to exclude certain groups, such as Asians, and ethnic enclaves established separate schools for the purpose of preserving, for example, traditional Chinese culture.

By the time Native Americans were granted U.S. citizenship in 1924, confinement on reservations and decades of forced assimilation had devastated Native American cultures and provided few successful educational programs. In 1928, a landmark report titled *The Problem of Indian Administration* recommended that Native American education be restructured. Among the recommendations were the building of day schools in Native American communities and the reform of boarding schools for Native American children. In addition, the report recommended that school curricula be revised to reflect tribal cultures and the needs of local tribal communities. Another fifty years passed before the recommendations began to be implemented.

World War II and Increasing Federal Involvement in Education

World War II created conditions in this country that led the federal government to fund several educational programs. One of these, the Lanham Act (1941), provided funding for: (1) the training of workers in war plants by U.S. Office of Education personnel; (2) the construction of schools in areas where military personnel and workers on federal projects resided; and (3) the provision of childcare for the children of working parents.

Another influential and extensive federal program in support of education was the Servicemen's Readjustment Act, popularly known as the **G.I. Bill of Rights**. Signed into law by President Franklin D. Roosevelt in 1944, the G.I. Bill has provided millions of veterans with payments for tuition and room and board at colleges and universities and at special schools. Similar legislation was later passed to grant educational benefits to veterans of the Korean and Vietnam conflicts. Not only did the G.I. Bill stimulate the growth of American colleges and universities, it also changed the character of the higher education student population. Generally, the returning veterans were older and more serious than students who had not served in the military.

How Did Education Change during the Modern Postwar Era (1945–present)?

Throughout our nation's history, three long-standing trends have characterized education. These trends may be grouped and summarized in terms of three general patterns, shown in Figure 3.2: Americanization, democratization, and the professionalization of teaching. At the same time, the decades since the end of World War II have seen a series of profound changes in U.S. education. These changes have addressed three as yet unanswered questions: (1) How can full and equal educational opportunity be extended to all groups in our culturally pluralistic society? (2) What knowledge and skills should be taught in our nation's schools? (3) How should knowledge and skills be taught?

The 1950s: Defense Education and School Desegregation

In 1957, the Soviet Union launched the world's first satellite, named *Sputnik*, into space. This event placed teachers and schools under intense scrutiny. Political leaders blamed the nation's education system for allowing the United States to be in second place in the "space race." According to their analysis, the Soviet Union was in first place because progressive education had weakened our system of education. For example, students in the United States were taught less science, mathematics, and foreign language than their European counterparts. Americans, asserted Vice

Figure 3.2   Three general patterns of trends in U.S. education.

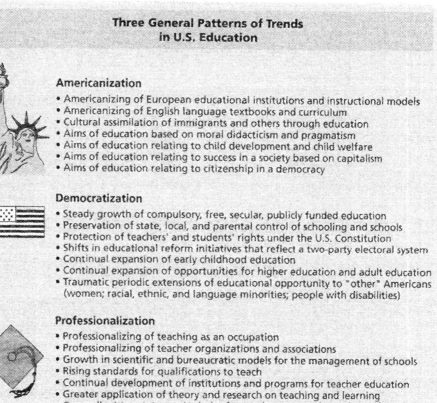

**Three General Patterns of Trends
in U.S. Education**

Americanization

- Americanizing of European educational institutions and instructional models
- Americanizing of English language textbooks and curriculum
- Cultural assimilation of immigrants and others through education
- Aims of education based on moral didacticism and pragmatism
- Aims of education relating to child development and child welfare
- Aims of education relating to success in a society based on capitalism
- Aims of education relating to citizenship in a democracy

Democratization

- Steady growth of compulsory, free, secular, publicly funded education
- Preservation of state, local, and parental control of schooling and schools
- Protection of teachers' and students' rights under the U.S. Constitution
- Shifts in educational reform initiatives that reflect a two-party electoral system
- Continual expansion of early childhood education
- Continual expansion of opportunities for higher education and adult education
- Traumatic periodic extensions of educational opportunity to "other" Americans
  (women; racial, ethnic, and language minorities; people with disabilities)

Professionalization

- Professionalizing of teaching as an occupation
- Professionalizing of teacher organizations and associations
- Growth in scientific and bureaucratic models for the management of schools
- Rising standards for qualifications to teach
- Continual development of institutions and programs for teacher education
- Greater application of theory and research on teaching and learning
- Generally rising status and salaries for teachers as members of a profession

Admiral H. G. Rickover in his 1959 book *Education and Freedom*, needed to recognize that "education is our first line of defense" (1959).

The federal government appropriated millions of dollars over the next decade for educational reforms. Through provisions of the **National Defense Education Act** of 1958, the U.S. Office of Education sponsored research and innovation in science, mathematics, modern foreign languages, and guidance. Out of their work came the new math; new science programs; an integration of anthropology, economics, political science, and sociology into new social studies programs; and renewed interest and innovations in foreign language instruction. Teachers were trained in the use of new methods and materials at summer workshops, schools were given funds for new equipment, and research centers were established. In 1964, Congress extended the act for three years and expanded Title III of the act to include money for improving instruction in reading, English, geography, history, and civics.

During the reform activity of the 1960s, public school enrollments rose dramatically. In 1950, about 25 million children were enrolled; in 1960, about 36 million; and in 1970, about 50 million. As a result of a decline in births, however, this trend stopped abruptly in the late 1970s. In the fall of 1979, for example, 41.5 million students were enrolled in K–12 classes, a decrease of 1,069,000 or 2.5 percent, from the year before (Rippa 1984).

The curriculum reform movement of the 1960s did not bear the positive results that its supporters hoped for. The benefits of the new federally funded programs reached only a small percentage of teachers. In regard to some of the new materials—those related to the new math, for example—teachers complained that the recommended approaches failed to take into account the realities of classroom life. Many of the materials, it turned out, were developed by persons who had little or no classroom experience. Thus, many teachers of the 1960s ignored the innovations and continued teaching as they had always done. In fact, this tendency for teachers to resist many educational reforms has continued into the present. As Diane Ravitch points out,

> A teacher whose career began in 1960 has lived through an era of failed revolutions. One movement after another arrived, peaked, and dispersed. Having observed the curriculum reform movement, the free school movement, the minimum competency movement, and, more recently, the back-to-basics movement, a veteran teacher may be excused for secretly thinking, when confronted by the next campaign to "save" the schools, "This too shall pass" (1985, 303).

The end of World War II also saw the beginning of school **desegregation**. On May 17, 1954, the U.S. Supreme Court rejected the "separate but equal" doctrine that had been used since 1850 as a justification for excluding African Americans from attending school with whites. In response to a suit filed by the NAACP on behalf of a Kansas family, Chief Justice Earl Warren declared that to segregate school children "from others of similar age and qualifications solely because of their race generates a feeling of inferiority as to their status in the community that may affect their hearts and minds in a way unlikely ever to be undone" (***Brown v. Board of Education of Topeka*** 1954).

The Supreme Court's decision did not bring an immediate end to segregated schools. Though the court one year later ordered that desegregation proceed with "all deliberate speed," opposition to school integration arose in school districts across the country. Some districts, whose leaders modeled restraint and a spirit of cooperation, desegregated peacefully. Other districts became battlegrounds, characterized by boycotts, rallies, and violence.

The 1960s: The War on Poverty and the Great Society

The 1960s, highlighted by the Kennedy administration's spirit of optimism and social responsibility, created a climate that supported change. Many classrooms became places for pedagogical experimentation and creativity reminiscent of the progressive era. Open education, team teaching, individualized instruction, flexible scheduling, and nongraded schools were among the innovations that teachers began to implement. These changes reflected a belief that teachers were capable professionals.

During the 1960s, several educators, influenced by the progressive education movement, published books that enhanced the image of teachers and teaching: A. S. Neill's *Summerhill* (1960), Sylvia Ashton-Warner's *Teacher* (1963), John Holt's *How Children Fail* (1964), Herbert Kohl's *36 Children* (1967), James Herndon's *The Way It Spozed to Be* (1969), and Jonathan Kozol's *Death at an Early Age* (1967). These books showed how effective teachers make instructional and curricular decision based on their understanding of how students learn.

The administrations of Presidents Kennedy and Johnson funneled massive amounts of money into a War on Poverty. Education was seen as the key to breaking the transmission of poverty from generation to generation. The War on Poverty developed methods, materials, and programs such as subsidized breakfast and lunch programs, Head Start, Upward Bound, and the Job Corps that would be appropriate for children who had been disadvantaged due to poverty.

The War on Poverty proved much more difficult to win than imagined, and the results of such programs nearly forty years later have been mixed. The three- to six-year-olds who participated in Head Start did much better when they entered public schools; however, academic gains appeared to dissolve over time. Although the Job Corps enabled scores of youth to avoid a lifetime of unemployment, many graduates returned to the streets where they eventually became statistics in unemployment and crime records. The education of low-income children received a boost in April 1965 when Congress passed the **Elementary and Secondary Education Act**. As part of President Johnson's Great Society program, the act allocated funds on the basis of the number of poor children in school districts. Thus schools in poverty areas that frequently had to cope with such problems as low achievement, poor discipline, truancy, and high teacher turnover rates received much needed assistance in addressing their problems.

In 1968, the Elementary and Secondary Education Act was amended with Title VII, the Bilingual Education Act. This act provided federal aid to low-income children "of limited English-speaking ability." The act did not spell out clearly what bilingual education might mean other than to say that it provided money for local school districts to "develop and carry out new and imaginative elementary and secondary school programs" to meet the needs of non-English-speaking children. Since the passing of Title VII, debate over the ultimate goal of bilingual education has been intense: Should it help students to make the *transition* to regular English-speaking classrooms, or should it help such students *maintain* their non-English language and culture?

The 1970s: Accountability and Equal Opportunity

The 1970s saw drops in enrollment, test scores, and public confidence in our nation's schools. At the same time, new educational policies called for equality of education for all in the United States. Troubled by the continued low academic

Technology in Teaching

History of education and the Internet

The Internet has increased dramatically the amount of information easily available to anyone with a computer. In a manner perhaps more dramatic than the invention of the printing press in the fifteenth century, the Internet brings limitless information and expertise to people around the globe.

On the Internet, you can find extensive information about the history of education, as well as an increasingly large collection of original primary sources, such as the *New England Primer* and the *McGuffey Reader*. Among the sites devoted to the history of education are the following:

- History of Education Society, maintained by the College of Education, Slippery Rock University of Pennsylvania (www.sru.edu/depts/scc/hes/hes.htm)
- History of Education Quarterly, maintained by the College of Education, Slippery Rock University of Pennsylvania (www.sru.edu/depts/scc/hes/heq2.htm)

- History of Education: Selected Moments of the 20th Century, maintained by The Ontario Institute for Studies in Education of the University of Toronto (OISE/UT) (www.fcis.oise.utoronto.ca/daniel_schugurensky/assignment1/)
- Blackwell History of Education Museum and Research Collections, maintained by Northern Illinois University (www.cedu.niu.edu/blackwell/)

NOTE: The above URLs were active when this book went to press. However, websites are frequently changed or withdrawn from the Internet. Also, because it is estimated that the amount of information in the world doubles every 900 days (Bitter and Pierson 2002) and about one million websites are added each month (Hobbes' Internet Timeline 2004), you should periodically use key words related to the history of education and your favorite search engine to gather the latest information and resources.

performance of many U.S. students, parents, citizen groups, and policy makers initiated a "back-to-basics" movement and called for increased teacher accountability.

Many school systems had to cope with financial crises during the 1970s. Public and private elementary school enrollments, instead of increasing as they had since 1940, declined by nearly five million during the 1970s (National Center for Education Statistics 1999). As a result of declining enrollments, schools received less state aid. Moreover, voters frequently failed to support referendums to increase school funding because they lacked confidence in the schools.

Some parents responded to perceived problems with U.S. education by establishing alternative schools or joining the home education movement. Parents with children in public schools demanded teacher **accountability**. In an effort to increase their effectiveness, many teachers were required to use various "teacher-proof" curriculum materials.

During the late 1960s and early 1970s, students increasingly questioned the relevance of what they were learning at school. Thousands protested against what they viewed as an unjust, undeclared war in Vietnam, and they spoke out against the oppression of minorities at home. Militant youth groups blamed irrelevant school curricula for not addressing social injustices.

In response to their critics, schools expanded curricular offerings and implemented new, creative approaches to teaching. These changes, however, were viewed with skepticism by many groups in society—taxpayers who accused the schools of extravagant spending; religious groups that questioned the values children were being taught; back-to-basics proponents who believed that students were not learning how to read, write, and compute; and citizens who were alarmed at rising crime, drug use, and violence in schools.

Despite the many criticisms lodged against teachers and schools, the reforms of the 1960s and 1970s resulted in positive changes that continue today. More young people graduate from high school now than in previous decades; more teachers have advanced training, school buildings are better equipped, and instructional methods and materials are both more relevant to learners and more diverse.

For people marginalized in U.S. society, several federal acts that were passed during the 1970s expanded their opportunities to receive quality education. Two of the most far-reaching acts were **Title IX** of the Education Amendments Act and the **Education for all Handicapped Children Act** (**Public Law 94-142**). Title IX, which took effect in 1975, stated that "no person in the United States shall, on the basis of sex, be excluded from participation in, be denied the benefits of, or be subjected to discrimination under any education program or activity receiving Federal financial assistance." Public Law 94-142, passed by Congress in 1975, extended greater educational opportunities to children with disabilities. This act (often referred to as the **mainstreaming** law) specifies extensive due process procedures to guarantee that children with special needs will receive a free, appropriate education in the least restrictive educational environment. Through the act's provisions, parents are involved in planning educational programs for their children.

The 1980s: A Great Debate

The first half of the 1980s saw a continuation, perhaps even an escalation, of the criticisms aimed at the schools during the two previous decades. In fact, Lee Shulman (1987) characterized much of the 1980s as an era of "teacher bashing." With the publication in 1983 of the report by the National Commission on Excellence in Education, *A Nation at Risk: The Imperative for Educational Reform*, a great national debate was begun on how to improve the quality of schools. *A Nation at Risk* and dozens of other national reports on U.S. schools gave evidence to some that the schools were failing miserably to achieve their goals. The following excerpt from the first paragraph of *A Nation at Risk* exemplifies the tone of many of these reports:

> Our Nation is at risk. Our once unchallenged preeminence in commerce, industry, science, and technological innovation is being overtaken by competitors throughout the world . . . the educational foundations of our society are presently being eroded by a rising tide of mediocrity that threatens our very future as a Nation and a people (National Commission on Excellence in Education, 1983).

Responses included more proposals for curriculum reform. Mortimer Adler's *Paideia Proposal* (1982) called for a core curriculum based on the Great Books. *High School: A Report on Secondary Education in America* (1983), written by Ernest Boyer for the Carnegie Foundation for the Advancement of Teaching, suggested strengthening the academic core curriculum in high schools, a recommendation that was widely adopted. In 1986, former Secretary of the U.S. Department of Education William Bennett advocated a rigorous high school curriculum that he described in *James Madison High* (1987). Educators at the middle school level began to create small learning communities, eliminate tracking, and develop new ways to enhance student self-esteem as a result of the Carnegie Council on Adolescent Development report *Turning Points: Preparing American Youth for the 21st Century* (1989). These and other reform reports that swept the nation during the 1980s made a lasting imprint on education in the United States.

The 1990s: Teacher Leadership

The push to reform schools begun in the 1980s continued throughout the 1990s, and teaching was transformed in dramatic ways. In response to challenges such as greater diversity, greater international competition, less support for public education, and decentralization and deregulation of schools, innovative approaches to teaching and learning were developed throughout the United States (see Figure 3.3). Teachers went beyond the classroom and assumed leadership roles in school restructuring and educational reform—roles that are examined more fully

Figure 3.3 The 1990s: A sampler of trends in education.

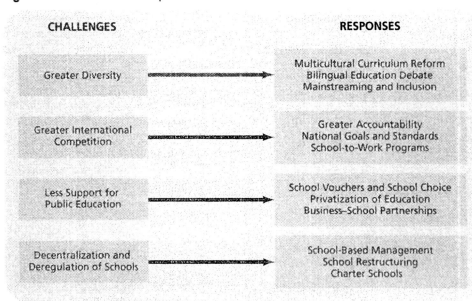

CHALLENGES	RESPONSES
Greater Diversity	Multicultural Curriculum Reform Bilingual Education Debate Mainstreaming and Inclusion
Greater International Competition	Greater Accountability National Goals and Standards School-to-Work Programs
Less Support for Public Education	School Vouchers and School Choice Privatization of Education Business–School Partnerships
Decentralization and Deregulation of Schools	School-Based Management School Restructuring Charter Schools

in Chapter 6. Through collaborative relationships with students, principals, parents, and the private sector, teachers changed the nature of their profession. As one high school teacher said in the late 1990s: "I see [change] happening. Not overnight, but I think it's going to. When I first started teaching in the early sixties, I would never have envisioned things changing as much as they have" (Grant and Murray 1999, 212).

The New Century: Continuing the Quest for Excellence

An excerpt from the mission statement of the International Centre for Educational Change at the Ontario Institute for Studies in Education captures well the world of teaching during the first decade of the new century—it is "a world of intensifying and rapid change . . . [characterized by] new technologies, greater cultural diversity, restructured approaches to administration and management, and a more sophisticated knowledge-base about teaching and learning." As educators work within this complex, exciting environment, their work will be enhanced if they acknowledge the ideas and events described in this chapter.

The United States has set for itself an education mission of truly ambitious proportions. To realize fully this mission during the new century will be difficult, but an examination of our history shows that it is not impossible. In little more than 380 years, our education system has grown from one that provided only a minimal education to an advantaged minority to one that now provides maximal educational opportunity to the majority. Clearly, the beginning of the new century provides ample evidence that our nation will not waver from its longstanding commitment to ensuring that all children have equal access to educational excellence.

Summary

What Were the European Antecedents of American Education?

- Many practices in today's schools had their origins in Europe where the role of education was to prepare children and youth for adulthood.

- Ancient Greeks believed that leisure should be used to reflect on practical and aesthetic values and to develop a well-rounded mind and body.

- Socrates questioned pupils to reveal errors in their thinking and to lead them to eternal truths.

- Plato, a student of Socrates, founded the Academy, often called the world's first university.

- Aristotle, a student of Plato, was a realist who believed that reality, knowledge, and value exist independent of the mind.

- Roman education, patterned after Greek education, consisted of the *ludus*, or elementary school, and a secondary or grammar school.

- Education in the European Middle Ages was mediated through the Roman Catholic Church. The Renaissance

- marked a rebirth of interest in Greco-Roman art, litera-ture, secular learning, and humanism.
- Four eighteenth-century European thinkers who influenced American education are Rousseau, Pestalozzi, Herbart, and Lancaster.

What Were Teaching and Schools Like in the American Colonies (1620–1750)?

- Colonial education was patterned after the British two-track system and its primary objective was to promote religion.
- Colonial teachers had low status, though respect increased with grade level.
- Puritans believed children were naturally corrupt and sinful and should be disciplined sternly at the dame schools, reading and writing schools, and Latin grammar schools common to the colonies.
- Mandated education in the United States had its origins in two colonial laws: the Massachusetts Acts of 1642 and 1647.
- At the end of the American Revolution, the few African Americans and Native Americans who were literate were taught at church-sponsored schools that were segregated by race.

What Were the Goals of Education during the Revolutionary Period (1750–1820)?

- During the Revolutionary Period, characterized by a de-clining European influence on American education, educa-tion in the new democracy was shaped by the ideas of Benjamin Franklin, Thomas Jefferson, and Noah Webster.
- Educational opportunities for women were often limited to preparing them for family life.

How Was the Struggle Won for State-Supported Common Schools (1820–1865)?

- Horace Mann, a strong advocate for state-supported, free common schools, believed that teachers should receive post secondary training in normal schools.

- The six-volume McGuffey reader, with its moral lessons and emphasis on virtue, determined much of what chil-dren learned at school.
- The Morrill Land-Grant Act, passed in 1862, provided federal land for colleges and set a precedent for federal involvement in education.

How Did Compulsory Education Change Schools and the Teaching Profession (1865–1920)?

- The spread of common schools and dramatic increases in their enrollments led to the use of scientific manage-ment techniques for their operation.
- Booker T. Washington, founder of the Tuskegee Institute, believed education could prepare African Americans to live peaceably with whites, while W. E. B. DuBois believed African Americans should educate them-selves for leadership positions and not accept inferior status.
- Kindergartens became common and used child-centered curricula patterned after German educator Friedrich Froebel's ideas.
- The National Education Association (NEA) and the Amer-ican Federation of Teachers (AFT) were founded to pro-fessionalize teaching and increase teachers' salaries and benefits.
- The NEA appointed the Committee of Ten and the Committee of Fifteen to make recommendations for the secondary and elementary school curricula, respectively.
- The Commission on the Reorganization of Sec-ondary Education, appointed by the NEA to reexamine the secondary curriculum in regard to students' individual differences, developed "seven cardinal principles" for schooling at all levels: health, command of fundamental processes (reading, writing, and computation), worthy home membership, vocation, citizenship, worthy use of leisure time, and ethical character.

What Were the Aims of Education during the Progressive Era (1920–1945)?

- John Dewey's Laboratory School at the University of Chicago, a model of progressive education, offered a curriculum based on children's interests and needs.

- Progressive educator Maria Montessori developed age-appropriate materials and teaching strategies that were implemented in the United States and throughout the world.

- Public criticism of progressive education led to its decline at the start of World War II.

- School enrollments became increasingly diverse as a result of immigration, and a goal of education was the rapid assimilation of all groups into an English-speaking Anglo-European culture.

How Did Education Change during the Modern Postwar Era (1945–present)?

- The Soviet Union's launching of *Sputnik* in 1957 sparked educational reform, particularly in science, mathematics, and foreign language education. Schools were ordered

to desegregate with "all deliberate speed" as a result of a 1954 decision by the Supreme Court in *Brown v. Board of Education of Topeka*.

- Innovative curricula and instructional strategies were used in many classrooms of the 1960s. The Elementary and Secondary Education Act of 1965, part of President Johnson's Great Society and War on Poverty programs, provided federal money to improve the education of poor children.

- Alarmed by declining test scores, the public became critical of schools during the 1970s and demanded accountability. An array of federal legislation was passed to provide equal educational opportunity for all students.

- *A Nation at Risk* and other reports during the 1980s addressed weaknesses in U.S. schools and sparked a "Great Debate" on how to improve U.S. education.

- In response to continuing challenges to education today, teachers are taking leadership roles in school restructuring, school governance, curriculum change, and other aspects of educational reform.

Key Terms and Concepts

academies, 99
accountability, 116
Brown v. Board of Education of Topeka, 114
Commission on the Reorganization of Secondary Education, 107
Committee of Fifteen, 107
Committee of Ten, 106
common schools, 102
dame schools, 94
desegregation, 114
Education for all Handicapped Children Act (Public Law 94-142), 117

Elementary and Secondary Education Act, 115
female seminaries, 99
Freedman's Bureau, 98
G.I. Bill of Rights, 112
horn book, 94
kindergarten, 106
Latin grammar school, 95
mainstreaming, 117
Massachusetts Act of 1642, 95
Massachusetts Act of 1647, 96
McGuffey readers, 103
monitorial system, 92

Montessori method, 110
Morrill Land-Grant Act, 104
National Defense Education Act, 113
normal school, 103
parochial schools, 94
Primer, 94
progressivism, 108
reading and writing schools, 94
scientific management, 105
Socratic questioning, 88
Title IX, 117

Reflective Application Activities

Discussion Questions

1. What does the history of textbooks tell us about education in the United States? What values and priorities do textbooks today seem to reflect in comparison to textbooks of the seventeenth, eighteenth, and nineteenth centuries?

2. Benjamin Franklin suggested that education is "the surest foundation" for happiness. To what extent do you agree or disagree with Franklin's statement?

Professional Journal

1. Reflect on the "daily school routine" you experienced as an elementary-aged child. How does that routine differ from that experienced by children in colonial schools? Recall how your teachers handled classroom discipline; how do those approaches differ from those used by colonial teachers? How do your views of children differ from those held by Puritan teachers during the colonial era? Do "remnants" of the Puritan influence on U.S. education still exist today?

2. In this chapter's opening scenario the last teacher to speak says, "I can't think of any real good that has come out of the federal government's involvement in education. Can you?" Drawing from the information presented in this chapter, write a memo to this teacher in which you respond to the teacher's question.

Online Assignments

1. Identify a trend or issue in education and then use the Internet to gather information about its roots in the past and impacts on teaching today. Consider, for example, the debate about the use of corporal punishment in the schools. Other areas to research include:

tax-supported schools
school desegregation
progressive education
higher education
early childhood education

equal educational opportunity for women
immigrant education
teacher education
educational technology
literacy

As your information accumulates, identify specific linkages between the past and present. Transcribe your notes into a brief narrative report and pool your findings with those of classmates.

2. Use online references to research in greater detail the contributions of a pioneer in education whose work is summarized in this chapter.

Observations and Interviews

1. Interview veteran teachers and administrators at a local school and ask them to comment on the changes in education that they have observed and experienced during their careers. In particular, compare their remarks to this chapter's discussion of education during the post-World War II era, using this chapter's description of the era to guide your questions. What events do respondents identify as having had the greatest impact on their teaching?

2. Visit a museum in your area for the purpose of examining some artifacts from out country's early educational history. Take notes on what you find and describe several of the artifacts to the rest of your class.

Professional Portfolio

This portfolio entry involves collaborating with classmates, school staff, and students to research the history of a school. The narrative will describe how the school and its culture have changed or persisted over time. You may wish to describe school characteristics such as the following:

- Participants and their characteristics
- Relationships among participants
- Groups and organizations within the school
- School customs and traditions
- Formal celebrations
- Symbols of membership, appreciation, and recognition
- Changes in the school's infrastructure and environment
- Significant events in the life of the school
- Significant events in the life of the community

Evidence for developing the history might include yearbooks, school and local newspapers, photographs, annual reports to parents, policy statements, curriculum materials, statistical data, and first-person accounts. In addition, you might examine school data over the years in the following categories: enrollment, test scores, funding, and additions to the original school building.

Members of the research team may also wish to interview graduates of the school and current and past teachers and staff. From their perspectives, how has the school changed? How do the comments of the oldest graduates about the school's culture compare with those of recent graduates? What was the influence of the principals and master teachers who led the school over the years?

As you and other members of the research team compile information about the school, identify major events dur-ing each 5–10 year period of the school's existence and place them on a timeline. For additional ideas on researching the history and culture of a school, review the discussion of schools as social institutions and school culture in Chapter 1. In addition, you may wish to examine historical case studies of schools such as Jacqueline Ancess's *Beating the Odds: High Schools as Communities of Commitment* (Teachers College Press, 2003), Tony Wagner's *How Schools Change: Lessons from Three Communities Revisited* (Routledge-Falmer, 2000), Gerald Grant's *The World We Created at Hamilton High* (Harvard University Press, 1988), or Daniel L. Duke's *The School That Refused to Die: Continuity and Change at Thomas Jefferson High School* (Teachers College Press, 1994).

4 Diversity in U.S. Education

Accomplished teachers recognize that in a multicultural nation students bring to the schools a plethora of abilities and aptitudes that are valued differently by the community, the school and the family.

—National Board for Professional Teaching Standards (NBPTS)

Yvette is twelve years old and lives with her older brother and younger sister in an apartment in the city. Yvette and her brother were born in Puerto Rico, and her sister was born in the United States. Yvette's mother and father brought the family to the mainland two years ago.

Three months ago, Yvette transferred into your class. It appears that the transition is difficult for her. Her work would improve if she got more involved, you think. However, she seems afraid to risk making mistakes, especially in reading and language arts.

Yvette seems to trust you, so you've decided to talk to her after school today. She usually waits in your classroom until her brother Juan arrives to walk her home.

You begin by asking, "How is school is going?"

As she speaks, timidly at first and then more openly and naturally, you realize that Yvette is still struggling to adjust to the challenges of living on the mainland. She misses her grandmother who lived with the family in Puerto Rico. She also says she does not speak English well enough. She is worried that the other children will tease her if she speaks out in class. You also learn that Yvette has missed school frequently because of bad headaches and stomach problems. When you ask Yvette if her parents are coming to the next PTA meeting, Yvette tells you they probably will not come because they do not speak English.

How can you get Yvette more involved in classroom activities? What strategies could you use to help her to increase her reading, speaking, and writing skills? How might you make Yvette's parents feel welcome and comfortable at the school?

Guiding Questions

1. How is diversity reflected in the culture of the United States?
2. What does equal educational opportunity mean?
3. What is meant by bilingual education?
4. What is multicultural education?
5. How is gender a dimension of multicultural education?

The above scenario shows how important it is for teachers to be sensitive to the needs of students from diverse cultural backgrounds. When you become a teacher in a multicultural classroom, you cannot develop a different curriculum for each group of students—that would be impossible and would place undue emphasis on differences among students. Instead, you can develop a curriculum that increases students' awareness and appreciation of the rich diversity in U.S. culture.

This chapter looks at cultural diversity in the United States and the challenges of equalizing educational opportunity for all students. Professional teachers see cultural diversity as an asset to be preserved and valued, not a liability. The United States derives strength from the **diversity** of its people, and *all* students should receive a high-quality education so that they may make their unique contributions to society.

How Is Diversity Reflected in the Culture of the United States?

The percentage of ethnic minorities in the United States has been growing steadily since the end of World War II. As Figure 4.1 shows, 28.4 million foreign-born peo-

Figure 4.1   Foreign-born population and percent of total population for the United States: 1850–2000.

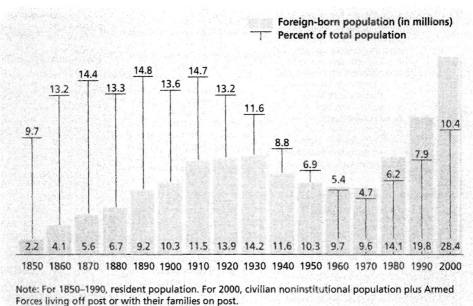

Note: For 1850–1990, resident population. For 2000, civilian noninstitutional population plus Armed Forces living off post or with their families on post.

Source: U.S. Census Bureau (2001), *Profile of the Foreign-born Population in the United States: 2000.* Washington, DC: U.S. Census Bureau, p. 9.

ple lived in the United States in 2000. The Census Bureau estimates that there is a net increase of one international migrant every thirty seconds.

New immigration and births to immigrants now account for more than three-fourths of U.S. population growth (Center for Immigration Studies, 2004). Twenty percent of U.S. senators are grandchildren of immigrants, a claim that can be made by no other nation in the world about its leading legislative body (Wirt and Kirst 1997). In addition, the Census Bureau estimates that

- By 2010, blacks and Hispanics will equal the number of whites.
- By 2025, half of U.S. youth will be white and half "minority."
- By 2050, no one group will be a majority among adults.

Increasing diversity in the United States is reflected, of course, in the nation's schools. In 2000, 39 percent of public school students were considered to belong to a minority group, an increase of 17 percent from 1972. This increase was largely due to the growth in the proportion of Hispanic students. In 2000, Hispanic students accounted for 17 percent of the public school enrollment, up by 11 percent from 1972. African Americans were 17 percent of the public school enrollment in 2000, up by 2 percent from 1972. The percentage of students from other racial and ethnic minority groups also increased, from 1 percent in 1972 to 5 percent in 2000 (National Center for Education Statistics 2002).

Increasing racial and ethnic diversity in student enrollments is resulting in more languages and cultures in the nation's public schools. Differences in student backgrounds offer opportunities to enhance the learning environment for all students; however, these differences can present challenges for schools. For example, in many parts of the country there is an increased demand for bilingual programs and teachers. Most school districts face a critical shortage of minority teachers. Moreover, teachers must develop curricula and strategies that address the needs and backgrounds of all students—regardless of their social class, gender, sexual orientation, or ethnic, racial, or cultural identity.

The Meaning of Culture

As pointed out in Chapter 1, one purpose of schools is to maintain the culture of the United States. But what is the U.S. culture? Is there a single culture to which everyone in the United States belongs? Before answering that question we must define the term *culture*. Simply put, **culture** is *the way of life* common to a group of people. It consists of the values, attitudes, and beliefs that influence their traditions and behavior. Culture also represents a way of interacting with and looking at the world. Though the United States was once viewed as a "melting pot" in which ethnic cultures would "melt" into one, ethnic and cultural differences have remained very much a part of life in the United States. Currently, a "salad-bowl" analogy captures more accurately the **cultural pluralism** of U.S. society. That is, the distinguishing characteristics of cultures are to be preserved rather than blended into a single culture.

Dimensions of Culture   Within the United States, cultural groups differ according to other distinguishing factors, such as religion, politics, economics, and geographic region. The regional culture of New England, for example, is quite different from that of the Southeast. Similarly, Californians are culturally different from Iowans.

However, everyone in the United States does share common dimensions of culture. James Banks, an authority on multicultural education, has termed this shared culture the "national macroculture" (2002). In addition to being members of the national macroculture, people in the United States are members of ethnic groups. An **ethnic group** is made up of individuals within a larger culture who share a self-defined racial or cultural identity and a set of beliefs, attitudes, and values. Members of an ethnic group distinguish themselves from others in the society by physical and social attributes. You should be aware also that the composition of ethnic groups can change over time, and that there is often as much variability within groups as between them.

Cultural Identity   In addition to membership in the national macroculture, each individual participates in an array of subcultures, each with its customs and beliefs. Collectively, these subcultures determine an individual's **cultural identity**, an overall sense of who one is. Other elements that can shape a person's cultural identity include age, racial identity, exceptionalities, language, gender, sexual orientation, income level, and beliefs and values. The importance of these elements differs among people. For some, their cultural identity is most strongly determined by their occupations; for others by their ethnicity; and for others by their religious beliefs.

Remember that your future students will have their own complex cultural identities, which are no less valid for being different. For some of them, these identities may make them feel "disconnected" from the attitudes, expectations, and values conveyed by the school. For example,

> Students who come from homes where languages other than English are the medium of communication, who share customs and beliefs unique to their cultural community and/or home countries, or who face the range of challenges posed by economic insecurity will not often find much of their family, community, or national existence reflected in the school setting. Often these students feel that school is itself foreign, alienating, and unrelated to their beliefs and concerns (Rice and Walsh 1996, 9).

As this chapter's Relevant Standards feature suggests, effective teachers understand the subtle differences in cultural identities among students. Such teachers create learning environments that enable all students to feel "connected to" their school experiences.

Language and Culture   Culture is embedded in language, a fact that has resulted in conflict among different groups in our society. Some groups support the preservation of ethnic cultures, yet they believe members of non-English-speaking groups must learn English if they are to function in U.S. society. Those who wish to pre-

Relevant Standards

Appreciation for Cultural Diversity

The following professional standards stress the teacher's role in meeting the needs of today's increasingly diverse student populations. Proficient teachers tailor their instruction based on their understanding of students' cultural backgrounds.

- "[Teacher candidates] understand language acquisition; cultural influences on learning; exceptionalities; diversity of student populations, families, and communities; and inclusion and equity in classrooms and schools." (National Council for Accreditation of Teacher Education [NCATE], 2002, 19. Standard 1: Candidate Knowledge, Skills, and Dispositions.)

- "Teachers are committed to students and their learning. (Core Proposition #1). [Accomplished teachers] are aware of the influence of context and culture on behavior. . . . [T]hey foster students' self-esteem, motivation, character, civic responsibility and their respect for individual, cultural, religious and racial differences." (National Board for Professional Teaching Standards [NBPTS], 2002, 3.)

- "The teacher understands how students' learning is influenced by individual experiences, talents, and prior learning, as well as language, culture, family and community values." (Interstate New Teacher Assessment and Support Consortium [INTASC], 1992, 18. "Disposition" statement for Principle #3: "The teacher understands how students differ in their approaches to learning and creates instructional opportunities that are adapted to diverse learners.")

- "Teacher . . . helps ensure that all students, particularly those traditionally underserved, are honored in the school." (Praxis Series, "distinguished" level of performance for Domain 4: Professional Responsibilities, Component 4f: Showing Professionalism.) (From Danielson 1996, 119)

serve linguistic diversity are also in conflict with those who wish to establish English as a national language.

Much of the debate has focused on **bilingual education**—using two languages as the medium of instruction. The purpose of bilingual education is to help students maintain their ethnic identity and become proficient in both English and the language of the home. Bilingual education also encourages assimilation into the mainstream culture and integrates the home language and culture with a new one. Some people are strongly opposed to bilingual education, and others support it as a short-term way to teach English to students.

Clearly, language diversity is an important dimension of U.S. cultural diversity. Many students come from homes where English is not spoken. About 4.4 million **limited English proficient** (**LEP**) students attended public schools in 1999–2000, or about 9.3 percent of the total enrollment (National Clearinghouse for English Language Acquisition 2002). The percentage of school-age children who speak a language other than English or have difficulty speaking English has more than doubled over the past two decades—from 2.8 percent to 5 percent (Brown 2002). LEP students have limited ability to understand, read, or speak English, and they have a first language other than English.

The public school LEP student enrollment for 1999–2000 was 27.3 percent higher than for 1997–98. California enrolled the largest number of public school LEP students, with 1.48 million, followed by Texas (0.55 million), Florida (0.24 million), New York (0.23 million), Illinois (0.14 million), and Arizona (0.13 million). In 1999–2000, states reported over four hundred languages spoken by LEP students nationwide, with 76 percent claiming Spanish as their native language. For 1998–99, thirty-six urban school districts enrolled ten thousand or more students identified as LEP (see Table 4.1).

Students differ among themselves not only regarding the first language spoken in the home, but also in the *language patterns* they acquire from the culture within which they are raised. Children from working-class backgrounds tend to develop "restricted" language patterns with their use of English, while children from middle-class backgrounds tend to develop more "elaborated" language patterns (Bernstein 1996; Heath 1983). In many cases, children encounter a mismatch between the language patterns used in the home and those they are expected to use in school. This mismatch can be "a serious stumbling block for working-class and nonwhite pupils" (MacLeod 1995, 18).

Students' language patterns became a topic of national debate in late 1996 when the Oakland, California, school district passed a resolution on "ebonics" (a blend of the words *ebony* and *phonics*), also known as "black English." The resolution recognized ebonics as the "primary language" of many of the district's 28,000 African American students and called for them to be taught in their primary language. The resolution also suggested that some students might be eligible for state and federal bilingual education or ESL money.

Critics of the ebonics resolution pointed out that "black English" is a nonstandard form of English or a dialect of English—not a foreign language. Other critics were concerned that students and teachers would be taught ebonics. In the midst of intense national debate, the district revised the resolution so that it no longer called for students to be taught in their "primary language." Instead, the district would implement new programs to move students from the language patterns they bring to school toward proficiency in standard English. Other dialects of English and their use in the classroom have been debated from time to time—for example, "Chicano English," "Cajun English," or Hawaiian Creole English (more popularly known as "pidgin English").

The Concept of Multiculturalism   Multiculturalism stresses the importance of seeing the world from different cultural frames of reference and valuing the rich array of cultures within a nation and within the global community. **Multiculturalism** affirms the need to create schools where differences related to race, ethnicity, gender, disability, and social class are acknowledged and all students are viewed as valuable resources for enriching the teaching–learning process. Furthermore, a central purpose of multiculturalism is to prepare students to live in a culturally plural-

Table 4.1 Which urban school districts in the United States have high LEP enrollments?

Rank	District	No. LEPs	Total Enrollment	% LEP
1	Los Angeles, CA[1]	310,955	688,574	45.2%
2	New York City, NY[1]	148,399	972,606	15.3%
3	Chicago, IL[1]	62,865	430,841	15.0%
4	Dallas, TX[1]	52,290	159,908	32.7%
5	Houston, TX[1]	49,345	191,765	25.7%
6	Miami-Dade, FL[1]	46,365	352,595	13.1%
7	Santa Ana, CA[2]	39,133	56,071	69.8%
8	San Diego, CA[1]	38,484	138,433	27.8%
9	Long Beach, CA[1]	31,225	89,214	35.0%
10	Clark County, NV[1]	26,896	203,579	13.0%
11	Fresno, CA[1]	25,473	78,258	32.6%
12	Garden Grove, CA[2]	22,972	46,916	49.0%
13	Broward County, FL[1]	20,091	225,619	8.9%
14	San Francisco, CA[1]	19,370	63,823	30.3%
15	Palm Beach, FL[2]	19,055	162,029	11.8%
16	Fort Worth, TX[1]	18,652	70,627	26.4%
17	Oakland, CA[1]	17,742	54,256	32.7%
18	Montebello, CA[2]	16,647	33,999	49.0%
19	Hillsborough, FL[1]	16,162	156,908	10.3%
20	Pomona, CA[2]	15,461	32,819	47.1%
21	El Paso, TX[2]	15,106	62,945	24.0%
22	Sacramento City, CA[1]	15,054	51,378	29.3%
23	Fairfax County, VA[2]	14,809	149,029	9.9%
24	St. Paul, MN[2]	14,783	45,325	32.6%
25	Denver, CO[1]	14,385	68,790	20.9%
26	Compton, CA[2]	13,175	29,409	44.8%
27	Glendale, CA[2]	12,790	30,312	42.2%
28	Ontario-Montclair, CA[2]	12,531	25,151	49.8%
29	Tucson, AZ[2]	12,345	66,234	18.6%
30	Anaheim, CA[2]	12,183	20,927	58.2%
31	San Bernardino, CA[2]	11,283	48,907	3.1%
32	Philadelphia, PA[2]	10,710	207,333	5.2%
33	Orange County, FL[1]	10,554	138,866	7.6%
34	Stockton City, CA[2]	10,401	36,124	28.8%
35	Salt Lake City, UT[1]	10,034	61,498	16.3%
36	Fontana, CA[2]	10,023	34,339	29.2%

[1]Data obtained from the Council of Great City Schools (www.cgcs.org).
[2]Data obtained from State Education Agency.
[3]Data obtained from Local Education Agency.

Source: Barron, V. (2001). National Clearinghouse for English Language Acquisition, September 2001. Retrieved at www.ncela.gwu.edu/aslencela/02districts.htm

istic world. This image of the world "contrasts sharply with cultural assimilation, or 'melting pot' images, where ethnic minorities are expected to give up their traditions and blend in or be absorbed by the mainstream society or predominant culture" (Bennett 2003, 14).

For teachers, multiculturalism also means actively seeking out experiences within other cultures that lead to increased appreciation for those ways of life. To provide such crosscultural experiences for students, several teacher education programs have developed "cultural immersion" experiences that enable prospective teachers to live in their students' neighborhoods and communities while student teaching. The University of Alaska-Fairbanks Teachers for Alaska Program, for example, enables students to live in remote Alaskan Native villages during their year-long student teaching experience. In the Urban Education Program of the Associated Colleges of the Midwest, prospective teachers live in a former convent in a multiracial, economically diverse neighborhood in Chicago. There the students teach and participate in structured activities that take them into the city's other ethnic neighborhoods. Students at Indiana University can choose among three unique student teaching experiences: the Native American Reservation Project, the Overseas Project, and the Bilingual/Bicultural Project. Through student teaching on a reservation, in another country, or on the Rio Grande border, students have a life-altering cultural immersion experience. As a student who participated in the Native American Reservation Project and now teaches high school in Indianapolis put it: "Before we went to the reservation, people [came] back to IU who said that it would change your life. We thought, 'Oh yeah, sure.' But it really does. A day doesn't go by when I don't think of those students, of that place" (Indiana University 1999).

Ethnicity and Race

By understanding the difference between ethnicity and race, you can provide students with learning experiences that reflect ethnic and racial diversity in meaningful ways. **Ethnicity** refers to a shared identity based on a "common national or geographic origin, religion, language, sense of peoplehood, common values, separate institutions, and minority or subordinate status" (Banks 2001, 84).

On the other hand, **race** is a subjective concept that is used to distinguish among human beings on the basis of biological traits and characteristics. However, anthropologists "reject the concept of race as a scientifically valid biological category and . . . they argue instead that 'race' is a socially constructed category" (Mukhopadhyay and Henze 2003, 670).

Numerous racial categories have been proposed, but because of the diversity among humans and the mixing of genes that has taken place over time, no single set of racial categories is universally accepted. Since many genetic factors are invisible to the naked eye (DNA, for example), noted anthropologist Ashley Montagu has suggested that there could be as few as three "races" (Negroid, Caucasoid, and Mongoloid) or as many as three hundred, depending on the kind and number of genetic features chosen for measurement. In his classic book, *Man's Most Dangerous Myth: The Fallacy of Race*, Montagu pointed out that

> It is impossible to make the sort of racial classification which some anthropologists and others have attempted. The fact is that all human beings are so . . . mixed with regard to origin that between different groups of individuals . . . "overlapping" of physical traits is the rule (1974, 7).

To reflect the realities of racial identities in the United States, the questionnaire for Census 2000 was changed so that people with a "mixed race" background could select "one or more races" for their racial identity. In addition, the "Spanish/Hispanic/Latino" category allowed respondents to choose among the following: Mexican, Mexican American, and Chicano; Puerto Rican; Cuban; and "other" Spanish/Hispanic/Latino. Similarly, respondents who self-identified as "Asian or Pacific Islander" had the following choices: Asian Indian, Chinese, Filipino, Japanese, Korean, Vietnamese, "other" Asian, Native Hawaiian, Guamanian or Chamorro, Samoan, and "other" Pacific Islander.

There are many ethnic groups in U.S. society, and everyone belongs to at least one. However, as James Banks points out:

> An individual is ethnic to the extent that he or she shares the values, behavioral patterns, cultural traits, and identification with a specific ethnic group. Many individuals have multiple ethnic attachments; others consider themselves "American" rather than ethnic.
>
> An individual's identity with his or her ethnic group varies significantly with the times in his or her life, with economic and social status, and with the situations and/or settings (Banks 2003, 15).

It is also clear that racial and ethnic identities in the United States are becoming more complex. We now know that "racial and ethnic identities derive their meanings from social and historical circumstances, that they can vary over time, and that they can sometimes even be slipped on and off like a change of clothing" (Coughlin 1993, A7). For example, a third-generation descendent of a Japanese immigrant may choose to refer to him- or herself as a Japanese American, an American, or an Asian American. Furthermore, it is evident that "specific racial categories acquire and lose meaning over time" (Coughlin 1993, A7), and the use of ethnic and racial labels and expressions of group membership is largely self-selected and arbitrary.

The Concept of Minorities

To understand the important concept of **minorities**, it may help to remember that even though the term *minority* technically refers to any *group* numbering less than half of the total population, in certain parts of the country "minorities" are actually the majority. However, more important than the numbers themselves is an appreciation of how many groups of people have continuously struggled to obtain full educational, economic, political, and social opportunities in society. Along with minority racial and ethnic groups, others who have traditionally lacked power in U.S. public life are immigrants, the poor, children and the elderly, non-English speakers, members of minority religions, and women. Groups that have been most frequently discriminated against in terms of the quality of education they have received include African Americans, Spanish-speaking Americans, Native Americans, Asian Americans, exceptional learners, people with disabilities, and females. There is mounting evidence that many students from these groups continue to receive a substandard education that does not meet their needs or help empower them to participate fully and equally in life in the United States.

Minority Groups and Academic Achievement   Minority-group students are disproportionately represented among students who have failed to master minimum competencies in reading, writing, and mathematics. It has been estimated that ethnic minority students are two to four times more likely than others to drop out of high school. In addition, "in many schools across the nation, racial and language minority students are overrepresented in special education and experience disproportionately high rates of suspension and expulsion" (Bennett 2003, 18).

"Modest growth in achievement among students from minority groups and from 'less advantaged' backgrounds" (Berliner and Biddle 1995, 27) was noted during the mid 1990s. However, 20 years after *A Nation at Risk* issued a bleak assessment of public schools in 1983, data indicated earlier achievement gains had been reversed (Lee 2002). For example, the National Assessment of Educational Progress showed that white fourth-graders were still three times more likely than African American and Hispanic students to be rated "proficient" in mathematics and reading (Hill, May 12, 2003).

When we consider the lower achievement levels of minority students, it is important to note the much higher incidence of poverty among minority families and the research showing that socioeconomic status—not race, language, or culture—contributes most strongly to students' achievement in school (Coleman et al. 1966; Jencks et al. 1972; Jencks and Phillips 1998; National Center for Education Statistics 1980). Understandably, it is difficult for poor children to learn well if they endure the stress of living in crime-ridden neighborhoods, dwelling in dilapidated homes, or going to school hungry.

Stereotyping and Racism   While teachers should expand their knowledge of and appreciation for the diverse cultural backgrounds of their students, they should also guard against forming stereotypes or overgeneralizations about those cultures. **Stereotyping** is the process of attributing behavioral characteristics to all members of a group. In some cases, stereotypes are formed on the basis of limited experiences with and information about the group being stereotyped, and the validity of these stereotypes is not questioned.

Within any cultural group that shares a broad cultural heritage, however, considerable diversity exists. For example, two Puerto Rican children who live in the same community and attend the same school may appear alike to their teachers when, in reality, they are very different. One may come from a home where Spanish is spoken and Puerto Rican holidays are observed; the other child may know only a few words of Spanish and observe only the holidays of the majority culture.

In addition to being alert for stereotypes they and others may hold, teachers should learn to recognize **individual racism**, the prejudicial belief that one's ethnic or racial group is superior to others. They should also be able to recognize **institutional racism**, which occurs when institutions "behave in ways that are overtly racist (i.e., specifically excluding people of color from services) or inherently racist (i.e., adopting policies that while not specifically directed at excluding people of color, nevertheless result in their exclusion)" (Randall 2001).

In light of the arbitrariness of the concept of race, James A. Banks points out, "In most societies, *the social significance of race is much more important than the presumed physical differences among groups*" (2003, 72, italics in original). Unfortunately, many people attach great importance to the concept of race. If you believe "that human groups can be validly grouped on the basis of their biological traits and that these identifiable groups inherit certain mental, personality, and cultural characteristics that determine their behavior" (Banks 2003, 73) then you hold racist beliefs. When people use such beliefs as a rationale for oppressing other groups, they are practicing racism. Appendix 4.1 presents a checklist for a small-group activity that can help you become more aware of individual and institutional racism.

As a teacher, you will not be able to eliminate stereotypic thinking or racism in society. However, you have an obligation to all your students to see that your curriculum and instruction are free of any forms of stereotyping or racism. At the end of this chapter, Professional Journal activity #1 (see page 164) will help you examine, and possibly reassess, your cultural attitudes and values and determine whether you have stereotypes about other cultural groups.

What Does Equal Educational Opportunity Mean?

Providing equal educational opportunity to all students means that teachers and schools promote the full development of students as individuals, without regard for race, ethnicity, gender, sexual orientation, socioeconomic status, abilities, or disabilities. More specifically, educators fulfill this important mission by continually evaluating the appropriateness of the curricular and instructional experiences they provide to each student.

The following sections review the progress that has been made to provide students from diverse groups with equal educational opportunity and present strategies for teaching in diverse classrooms. Strategies for each group draw from research that suggests that particular learning styles *may be* associated with specific ethnic groups in U.S. society (Bennett 2003; Hale-Benson 1986; Shade 1982). These strategies should not lead you to assume, however, that *all* students from a certain group learn in a particular way. As Christine I. Bennett, an expert on multicultural education, points out:

> The notion that certain learning styles are associated with different ethnic groups is both promising and dangerous. Promise lies in the realization that low academic achievement among some ethnic minorities may sometimes be attributed to conflicts between styles of teaching and learning, not low intelligence. This leads to the

possibility that teachers will alter their own instructional styles to be more responsive to the learning needs of students. Danger lies in the possibility that new ethnic stereotypes will develop while old ones are reinforced, as in "Blacks learn aurally," "Asians excel in math," "Mexican American males can't learn from female peer tutors," and "Navajos won't ask a question or participate in a discussion" (2003, 67).

Anglo-European Americans are omitted from this review, not because students from this very diverse group always have had equal educational opportunities, but because this group represents the historically dominant culture. To a great extent, it has determined the curricular and instructional practices found in schools.

Like the other groups discussed, however, "Anglo-European American" is not a single, monolithic culture. Americans whose ethnic heritage is English, Polish, German, Italian, Irish, Czechoslovakian, Russian, or Swedish, for example, often differ greatly in religious and political traditions, beliefs, and values. Their individual ethnic identity may or may not be strengthened by recent immigrants from their country of origin. European ethnics have, nevertheless, assimilated into the mainstream U.S. society more completely than others.

Education and African Americans

Of the more than 287 million persons living in the United States, approximately 13 percent are African Americans. According to U.S. Census Bureau projections, the African American population in the United States is expected to increase from 36 million (13 percent of the total population) in 2001 to 45 million (14 percent of the total) in 2020, and then to 55 million (15 percent of the total) in 2040. The incidence of social problems such as unemployment, crime, drug abuse, poverty, inadequate housing, and school dropouts is proportionally greater for African Americans than for whites. The struggle of African Americans to improve their quality of life after the end of slavery has been hampered for generations by persistent racism, discrimination, poverty, crime, unemployment, and underemployment.

The civil rights movement of the 1960s and 1970s made it clear that African Americans had been denied full access to many aspects of U.S. life, including the right to a good education. A 1976 report by the United States Commission on Civil Rights, for example, revealed that a Southern school district in the 1930s spent nearly eighteen times as much for the education of white pupils as it did for the education of African Americans.

The Desegregation Era   Perhaps the most blatant form of discrimination against African Americans has been school segregation and unequal educational opportunity. As you learned in the previous chapter, the attempt was made to justify segregation by the idea of separate-but-equal schools. It was not until the National Association for the Advancement of Colored People (NAACP) brought suit on behalf of a Kansas family (*Brown v. Board of Education of Topeka, Kansas*) in 1954 that the concept of separate-but-equal schools was decidedly struck down.

The parents of Linda Brown felt that the education their fourth-grader was receiving in the segregated Topeka schools was inferior. When their request that she be transferred to a white school was turned down, they filed suit. In a landmark decision, the U.S. Supreme Court ruled that segregated schools are "inherently unequal" and violate the equal protection clause of the Fourteenth Amendment. U.S. citizens, the justices asserted, have a right to receive an equal opportunity for education.

As a result of opportunities created during the civil rights movement, a substantial number of African Americans are now members of the middle class. Affirmative action programs have enabled many African Americans to attain high-ranking positions in the business, medical, legal, and educational professions. Such gains lead to the observation that

> [A]ny accurate and sophisticated description of the status of African Americans . . . must describe not only the large percentage of Blacks who are members of the so-called underclass, but also the smaller and significant percentage of African Americans who have entered the middle and upper classes and who function in the mainstream society. Many of the children of the new middle class are not only unacquainted with poverty, but also have been socialized in mainstream middle- and upper-class communities. They have little first-hand experience with traditional African American culture (Banks and Banks 1997, 228–229).

What is the legacy of school desegregation today? What are some outcomes of education research and curriculum reform related to the African American experience?

Resegregation of Schools in the United States   As the United States continues to become more ethnically and racially diverse, there is evidence that schools have been "resegregating" since 1990, according to *Resegregation in American Schools*, a Harvard University report released in June 1999 (Orfield and Yun 1999). The report included the following findings:

- Latinos attend the most severely segregated schools (see Figure 4.2).
- Since the late 1980s, schools in the South have been resegregating.
- As African Americans and Latinos move to the suburbs, they are attending segregated schools, especially in urban areas.
- States with a high proportion of African American students made progress toward desegregation in the 1970s; however, all showed increases in school segregation between 1980 and 1996.
- Segregated schools, with the exception of those for white students, tend to have a high concentration of poverty, which has a negative influence on student achievement.

One reason for the trend back to resegregation has been Supreme Court rulings that removed judicial supervision of school districts' efforts to desegregate—for example, *Board of Education of Oklahoma City Public Schools v. Dowell*, 1991;

Figure 4.2   Percent of African American and Latino students in 50–100% minority schools, 1968–1996.

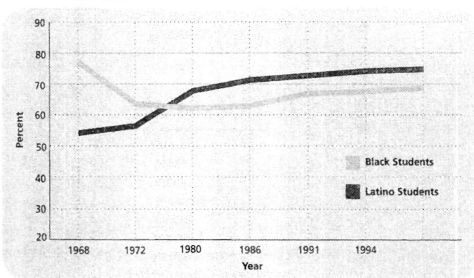

Source: Gary Orfield and John T. Yun, *Resegregation in American Schools.* Cambridge, MA: The Civil Rights Project, Harvard University, June 1999. Used by permission of the publisher.

Freeman v. Pitts, 1992; and *Brown v. Unified School District No. 501*, 1999. In addition, the Supreme Court ruled in *Missouri v. Jenkins*, 1995, that Kansas City schools did not have to maintain desegregation through a magnet school approach until actual benefits for African American students were shown. Such rulings by the Supreme Court prompted the filing of many lawsuits to end desegregation in several large school districts.

The Learning Needs of African American Students   Research on factors related to students' success in school suggests that schools are monoethnic and do not take into account the diverse needs of ethnic minority-group students (Bennett 2003). In the case of African American students, the failure of the school curriculum to address their learning needs may contribute to high dropout rates and below-average achievement. For example, research indicates that teaching strategies that emphasize cooperation—not competition—often result in higher achievement among African American (and Mexican American) students (Aronson and Gonzalez 1988). In addition, it has been suggested that because many African Americans have grown up in an oral tradition, they may learn better through oral/aural activities—for example, reading aloud and listening to audiotapes (Bennett 2003). However, one should not assume that all African Americans learn better aurally.

Afrocentric Schools   To address the educational inequities that African American and other minority-group students may experience as a result of segregation, many communities have tried to create more ethnically and racially diverse classrooms through the controversial practice of busing students to attend schools in other neighborhoods. Also, some African Americans have recently begun to call for **Afrocentric schools**—that is, schools that focus on African American history and cultures for African American pupils. Proponents believe that the educational needs of African American students can be met more effectively in schools that offer Afrocentric curricula and build on the strengths of the African American community.

Private Afrocentric schools, or "black academies," have sprung up across the country in recent years, many supported by the growing number of African Americans who practice Islam. Curricula in these schools emphasize the people and cultures of Africa and the history and achievements of African Americans. Teaching methods are often designed for culture-based learning styles, such as choral response, learning through movement, and sociality. For example, at the elementary-level African American Academy in Seattle, a teacher uses African drums to help students learn geography. The following statement serves as the vision of the Academy: "We the staff, parents, scholars [students], and community make up the Village of the African American Academy of Seattle Public Schools. We shall persevere in the scholarly traditions of our ancestors that enriched civilizations around the world, that gave birth to leaders, and provided knowledge of our beauty, unity and hope extending from our elders to our present and future generations" (African American Academy 2003).

Education and Latino and Hispanic Americans

The Hispanic American population, the fastest growing minority group in the United States, accounts for about 10 percent of the population, and it has been estimated that an additional five million illegal aliens who speak Spanish may be in the country. Census Bureau data show that Hispanic Americans increased by almost 10 percent between 2000 and 2002. By 2010, the Hispanic population is expected to be 14 percent, surpassing African Americans as the nation's largest minority group. The U.S. Census Bureau estimates that the Hispanic American population in the United States will increase from 32 million (12 percent of the total population) in 2001 to 52 million (16 percent of the total) in 2020, and then to 80 million (22 percent of the total) in 2040.

Included in the category of Hispanic Americans are people who call themselves Latinos and Chicanos and who report their ancestry as Mexican, Puerto Rican, Cuban, Central American, or South American. Five states have populations that are more than 10 percent Hispanic: California, Texas, New Mexico, Arizona, and Colorado. Many states have passed English-only laws and made efforts to restrict Hispanic immigrants' access to education. Prior to 1983, six states had English-language laws; however, efforts by political action groups such as U.S. English, founded by the late Senator S. I. Hayakawa of California in 1983, were instrumental in getting English-only laws passed in 25 states by 1999, including California and Colorado. Arizona's 1988 Official English amendment was overturned by the Arizona State Supreme Court in 1998. In addition, California voters approved Proposition 187 in 1994, which prevents public schools from educating the children of illegal aliens.

Socioeconomic Factors   Although some Spanish-speaking immigrants come to the United States hoping to escape a life of poverty in their home country, many others come because they have relatives in the United States or they wish to take advantage of business opportunities in this country. For those Spanish-speaking immigrants who lack job skills and have little education, however, adjusting to the complexities and demands of life in the United States may be difficult.

Socioeconomic factors affect the education of some Hispanics, such as the children of migrant farm workers. Among the estimated one million or so migrant farm workers in this country, more than 70 percent are Spanish speaking. The dropout rate among all migrant workers is 90 percent, and 50 percent leave school before finishing the ninth grade (Bennett 2003). Migrant children are handicapped by the language barrier, deprivation resulting from poverty, and irregular school attendance. Some states have educational intervention programs in place for reaching this group.

The Learning Needs of Spanish-Speaking Students   What can easily happen to Spanish-speaking learners if they are taught by teachers who are not sensitive to their learning needs is illustrated in Christine I. Bennett's portrait of Jesús, an LEP student:

> *Jesús Martinez was a bright, fine-looking six-year-old when he migrated with his family from Puerto Rico to New York City. At a time when he was ready to learn to read and write his mother tongue, Jesús was instead suddenly thrust into an English-only classroom where the only tool he possessed for oral communication (the Spanish language) was completely useless to him. Jesús and his teacher could not communicate with each other because each spoke a different language and neither spoke the language of the other. Jesús felt stupid, or retarded; his teacher perceived him to be culturally disadvantaged and beyond her help. However, she and the school officials agreed to allow him to "sit there" because the law required that he be in school (2003, 8).*

Bennett also captures well the dilemma that many Spanish-speaking LEP students find themselves in: "Students with limited English proficiency are often caught up in conflicts between personal language needs—for example, the need to consolidate cognitive skills in the native language—and a sociopolitical climate that views standard English as most desirable and prestigious" (2003, 271). The degree to which students from Spanish-speaking backgrounds are motivated to learn English varies from group to group. Mexican American students who live in the southwest may retain the Spanish language to maintain ties with family and friends in Mexico. Recently arrived Cubans, on the other hand, may have a stronger motivation to learn the language of their new country. In regard to what they wish

What effects has the growing Hispanic population in the United States had on schools both throughout the country as well as in some states in particular? Why might some Hispanic Americans prefer assimilation over bilingual education for their children?

to learn, children take their cues from the adults around them. If their parents or guardians and friends and relatives have learned English and are bilingual, then they will be similarly motivated. Many Hispanic Americans who value assimilation over their traditional culture favor English-only education.

However, the limited English proficiencies of many children raised in native Spanish-speaking families contribute significantly to the difficulties they have in school. To address the needs of these students, federally funded bilingual-bicultural programs encourage teachers to view bicultural knowledge as a bridge to the school's curriculum. Bilingual education is examined in detail later in this chapter.

Education and Asian Americans and Pacific Islanders

Asian Americans and Pacific Islanders represent about 4 percent of the total population of the United States. Census Bureau data show that the Asian American population increased by 9 percent between 2000 and 2002, almost as much as the Hispanic American population. The U.S. Census Bureau estimates that the Asian and Pacific Islander population in the United States will increase from 11.6 million (4 percent of the total population) in 2001 to 19.6 million (6 percent of the total) in 2020, and then to 29 million (8 percent of the total) in 2040.

Asian Americans and Pacific Islanders comprise at least 34 ethnic groups that speak more than 300 languages and dialects (Asian Americans/Pacific Islanders in Philanthropy 1997). The group is tremendously diverse and includes people from South Asia, primarily Bangladesh, India, and Pakistan; Southeast Asia, including Indochina (Laos, Thailand, Indonesia, Malaysia, and Vietnam) and the Philippines; East Asia, including China, Hong Kong, Japan, Korea, and Taiwan; and the Pacific Islands, including Hawaii, Guam, and Samoa. About 55 percent of the total Asian American and Pacific Islander population lives in the western United States, compared to 22 percent of the total population (U.S. Census Bureau 2002).

Historical, Cultural, and Socioeconomic Factors   The three largest Asian American groups are Chinese (23.8 percent of Asian Americans), Filipinos (20.4 percent), and Japanese (12.3 percent) (U.S. Census Bureau 1998). Although these groups differ significantly, each "came to the United States seeking the American dream, satisfied important labor needs, and became victims of an anti-Asian movement designed to prevent their further immigration to the United States. [They] also experienced tremendous economic, educational, and social mobility and success in U.S. society" (Banks 2003, 413).

The California gold rush of 1849 brought the first immigrants from Asia, Chinese men who worked in mines, on railroads, and on farms, and who planned to return to their families and homeland. Early Chinese immigrants encountered widespread discrimination in their new country, with anti-Chinese riots occurring in San Francisco, Los Angeles, and Denver between 1869 and 1880. In 1882, Congress passed the Immigration Act, which ended Chinese immigration until 1902. The Chinese were oriented toward maintaining traditional language and religion and established tight-knit urban communities, or "Chinatowns." Recently, many upwardly mobile, professional Chinese Americans have been assimilated into suburban communities, while newly arrived, working-class immigrants from China and Hong Kong are settling in redeveloped Chinatowns.

Japanese immigrants began to arrive in Hawaii and the U.S. mainland in the late 1800s; most worked in agriculture, fisheries, the railroads, or industry and assimilated rapidly despite racial discrimination. The San Francisco Board of Education, for example, began to segregate all Japanese students in 1906, and the Immigration Act of 1924 ended Japanese immigration until 1952. During World War II, the United States was at war with Japan. In response to war hysteria over the "yellow peril," the United States government interned 110,000 Japanese Americans, most of them American born, in ten detention camps from 1942 to 1946. Since World War II, Japan has developed into one of the world's leading economic and technological powers—an accomplishment that has contributed, no doubt, to a recent decline in Japanese immigration to the United States.

Filipinos began to immigrate to Hawaii and the mainland as field laborers during the 1920s. They, too, encountered racism; in 1934 Congress passed the Tydings-McDuffie Act, which limited Filipino immigration to the United States to 50 persons annually. The following year, President Franklin Roosevelt signed the Repatriation Act, which provided free transportation to Filipinos willing to return to the Philippines. While most early Filipino immigrants had little education and low income, recent immigrants have tended to be professional, technical workers who hope to obtain employment in the United States more suitable for their education and training than they could in the Philippines (Banks 2003).

Teachers' Concerns about Asian American Students   Asian Americans are frequently stereotyped as hard working, conscientious, and respectful of authority, what Sue and Sue (1999) term a "model minority." In fact, 42.2 percent of Asian Americans 25 years and over have a bachelor's degree or more, compared to 23.9 percent of the total population (U.S. Census Bureau 1999). The unreliability of such stereotypes notwithstanding, Asian American parents do tend to require their children to respect authority and value education. However, "for many Asian American students, this image is a destructive myth," according to a report titled *An Invisible Crisis: The Educational Needs of Asian Pacific American Youth.* "As their schools fail them, these children become increasingly likely to graduate with rudimentary language skills, to drop out of school, to join gangs, or to find themselves in the low-paying occupations and on the margins of American life" (Asian Americans/Pacific Islanders in Philanthropy 1997). Families often pressure children to be successful academically through sacrifice and hard work. At the same time, there has been an increase in the number of Asian American youth who are in conflict with their parents' way of life. Leaders in Asian American communities have expressed concern about increases in dropout rates, school violence, and declining achievement. Some Indochinese Americans, for example, face deep cultural conflict in schools. Values and practices that are accepted in U.S. culture, such as dating and glorification of the individual, are sources of conflict between many Indochinese students and their parents.

Teachers need to be sensitive to cultural conflicts that may contribute to problems in school adjustment and achievement for Asian American students and realize that

> Stereotypes about Asian "whiz kids" and jealousy over the relatively high percentages of Asian Americans in the nation's colleges and universities may blind some non-Asian parents, fellow students, and teachers to the deep cultural conflict many Southeast Asian Americans face in our schools (Bennett 2003, 157).

To help Asian American students adjust to the U.S. culture, Qiu Liang offers teachers the following advice based on his school experiences as a Chinese immigrant:

> [Teachers] should be more patient [with an immigrant child] because it is very difficult for a person to be in a new country and learn a new language. Have patience.
> If the teacher feels there is no hope in an immigrant child, then the child will think, "Well, if the teacher who's helping me thinks that I can't go anywhere, then I might as well give up myself" (Igoa 1995, 99–100).

Similarly, Dung Yoong offers these recommendations based on her educational experiences as a Vietnamese immigrant:

> Try to get them to talk to you. Not just everyday conversation, but what they feel inside. Try to get them to get that out, because it's hard for kids. They don't trust—I had a hard time trusting and I was really insecure because of that.
> [P]utting an immigrant child who doesn't speak English into a classroom, a regular classroom with American students, is not very good. It scares [them] because it is so different. [Teachers] should start [them] slowly and have special classes where the child could adapt and learn a little bit about American society and customs (Igoa 1995, 103).

Education and Native Americans and Alaskan Natives

Native Americans and Alaskan Natives peopled the Western hemisphere more than 12,000 years ago. Today, they represent less than 1 percent of the total U.S. population, or about two million people (U.S. Census Bureau 2002). This group consists of 517 federally recognized and 365 state-recognized tribes, each with its own language, religious beliefs, and way of life. The four largest groups are the Cherokee Nation of Oklahoma, over 281,000 members; the Navajo Nation, 269,000; the Sioux Nation, 108,000; and the Chippewa Nation (U.S. Census Bureau 2002).

Approximately 760,000 Native Americans live on 275 reservations located primarily in the West. More than half of the Native American and Alaskan Native population lives in six states: Alaska, Arizona, California, New Mexico, Oklahoma, and Washington (Manning and Baruth 1996). Though most Native Americans live in cities, many are establishing connections with reservation Indians as a means of strengthening their cultural identities.

Native Americans are an example of the increasing ambiguity of racial and ethnic identities in the United States. For example, controversy exists over who is Native American. "Some full-blooded native people do not regard a person with one-quarter native heritage to qualify, while others accept 1/128" (Bennett 2003, 138). While most Native Americans consider a person with one-quarter or more tribal heritage to be a member, the U.S. Census Bureau considers anyone who claims native identity to be a member. An expert on Native Americans and Alaskan Natives, Arlene Hirschfelder (1986), points out that fifty-two legal definitions of Native Americans have been identified. Native Americans were declared U.S. citizens in 1924, and native nations have been recognized as independent, self-governing territories since the 1930s (Bennett 2003).

Historical, Cultural, and Socioeconomic Factors   Perhaps more than any other minority group, Native Americans have endured systematic long-term attempts to eradicate their languages and cultures. Disease, genocide, confinement on reservations, and decades of forced assimilation have devastated Native American cultures. In 1492, native people used 2 billion acres of land; currently, they own about 94 million acres of land, or about 5 percent of U.S. territory (Bennett 2003). Today, the rates of unemployment, poverty, and lack of educational attainment among Native Americans are among the nation's highest. Since the 1970s, however, there has been a resurgence of interest in preserving or restoring traditional languages, skills, and land claims.

There are hundreds of Native American languages, which anthropologists have attempted to categorize into six major language families (Banks 2002). Older tribal members fluent in the original tribal language and younger members often speak a form of so-called "reservation English." The challenge of educating Native Americans from diverse language backgrounds is further complicated by the difference in size of various Native American populations. These range from the more than 280,000 Cherokee to the 650 or so members of the Havasupi tribe of Arizona. As a result of the extreme diversity among Native Americans, it has even been suggested that "There is no such thing as an 'Indian' heritage, culture, or value system. [N]avajo, Cherokee, Sioux, and Aleut children are as different from each other in geographic and cultural backgrounds as they are from children growing up in New York City or Los Angeles" (Gipp 1979, 19).

Education for Native American children living on reservations is currently administered by the federal government's Bureau of Indian Affairs (BIA). The **Indian Education Act of 1972** and its **1974 amendments** supplement the BIA's educational programs and provide direct educational assistance to tribes. The act seeks to improve Native American education by providing funds to school districts to meet the special needs of Native American youth, to Indian tribes and state and local education agencies to improve education for youth and adults, to colleges and universities for the purpose of training teachers for Indian schools, and to Native American students to attend college.

Research on Native American Ways of Knowing   Considerable debate has occurred over the best approaches for educating Native Americans. For example, Banks points out that "since the 1920s, educational policy for Native Americans has vacillated between strong assimilationism to self-determination and cultural pluralism" (2001, 22). In any case, the culture-based learning styles of many Native Americans and Alaskan Natives differ from that of other students. The traditional upbringing of Native American children generally encourages them to develop a view of the world that is holistic, intimate, and shared. "They approach tasks visually, seem to prefer to learn by careful observation which precedes performance, and seem to learn in their natural settings experientially" (Swisher and Deyhle 1987, 350). Bennett suggests the following guideline to ensure that the school experiences of Native American students are in harmony with their cultural backgrounds: "An effective learning environment for Native Americans is one that does not single out the individual but provides frequent opportunities for the teacher to interact privately with individual children and with small groups, as well as opportunities for quiet, persistent exploration" (2003, 212).

Increasingly, Native Americans are designing multicultural programs to preserve their traditional cultures and ways of knowing. Although these programs are sometimes characterized as emphasizing separatism over assimilation, for many

What factors contribute to below-average achievement levels of Native American children? How do forces toward assimilation and cultural preservation coexist in the Native American experience?

Native Americans they are a matter of survival. The Heart of the Earth Survival School in Minneapolis, for example, was created to preserve the languages and cultures of the northern Plains Indians. Native American teachers at the school provide bilingual instruction in Ojibwe and Dakota. Students are encouraged to wear traditional dress and practice traditional arts, such as drumming and dancing.

Cultural preservation is also the primary concern at Alaskan Native schools in remote parts of western Alaska and Cherokee schools in the Marietta Independent School District of Stillwell, Oklahoma. In Alaska, elders come into the classroom to teach children how to skin a seal, an education that few Alaskan Native children receive today at home. In an effort to keep the Cherokee language alive, students at the Lost City School near Tulsa, Oklahoma, learn Cherokee, one of the many endangered Native American tongues. In Oklahoma, fewer than 8,000 of the 100,000 Cherokees can speak the language fluently, and most of those are over 45 (Burns, September 20, 2003).

What Is Meant by Bilingual Education?

Bilingual education programs are designed to meet the learning needs of students whose first language is not English by providing instruction in two languages. Regardless of the instructional approach used, one outcome for all bilingual programs is for students to become proficient in English. Additionally, students are encouraged to become **bicultural**, that is, able to function effectively in two or more linguistic and cultural groups.

In 1968, Congress passed the Bilingual Education Act, which required that language-minority students be taught in both their native language and English. In response to the Act, school districts implemented an array of bilingual programs that varied greatly in quality and effectiveness. As a result, many parents filed lawsuits, claiming that bilingual programs were not meeting their children's needs.

In 1974, the Supreme Court heard a class action suit (*Lau v. Nichols*) filed by 1,800 Chinese students in San Francisco who charged that they were failing to learn because they could not understand English. The students were enrolled in all-English classes and received no special assistance in learning English. In a unanimous ruling, the Court asserted that federally funded schools must "rectify the language deficiency" of students who "are certain to find their classroom experiences wholly incomprehensible." That same year, Congress adopted the Equal Educational Opportunity Act (EEOA), which stated in part that a school district must "take appropriate action to overcome language barriers that impede equal participation by its students in its instructional programs."

While most bilingual programs serve Latino and Hispanic American students, there is an increasing need for bilingual teachers who are proficient in a variety of second languages. In fact, many school districts are offering salary bonuses for bilingual teachers.

Bilingual programs are tremendously varied and reflect "extreme differences in student composition, program organization, teaching methodologies and approaches, and teacher backgrounds and skills" (Griego-Jones 1996, 115). Generally, however, four types of bilingual education programs are currently available to provide special assistance to the 3.5 million language-minority students in the United States (see Figure 4.3). Only about 315,000 students actually participate in some kind of bilingual program.

Research and Debate on Bilingual Programs

Research on the effectiveness of bilingual programs is mixed (Rothstein 1998). Some who have examined the research conclude that bilingual programs have little effect on achievement (Baker 1991; Rossell 1990; Rossell and Baker 1996). Others have found that well-designed bilingual programs do increase students' achievement and are superior to monolingual programs (Cziko 1992; Nieto 1992; Schmidt 1991; Trueba, Cheng, and Kenji 1993; Willig 1987).

Considerable debate surrounds bilingual programs in the United States. Those in favor of bilingual education make the following points:

- Students are better able to learn English if they are taught to read and write in their native language.
- Bilingual programs allow students to learn content in their native language rather than delaying that learning until they master English.
- Further developing competencies in students' native languages provides important cognitive foundations for learning English and academic content.

Figure 4.3 Four types of bilingual education programs.

Four Types of Bilingual Education Programs

Immersion programs: Students learn English and other subjects in classrooms where only English is spoken. Aides who speak the first language of students are sometimes available, or students may also listen to equivalent audiotaped lessons in their first language.

Transition programs: Students receive reading lessons in their first language and lessons in English as a Second Language (ESL). Once they sufficiently master English, students are placed in classrooms where English is spoken and their first language is discontinued.

Pull-out programs: On a regular basis, students are separated from English-speaking students so that they may receive lessons in English or reading lessons in their first language. These are sometimes called sheltered English programs.

Maintenance programs: To maintain the student's native language and culture, instruction in English and instruction in the native language are provided from kindergarten through twelfth grade. Students become literate.

In recent elections, education has been at the forefront of candidate debates, with bilingual education at the center of many candidates' platforms. Why do you think bilingual education creates such a schism among Americans?

- Second-language learning is a positive value and should be as valid for a Spanish-speaker learning English as for an English-speaker learning Spanish.
- Bilingual programs support students' cultural identity, social context, and self-esteem.

On the other hand, those opposed to bilingual programs make the following points:

- Public schools should not be expected to provide instruction in all the first languages spoken by their students, nor can schools afford to pay a teacher who might teach only a few students.
- The cost of bilingual education is high. Bilingual programs divert staff and resources away from English-speaking students.
- If students spend more time exposed to English, they will learn English more quickly.
- Bilingual programs emphasize differences among and barriers between groups; they encourage separateness rather than assimilation and unity.
- Bilingual education is a threat to English as the nation's first language.

Advice for Monolingual Teachers

Although the future of bilingual education in the United States is uncertain, teachers must continue to meet the needs of language-minority students. These needs are best met by teachers who speak their native language as well as English.

However, this is often not possible, and monolingual teachers will find increasing numbers of LEP students in their classrooms. See Appendix 4.2, "Creating Classroom Environments That Support Second-Language Learners," and Appendix 4.3, "Strategies for Enhancing the Learning and Literacy of Second-Language Learners" at the end of this chapter. Developed by bilingual/ESL education expert Gisela Ernst and her colleagues, these strategies can be used whether or not a teacher is bilingual.

What Is Multicultural Education?

Multicultural education is committed to providing all students—regardless of socioeconomic status, gender, sexual orientation or ethnic, racial, or cultural backgrounds—with equal opportunities to learn in school. Multicultural education is based on the fact that students do not learn in a vacuum—their culture predisposes them to learn in certain ways. And finally, multicultural education recognizes that current school practices have provided, and continue to provide, some students with greater opportunities for learning than students who belong to other groups. The suggestions in this chapter's appendices are examples of multicultural education in practice.

As multiculturalism has become more pervasive in U.S. schools, controversy over the need for multicultural education and its purposes has emerged. Carl Grant has identified as "myths" the following six arguments against multicultural education: "(1) It is both divisive and so conceptually weak that it does little to eliminate structural inequalities; (2) it is unnecessary because the United States is a melting pot; (3) multiculturalism—and by extension multicultural education—and political correctness are the same thing; (4) multicultural education rejects the notion of a common culture; (5) multicultural education is a 'minority thing'; and (6) multicultural education will impede learning the basic skills" (1994, 5). Though multicultural education is being challenged by those who promote these beliefs, public dialogue and debate about how schools can more effectively address diversity is healthy—an indicator that our society is making real progress toward creating a culture that incorporates the values of diverse groups.

Dimensions of Multicultural Education

According to James A. Banks, "Multicultural education is a complex and multidimensional concept" (Banks 2001, 5). More specifically, Banks suggests that multicultural education may be conceptualized as consisting of five dimensions: (1) content integration; (2) knowledge construction; (3) prejudice reduction; (4) an equity pedagogy; and (5) an empowering school culture (see Figure 4.4). As you progress through your teacher-education program and eventually begin to prepare curriculum materials and instructional strategies for your multicultural classroom, remember that integrating content from a variety of cultural groups is just one dimension of multicultural education. Multicultural education is not "something that is done at a certain time slot in the school day where children eat with

Figure 4.4 Banks's dimensions of multicultural education.

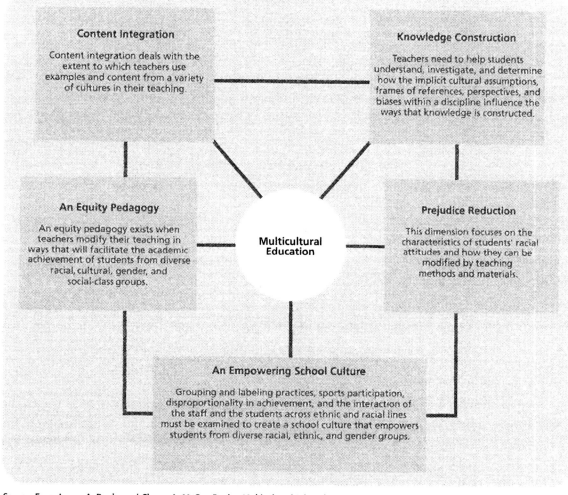

chopsticks or listen to Peruvian music. . . . [It is] something that is infused throughout the school culture and practiced daily" (Henry 1996, 108).

Multicultural education promotes students' positive self-identity and pride in their heritage, acceptance of people from diverse backgrounds, and critical self-assessment. In addition, multicultural education can prompt students, perhaps with guidance from their teachers, to take action against prejudice and discrimination within their school. Indeed, as Joel Spring says, "multicultural education should create a spirit of tolerance and activism in students. An understanding of other cultures and of differing cultural frames of reference will . . . spark students to actively work for social justice" (1998, 163). For example, students might reduce the marginalization of minority-group students in their school by inviting them to participate in extracurricular and after-school activities.

Multicultural Curricula

As a teacher you will teach students who historically have not received full educational opportunity—students from the many racial and ethnic minority groups in the United States, students from low-income families or communities, students with exceptional abilities or disabilities, students who are gay or lesbian, and students who are male or female. You will face the challenge of reaching out to all students and teaching them that they are persons of worth who can learn. The Teachers' Voices feature on page 153 presents two teachers' suggestions for beginning teachers to follow in multicultural classrooms.

In your diverse classroom your aim is not to develop a different curriculum for each group of students—that would be impossible and would place undue emphasis on differences among students. Rather, your curriculum should help increase students' awareness and appreciation of the rich diversity in U.S. culture. A **multicultural curriculum** addresses the needs and backgrounds of all students regardless of their cultural identity. As Banks suggests, the multicultural curriculum "enable[s] students to derive valid generalizations and theories about the characteristics of ethnic groups and to learn how they are alike and different, in both their past and present experiences. . . . [It] focus[es] on a range of groups that *differ* in their racial characteristics, cultural experiences, languages, histories, values, and current problems" (2003, 16). Teachers who provide multicultural education recognize the importance of asking questions such as those posed by Valerie Ooka Pang: "Why is a child's home language important to keep? What strengths does culture give children? What impact does culture have on learning? What does racism, sexism, or classism look like in schools?" (1994, 292).

In developing a multicultural curriculum, you should be sensitive to how your instructional materials and strategies can be made more inclusive so that they reflect cultural perspectives, or "voices," that previously have been silent or marginalized in discussions about what should be taught in schools and how it should be taught. "Non-dominant groups representing diversity in the school whose voices traditionally have not been heard include those defined by race, language, gender, sexual orientation, alternative family structures, social class, disability, bilingualism, and those with alien or refugee status" (Henry 1996, 108). Effective teachers attend to these previously unheard voices not as an act of tokenism but with a genuine desire to make the curriculum more inclusive and to "create space for alternative voices, not just on the periphery but in the center" (Singer 1994, 286).

Multicultural Instructional Materials and Strategies

To create classrooms that are truly multicultural, teachers must select instructional materials that are sensitive, accurately portray the contributions of ethnic groups,

Teachers' Voices   Putting Research and Theory into Practice

Celebrating Diversity in the Classroom

Neal A. Glasgow and Cathy D. Hicks

Frequently it is beginning teachers who find themselves with the most diverse classroom. It is of the utmost importance that these teachers are prepared for crosscultural, inclusive instruction. Classes in teacher education programs must include information about the characteristics of prejudice and racism, provide successful examples of teaching ethnic- and language-minority students, and ingrain instruction that provides both social support for students and an intellectual challenge.

Teachers must also be sensitive to issues involving money. Perhaps every child in class wouldn't be able to afford the cost of a field trip. For one high school that was considering putting ATM machines on campus, the realization of the ways this could further divide students into "haves" and "have-nots" caused administrators to rethink their decision.

Teachers should consult with experienced exemplary veteran teachers or school administrators before meeting with parents of immigrant students to determine if a translator might be needed or if there is any specific information about that student's family culture which might assist the teacher in having a successful meeting. The same is true for a student with disabili-

ties. The special education teacher and the IEP (individual education program) can provide beneficial information to the novice teacher. The more a teacher is sensitive to the richness of the diversity in the classroom, the more successful and equitable today's classrooms will become.

Questions

1. When you think about the diverse students whom you will teach, what are your concerns?
2. What knowledge and abilities do you *now* have that will enable you to be successful at "celebrating diversity" in your classroom?
3. What additional knowledge and abilities do you plan to develop? How will you develop those?

Neal A. Glasgow teaches biology and art at San Dieguito Academy High School, a public high school of choice in California. *Cathy D. Hicks* is the Beginning Teacher Support and Assessment (BTSA) Coordinator for the San Dieguito Union High School District in California. The preceding is excerpted from their book, *What Successful Teachers Do: Research-Based Classroom Strategies for New and Veteran Teachers.* (Thousand Oaks, CA: Corwin Press, Inc., 2003), pp. 129–130.

---

and reflect diverse points of view. Teachers must also recognize that "[s]ome of the books and other materials on ethnic groups published each year are insensitive, inaccurate, and written from mainstream and insensitive perspectives and points of view" (Banks 2003, 111). Some guidelines for selecting multicultural instructional materials follow:

- Books and other materials should accurately portray the perspectives, attitudes, and feelings of ethnic groups.
- Fictional works should have strong ethnic characters.
- Books should describe settings and experiences with which all students can identify and yet should accurately reflect ethnic cultures and lifestyles.

Figure 4.5   Essential knowledge and skills for successful teaching in a diverse society.

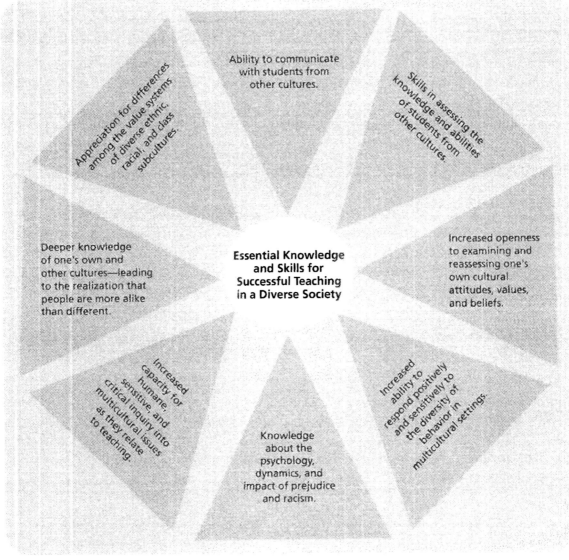

Source: Adapted from Forrest W. Parkay and Henry T. Fillmer, "Improving Teachers' Attitudes toward Minority-Group Students: An Experiential Approach to Multicultural Inservice," *New Horizons Journal of Education,* November 1984, pp. 178–179.

- The protagonists in books with ethnic themes should have ethnic characteristics but should face conflicts and problems universal to all cultures and groups.
- The illustrations in books should be accurate, ethnically sensitive, and technically well done.
- Ethnic materials should not contain racist concepts, clichés, phrases, or words.

- Factual materials should be historically accurate.
- Multiethnic resources and basal textbooks should discuss major events and documents related to ethnic history (Banks 2003, 127).

Yvonne Wilson, a first-grade teacher in Talmoon, Minnesota, and an Ojibwe Indian, points out that a teacher's willingness to learn about other cultures is very important to students and their parents:

> *People in the community know if you are trying to understand their culture. Students also see it. Becoming involved—going to a powwow or participating in other cultural events—shows people that here is a teacher who is trying to learn about our culture.*

Participating wholeheartedly in crosscultural experiences will help you to grow in the eight areas outlined in Figure 4.5 as essential for successful teaching in a diverse society.

How Is Gender a Dimension of Multicultural Education?

Though it may be evident that gender affects students' learning in many ways, it may not be evident that gender is an important dimension of multicultural education. However, as Tozer, Violas, and Senese point out:

> Traditional definitions of culture have centered around the formal expression of a people's common existence—language, art, music, and so forth. If culture is more broadly defined to include such things as ways of knowing, ways of relating to others, ways of negotiating rights and privileges, and modes of conduct, thought, and expression, then the term "culture" applies not only to ethnic groups but to people grouped on the basis of gender. [G]ender entails cultural as well as physiological dimensions (1993, 310).

Gender Differences

Cultural differences between males and females are partially shaped by society's traditional expectations of them. Through **sex role stereotyping**, families, the media, the schools, and other powerful social forces condition boys and girls to act in certain ways regardless of abilities or interests. As Chapter 1 pointed out, one aim of schools is to socialize students to participate in society. One dimension of the **sex role socialization** process conveys to students certain expectations about the way boys and girls are "supposed" to act. Girls are supposed to play with dolls, boys with trucks. Girls are supposed to be passive, boys active. Girls are supposed to express their feelings and emotions when in pain, boys to repress their feelings and deny pain.

Students may be socialized into particular gender-specific roles as a result of the curriculum materials they use at school. By portraying males in more dominant, assertive ways and portraying females in ways that suggest that they are passive and helpless, textbooks can subtly reinforce expectations about the way girls and boys "should" behave. Within the last few decades, though, publishers of curriculum materials have become more vigilant about avoiding these stereotypes.

Case for
Reflection
Developing Group Unity in a Diverse Classroom

You are a first-year teacher at a school in a low socioeconomic neighborhood. The school is 30 years old and the surrounding neighborhood consists of homes that are much older. The neighborhood, located in a large metropolitan area, is ethnically and racially diverse. The school's enrollment is approximately 60 percent Anglo-European American, 20 percent African American, 15 percent Latino and Hispanic, and 5 percent Asian American.

It is the first day of school, and students are just now entering your classroom. There is a lot of talking, joking, and good-natured horseplay.

This year, you have set up your classroom for cooperative learning. Five octagonal tables are distributed evenly around the room. Students at each table will make up a "team." Though students will work in teams, you plan to de-emphasize competition among the teams. Instead, you want the entire class to see itself, eventually, as one, unified "team."

As the students select tables at which to sit, you notice that they are clustering themselves into four distinct racial groups. After taking their seats, most of the students continue to talk with the other students at their table. The Anglo-European American students are seated at two tables; the African American, Latino and Hispanic, and Asian American students are seated, separately, at the remaining three tables.

"Welcome to my class," you begin. "We are going to have a great year together!"

The students gradually quiet down and give you their attention. You continue with a brief overview of what students will learn in your class that year. Following the overview, you ask each student to introduce him- or herself to the class.

As students introduce themselves, you are thinking about how students have obviously used race as a criteria for choosing a table at which to sit. Your preference is for students to choose work tables for the year. Assigning tables might minimize the tendency of students to cluster by race, you realize. However, that would work against the democratic classroom climate you hope to create. Also, your hunch is that interaction among students would still reflect racial group membership, regardless of assigned seats.

You are well aware that during the next few days you will set the tone for the new school year. What can you do during that time to encourage students to interact as much as possible across racial groups? What can you do throughout the school year to encourage cohesiveness in your diverse classroom?

Questions

1. In the preceding case, your students have divided themselves into groups according to race. Assuming they are allowed to form small groups on their own, what other criteria might students use to determine group membership?
2. Why do you think students often prefer to work with classmates who are from the same racial group?
3. With reference to the grade level and subject area for which you are preparing to teach, what instructional activities would encourage students to see themselves as *one* cohesive group, rather than several small groups formed according to race, ethnicity, gender, ability, socioeconomic status, or other criteria?

Technology in Teaching

Does gender equity exist in the use of educational technology?

Considerable evidence indicates that boys tend to have more experience with and positive attitudes toward computer technology than girls (Bitter and Pierson 1999; Comber et al. 1997; Hammett 1997; Valenza 1997; Whitley 1997). In addition, boys participate in more elective technology courses and activities than girls. A partial explanation for this difference may stem from the fact that "Software generally tends to emphasize male-dominated activities. Games often include violence and competition as motivation. These software characteristics tend to attract males" (Bitter and Pierson 1999, 240). Also, some computer software and online advertisements promote gender stereotypes (Knupfer 1998). In addition, Cornelia Brunner and Dorothy Bennett (1997) suggest that the attitude of girls toward technology might reflect a tendency in schools to celebrate the speed and power of the machine (the "masculine view") rather than the social function of technology (the "feminine view").

In any case, as the use of technologies continues to become more widespread in society and schools, teachers must make a special effort to ensure that girls have equal access to technology and that their technology-related experiences are positive and growth enhancing. What steps will you take to ensure that your use of technology reflects gender equity? How will you encourage your students, regardless of gender, to acquire additional knowledge and skills with computers?

Gender and Education

As noted in Chapter 3, it was not until Title IX of the Education Amendments Act was passed in 1972 that women were guaranteed equality of educational opportunity in educational programs receiving federal assistance. Title IX has had the greatest impact on athletic programs in schools. On the thirtieth anniversary of Title IX, U.S. Secretary of Education Roderick Paige stated:

> Without a doubt, Title IX has opened the doors of opportunity for generations of women and girls to compete, to achieve, and to pursue their American dreams. In 1971, before Title IX went into effect, more than 294,000 girls participated in high school sports. Last year, that number exceeded 2.7 million—an 847 percent increase (U.S. Department of Education, news release, June 27, 2002).

The law requires that both sexes have equal opportunities to participate in and benefit from the availability of coaches, sports equipment, resources, and facilities. For contact sports such as football, wrestling, and boxing, sports that were not open to women, separate teams are allowed.

The right of females to equal educational opportunity was further enhanced with the passage of the **Women's Educational Equity Act (WEEA)** of 1974. This act provides the following opportunities:

• Expanded math, science, and technology programs for females

- Programs to reduce sex-role stereotyping in curriculum materials
- Programs to increase the number of female educational administrators
- Special programs to extend educational and career opportunities to minority, disabled, and rural women
- Programs to help school personnel increase educational opportunities and career aspirations for females
- Encouragement for more females to participate in athletics

Despite reforms stemming from WEEA, several reports in the early 1990s criticized schools for subtly discriminating against girls in tests, textbooks, and teaching methods. Research on teacher interactions in the classroom seemed to point to widespread unintentional gender bias against girls. Two of these studies, *Shortchanging Girls, Shortchanging America* (1991) and *How Schools Shortchange Girls* (1992), both commissioned by the American Association of University Women (AAUW), claimed that girls were not encouraged in math and science and that teachers favored boys' intellectual growth over that of girls.

Since the mid-1990s, however, gender equity studies have had more mixed findings. In their analysis of data on achievement and engagement of 9,000 eighth-grade boys and girls, University of Michigan researchers Valerie Lee, Xianglei Chen, and Becky A. Smerdon (1996) concluded that "the pattern of gender differences is inconsistent. In some cases, females are favored; in others males are favored." Similarly, University of Chicago researchers Larry Hedges and Amy Nowell found in their study of thirty-two years of mental tests given to boys and girls that, while boys do better than girls in science and mathematics, they were "at a rather profound disadvantage" in writing and scored below girls in reading comprehension (Hedges 1996, 3).

Additional research and closer analyses of earlier reports on gender bias in education were beginning to suggest that boys, not girls, were most "shortchanged" by the schools (Sommers 1996). Numerous articles as well as a 1999 PBS series that began with a program titled "The War on Boys" challenged the conclusions of the earlier AAUW report, *How Schools Shortchange Girls*. Other commentary discounted gender bias in the schools as a fabrication of radical feminism. Among the first to put forth this view was Christina Hoff Sommers's (1994) controversial book, *Who Stole Feminism? How Women Have Betrayed Women*; and, four years later, Judith Kleinfeld's (1998) *The Myth That Schools Shortchange Girls: Social Science in the Service of Deception* and Cathy Young's (1999) *Ceasefire! Why Women and Men Must Join Forces to Achieve True Equality.*

To examine gender issues in the public schools, *The Metropolitan Life Survey of the American Teacher, 1997* surveyed 1,306 students in grades 7–12 and interviewed 1,035 teachers in grades 6–12. The analysis of data indicated that:

(1) contrary to the commonly held view that boys are at an advantage over girls in school, girls appear to have an advantage over boys in terms of their future plans, teachers' expectations [see Figure 4.6], everyday experiences at school and interactions

Figure 4.6 Teachers' opinions on who aims higher: boys or girls.

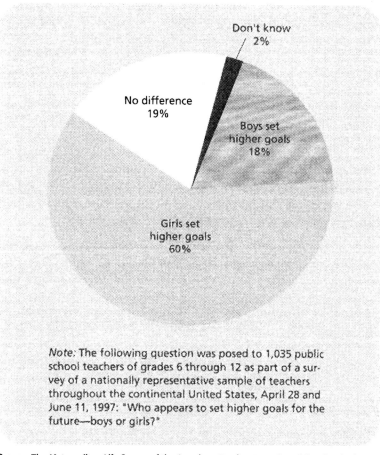

Note: The following question was posed to 1,035 public school teachers of grades 6 through 12 as part of a survey of a nationally representative sample of teachers throughout the continental United States, April 28 and June 11, 1997: "Who appears to set higher goals for the future—boys or girls?"

Source: The Metropolitan Life Survey of the American Teacher 1997: Examining Gender Issues in Public Schools. New York: Louis Harris and Associates, Inc., 1997, p. 52.

in the classroom; (2) minority girls [African Americans and Hispanics only] hold the most optimistic views of the future and are the group most likely to focus on education goals; (3) minority boys are the most likely to feel discouraged about the future and the least interested in getting a good education; and (4) teachers nationwide view girls as higher achievers and more likely to succeed than boys. [These] findings appear to contradict those from other studies which conclude that girls have lower expectations than boys, feel less confident, perceive competitiveness as a barrier to learning and believe that society discourages them from pursuing their goals (Louis Harris and Associates 1997, 3).

To shed light on gender differences in academic achievement, Warren Willingham and Nancy Cole (1997) conducted a seminal study of the scores of 15 million students in the fourth, eighth, and twelfth grades on hundreds of standardized exams used by schools and college placement exams such as the SAT. Contrary to long-standing assumptions that there are pronounced differences between the performance of males and females on standardized tests, their study found that "there is not a dominant picture of one gender excelling over the other and, in fact, the average performance difference across all subjects is essentially zero." Boys and girls, Willingham and Cole found, were fairly evenly matched in verbal and abstract reasoning, math computation, and the social sciences. The superiority of boys in math and science was found to be surprisingly slight and "significantly smaller than 30 years ago." Boys were found to have a clear advantage in mechanical and electronic ability and knowledge of economics and history, while girls had a clear advantage in language skills, especially writing, and a "moderate edge" in short-term memory and perceptual speed. Furthermore, the authors concluded that gender differences in test scores are not the result of bias in the exams; instead, the differences are genuine and would be reflected also in more carefully designed tests.

International Comparisons   A comparison of the academic achievement of boys and girls in 42 countries conducted by the Paris-based Organization for Economic Cooperation and Development (OECD) (2003) found that girls are better readers than boys, and they have higher expectations than boys of holding good jobs someday. In the United States, 15-year-old girls scored an average of 518 on the study's reading test while boys scored an average of 490. Their gap of 28 points is close to the worldwide average of 32. In math, 15-year-old boys scored higher than girls in about half of industrialized countries. Boys are "marginally but not significantly" ahead in the United States, the study found (Potrikus, September 28, 2003).

The OECD study results parallel U.S. reports showing higher achievement for girls. For example, in the United States, three of five members of high schools' National Honor Societies today are girls; girls outnumber boys 124 to 100 in advanced-placement courses; and girls also tend to make better grades.

Gender-Fair Classrooms and Curricula

Although research and debate about the bias boys and girls encounter in school will no doubt continue, it is clear that teachers must encourage girls and boys to develop to the full extent of their capabilities and provide them an education that is free from **gender bias**—subtle favoritism or discrimination on the basis of gender.

Following is a list of basic guidelines for creating a **gender-fair classroom**. Adherence to these guidelines will help teachers "address the inequities institutionalized in the organizational structure of schools, the curriculum selected to be taught, the learning strategies employed, and their ongoing instructional and informal interactions with students" (Stanford 1992, 88).

- Become aware of differences in interactions with girls and boys.
- Promote boys' achievement in reading and writing and girls' achievement in mathematics and science.

- Reduce young children's self-imposed sexism.
- Teach about sexism and sex role stereotyping.
- Foster an atmosphere of collaboration between girls and boys.

Sexual Orientation   In addition to gender bias, some students experience discrimination on the basis of their sexual orientation. To help all students realize their full potential, teachers should acknowledge the special needs of gay, lesbian, and bisexual students for "there is an invisible gay and lesbian minority in every school, and the needs of these students [a]re often unknown and unmet" (Besner and Spungin 1995, xi). One study of 120 gay and lesbian students ages fourteen to twenty-one found that only one-fourth said they were able to discuss their sexual orientation with school counselors, and less than one in five said they could identify someone who had been supportive of them (Tellijohann and Price 1993). Moreover, a similar study of lesbian and gay youth reported that 80 percent of participants believed their teachers had negative attitudes about homosexuality (Sears 1991).

Based on estimates that as much as 10 percent of society may be homosexual, a high school with an enrollment of 1,500 might have as many as 150 gay, lesbian, and bisexual students (Besner and Spungin 1995; Stover 1992). The National Education Association, the American Federation of Teachers, and several professional organizations have passed resolutions urging members and school districts to acknowledge the special needs of these students.

The nation's first dropout prevention program targeting gay, lesbian, and bisexual students was implemented in the Los Angeles school system. Known as Project 10, the program focuses on education, suicide prevention, dropout prevention, creating a safe environment for homosexual students, and HIV/AIDS education (Uribe and Harbeck 1991). In 1993, Massachusetts became the first state to adopt an educational policy prohibiting discrimination against gay and lesbian students and teachers. At one Massachusetts high school, gay and straight students created the Gay-Straight Alliance (GSA), a school-sanctioned student organization that gives students a safe place to discuss sexual orientation issues (Bennett 1997).

In 2003 about 100 students enrolled in The Harvey Milk School, the nation's first public high school for gay, lesbian, bisexual and transgender students. Housed in an office building in New York City, Harvey Milk is named after California's first elected gay official—a member of the Board of Supervisors in San Francisco—who was assassinated after less than a year in office. New York City also co-sponsors after-school programs such as art and music, and counseling and support services for as many as 2,000 gay and lesbian students (Ferguson, August 30, 2003).

Homosexual students can experience school-related problems and safety risks. The hostility gay, lesbian, and bisexual youth can encounter may cause them to feel confused, isolated, and self-destructive (Alexander 1998; Anderson 1997; Edwards 1997; Jones 1999; Jordan, Vaughan, and Woodworth 1997). Teachers and other school personnel can provide much-needed support. Informed, sensitive, and caring teachers can play an important role in helping all students develop to their full potential. Such teachers realize the importance of recognizing diverse perspectives, and they create inclusive classroom environments that encourage students to respect differences among themselves and others and to see the contributions that persons from all groups have made to society.

Summary

How Is Diversity Embedded in the Culture of the United States?

- The percentage of ethnic minorities in the United States has been growing steadily since World War II. By 2025, half of U.S. youth will be white and half "minority"; and by 2050, no one group will be a majority among adults in the United States. Currently, the majority of students in several states and many urban districts are from groups traditionally thought of as minority.

- Culture is defined as the way of life common to a group of people, including beliefs, attitudes, habits, values, and practices.

- Dimensions of cultural identity include beliefs, attitudes, and values; racial identity; exceptionalities; language; gender; ethnicity; income level; and occupation.

- Ethnicity refers to a commonly shared racial or cultural identity and a set of beliefs, values, and attitudes. The concept of *race* is used to distinguish among people on the basis of biological traits and characteristics. A minority group is a group of people who share certain characteristics and are fewer in number than the majority of a population.

- The lower achievement levels of certain minority-group students compared to those of their Anglo-European American and Asian American counterparts reflect the strong connection between socioeconomic status (SES) and achievement, since the incidence of poverty is highest among minority families.

- Stereotyping is the process of attributing certain behavioral characteristics to all members of a group, often on the basis of limited experiences with and information about the group being stereotyped. Individual racism is the prejudicial belief that one's own ethnic or racial group is superior to others, and institutional racism refers to laws, customs, and practices that lead to racial inequalities.

What Does Equal Educational Opportunity Mean?

- Equal educational opportunity means that teachers promote the full development of students without regard for race, ethnicity, gender, sexual orientation, socioeconomic status, abilities, or disabilities.

- Past evidence indicates that four minority groups in the United States have been denied equality of educational opportunity through various forms of racism, discrimination, and neglect: African Americans, Latino and Hispanic Americans, Asian Americans and Pacific Islanders, and Native Americans and Alaskan Natives. Teachers can meet the needs of students from these groups by becoming familiar with their cultural and linguistic backgrounds and learning styles.

- In spite of increasing diversity in the United States, there has been a trend since 1990 for schools to "resegregate," perhaps as a result of Supreme Court rulings that removed judicial supervision of school district efforts to desegregate.

What Is Meant by Bilingual Education?

- Bilingual education programs provide instruction in a student's first language and English. The goal of bilingual programs is for students to learn English and become bicultural, able to function effectively in two or more linguistic/cultural groups. Four approaches to bilingual education are immersion, maintenance, pull-out, and transition programs.

- Some research has found that bilingual programs have a positive effect on achievement, while others have found little effect. In light of inconclusive outcomes and mixed support, there has been a continuing debate over bilingual education in the United States.

What Is Multicultural Education?

- Five dimensions of multicultural education have been suggested: content integration, knowledge construction, prejudice reduction, an equity pedagogy, and an empowering school culture.

- A multicultural curriculum addresses the needs and backgrounds of all students—regardless of their cultural identity—and expands students' appreciation for diversity. Effective multicultural materials and instructional strategies include the contributions of ethnic groups and reflect diverse points of view or "voices" that previously may have been silenced or marginalized in society.

How Is Gender a Dimension of Multicultural Education?

- Gender includes ways of knowing and "modes of conduct, thought, and expression"; these are dimensions of culture.

- The behavior of boys and girls in our society is influenced by *sexism, sex role socialization*, and *sex role stereotyping*.

- Both boys and girls experience inequities in the classroom; teachers, however, can provide both sexes with an education free of *gender bias* by creating gender-fair classrooms and curricula.

- Teachers should acknowledge the special needs of students who are gay, lesbian, or bisexual, and provide them with safe, supportive learning environments.

Key Terms and Concepts

Afrocentric schools, 139
bicultural, 147
bilingual education, 129
cultural identity, 128
cultural pluralism, 127
culture, 127
diversity, 126
ethnic group, 128
ethnicity, 132

gender bias, 160
gender-fair classroom, 160
Indian Education Act of 1972 and
  1974 Amendments, 145
individual racism, 135
institutional racism, 135
limited English proficiency (LEP),
  129
minorities, 133

multicultural curriculum, 152
multicultural education, 150
multiculturalism, 130
race, 132
sex role socialization, 155
sex role stereotyping, 155
stereotyping, 134
Women's Educational Equity Act
  (WEEA), 157

Reflective Application Activities

Discussion Questions

1. What are the characteristics of those who are effective in teaching students from cultural backgrounds other than their own? Which of these characteristics can be acquired or developed further through education or training experiences?

2. What are the problems inherent in a multiethnic society? In what ways does ethnicity affect the school population? What are the strengths that can be gained from cultural diversity?

Professional Journal

1. What is your cultural identity? To what subcultures do you belong, and how do these contribute to your cultural identity?

2. As this chapter points out, "through sex role stereotyping families, the media, the schools, and other powerful social forces condition boys and girls to act in certain ways regardless of abilities or interests." As a teacher, how can you minimize the effects of sex role stereotyping?

Online Assignments

1. Conduct an online keyword search for sources of information on one or more of the following diversity topics from Chapter 4. Share your findings with classmates before narrowing your search:

   bilingual education

   English as a Second Language (ESL)

   English for Students of Other Languages (ESOL)

   gender equity

   multicultural education

2. Using one of the diversity topics above, go online to gather current national and state statistics related to that topic. For example, you may gather relevant data at one or more of the following sites:

   International Assessment of Educational Progress (IAEP)

   National Assessment of Educational Progress (NAEP)

   National Center for Education Statistics

   National Data Resource Center

   U.S. Census Bureau

Observations and Interviews

1. If possible, visit a school that has an enrollment of students whose cultural or socioeconomic backgrounds differ from your own. What feelings and questions about these students emerge as a result of your observations? How might your feelings affect your effectiveness as a teacher? How might you go about finding answers to your questions?

2. Interview a teacher at the school identified in the above activity. What special satisfactions does he or she experience from teaching at the school? What significant problems relating to diversity does he or she encounter, and how are they dealt with?

Professional Portfolio

Prepare an annotated directory of local resources for teaching students about diversity, implementing multicultural curricula, and promoting harmony or equity among diverse groups. For each entry, include an annotation—that is, a brief description of the resource materials and their availability.

Resources for your personalized directory should be available through local sources such as your university library, public library, community agencies, and so on. Among the types of resources you might include are the following:

- Films, videos, audiocassettes, books, and journal articles
- Simulation games designed to improve participants' attitudes toward diversity
- Motivational guest speakers from the community
- Ethnic museums and cultural centers
- Community groups and agencies dedicated to promoting understanding among diverse groups
- Training and workshops in the area of diversity

Appendix 4.1
Can You Recognize Racism?

INSTRUCTIONS

First work alone. Put a check before each statement you think is an example of racism. Then work with your small group and try to agree on the examples of racism. (Your group will receive a packet of statement cards to make the task easier). Choose one member of your group to share your decisions with everyone.

1. Which of the following quotations or descriptive statements are examples of racism? Indicate these with a check.

   _____ "A black family moved into our neighborhood this week."

   _____ The principal interviewed two equally outstanding candidates, one black and the other Latino. She selected the black teacher because her school had several Latino teachers but no black teachers.

   _____ In 1882 immigration laws excluded the Chinese, and the Japanese were excluded in 1908.

   _____ During the 1960s civil rights movement, Mrs. Viola Liuzzo, a white civil rights worker from Michigan, was shot by white southern segregationists.

   _____ Between 1892 and 1921 nearly 2,400 African Americans were lynched by vigilante mobs who were never brought to justice.

   _____ "The best basketball players on our team this year are black."

   _____ The band director discouraged black students from playing the flute or piccolo because he believed it was too difficult for them to excel on these instruments.

   _____ When Mrs. Wallace, an African American woman from Detroit, visited a predominantly white university in northern Michigan to see her son play basketball, she was seriously injured in a car accident. She refused a blood transfusion because she was afraid of being contaminated by white blood.

   _____ When Stacey Russell, an African American undergraduate, went through rush, the girls of an all-white sorority decided not to pledge her because several members threatened to move out if they did.

   _____ The geography textbook described the peoples of Nigeria as primitive and underdeveloped.

   _____ The children who attended an elementary school in southwest Texas spoke only Spanish at home. When they came to school all the books and intelligence tests were in English. Nearly all of the children were placed in remedial classes or in classes for the mentally retarded.

   _____ Mr. Jones said, "It is true that Indians who still live on reservations live in extreme poverty. But this is because they refuse to give up their traditions and a culture which is obsolete in the modern world."

   _____ The U.S. Constitution allowed each slave to be counted as three-fifths of a person.

   _____ The reporter wrote that "Toni Morrison is a brilliant writer who accurately portrays much of the black experience in America."

Source: From Christine I. Bennett, *Comprehensive Multicultural Education: Theory and Practice*, 4th ed. Boston: Allyn and Bacon, 1999, pp. 312–314. Copyright © 1999 by Allyn and Bacon. Reprinted by permission.

_____ When John brought home a new friend, his father was shocked and angry. Peter, the new friend, was of Japanese origin and John's father had been seriously wounded by the Japanese in World War II. John's father refused to allow Peter to visit again.

_____ In 1896 the Supreme Court ruled that separate facilities for the races were legal as long as they were _equal_. This resulted in separate schools, churches, restaurants, restrooms, swimming pools, theaters, doctors' offices, neighborhoods, Bibles used in court, and so forth.

_____ When Mary Addams wanted to find a place in the school cafeteria, the only vacant chair was at a table seating five black girls. Mary, who is white, was afraid to join them.

_____ In California today, approximately 10 percent of the population is black, while 41 percent of those in prison are black. Blacks generally have more financial difficulty than whites in hiring a lawyer and plea bargaining.

2. Select one member to write your group's decisions below on the decision sheet and another person to share the results with the rest. Be prepared to explain your reasons if necessary.

    a. The following statements are examples of either individual or institutional racism: (Write numbers and a word or two for description, and arrange them according to those that refer to racist individuals or to racist policies and institutions.)

                Individual Racism   **Institutional Racism**

    b. The group's definition of racism is:

    c. The main difference between individual and institutional racism is:

    d. Examples of individual and institutional racism in our community are:

        Individual racism:

        Institutional racism:

Appendix 4.2
Creating Classroom Environments that Support Second-Language Learners

CLASSROOM ENVIRONMENT AND ATTITUDE

1. Relax and enjoy. Language is more caught than taught. Your relaxed, receptive, interested concern will be the magical ingredient for enhancing the teaching and learning process.
2. Provide a warm, encouraging environment in which help is readily available to LEP students.
3. Books that are sensitive to the adjustments of the new student can be shared with the class (e.g., *Crow Boy* by Yashima; *I Hate English* by Levine, *What Does the Rooster Say, Yoshio?* by Battles).
4. Fill the room with meaningful, relevant print. These are springboards for discussion and rudiments of second-language literacy.
5. Label as many objects in the classroom as possible and invite your students to provide labels in their own language.
6. Increase possibilities for success by using a satisfactory/unsatisfactory option for grading until students are able to successfully complete classroom assignments.
7. Try to avoid anglicizing your students' names. Sometimes their names are the only connection they have with their native language, culture, and country.

CROSS-CULTURAL COMMUNICATION AND UNDERSTANDING

1. Become informed about the different cultures and languages represented in your classroom. This can be done by designing activities wherein your students become the "experts" by sharing part of their culture with the class.
2. If you find a student's behavior to be unusual or disconcerting, you might ask students or parents to clarify its meaning (e.g., Native American and Asian American students avoid eye contact with authority figures out of respect). This could prevent misunderstandings further down the road.
3. Try to talk individually with your students as much as possible. This lets them know you are interested in them as individuals, not just as students.
4. Avoid forcing students to speak and allow a wait time for students to answer.
5. LEP students need instruction to be clear and interesting. By using exaggerated facial expressions, a slower speech rate, abundance of gestures, and enunciating clearly you can reach more students. Many times our expressions and gestures can help students understand what we are saying when our words do not.
6. Try to incorporate tutors who speak students' native languages.
7. Start by asking questions (backed by visual aids) that can be answered with *yes* or *no*. Then move, little by little, to questions requiring slightly longer answers.

Source: Gisela Ernst, Margaret Castle, and Lauren C. Frostad, "Teaching in multilingual/multicultural settings: Strategies for supporting second-language learners." *Curriculum in Context* (Fall/Winter 1992), 14–15. Used by permission of the authors and the publisher.

Appendix 4.3
Strategies for Enhancing the Learning and Literacy of Second-Language Learners

INSTRUCTIONAL TECHNIQUES AND STRATEGIES

1. Whenever possible, try to use a variety of formats that go beyond the traditional lecture format. This will enable you to target different learning styles in your classroom.
2. Organize, when possible, cooperative learning activities. Small groups give second-language learners a chance to use their second-language skills in a nonthreatening environment.
3. The use of videos, films, drama/role plays, manipulatives (great for math), pictures, artifacts, posters, music, nursery rhymes, games, filmstrips, maps, charts, and fieldtrips can enhance teaching and learning.
4. Your school ESL specialist is a wonderful source of knowledge and information about what to do and what materials to use with your LEP students.
5. Encourage students to indicate when they are confused or do not understand. Students may feel more comfortable indicating understanding rather than acknowledging confusion.
6. When testing we need to be sensitive to students' cultural background. Culturally biased tests are a major hurdle for second language learners. Standardized tests can be a common culprit. Misinterpreting terms, directions, or situational cues can cause your students' test performance to drop drastically.
7. When planning lessons or assignments, think about the following questions: What background knowledge do students have? Will the assignment use academic language or critical thinking skills unfamiliar to your students?
8. Restate, rephrase, summarize, and review frequently.

Source: Gisela Ernst, Margaret Castle, and Lauren C. Frostad, "Teaching in multilingual/multicultural settings: Strategies for supporting second-language learners." *Curriculum in Context* (Fall/Winter 1992), 14–15. Used by permission of the authors and the publisher.

LITERACY AND ORAL LANGUAGE DEVELOPMENT

1. Keep in mind specialized vocabulary that is content specific. Each content area has specific terminology that can confuse most second-language learners. Math, for example, has several terms for the function of addition (e.g., add, plus, combine, sum, increased by).
2. Whenever possible define key terms in several ways.
3. Make use of pictionaries.
4. Encourage the use of bilingual dictionaries, materials, and content-area books in students' first language. They can help students understand new concepts both in their native language and in English.
5. Consult with your media specialist for books appropriate for students' reading/comprehension level.

5 Social Realities and Today's Schools

Thousands of children die every year, and millions are at risk because of poverty, family structure, lack of parental employment, or risky behavior.

—Kids Count Data Book 2003, p. 38
The Annie E. Casey Foundation

Carla is in her tenth year as a social studies teacher at Metropolitan School. Metro is located in a large industrial city in the Midwest. The school is in the center of a low- to middle-income area known as Uptown and has an enrollment of almost 2,300 students. About 75 percent of these are African Americans, with the remaining 25 percent about evenly divided between Mexican Americans and Anglo European Americans. Metro has a reputation for being "difficult"—a label the school has been unable to shed.

Carla lives with her twelve-year-old son in a condominium on the edge of the Uptown area. Carla believes that teachers have an obligation to society to address social issues. Several months ago, for example, Carla was the center of controversy when she began a two-week unit on homelessness in the Uptown area. The unit stressed the impact of homelessness on children and youth. She had two homeless people visit her classes, and her students participated in role plays and debates that focused on how homelessness impacts families.

Some of Carla's colleagues are skeptical about her methods. They believe she does her students a disservice by reducing the amount of time spent on "academics." They point out that Metro parents want their children to learn the traditional basics. Schools, they maintain, should not become involved in social issues like homelessness.

Another group of teachers is very supportive of Carla. They remind her detractors that students are highly involved in her classroom and that several potential dropouts have decided to remain in school because of Carla's willingness to address contemporary social issues in the classroom.

Today Carla and two other teachers are talking in the teachers' lounge about the results of a schoolwide survey Carla's third-period class did on students' awareness of homelessness in the Uptown area. "My kids are really disturbed about the lack of awareness of homelessness in our neighborhood," Carla says. "We're thinking about starting a schoolwide awareness campaign about homelessness. We might submit a proposal to the board of education to provide homeless and low-income families with social services in the school—job training, a health clinic, things like that."

"That's all well and good," says one teacher. "But I don't see where all of this is going to lead. Our responsibility as teachers is to give our kids the knowledge they need to get a better job. We need to give them the basics so they have a chance of getting out of Uptown. That's what their parents want—they don't want us getting their kids involved in delivering social services. Besides, a lot of other agencies, like neighborhood health clinics and career counseling centers are addressing these issues."

What are the social issues that impact students' learning and place them at risk of dropping out of school? What is the role of schools regarding those issues? Should teachers focus on social issues like homelessness in the classroom? If you were Carla, what would you say to this teacher?

Guiding Questions

1. Which students are at risk in our society?

2. What social issues impact schools and place students at risk?

3. How are schools addressing social issues?

4. How can home/school/community partnerships help students learn?

The conflict between Carla and her fellow teacher highlights a major challenge confronting our nation's schools—how can schools address social issues that place students at risk? Those who disagree with Carla's approach to teaching social studies tend to believe that she should teach only content to students. Carla and her supporters, however, believe teachers have an obligation to address domestic social problems. As this chapter's Relevant Standards feature suggests, effective teachers understand how social issues influence student learning.

Which Students Are at Risk in Our Society?

An increasing number of young people live under conditions characterized by extreme stress, chronic poverty, crime, and lack of adult guidance. In fact, "in almost every community in America, growing numbers of kids live in a socially toxic environment" (Garbarino 1999, 19). That environment compels many to drop out of school.

Frustrated, lonely, and feeling powerless, many of today's youth escape into music with violence-oriented and/or obscene lyrics, violent video games, cults, movies and television programs that celebrate gratuitous violence and sex, and cruising shopping malls or "hanging out" on the street. Others turn also to crime, gang violence, promiscuous sex, or substance abuse. Not surprisingly, these activities place many young people at risk of dropping out of school. In fact, it is estimated that the following percentages of fourteen-year-olds are likely to exhibit one

Relevant Standards

Awareness of How Social Issues Influence Student Learning

The following professional standards stress the need for teachers to be aware of how social issues influence student learning. Based on their understanding of these issues, teachers develop relationships with the larger community that support students' cognitive, emotional, social, and physical well-being.

- "[Teacher candidates] foster relationships with school colleagues, parents and families, and agencies in the larger community to support students' learning and well being." (National Council for Accreditation of Teacher Education [NCATE], 2002, 18. Standard 1: Candidate Knowledge, Skills, and Dispositions.)

- "Teachers are members of learning communities. (Core Proposition #5). The effects of culture, language, and parental education, income and aspirations influence each learner. Teachers are alert to these effects and tailor their practice accordingly to enhance student achievement." (National Board for Professional Teaching Standards [NBPTS], 2002, 20).

- "The teacher understands how factors in the students' environment outside of school (e.g., family circumstances, community environments, health and economic conditions) may influence students' life and learning." (Interstate New Teacher Assessment and Support Consortium [INTASC], 1992, 33. "Knowledge" statement for Principle #10: "The teacher fosters relationships with school colleagues, parents, and agencies in the larger community to support students' learning and well-being.")

- "Highly professional teachers care deeply for the well-being of their students and step in on their behalf when needed. They are aware of, and alert to, the signs of physical abuse and drug and alcohol abuse. They may locate a winter coat for a child or discuss a student's future plans with the student and her parents." (Praxis Series, Domain 4: Professional Responsibilities, Component 4f: Showing Professionalism.) (From Danielson 1996, 118)

or more at-risk behaviors (substance abuse, sexual behavior, violence, depression, or school failure) and to experience serious negative outcomes as a result: 10 percent at very high risk, 25 percent at high risk, 25 percent at moderate risk, 20 percent at low risk, and 20 percent at no risk (Dryfoos 1998).

School Drop Outs

Grouped by gender, race, ethnicity, family income, age, and region, students drop out of school at varying rates. Table 5.1, for example, shows that the dropout rate for Hispanic students in 2000 was higher than the rates for other groups. Also, African American students dropped out of school more frequently than their white peers. Lastly, the data reveal that students from low-income families are more likely to drop out than their counterparts from middle- and high-income families. **Students at risk** of dropping out tend to get low grades, perform below grade level academically, are older than the average student at their grade level because of previous retention, and have behavior problems in school.

Table 5.1 Event dropout rates and number and distribution of fifteen- through twenty-four-year-olds who dropped out of grades 10–12, by background characteristics: October 2000

Characteristic	Event Dropout Rate (percent)	Number of Event Dropouts (thousands)	Population Enrolled (thousands)	Percent of All Dropouts	Percent of Population Enrolled
Total	4.8	488	10,126	100.0	100.0
Sex					
Male	5.5	280	5,087	57.4	50.2
Female	4.1	208	5,039	42.6	49.8
Race/ethinicity[1]					
White, non-Hispanic	4.1	276	6,786	56.6	67.0
Black, non-Hispanic	6.1	91	1,510	18.6	14.9
Hispanic	7.4	100	1,351	20.5	13.3
Asian/Pacific Islander	3.5	13	379	2.7	3.7
Family income[2]					
Low income	10.0	141	1,408	28.9	13.9
Middle income	5.2	298	5,728	61.1	56.6
High income	1.6	48	2,990	9.9	29.5
Age[3]					
15–16	2.9	84	2,924	17.2	28.9
17	3.5	121	3,452	24.8	34.1
18	6.1	165	2,721	33.8	26.9
19	9.6	70	724	14.3	7.1
20–24	16.1	49	305	10.0	3.0
Region					
Northeast	3.9	73	1,849	15.0	18.3
Midwest	4.4	109	2,481	22.3	24.5
South	6.2	220	3,543	45.1	35.0
West	3.8	86	2,253	17.6	22.2

[1]Due to small sample sizes, American Indians/Alaska Natives are included in the total but are not shown separately.
[2]Low income is defined as the bottom 20 percent of all family incomes for 2000; middle income is between 20 and 80 percent of all family incomes; and high income is the top 20 percent of all family incomes.
[3]Age when a person dropped out may be one year younger, because the dropout event could occur at any time over a twelve-month period.

Note: Because of rounding, detail may not add to totals.

Source: U.S. Department of Commerce, U.S. Census Bureau, Current Population Survey, October 2000.

Many youth take more than the typical four years to complete high school, or they eventually earn a high school equivalency certificate (GED). If these alternative routes to high school completion are considered, however, there are still significant differences among racial/ethnic groups. For example, in 2000, 91.8 percent of whites between the ages of eighteen and twenty-four had completed high school, compared to 83.7 percent of African Americans and 64.1 percent of Latinos (U.S. Department of Commerce, U.S. Census Bureau 2000).

Life Settings of Children at Risk

Many children in the United States live in families that help them grow up healthy, confident, and skilled, but many do not. Instead, their life settings are characterized by problems of alcoholism or other substance abuse, family or gang violence, unemployment, poverty, poor nutrition, teenage parenthood, and a history of school failure. Such children live in communities and families that have many problems and frequently become dysfunctional, unable to provide their children with the support and guidance they need. According to *Kids Count Data Book, 2003*, ". . . thousands of children die every year, and millions are at risk because of poverty, family structure, lack of parental employment, or risky behavior . . . [their] futures are in jeopardy because their lives are filled with risks" (Annie E. Casey Foundation 2003, 38).

Children at risk are from families of all ethnic and racial groups. As Marian Wright Edelman (November 9, 1997, B5), founder and president of the Children's Defense Fund, said:

> Since 1973, families headed by someone younger than 30 have suffered a collapse in the value of their incomes, a surge in poverty, and a stunning erosion of employer-provided health benefits for their children. . . . Virtually every category of young families with young children has suffered major losses in median incomes: whites (22 percent), Hispanics (28 percent), and blacks (46 percent). . . . Low-income children are two or three times more likely to suffer from health problems, including infant death, iron deficiency, stunted growth, severe physical or mental disabilities, and fatal accidental injuries. . . . [T]he risk of students falling behind in school goes up by 2 percentage points for every year spent in poverty.

The life experiences of students at risk of dropping out can be difficult for teachers to imagine. Encountering the realities of poverty for the first time can be upsetting, as the following comments by a student teacher in an inner-city third-grade classroom illustrate:

> *Roughly 85 percent of [students are] living in poverty. The entire school population is eligible for free or reduced lunch. I was horrified. I guess I was a little ignorant of other people's situations.*
> *[Some] students came in wearing the same clothes for a week. Others would come in without socks on. No pencils, crayons, scissors, or glue. Some without breakfast, lunch, or a snack. My heart bled every day. I found myself becoming upset about their lives. I even found myself thinking about them at night and over the weekend. [I] noticed that they were extremely bright students, but their home life and economic status hindered them*

from working to their potential. Some of my students couldn't even complete their home-work because they had no glue, scissors, or crayons at home (Molino 1999, 55).

Read the following actual cases of two students at risk. Imagine that you are their teacher and have learned about their personal circumstances. How comfortable would you be with such information? Would that information affect they way you react to these students in the classroom? How? What might be the consequences of your reactions?

Eric has a three-year-old brother. His mother is on welfare and stays at home. On weekends, she goes out and Eric stays with his brother. To reward Eric, she allows him to drink hard liquor.

Five years ago, Eric's mother lived with a man who was very abusive. One night he beat her severely. Eric was afraid for his mother, so he grabbed a knife and stuck it in the man's neck. Eric was ten years old.

Kathy's mother is in a wheel chair. She was in a car that was run over by a logging truck and has to go to the hospital several times a year for operations. During those times, Kathy becomes very worried and has difficulty concentrating on her work. She is some-times suicidal and states that she wants to die before her mother does. Having almost lost her, eleven-year-old Kathy cannot stand the thought that her mother might die.

Kathy's parents sometimes go away for the weekend and leave her alone. At those times, she seems to get into the most trouble. After school, for example, she runs over to the high school to smoke cigarettes with the high school crowd. Kathy loves both her parents a lot, and she craves attention from them.

Challenges for Students at Risk

Students at risk of dropping out frequently come from families of relatively low socioeconomic status. Quite often, students at risk are members of a minority group. In addition to lacking the basic necessities, such as clothing and food that most people take for granted, minority at-risk students may also have to contend with intangible obstacles. They may be unable to "fit in." Language barriers, con-flicts with fellow students and teachers, racism and discrimination, and the inabil-ity to reach teacher- and school-established expectations are problems that community, state, and federal assistance programs cannot easily overcome.

Peers often see at-risk students as unsociable and different, which results in their excluding them from social acceptance in school—acceptance that is so neces-sary for positive self-esteem and success. Teachers often grow frustrated at their fre-quent inability to reach these students. The tendency to ignore their needs and to force them to conform to standards others are required to reach is strong. Without much-needed guidance and support from their peers and teachers, school for at-risk students can become an inhospitable place to return to day after day. The results are students who permanently drop out of school.

What Social Issues Impact Schools and Place Students at Risk?

A complex and varied array of social issues impact schools. Not only do these problems detract from the ability of schools to educate students, schools are often charged with the difficult (if not impossible) task of providing a front-line defense against such problems. The following sections examine several societal problems that directly influence schools, teachers, and students.

Children and Poverty

Although the United States is one of the richest countries in the world, it has by no means achieved an enviable record in regard to poverty among children (see Table 5.2 on page 178). According to the *Kids Count Data Book, 2003*, 17 percent of children live in families below the poverty line, and 24 percent live with parents who do not have full-time, year-round employment. In the District of Columbia, 29 percent live in poverty, 26 percent in New Mexico, and 26 percent in Louisiana (Annie E. Casey Foundation 2003). During 2002, the nation's flagging economy sent 1.4 million more people into poverty, and nearly half of the newly impoverished were children (U.S. Census Bureau 2003).

In the United States, there is a tremendous gap between rich and poor. Similarly, the gap between "rich schools" and "poor schools" is widening in many communities. Poor children attend poor schools, and their school experiences may cause them to become disenfranchised from school and society. These children, when they become adults, often continue to perpetuate the cycle of poverty.

Homelessness

Despite America's high standard of living, homelessness is a major social problem. Prior to the 1980s, homelessness was largely confined to the poorest areas of the nation's largest cities. Since then, changes in social policies such as welfare, minimum wages, and affordable housing—coupled with economic upheavals and continued unequal distribution of wealth—have swelled the numbers of homeless. In addition, homelessness is moving beyond cities to rural areas where single mothers (often migrant farm workers) and their children make up the largest percentage of the homeless population (National Coalition for the Homeless 2003).

Each year about 1 percent of the U.S. population—two to three million people—experience homelessness. Children are the fastest growing segment of the homeless; they constitute about 39 percent of the homeless population (National Coalition for the Homeless 2003).

Sixty percent of homeless women and 41 percent of homeless men have minor children (U.S. Department of Health and Human Services 2002). And, not surprisingly, the incidence of child abuse, poor health, underachievement in school, and attendance problems is higher among these children than it is among children with homes. Compared to children with permanent residences, homeless children are nine times more likely to repeat a grade, four times as likely to drop out of school, three times more likely to be placed in special education programs, and two times as likely to score lower than average on standardized tests (Homes for the Homeless 1999).

About half of all homeless children do not attend school regularly (Cunningham 2003). A host of barriers can make it difficult for them to attend school. First, is the need to overcome health problems, hunger, and difficulty obtaining clothing

Table 5.2   Profile of children in the United States

Indicators of Child Well-Being	Trend Data 1990	2000
Percent low birth-weight babies	7.0%	7.6%
Infant mortality rate (deaths per 1,000 live births)	9.2	6.9
Child death rate (deaths per 100,000 children ages 1–14)	31	22
Rate of teen deaths rate by accident, homicide, and suicide (deaths per 100,000 teens ages 15–19)	71	51
Teen birth rate (births per 1,000 females ages 15–17)	37	27
Percent of teens who are high school dropouts (ages 16–19)	10%	9%
Percent of teens not attending school and not working (ages 16–19)	10%	8%
Percent of children living with parents who do not have full-time, year-round employment	30%	24%
Percent of children in poverty (data reflect poverty in the previous year)	20%	17%
Percent of families with children headed by a single parent	24%	28%

Education		
Children under age 6 in paid child care while parents work: 2000		26%
3- and 4-year-olds enrolled in nursery school, preschool, or kindergarten		49%
4th-grade students who scored below basic science level		36%

Economic Condition of Families		
Median income of families with children: 2000		$50,000
Children in extreme poverty (income below 50% of poverty level): 2000		7%
Female-headed families receiving child support or alimony: 2000		36%
Households eligible for Food Stamps, but not receiving them		41%
Children without Internet access at home		52%
Children without a telephone at home		3%
Children without a vehicle at home		7%

Child Health		
Children without health insurance: 2000		12%
2-year-olds who were immunized: 2000		79%

Children in Low-Income Working Families		
Low-income households with children where housing costs exceed 30% of income		59%

Neighborhood		
Children in neighborhoods with a high poverty rate (above 18.6%)		23%
Children in neighborhoods with a high rate of males not in the labor force (above 38.1%)		14%
Children in neighborhoods with a high rate of female-headed families (above 35.2%)		17%
Children in neighborhoods with a high rate of high school dropouts (above 14.7%)		25%

Source: Kids Count Data Book, 2003. (2003). Baltimore: Annie E. Casey Foundation.

and school supplies. Second, providing documentation for school enrollment is often difficult for homeless guardians. School districts are often reluctant to eliminate requirements for birth certificates, immunization records, and documentation of legal guardianship. Third, homeless shelters and other temporary housing may not be on regular school district bus routes, making it difficult for homeless children to get to and from school. Lastly, homeless children can be difficult to identify—they are often highly mobile and may not wish to be identified.

The school attendance patterns of homeless children often affect their learning. For example, homeless families in New York City typically move two times a year, or 12 times the rate of the "average" U.S. family (Holloway December 2002/January 2003). Furthermore, each year 41 percent of homeless children attend at least two different schools; 28 percent attend two or three schools; and another 13 percent attend at least four different schools (Duffield 2001). Frequent transfers and difficulties enrolling in school result in homeless children losing an average of three weeks of school each year (Holloway December 2002/January 2003).

Homeless children face significant obstacles to learning, and their in-school behavior often reflects many developmental, psychological and behavioral problems. They frequently have short attention spans, experience separation anxiety and withdrawal that prohibits them from active class participation, are sometimes overly aggressive and in general, display poor social interaction skills with peers and adults. Homeless children suffer low self-esteem issues, and, compared to children with homes, children living in homeless shelters are almost 20 times more likely to experience depression (Rafferty, 1997). Homeless children are also more likely to experience sleep disorders which interfere with their ability to learn. Furthermore, they often experience delays in gross motor, speech, and language development, particularly if they are homeless during their preschool years. As a result, homeless children are frequently below grade level in reading and comprehension skills and are typically two or more years over the usual age for their grade (Pawlas, 1994).

In addition to the preceding challenges, the majority of homeless parents are not well equipped to help their children in school. Approximately two-thirds of homeless parents left school by the tenth grade, and, on average, they read at a sixth-grade level. Homeless parents also frequently lack a support network (other parents, neighborhood groups, and parent–teachers associations) that provides information about their children's education and enables them to voice concerns about their children's development and education.

The nation's first law to provide assistance to homeless persons, particularly children, was passed in 1987. The McKinney Act (recently named the McKinney-Vento Act) requires states to provide homeless children with free public education. According to the **McKinney-Vento Act**, schools must remove obstacles to school registration for homeless students—requirements for residency, guardianship, immunization, and previous school records—as well as provide transportation to and from school. In addition, the Act requires that each school district have a liaison whose responsibility is to help identify homeless students and to ensure their success in school.

This chapter's Teachers' Voices profiles an elementary school principal who began a project titled TEAMWork to meet the needs of homeless students at her school.

Family Stress

The stress placed on families in a complex society is extensive and not easily handled. For some families, such stress can be overwhelming. The structure of families who are experiencing the effects of financial problems, substance abuse, or violence, for example, can easily begin to crumble. Children in these families are more likely to experience difficulties in school.

The National Clearinghouse on Child Abuse and Neglect (NCCAN) reported that Child Protective Service (CPS) agencies investigated three million reports of alleged child maltreatment, involving five million children in 2000. Of these children, CPS determined that about 879,000 were victims of child maltreatment. Almost two-thirds of child victims (63 percent) suffered neglect (including medical neglect); 19 percent were physically abused; 10 percent were sexually abused; and 8 percent were psychologically maltreated (National Clearinghouse on Child Abuse and Neglect 2002). Clearly, the burden of having to cope with such abuse in the home environment does not prepare a child to come to school to learn.

Stress within the family can have a significant negative effect on students and their ability to focus on learning while at school. Such stress is often associated with health and emotional problems, failure to achieve, behavioral problems at school, and dropping out of school.

With the high rise in divorce and women's entry into the workforce, family constellations have changed dramatically. No longer is a working father, a mother who stays at home, and two or three children the only kind of family in the United States. The number of single-parent families, stepparent families, blended families, and extended families has increased dramatically during the last decade. Three million children are now being raised by their grandparents, and an equal number are raised by same-sex parents (Hodgkinson 2002). Table 5.2 shows that 28 percent of families with children were headed by a single parent in 2000. Of these children, 20 percent lived with only their mothers, about 4 percent lived with only their fathers, and four percent with neither parent (Federal Interagency Forum on Child and Family Statistics 2003).

Family structure and the well-being of children have also changed due to increased births to unmarried women. Children of unmarried mothers are at risk of having low birth weight, higher infant mortality, and other problems. Compared with children of married mothers, they are more likely to live in poverty and have limited social, emotional, and financial resources available to them (Federal Interagency Forum on Child and Family Statistics 2003). While only 8.4 percent of women who give birth in marriage are poor, 30 percent of those who give birth outside of marriage are poor (Lichter and Graefe 2001).

Just as there is diversity in the composition of today's families, so, too, there is diversity in the styles with which children are raised in families. Because of the number of working women and single-parent homes, an alarming number of chil-

Teachers'
Voices   Putting Research and Theory into Practice

There's No Place Like School

Juanita Fagan

At 7:15 on Monday morning Jason and his sister Jill get out of their father's beat-up 1962 Buick and run for the front door of the school. Inside, they head for the warm library where they can watch TV until school begins. Jason and Jill are homeless children. Their family lives in a deserted cabin that has no running water or electricity. Most nights, Jason sleeps in the car with his father while Jill and their mother sleep on the floor of the cabin. On weekends, Jason helps his father cut and stack firewood to earn money for the family.

Jason and Jill are two of 28 kids, ranging from kindergarten to grade 5, who [are] homeless children at Williams Elementary School, a small, rural PreK–5 school in southwest Oregon, where more than three-fourths of the children live in poverty.

At 7:30 A.M., Wes [an adult who serves as a student advocate] comes to the library to pick up Jason and walk him to the boys' bathroom in the gym, where there is a shower stall, washer and dryer, and a folded pile of donated clothing. After a hot shower and dressed in clean clothes, Jason joins his classmates in the cafeteria for breakfast.

Mindi, another student advocate, handles the clothes bank and supervises showers for the girls. She works an hour a day beyond her Title I job duties to meet the hygiene needs of our homeless children, including dispensing lice shampoo to their families and coordinating regular checks for head lice.

At 2:15 P.M. [Jason] is standing in front of his fourth-grade class with his social studies report, answering questions from his classmates. His hair is neatly combed, his face and hands are clean, and his mind has been focused all day on his schoolwork. At 2:30, he leaves the classroom and heads for the office. The dirty clothes he wore to school are now clean and neatly folded on the nurse's bed. He removes the clothes he's worn all day and puts on his clean hand-me-downs. It's been a good day for Jason. But most important, he feels like any other fourth grader in the school. He may not have a real home to go to, but he knows that there are those who really care about him in school. They are family, and this is home.

Questions

1. What challenges do homeless students face daily when they come to school?
2. How can teachers make homeless students feel supported while they are at school?
3. Fagan gives examples of how student advocates work with homeless students; in what additional ways can student advocates support homeless students?

Juanita Fagan is principal of Williams Elementary School in Williams, Oregon. Her article appeared in *Principal*, May 2001, pp. 36–37.

dren are unsupervised during much of the day. Between 3 P.M. and 8 P.M. is the most likely time for youth to engage in risk-taking or delinquent behaviors or to be victims of a crime (Cunningham 2003).

It has been estimated that there may be as many as six million such **latchkey children** younger than thirteen (Hopson, Hopson, and Hagen 2002). Left alone after school, these children are more likely to use drugs and alcohol, receive poor grades, and drop out of school than their peers who have adult supervision after school. To meet the needs of latchkey children, many schools offer before- and after-school programs.

In addition, many middle-class couples are waiting longer to have children. Although children of such couples may have more material advantages, they may be "impoverished" in regard to the reduced time they spend with their parents. To maintain their lifestyle, these parents are often driven to spend more time developing their careers. As a result, the care and guidance their children receive is inadequate, and "sustained bad care eventually leads to a deep-seated inner sense of insecurity and inadequacy, emotional pain, and a troublesome sense of self" (Comer 1997, 83). To fill the parenting void that characterizes the lives of an increasing number of children from all economic classes, schools and teachers are being called on to play an increased role in the socialization of young people.

Substance Abuse

One of the most pressing social problems confronting today's schools is the abuse of illegal drugs, tobacco, and alcohol. Though drug abuse by students moved from the top-ranked problem facing local schools according to the 1996 Gallup Poll of the public's attitudes toward the public schools to the fourth-ranked problem in the 2003 poll, drug use among students remains at alarming levels. The University of Michigan's Institute for Social Research (2002) reported that, in 2001, 54 percent of students had tried an illicit drug by the time they finished high school. Figure 5.1

Figure 5.1   Trends in illicit drug use: eighth-, tenth-, and twelfth-graders.

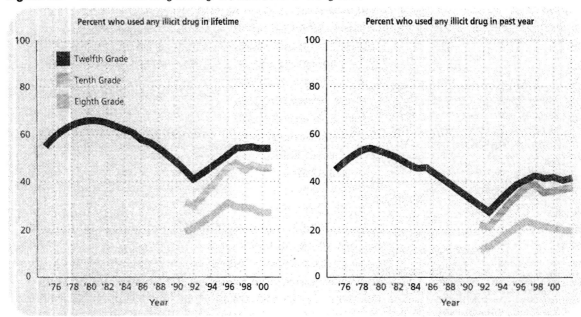

Source: Monitoring the Future: National Results on Adolescent Drug Use. The University of Michigan: Institute for Social Research, 2002.

shows trends in illicit drug use among eighth-, tenth-, and twelfth-graders between 1976 and 2000.

The Institute also found that alcohol use remains extremely widespread among today's youth. Eighty percent of students have consumed alcohol (more than just a few sips), and 51 percent have done so by eighth grade. Sixty-four percent of the twelfth-graders and 23 percent of the eighth-graders report having been drunk at least once in their life. It has been suggested that alcohol use among adolescents is the nation's number one health problem (Maney et al. 2002).

The use of drugs among young people varies from community to community and from year to year, but overall it is disturbingly high. Mind-altering substances used by young people include the easily acquired glue, white correction fluid, and felt marker, as well as marijuana, amphetamines, and cocaine. The abuse of drugs not only poses the risks of addiction and overdosing, but is also related to problems such as HIV/AIDS, teenage pregnancy, depression, suicide, automobile accidents, criminal activity, and dropping out of school. For an alarming number of young people, drugs are seen as a way of coping with life's problems.

Violence and Crime

The rate of victimization in U.S. schools has decreased since 1992, according to *Indicators of School Crime and Safety, 2003*, jointly published by the Bureau of Justice Statistics and the National Center for Education Statistics. However, students ages 12–18 were victims of about 764,000 violent crimes and 1.2 million crimes of theft at school in 2001 (Bureau of Justice Statistics and the National Center for Education Statistics 2003). Seventy-one percent of public schools experienced one or more violent incidents, while 36 percent reported one or more such incidents to the police. Figure 5.2 on page 184 shows the percentage of public schools, by level, with various types of crime and the percentage that reported crimes to the police.

In addition, the U.S. Department of Justice estimates that there are more than 30,500 gangs and approximately 816,000 gang members (Moore and Terrett 1999). According to *Indicators of School Crime and Safety, 2003*, 22 percent of students in public schools reported that there were street gangs in their schools, compared with 5 percent in private schools. Urban students were more likely to report street gangs at their schools (29 percent) than were suburban and rural students (18 percent and 13 percent, respectively).

Gang membership is perceived by many youth as providing them with several advantages: a sense of belonging and identity, protection from other gangs, opportunities for excitement, or a chance to make money through selling drugs or participating in other illegal activities. Though few students are gang members, a small number of gang-affiliated students can disrupt the learning process, create disorder in a school, and cause others to fear for their physical safety. Strategies for reducing the effects of gang activities on schools include the identification of gang members, implementing dress codes that ban styles of dress identified with gangs, and quickly removing gang graffiti from the school.

Since 1996, the nation's concern about school crime and safety heightened as a result of a string of school shootings. Among the communities that had to cope

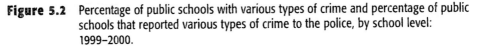

Figure 5.2 Percentage of public schools with various types of crime and percentage of public schools that reported various types of crime to the police, by school level: 1999–2000.

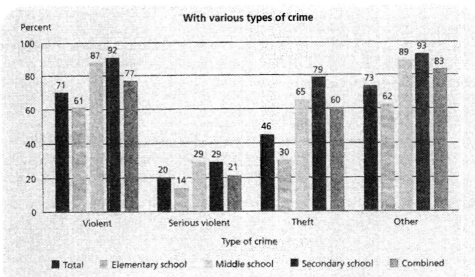

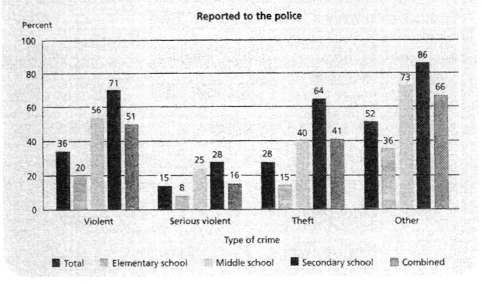

NOTE: Violent incidents include rape, sexual battery other than rape, physical attack or fight with or without a weapon, threat of physical attack with or without a weapon, and robbery with or without a weapon. Serious violent incidents include rape, sexual battery other than rape, physical attack or fight with a weapon, threat of physical attack with a weapon, and robbery with or without a weapon. Other incidents include possession of a firearm or explosive device, possession of a knife or sharp object, distribution of illegal drugs, possession or use of alcohol or illegal drugs, sexual harassment or vandalism. Principals were asked to report crimes that took place in school buildings, on school grounds, and on school buses during normal school hours and at school-sponsored events or activities.
Source: Indicators of School Crime and Safety, 2003. Washington, DC: Bureau of Justice Statistics and National Center for Education Statistics, p. 21.

The graffiti on this school's walls suggests the presence of gang activity. Why do young people join gangs? What can schools do to minimize gang-related activities in and around the school?

with such tragic incidents were Moses Lake, Washington (1996); Pearl, Mississippi (1997); West Paducah, Kentucky (1997); Jonesboro, Arkansas (1998); Springfield, Oregon (1998); Littleton, Colorado (1999); Conyers, Georgia (1999); and Santee and El Cajon, California (2001). Since the recurring question after each instance of horrific school violence was Why? there was a renewed effort to understand the origins of youth violence.

In *Lost Boys: Why Our Sons Turn Violent and How We Can Save Them*, James Garbarino (1999, 217–230) points out that some boys have had personal life experiences that may eventually drive them to commit horrific, violent acts. He suggests ten "facts of life" that may compel some boys to commit violence:

1. Child maltreatment leads to survival strategies that are often antisocial and/or self-destructive.

2. The experience of early trauma leads boys to become hypersensitive to arousal in the face of threat and to respond to such threats by disconnecting emotionally or acting out aggressively.

3. Traumatized kids require a calming and soothing environment to increase the level at which they are functioning.

4. Traumatized youth are likely to evidence an absence of future orientation.

5. Youth exposed to violence at home and in the community are likely to develop juvenile vigilantism, in which they do not trust an adult's capacity and motivation to ensure safety, and as a result believe they must take matters into their own hands.

6. Youth who have participated in the violent drug economy or chronic theft are likely to have distorted materialistic values.

7. Traumatized youth who have experienced abandonment are likely to feel life is meaningless.

8. Issues of shame [and humiliation] are paramount among violent youth . . . [they] share a common sense of inner crisis, a crisis of shame and emptiness. These boys are ashamed of who they are inside, and their efforts to compensate for that shame drive their violence.

9. Youth violence is a boy's attempt to achieve justice as he perceives it.

10. Violent boys often seem to feel they cannot afford empathy.

Each widely publicized account of school violence revitalizes the nation's ongoing debate about gun control measures; the influence of violence in television, movies, and point-and-shoot video games; and steps that parents, schools, and communities could take to curb school crime and violence. Some school districts have implemented **zero-tolerance policies** for any weapons (handguns, knives, and, in some cases, fingernail files) and any drugs in school (cocaine, marijuana, alcohol, and, in some cases, over-the-counter medicines like Tylenol or Modol). Figure 5.3 shows the percentage of schools reporting various types of security measures.

Figure 5.3   Percent of schools reporting various types of security measures, 1996–97.

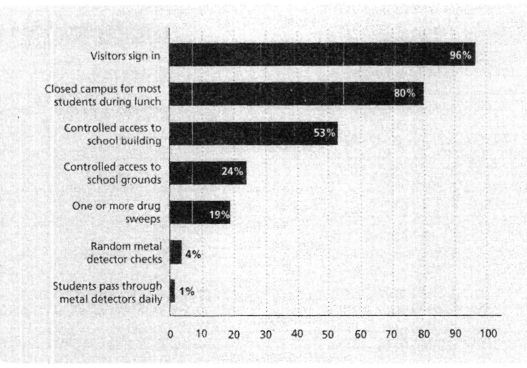

Source: Indicators of School Crime and Safety, 2001. Washington, DC: U.S. Department of Justice.

Case for
Reflection

Dealing with School Violence

Jeff Banks, a history teacher at Southside High School, enters the faculty lunchroom and sees his friends, Sue Anderson, Nancy Watkins, and Bret Thomas, at their usual table in the corner. Southside is located in a medium-sized city in the Southeast. The school, in the center of a low- to middle-income area known as Lawndale, has an enrollment of almost 1,900 students. About 70 percent of these self-identify as Anglo-European Americans, with the remaining 30 percent about evenly divided between African Americans and Mexican Americans.

Southside has a reputation for being a "good" school—students are respectful, for the most part, of their teachers. The consensus among teachers is that most Southside parents recognize that education is the key if their children are to "better themselves" and move out of Lawndale.

Jeff hears them talking about shooting rampages at two high schools in the San Diego, California, area. In the first case, the shooter fired shots from the bathroom, killing two students and wounding thirteen others. In the second, about three weeks later, the shooter walked confidently through the hallway shooting as he went. He wounded three students and two teachers.

The incidents are eerily reminiscent of the carnage that took place at a high school in Colorado a few years ago. In that instance, two boys chose Adolph Hitler's birthday to go on a shooting rampage, resulting in the deaths of twelve fellow students, one teacher, and themselves.

"It's so scary," Sue says, "Who knows, something like that could happen right here at Southside. We have no idea what kids have to deal with today."

"Yeah, we have no idea who might snap," says Bret. "Lately it seems to be a kid that no one would have expected. Quiet, polite, good student—you just never know."

"In some cases, that's true," Jeff says, placing his lunch tray on the table and then sitting down between Sue and Bret. "But a lot of time there are signs. A lot of these kids are loners and outcasts; they're into violent video games, cults, drugs, guns, you name it."

"What I want to know," says Sue, "is how we can prevent something like that from happening here? Since the Colorado shootings, there have been bomb scares, threats, guns confiscated at dozens of schools around the country."

"Well, I don't think metal detectors, more police in schools, and zero-tolerance policies are the answers," says Bret. "The question is why are kids doing this?"

"Right, how can we prevent things like this?" says Jeff.

"If we're going to change things," says Sue, "we've got to figure out ways to identify and help kids who feel so desperate that they turn to violence."

"Well, that's all well and good," says Nancy with a sigh. "But I don't see where all of this is going to lead. Our responsibility as teachers is to educate our kids. We're not psychiatrists or social workers. We can't change society. Besides, we've got youth agencies, centers for families in crisis, and all kinds of social service agencies."

Questions

1. Should teachers play a role in addressing social problems such as violence in our society?
2. What would you say to a teacher who expresses views such as Nancy's?

Figure 5.4 Recognizing violence warning signs in others.

Recognizing Violence Warning Signs in Others

If you see these immediate warning signs, violence is a serious possibility:
- Loss of temper on a daily basis
- Frequent physical fighting
- Significant vandalism or property damage
- Increase in use of drugs or alcohol
- Increase in risk-taking behavior
- Detailed plans to commit acts of violence
- Announcing threats or plans for hurting others
- Enjoying hurting animals
- Carrying a weapon

If you notice the following signs over a period of time, the potential for violence exists:
- A history of violent or aggressive behavior
- Serious drug or alcohol use
- Gang membership or strong desire to be in a gang
- Access to or fascination with weapons, especially guns
- Threatening others regularly
- Trouble controlling feelings like anger
- Withdrawal from friends and usual activities
- Feeling rejected or alone
- Having been a victim of bullying
- Poor school performance
- History of discipline problems or frequent run-ins with authority
- Feeling constantly disrespected
- Failing to acknowledge the feelings or rights of others

Source: MTV and American Psychological Association, *Warning Signs: A Violence Prevention Guide for Youth from MTV and APA.* New York: MTV. Washington, DC: American Psychological Association, n.d.

The increased use of guns by children and youth to solve conflicts is one consequence of the "gun culture" in the United States, in which it is estimated that nearly 40 percent of homes have at least one gun (Garbarino 1999). On the issue of television violence, the American Psychological Association reviewed research studies and concluded that television violence *alone* is responsible for up to 15 percent of all aggressive behavior by children and youth (Garbarino 1999). Lastly, David Grossman, a military psychologist, and his colleague pointed out that violent point-and-shoot video games are similar to those used to "desensitize" soldiers to shoot at human figures (Grossman and Siddle 1999).

As a result of the school shootings listed earlier and the public's concern with school crime and violence, many schools developed crisis management plans to cope with violent incidents on campus. Schools also reviewed their ability to provide students, faculty, and staff with a safe environment for learning; for example, Appendix 5.1 presents a "School Safety Checklist" excerpted from the National Education Association's *School Safety Check Book*. Additionally, to help troubled youth *before* they commit violence, the American Psychological Association, in collaboration with MTV, developed a set of warning signs, as shown in Figure 5.4 (p. 188).

Teen Pregnancy

Each year more than one million U.S. teenagers (four out of ten teenagers) become pregnant, and about 85 percent of these pregnancies are unintended (Brown 2002). This figure includes about 18 percent of all African American women ages fifteen to nineteen, 16 percent of Latina women, and 8 percent of Anglo-European women (Alan Guttmacher Institute 1999). Indeed, most teachers of adolescents today may expect to have at least some students who are, or have been, pregnant.

Since peaking in 1990, the teenage pregnancy, birth, and abortion rates have declined, largely the result of more effective contraceptive practices among sexually active teenagers (Alan Guttmacher Institute 1999). Nevertheless, teen pregnancies remain a serious problem in society. Because the physical development of girls in adolescence may not be complete, complications can occur during pregnancy and in the birthing process. Also, adolescents are less likely to receive prenatal care in the crucial first trimester; they tend not to eat well-balanced diets; and are not free of harmful substances such as alcohol, tobacco, and drugs, which are known to be detrimental to a baby's development.

Teenage mothers "are at risk for chronic educational, occupational, and financial difficulties, and their offspring are also at risk for medical, educational, and behavioral problems" (Durlak 1995, 66). Most teen mothers drop out of school, forfeiting their high school diplomas and limiting their access to decent, higher-paying jobs. Moreover, a disproportionate number of teen mothers are dependent on welfare, with one-fourth receiving financial aid and one-third receiving food stamps (Cunningham 2003). Teen mothers and their children stay at the bottom of the economic ladder, and they may be marginalized by their peers and by their communities.

Suicide among Children and Youth

The increase in individual and multiple suicides is alarming. The National Institute for Mental Health (1999) reported that suicide is the third leading cause of death

Pregnant teenagers often drop out of school. What can schools do to encourage pregnant teenagers to stay in school and graduate? What challenges do teen mothers face, especially if they do not graduate?

among youth ages fifteen to twenty-four and accounts for more than four thousand deaths yearly for this group. The Institute also estimated that there are eight to twenty-five attempted suicides for one completion.

Although female students are almost two times more likely than male students to have seriously considered attempting suicide during the preceding twelve months, about six times as many male students as females actually commit suicide. Latino students are about two times more likely than white students to attempt suicide, and students in grade nine are about four times more likely than students in grade twelve to make a suicide attempt that requires medical attention (Centers for Disease Control and Prevention 1998). Also, lesbian and gay youth are two to three times more likely to attempt suicide than their heterosexual peers, and they account for up to 30 percent of all completed suicides among youth (Besner and Spungin 1995).

How Are Schools Addressing Social Issues?

One of the most vocal advocates of the role of schools in solving social problems was George S. Counts, who said in his 1932 book *Dare the School Build a New Social Order?* that "if schools are to be really effective, they must become centers for the building, and not merely the contemplation, of our civilization" (12). Many people, however, believe that schools should not try to build a new social order. They should be concerned only with the academic and social development of students—not with solving society's problems. Nevertheless, the debate over the role of schools in regard to social problems will continue to be vigorous.

Technology in Teaching

Are up-to-date technologies being used effectively in low-income urban schools?

According to two recent reports (Lonergan, 2001, and Education Writers Association, 2001), the gap in the availability of computers and Internet access between affluent and poor schools has decreased dramatically since the early 1990s. For example, federal funding has enabled low-income schools in Chicago, Milwaukee, Detroit, and Cleveland to acquire extensive telecommunications networks and high-speed bandwidth to support audio, video, and data transmissions.

However, in poorer urban school districts, funding and time to train teachers to use technology are often lacking. Furthermore, teachers in low-income schools often use computers for drill and practice only, rather than for research and inquiry as do teachers in wealthier schools. Teachers assume that children need to learn basic skills through drill and practice before they can move on to higher-order problem solving. In addition, pressure to do well on standardized tests has led teachers to use drill-and-practice software rather than software that promotes critical thinking and reasoning.

What technologies do you think should be available to *all* students to enhance their learning? What technologies should be available to *all* teachers? What would be the impact on *your* current ability to learn if you had access only to outdated equipment, or none at all? What leadership roles can teachers in urban schools take to increase their students' access to advanced technologies?

Sources: James M. Lonergan, "Preparing Urban Teachers to Use Technology for Instruction." ERIC Digest, Number 168, October 2001, and *New Networks, Old Problems: Technology in Urban Schools,* Education Writers Association, 2001. Available from the Education Writers Association, 1331 H Street NW #307, Washington, DC 20005, (202) 637-9700; fax (202) 637-9707; ewa@ewa.org.

Responding to the needs of at-risk students will be a crucial challenge for schools, families, and communities during the twenty-first century. Since most children attend school, it is logical that this preexisting system be used for reaching large numbers of at-risk children (and, through them, their families).

During the last decade, many school districts have taken innovative steps to address societal problems that impact students' lives. Schools have served in the battle against social problems by offering an array of health, education, and social service programs. Schools provide breakfasts, nutritional counseling, diagnostic services related to health and family planning, after-school child care, job placement, and sex and drug education, to name a few.

Though programs that address social problems are costly, most of the public believes that schools should be used for the delivery of health and social services to students and their families. However, there has been disagreement about the extent to which school facilities should be used for anything but meeting students' educational needs. For example, the Committee for Economic Development (1994, 1) stated, "Schools are not social service institutions; they should not be asked to solve all our nation's social ills and cultural conflicts." In isolated instances, community groups and school boards have resisted school-based services such as family planning clinics and mental health services. However, increases in state funding and foundation support to provide school-based health, mental health, and social services have tended to dissipate most of this resistance (Dryfoos 1998).

Under pressure to find solutions to increasing social problems among children and adolescents, educators have developed an array of intervention programs. In general, the aim of these programs is to address the behavioral, social, and academic adjustment of at-risk children and adolescents so they can receive maximum benefit from their school experiences.

The following sections describe five intervention strategies that have proven effective in addressing academic, social, and behavioral problems among children and adolescents: peer counseling and peer mediation, full-service community schools, school-based interprofessional case management, compensatory education, and alternative schools and curricula. Also see Appendix 5.2, Selected Resources for Meeting Needs of Students Placed at Risk—a list of publications, organizations, and online locations that are good sources of information on the problems children and youth may encounter.

Peer Counseling and Peer Mediation

To address the social problems that affect students, some schools have initiated student-to-student peer counseling programs—usually monitored by a school counselor or other specially trained adult. In **peer counseling** programs, students can address problems and issues such as low academic achievement, interpersonal problems at home and at school, substance abuse, and career planning. Evidence indicates that both peer counselors and students experience increased self-esteem and greater ability to deal with problems.

When peer counseling is combined with cross-age tutoring, younger students can learn about drugs, alcohol, premarital pregnancy, delinquency, dropping out, HIV/AIDS, suicide, and other relevant issues. Here the groups are often college-age students meeting with those in high school, or high school students meeting with those in junior high school or middle school. In these preventative programs, older students sometimes perform dramatic episodes that portray students confronting problems and model strategies for handling the situations presented.

Peer mediation programs are similar to peer counseling programs. The focus of **peer mediation** is on cultivating a classroom climate in which students influence one another to be more accepting of differences, instead of solving problems per se. In some peer mediation programs, students participate in role plays and simulations to help them develop empathy, social skills, and awareness of prejudice.

An example of peer mediation is at John Marshall Middle School, in Long Beach, California, where students increase their understanding of cultural differences by learning about peer mediation. Students become "Diversity Ambassadors" by attending workshops on peer mediation, cultural diversity, tolerance, and con-

What approach to the education of students at risk does the scene in this photograph represent? What other risk factors affect children and youths? What are some other effective approaches for helping students at risk to succeed in school?

flict resolution. The workshops focus on issues of racial and ethnic barriers for fellow students. The Diversity Ambassadors host a school assembly on school violence in partnership with the Long Beach Police Department's Gang Unit. Marshall teachers and students report that the Diversity Ambassadors have improved the school climate (Learning In Deed, 2004).

Full-Service Community Schools

In response to increasing numbers of at-risk students, many schools are serving their communities by integrating educational, medical, social and/or human services. **Full-service community schools**, often called "community schools," operate in a public school building before, during, and after school, seven days a week, all year long. Often located in low-income urban areas, community schools integrate educational, medical, social, and/or human services to meet the needs of children and their families. (See this chapter's Appendix 5.3 for a "Family Needs Assessment" used at many community schools).

Community schools involve collaborative partnerships among school districts, departments of public health, hospitals, and various nonprofit organizations. At full-service community schools, students and their families can receive health screening, psychological counseling, drug prevention counseling, parent education, child rearing, and family planning information. Parents and community members also participate in adult education and job training programs at the school, as well as use the school as a site to solve community problems.

The Institute of Educational Leadership's Coalition for Community Schools has identified nine essential elements for effective community schools:

1. *Clear vision and goals* as well as ways to measure effectiveness
2. A *full-time community school coordinator* to provide leadership for planning, management, and collaboration
3. A source of *flexible funding* to attract new partners and allow the partnership to respond to urgent priorities
4. *Sufficient programs, services, and resources* at the school site to achieve desired results
5. *Effective, research-based, service-delivery strategies* coordinated at the community school
6. *Integration of after-school programs and community-based learning experiences* with the school curriculum
7. *Engaged community leadership* at the school site and at the community or school-district level
8. *Technical assistance and professional development* to support quality services
9. *Adequate and accessible facilities.* (Institute for Educational Leadership 2002, 16).

Community Schools and Student Learning   An evaluation of forty-eight community school programs indicates that they contribute to improved student achievement. Moreover, they are linked to increased attendance and reduced levels of high-risk behaviors (e.g., drug use and sexual activity). In addition, since community schools support families, family involvement in school programs increases and family functioning improves (Dryfoos and Maguire 2002). For example, an evaluation of three public community schools in Chicago found that:

- Reading scores improved at rates exceeding the citywide average at all three participating schools.
- Parents reported an increase in the number of adults in after-school programs who could be trusted to help their child with a serious problem.
- Teachers reported an increase in the number of adults in after-school programs who know children in the school well as individuals (Whalen 2001).

Another benefit of community schools is that they encourage parents to view the school positively; thus, parents are more likely to support the school in maintaining high expectations for learning and appropriate behavior. Community schools also directly support the work of teachers in the classroom. As the Institute for Educational Leadership's Coalition of Community Schools points out:

> Teachers in community schools teach. They are not expected to be social workers, mental health counselors, or police officers. Partner organizations do this work, providing teachers with essential support, helping them recognize and respond effectively to student problems, and connecting students and their families with needed community services and opportunities (2002, 6).

In Washington State, an evaluation of community schools found that 84 percent of the educators surveyed reported that their school environments were more supportive of learning as a result of integrated education, health, and social service systems (RMC Research Corporation, 2001). Similarly, 78 percent of school personnel involved with community schools in Dallas, Texas, indicated that the in-school behavior of students served by the centers improved (Hall, 2001).

One example of a full-service community school is award-winning Salome Urena Middle Academy (SUMA), a middle school serving a Dominican community in Washington Heights, New York. Open six days per week, fifteen hours per day, year round, SUMA offers before-school and after-school child care. Through seventy-five partnerships with various community groups and agencies, SUMA offers a comprehensive, integrated array of programs and services to children and their families. Students may enroll in their choice of four academies—business; community service; expressive arts; and mathematics, science, and technology. A Family Institute offers English as a second language, Spanish, aerobics, and entrepreneurial skills. At a Family Resource Center, social workers, paraprofessionals, parents, and other volunteers offer help with immigration, employment, and housing. Next to the Family Resource Center, a clinic provides dental, medical, and mental health services. Each year, the school's more than 1,200 students, their parents, and siblings are served at a cost significantly less than the per-pupil expenditures in most suburban schools. Moreover, according to an evaluation conducted by Fordham University, the school has realized a significant increase in attendance, a major reduction in misbehavior, and a modest increase in test scores (Dryfoos 1994, 1998; Karvarsky 1994).

School-Based Interprofessional Case Management

To respond to the needs of at-risk students, it has been suggested that schools "will need to reconceptualize the networks of community organizations and public services that might assist, and they will need to draw on those community resources" (Edwards and Young 1992, 78). One such approach to forming new home/school/community partnerships is known as **school-based interprofessional case management**. The approach uses professionally trained case managers who work directly with teachers, the community, and the family to coordinate and deliver appropriate services to at-risk students and their families. The case management approach is based on a comprehensive service delivery network of teachers, social agencies, and health service agencies.

One of the first case-management programs in the country is operated by the Center for the Study and Teaching of At-Risk Students (C-STARS) and serves twenty school districts in the Pacific Northwest. Center members include Washington State University, the University of Washington, a community-based organization, and Washington State's Department of Social and Health Services. Working with teachers and other school personnel, an interprofessional case management team fulfills seven functions to meet the needs of at-risk students: assessment, development of a service plan, brokering with other agencies, service implementation and coordination, advocacy, monitoring and evaluation, and mentoring.

C-STARS also provides a combination of the following services customized to the specific needs of each community: after school educational programs, summer school programs, recreational activities, social and health services, case management services for students and families, and Parent Resource Centers offering educational opportunities, such as ESL, computer literacy, and leadership training. C-STARS program evaluation data have shown significant measurable improvements in student's attendance, academic performance, and school behavior.

Compensatory Education

To meet the learning needs of at-risk students, several federally funded **compensatory education programs** for elementary and secondary students have been developed, the largest of which is Title I. Launched in 1965 as part of the Elementary and Secondary Education Act (ESEA) and President Lyndon Johnson's Great Society education program, Title I (called Chapter I between 1981 and 1994) was designed to improve the basic skills (reading, writing, and mathematics) of low-ability students from low-income families. Each year, more than five million students (about 10 percent of enrollments) in nearly all school districts benefit from Title I programs. The Educational Excellence for All Children Act of 1999, former President Clinton's plan for reauthorizing the Elementary and Secondary Education Act, including Title I, called for dramatic new steps to improve education for at-risk students. The $8 billion program called for an end to "social promotion" in schools and higher standards for teacher quality and training.

Students who participate in Title I programs are usually taught through "pull-out" programs, in which they leave the regular classroom to receive additional instruction individually or in small groups. Title I teachers, sometimes assisted by an aide, often have curriculum materials and equipment not available to regular classroom teachers.

Research on the effectiveness of Title I programs has been inconclusive, with some studies reporting achievement gains not found in other studies. Recent research has found positive effects on students' achievement in the early grades, but these gains tend to dissipate during the middle grades. The pattern of short-lived gains is strongest for students attending urban schools that serve a high proportion of families in poverty (Levine and Levine 1996). Some critics of Title I and other compensatory education programs such as Head Start for preschool children, Success for All for preschool and elementary children, and Upward Bound for high school students argue that they are stopgap measures at best. Instead, they maintain, social problems such as poverty, the breakdown of families, drug abuse, and crime that contribute to poor school performance should be reduced.

Alternative Schools and Curricula

To meet the needs of students at risk of education failure because of poor grades, truancy, disruptive behavior, or pregnancy, many school districts have developed alternative schools and curricula. These programs are designed to minimize students' high-risk behavior and address concerns about violence, weapons, and drugs in schools. Despite the need for such programs, only about 40 percent of school districts have alternative programs for at-risk students. Sixty-five percent of these districts had only one alternative school during the 2000–01 school year and were unable to meet the demand for alternative schools (Kleiner, Porch, and Farris 2002).

Usually, an **alternative school** is a small, highly individualized school separate from the regular school; in other cases, the alternative school is organized as a **school-within-a-school**. Alternative school programs usually provide remedial instruction, some vocational training, and individualized counseling. Since they usually have much smaller class sizes, alternative school teachers can monitor students' progress more closely and, when problems do arise, respond more quickly and with greater understanding of student needs.

One exemplary alternative school is the Buffalo Alternative High School serving at-risk seventh- to twelfth-grade students in the Buffalo, New York, Public School District. To reach students who are not successful at regular schools, the Buffalo program offers individualized instruction, small class sizes, and various enrichment programs delivered in what school staff describe as a "supportive, noncoercive, nontraditional setting." Most students are expected to return to their regular schools after a minimum of four weeks. Students must earn six hundred "points" (based on attendance, punctuality, attitude, behavior, and performance) to return to their regular school.

In addition, the Buffalo Alternative High School operates eight satellite schools in nonschool buildings throughout Buffalo. Among these programs are:

- *SAVe (Suspension Avoidance Vehicle)*—a two-week program students complete before returning to their sending school or enrolling in the Alternative High School
- *City-as-School*—students serve as interns in the public and private sectors and earn academic credit
- *SMART (Students Moving Ahead Through Remediation Testing)*—seventh- and eighth-grade students held behind can qualify for promotion to the appropriate grade
- *Bilingual Satellite*—educational services provided to Spanish-speaking students

Another exemplary alternative school is the Beard Alternative School in Syracuse, New York. Students address important community issues such as hunger, domestic violence, the criminal justice system, racism and gender issues. In partnership with the Center for Community Alternatives and Communities United to Rebuild Neighborhoods, students maintain a flower and vegetable garden on the city's southwest side. The students also publish a biannual student newspaper (*Beard News*) that deals with topics relevant to students' lives. Students also participate in classroom learning experiences based on their volunteer activities (Learning in Deed 2004).

While they don't work in alternative school settings, many highly effective regular teachers have developed alternative curricula to meet the unique learning needs of students at risk. Many teachers, for example, link students' learning to the business, civic, cultural, and political segments of their communities. The rationale is that connecting at-risk students to the world beyond their schools will enable them to see the relevance of education.

Out-of-School Time (OST) Activities

One approach to reducing high-risk behaviors among youth is to involve them in out-of-school time (OST) activities (often called "extracurricular activities"). **Out-of-school time (OST) activities** support and promote youth's development because they: (1) place youth in safe environments; (2) prevent youth from engaging in delinquent activities; (3) teach youth general and specific skills, beliefs, and behaviors; and (4) provide opportunities for youth to develop relationships with peers and mentors (Simpkins 2003). OST programs provide opportunities for growth and development at times when youth are unsupervised and might be tempted to engage in risky behaviors.

Frequently, children living in poverty don't have the same opportunities as other children to participate in music and dance, sports programs, and other out-of-school activities. Students who spend one to four hours in out-of-school activities each week are 49 percent less likely to use drugs and 37 percent less likely to become teen parents than their peers who do not participate in such activities. However, out-of-school programs met only 25 percent of the demand in urban areas during 2002 (Little and Harris 2003).

How Can Home/School/Community Partnerships Help Students Learn?

The previous section examined *intervention* programs schools have developed to ensure the optimum behavioral, social, and academic adjustment of at-risk children and adolescents to their school experiences. This section describes innovative, community-based partnerships that some schools have developed recently to *prevent* social problems from hindering students' learning.

The range of school-community partnerships found in today's schools is extensive. For example, as the "Interactive Organizational Model" in Figure 5.5 illustrates, Exeter High School in suburban Toronto has developed partnerships with thirteen community organizations and more than one hundred employers. Through Exeter's Partners in Learning program, business, industry, service clubs, and social service agencies make significant contributions to students' learning.

The Community as a Resource for Schools

To assist schools in addressing the social problems that impact students, many communities are acting in the spirit of a recommendation made by the late Ernest Boyer: "Perhaps the time has come to organize, in every community, not just a *school* board, but a *children's* board. The goal would be to integrate children's services and build, in every community, a friendly, supportive environment for chil-

Figure 5.5 Exeter High School interactive organizational model.

Student Activities and Clubs
- Ambassadors
- Art
- Band/Choir/Chamber Band/Stage Band
- Bowling
- Chess
- Culinary
- Design
- Drama
- Fish-On
- Interact (Junior Rotarians)
- Math Clinic
- OSAID
- Outers
- Sign Language
- Ski
- Squash
- Technology
- Weight Training
- Welding
- Woodworking
- Youth Alive

Support Staff
- Secretarial
- LAN Administrator
- Custodial

Departments
- Art
- Business
- English
- Family Studies
- Geography
- History
- Library Media
- Mathematics
- Modern
- Music
- Physical & Health Education
- Science
- Technology
- Special Education
- Student Services
- Work Education

Community Groups
- Exeter Citizenship
- Exeter Intergenerational
- Tech Advisory
- Music Advisory
- OISE/U of T
- Ontario Hydro
- Durham Regional Police
- C.A.M.C.
- McDonalds
- Durham Health and the Youth Council
- Rogers
- Cablesystem
- School Town Library
- Bell Canada Pioneers
- Over 100 employers for Work Education Program

MISSION STATEMENT

Exeter High School is committed to excellence through innovative academic and technological programming within a culture of mutual respect, community involvement, and partnerships.

School Growth Team

Administration Team

Department Heads

Student Council

School Community Council

Student Athletic Associations
- Alpine Skiing
- Archery
- Badminton
- Baseball
- Cross Country Running
- GoH
- Field Hockey
- Hockey
- Soccer
- Softball
- Swimming
- Tennis
- Track & Field
- Volleyball
- Wrestling

Task Forces
- Integrated Curriculum
- Curriculum Focus Day
- Exam Scheduling
- Staff Supervision

Committees
- Ethnocultural
- P.D.
- Beautification
- Safe Schools
- Wellness
- Evaluation
- Specialization Years
- Public Relations
- Site Management Team
- Schoolwide Action
- Research
- Health & Safety
- New Teachers
- Computers

Activity Groups
- Breakfast Club
- Food and Toy Drive
- Graduation/Junior Awards
- Open House
- Picture Day
- Sunshine Club
- Transition Years
- United Way
- School Profile
- Citizenship
- Intergenerational
- Yearbook

Liaison Groups
- Group 1
- Group 2
- Group 3
- Group 4
- Group 5
- Group 6
- Group 7
- Group 8

Source: Gordon Cawelti, Portaits of Six Benchmark Schools: Diverse Approaches to Improving Student Achievement. Arlington, VA: Educational Research Service, 1999, p. 32. Used with permission.

dren" (Boyer 1995, 169). In partnerships between communities and schools, individuals, civic organizations, or businesses select a school or are selected by a school to work together for the good of students. The ultimate goals of such projects are to provide students with better school experiences and to assist students at risk.

Civic Organizations To develop additional sources of funding, many local school districts have established partnerships with community groups interested in improving educational opportunities in the schools. Some groups raise money for schools. The American Jewish Committee and the Urban League raised funds for schools in Pittsburgh, for example. Other partners adopt or sponsor schools and enrich their educational programs by providing funding, resources, or services.

One example of partnerships with community groups involved the Phenix City (Alabama) Schools. Students worked with civic organizations to raise awareness among students and community members about important health issues. The Healthcare Science and Technology (HST) Department and the Western District medical/dental associations taught preventive health skills, including hand washing and oral hygiene, to all kindergarten, first-grade, and special education students in the Phenix City School System. Working with the civic organizations, the students developed and prepared all materials used in the training programs. In addition, students collaborated with the organizations to provide the community with educational programs on diabetes, and they offered blood sugar screenings to the community (Learning in Deed 2004).

Volunteer Mentor Programs Mentorship is a trend in community-based partnerships today, especially with students at risk. Parents, business leaders, professionals, and peers volunteer to work with students in neighborhood schools. Goals might include dropout prevention, high achievement, improved self-esteem, and healthy decision making. Troubleshooting on lifestyle issues often plays a role, especially in communities plagued by drug dealing, gang rivalry, casual violence, and crime. Mentors also model success.

Some mentor programs target particular groups. For instance, the Concerned Black Men (CBM), a Washington, D.C.-based organization with fifteen chapters around the country, targets inner-city African American male youth. More than five hundred African American men in diverse fields and from all walks of life participate as CBM mentors to students in area schools. Their goal is to serve as positive adult male role models for youth, many of whom live only with their mothers or grandmothers and lack male teachers in school. To date, CBM has given cash awards and scholarships to more than four thousand youth selected on the basis of high academic achievement, motivation, leadership in academic and nonacademic settings, and community involvement.

CBM volunteer mentors receive training and attend class every day, working as teachers' aides, contributing materials, arranging field trips, and running an after-school program for latchkey children. Many volunteers started working with first-

and second-graders and saw these same children all the way though their elementary school years. The program's good results have made it a model for mentorship programs in other schools.

Corporate–Education Partnerships   Business involvement in schools has taken many forms, including, for example, contributions of funds or materials needed by a school, release time for employees to visit classrooms, adopt-a-school programs, cash grants for pilot projects and teacher development, educational use of corporate facilities and expertise, employee participation, student scholarship programs, and political lobbying for school reform. Extending beyond advocacy, private sector efforts include job initiatives for disadvantaged youth, inservice programs for teachers, management training for school administrators, minority education and faculty development, and even construction of school buildings.

Business-sponsored school experiments focus on creating model schools, laboratory schools, or alternative schools that address particular local needs. In Minneapolis, for example, the General Mills Foundation has provided major funding to create the Minneapolis Federation of Alternative Schools (MFAS), a group of several schools designed to serve students who have not been successful in regular school programs. The goals for students who attend MFAS schools include returning to regular school when appropriate, graduating from high school, and/or preparing for postsecondary education or employment.

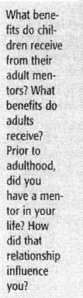

What benefits do children receive from their adult mentors? What benefits do adults receive? Prior to adulthood, did you have a mentor in your life? How did that relationship influence you?

In addition to contributing more resources to education, chief executive officers and their employees are donating more time; 83 percent of the top managers surveyed by a recent *Fortune* poll said they "participate actively" in educational reform, versus 70 percent in 1990. At Eastman Kodak's Rochester, New York, plant, for example, hundreds of employees serve as tutors or mentors in local schools. In some dropout prevention programs, businessmen and businesswomen adopt individual students, visiting them at school, eating lunch with them once a week, meeting their families, and taking them on personal field trips.

Schools as Resources for Communities

A shift from the more traditional perspective of schools is the view that schools should serve as multipurpose resources *for* the community. By focusing not only on the development of children and youth, but also on their families as well, schools ultimately enhance the ability of students to learn. As Ernest Boyer (1995, 168) put it, "No arbitrary line can be drawn between the school and life outside. Every [school] should take the lead in organizing a *referral service*—a community safety net for children that links students and their families to support agencies in the region—to clinics, family support and counseling centers, and religious institutions."

Beyond the School Day   Many schools and school districts are serving their communities by providing educational and recreational programs before and after the traditional school day and during the summers. Increasingly, educational policymakers recognize that the traditional school year of approximately 180 days is not the best arrangement to meet students' learning needs. As the RCM Research Corporation, a nonprofit group that studies issues in educational change, points out: "Historically, time has been the glue that has bonded the traditions of our public school system—i.e., the Carnegie units, equal class periods, no school during summer months, 12 years of schooling, etc.—and, as a result, the use of time has become sacrosanct, 'We have always done it this way!' How time is used by schools often has more to do with administrative convenience than it does with what is best educationally for the student" (RCM Research Corporation 1998).

Proposals for year-round schools and educationally oriented weekend and after-school programs address the educational and developmental needs of students impacted by social problems. According to the National Association for Year-Round Education, 1,646 year-round schools served 1.3 million students in 1992; by 2003, 3,181 year-round schools served 2.3 million students. In Austin, Texas, for example, schools can participate in an Optional Extended Year (OEY) program that allows them to provide additional instruction in reading and mathematics to students at risk of being retained a grade. Schools participating in OEY can choose from among four school day options: (1) extended day; (2) extended week; (3) intersession of year-round schools; and (4) summer school (Idol 1998; Washington 1998).

Programs that extend beyond the traditional school day also address the needs of parents and the requirements of the work world. As an elementary teacher in

Missouri said, "Many of my students just hang around at the end of every day. They ask what they can do to help me. Often there's no one at home, and they're afraid to go home or spend time on the streets" (Boyer 1995, 165).

After-school educational and recreational programs are designed to: (1) provide children with supervision at times when they might become involved in antisocial activities; (2) provide enrichment experiences to widen children's perspectives and increase their socialization; and (3) improve the academic achievement of children not achieving at their potential during regular school hours (Fashola 1999). Ernest Boyer argued that schools should adapt their schedules to those of the workplace so that parents could become more involved in their children's education, and that businesses, too, should give parents more flexible work schedules. Drawing on the model of Japan, Boyer suggested that the beginning of the school year could be a holiday to free parents to attend opening day ceremonies and celebrate the launching and continuation of education in the same way that we celebrate its ending.

For several years, the After-School Plus (A+) Program in Hawaii has operated afternoon enrichment programs from 2:00 to 5:00 for children in kindergarten through sixth grade. The children, who are free to do art, sports, drama, or homework, develop a sense of *ohana*, or feeling of belonging. Currently, 178 program sites serve nearly 22,000 students (National Governors' Association & NGA Center for Best Practices 2002). Since the mid-1970s, schools in Buena Vista, Virginia, have operated according to a Four Seasons Calendar that includes an optional summer enrichment program. Buena Vista's superintendent estimates that the district saves more than $100,000 a year on retention costs; though some students take more time, they are promoted to the next grade (Boyer 1995).

Although some research indicates that extended school days and school calendars have a positive influence on achievement (Center for Research on Effective Schooling for Disadvantaged Students 1992; Gandara and Fish 1994), the Center for Research on the Education of Students Placed at Risk (CRESPAR) at Johns Hopkins University concluded that "there is no straightforward answer to the question of what works best in after-school programs" (Fashola 1999). According to CRESPAR, few studies of the effects of after-school programs on measures such as achievement or reduction of antisocial behavior meet minimal standards for research design. Nevertheless, CRESPAR found that after-school programs with stronger evidence of effectiveness had four elements: training for staff, program structure, evaluation of program effectiveness, and planning that includes families and children (Fashola 1999).

Social Services   In response to the increasing number of at-risk and violence-prone children and youth, many schools are also providing an array of social services to students, their families, and their communities. The following comments by three female students highlight the acute need for support services for at-risk youth who can turn to aggression and violence in a futile attempt to bolster their fragile self-esteem and to cope with the pain in their lives. All three girls have been involved in violent altercations in and around their schools, and all three frequently use alcohol and illegal drugs. Fifteen-year-old "Mary" has been physically abused by both her father and mother, and she was raped when she was fourteen. "Linda," also fifteen years old, was sexually molested during a four-year period by a family acquaintance, and she endures constant physical and psychological abuse from her father. Fourteen-year-old "Jenny" is obsessed with death and suicide, and she aspires to join a gang.

> When you're smoking dope, you just break out laughing, you don't feel like punching people because it's just too hard. It takes too much. . . . You're mellow. . . . You just want to sit there and trip out on everybody. . . . It's even good for school work. When I used to get stoned all the time last year, I remember, I used to sit in class and do my work because I didn't want the teacher to catch me, and this year I'm getting failing marks 'cause I'm not doing my work 'cause I'm never stoned (Mary).

> I just know I got a lot of hatred. . . . And there's this one person [Jenny], and it just kinda happened after she mouthed me off, I was just like totally freaked with her and now I just want to slam her head into something. I wanna shoot her with a gun or something. I wanna kill her. . . . If I could get away with it I'd kill her. I wouldn't necessarily kill her, but I'd get her good. I just want to teach her a lesson. I'd beat the crap out of her. She's pissed me off so badly. I just want to give her two black eyes. Then I'd be fine. I'd have gotten the last word in (Linda).

> I like fighting. It's exciting. I like the power of being able to beat up people. Like, if I fight them, and I'm winning, I feel good about myself, and I think of myself as tough. . . . I'm not scared of anybody, so that feels good. My friends are scared of a lot of people, and I go "Oh yeah, but I'm not scared of them. . . . All these people in grade eight at that junior high are scared of me, they don't even know me, and they're scared of me. It makes me feel powerful" (Jenny) (Artz 1999, 127, 136, 157).

Although some believe that schools should not provide social services, an increase in the number of at-risk students like Mary, Linda, and Jenny suggest that the trend is likely to continue. In Seattle, a referendum required that a percentage of taxes be set aside to provide services to elementary-age children. In Florida, Palm Beach County officials created the Children's Services Council to address sixteen areas, from reducing the dropout rate to better child care. From parent support groups, to infant nurseries, to programs for students with special needs, the council has initiated scores of projects to benefit the community and its children.

Summary

Which Students Are At Risk in Our Society?

- In response to life experiences characterized by extreme family stress, poverty, crime, and lack of adult guidance, a growing number of youth are at risk of dropping out of school.

- Students from low-income families are more likely to drop out, as are students who are members of minority groups.

- Children at risk, who represent all ethnic and racial groups and all socioeconomic levels, tend to get low grades, underachieve, be older than other students at the same grade level, and have behavior problems at school.

- Minority at-risk students may have to contend with intangible obstacles such as language barriers, conflicts with fellow students and teachers, and racism and discrimination.

What Social Issues Impact Schools and Place Students at Risk?

- Among the many social problems that impact the school's ability to educate students are poverty, homelessness, family stress, substance abuse, violence and crime, teen pregnancy, and suicide.

How Are Schools Addressing Social Issues?

- Schools have developed intervention and prevention programs to address social problems. Three effective intervention programs are peer counseling and peer mediation, full-service community schools, and school-based interprofessional case management.

- Since 1965, an array of federally funded compensatory education programs has provided educational services to improve the basic skills of low-ability students from low-income families.

- Many school districts have developed alternative schools or schools-within-a-school that provide highly individualized instructional and support services for students who have not been successful in regular schools. Also, highly effective teachers modify their techniques and develop alternative curricula to meet the needs of students at risk.

- One approach to reducing high-risk behaviors among youth is to involve them in out-of-school time (OST) activities.

How Can Home/School/Community Partnerships Help Students Learn?

- Communities help schools address social problems that hinder students' learning by providing various kinds of support.

- Civic organizations raise money for schools, sponsor teams, recognize student achievement, award scholarships, sponsor volunteer mentor programs, and provide other resources and services to enrich students' learning.

- Corporate–education partnerships provide schools with resources, release time for employees to visit schools, scholarships, job initiatives for disadvantaged youth, inservice programs for teachers, and management training for school administrators.

- Schools serve as resources for their communities by providing educational and recreational programs before and after the school day, and by providing health and social services.

Key Terms and Concepts

Reflective Application Activities

Discussion Questions

1. Controversy exists over the use of the term *at-risk students*; some suggest that the term implies that students are to "blame" for their circumstances. Why do they view the term in this manner? Alternative terms such as *schools at risk* and *students placed at risk* have been suggested. Are these terms more acceptable?

2. Select one of the social problems addressed in this chapter. What steps might be taken to solve that problem? Which of those steps might be undertaken by schools? Is it unrealistic to believe that schools can provide leadership for social improvement?

Professional Journal

1. Write a short paper based on your own high-school experience, addressing the following:

   - Who constituted the at-risk population?
   - What percentage of the school population would you have considered at risk? How did this affect the overall school program?
   - What special considerations were made for at-risk students?
   - Describe the personalities or actions of any teachers or counselors who were dedicated to helping this population succeed.
   - Describe one success story involving an at-risk student from your school experience.
   - Describe one failure. What might have changed that failure to success?

2. What are the characteristics of teachers who effectively meet the needs of students placed at risk? Which of those characteristics do you possess? How can you develop those characteristics more fully as you progress through your teacher education program?

Online Assignments

1. Gather data on the Internet about children and/or adolescents that reflect issues of health, safety, and welfare in your state. State government databases are good places to start. Narrow your search to one of the following areas:

   - childhood poverty and homelessness
   - student nutrition and health
   - teen pregnancy
   - sexual harassment in school
   - child abuse and neglect
   - student drug, alcohol, and tobacco abuse
   - school violence and crime
   - truancy
   - juvenile delinquency
   - suicide among children and youth

2. Go to the home page for the National Education Association (NEA). From there, click on the link to "NEA's Legislative Action Center." At that site, gather information about federal or state legislation that addresses meeting the educational needs of students at risk. Then, using the online tools available at that site, send an e-mail message to Congress or one of your state's legislators explaining your position regarding that legislation.

Observations and Interviews

1. Visit a school and interview several teachers in regard to the social issues that impact their teaching. How have the teachers responded to these social issues? From their point of view, what resources would enable them to respond more effectively to these issues?

2. Interview a social worker in your community. According to him or her, what kind of relationship should exist between the schools and social service agencies?

Professional Portfolio

Review the list of organizations presented in Appendix 5.2, "Selected Resources for Meeting Needs of Students Placed at Risk" at the end of this chapter. Visit the websites for a few of those organizations (or others that address the needs of at-risk youth) and compile a set of materials (publications, instructional strategies, videos, training materials, etc.) that address one social issue that places students at risk.

Appendix 5.1
School Safety Checklist

Give your school a thorough crime prevention inspection now. Use this checklist as a guideline to determine
your school's strengths and weaknesses.

	Yes	*No*
1. Is there a policy for dealing with violence and vandalism in your school? (The reporting policy must be realistic and strictly adhered to.)	_____	_____
2. Is there an incident reporting system?	_____	_____
3. Is the incident reporting system available to all staff?	_____	_____
4. Is there statistical information available as to the scope of the problems at your school and in the community?	_____	_____
5. Have the school, school board and administrators taken steps or anticipated any problems through dialogue?	_____	_____
6. Does security fit into the organization of the school? (Security must be designed to fit the needs of the administration and made part of the site.)	_____	_____
7. Are the teachers and administrators aware of laws that pertain to them? To their rights? To students' rights? Of their responsibility as to enforcement of and respect for rules, regulations, policies, and the law?	_____	_____
8. Is there a working relationship with your local law enforcement agency?	_____	_____
9. Are students and parents aware of expectations and school discipline codes?	_____	_____
10. Are there any actual or contingency action plans developed to deal with student disruptions and vandalism?	_____	_____
11. Is there a policy as to restitution or prosecution of perpetrators of violence and vandalism?	_____	_____
12. Is there any in-service training available for teachers and staff in the areas of violence and vandalism and other required reporting procedures?	_____	_____
13. Is there a policy for consistent monitoring and evaluation of incident reports?	_____	_____
14. Is the staff trained in standard crime prevention behavior?	_____	_____

Source: Excerpted from *The School Safety Check Book* by the National School Safety Center, 141 Duesenberg Dr., Suite 16,
Westlake Village, CA, 91362, www.nsscl.org.

Appendix 5.2
Selected Resources for Meeting Needs of Students Placed at Risk

ORGANIZATIONS

American Red Cross
431 18th Street NW
Washington, DC 20006
(703) 206-6750

Center for Research on the Education of Students Placed At Risk
Johns Hopkins University
3003 North Charles Street, Suite 200
Baltimore, MD 21218
(410) 516-8800

Child and Family Policy Center
218 6th Avenue Suite 1021
Des Moines, IA 50309-4006
(515) 280-9027

Children's Defense Fund
25 E Street, NW
Washington, DC 20001
(202) 628-8787

The Family Resource Coalition of America
200 South Michigan Avenue
Chicago, IL 60604
(312) 341-0900

Foundation for Child Development
345 E. 46th Street Suite 700
New York, NY 10017
(212) 697-3150

National Coalition of Hispanic and Human Service Organizations
1501 16th Street
NW Washington, DC 20036
(202) 387-5000

National Community Education Association
3929 Old Lee Highway, Suite 91A
Fairfax, VA 22030
(703) 359-8973

National Institute on the Education of At-Risk Students
U.S. Department of Education
OERI/At-Risk Room
610 555 New Jersey Avenue, NW
Washington, DC 20208-5521

BOOKS ON TEACHING STUDENTS AT RISK

1. Barr, R. D., and Parrett, W. H. (1995). *Hope at Last for At-Risk Youth.* Boston: Allyn and Bacon.
2. Bempechat, J. (1998). *Against the Odds: How "At-risk" Children Exceed Expectations.* San Francisco: Jossey-Bass.
3. Calfee, C., Wittwer, F., and Meredith, M. (1998). *Building a Full-Service School: A Step-by-Step Guide.* San Francisco: Jossey-Bass.
4. Canfield, J., and Siccone, F. (1994). *101 Ways to Develop Student Self-Esteem and Responsibility.* Boston: Allyn and Bacon.
5. Comer, J. P. (1997). *Waiting for a Miracle: Why Schools Can't Solve Our Problems—And How We Can.* New York: Dutton.
6. Deiredre, K. (1993). *Last Chance High: How Girls and Boys Drop In and Out of Alternative Schools.* New Haven, CT: Yale University Press.
7. Dryfoos, J. G. (1998). *Safe Passage: Making It Through Adolescence in a Risky Society.* New York: Oxford University Press.
8. Gonzalez, V., Brusca-Vega, R., and Yawkey, T. (1997). *Assessment and Instruction of Culturally and Linguistically Diverse Students with or At-risk of Learning Problems: From Research to Practice.* Boston: Allyn and Bacon.
9. Henderson, N., and Milstein, M. M. (1996). *Resiliency in Schools: Making It Happen for Students and Educators.* Thousand Oaks, CA: Corwin Press.

10. Horn, L. J., Chen, X., and Adelman, C. *Toward Resiliency: At-risk Students Who Make It to College.* Washington, DC: U.S. Department of Education.

11. Johnson, D. W., and Johnson, R. T. (1995). *Reducing School Violence through Conflict Resolution.* Alexandria, VA: Association for Supervision and Curriculum Development.

12. Johnson, D. W., Johnson, R. T., and Holubec, E. J. (1994). *The New Circles of Learning: Cooperation in the Classroom and School.* Alexandria, VA: Association for Supervision and Curriculum Development.

13. Kennedy, R. L., and Morton, J. H. (1999). *A School for Healing: Alternative Strategies for Teaching At-risk Students.* New York: P. Lang.

14. Knapczyk, D. R., and Rodes, P. (1996). *Teaching Social Competence: A Practical Approach for Improving Social Skills in Students At-Risk.* Pacific Grove, CA: Brooks/Cole.

15. Kohn, A. (1996). *Beyond Discipline: From Compliance to Community.* Alexandria, VA: Association for Supervision and Curriculum Development.

16. Lane, K., Richardson, M. D., and Van Berkum, D. W. (Eds.). (1996). *The School Safety Handbook: Taking Action for Student and Staff Protection.* Lancaster, PA: Technomic Publishing Company.

17. Manning, H. L., and Baruth, L. G. (1995). *Students at Risk.* Boston: Allyn and Bacon.

18. Mendrinos, R. B. (1997). *Using Educational Technology with At-Risk Students: A Guide for Library Media Specialists and Teachers.* Westport, CT: Greenwood Press.

19. National Institute on the Education of At-Risk Students. (2000). *Get to School Safely!* Washington, DC: Author.

20. Peterson, S. L. (1998). *At-risk Students: Tools for Teaching in Problem Settings.* San Francisco: International Scholars Publications.

21. Porro, B. (1996). *Talk It Out: Conflict Resolution in the Elementary Classroom.* Alexandria, VA: Association for Supervision and Curriculum Development.

22. Reglen, G. (1998). *Mentoring Students at Risk: An Underutilized Alternative Education Strategy for K–12 Teachers.* Springfield, IL: Charles C. Thomas Publishers.

23. Ross, G. R. (1994). *Treating Adolescent Substance Abuse: Understanding the Fundamental Elements.* Boston: Allyn and Bacon.

24. Rossi, R. J., and Stringfield, S. C. (1997). *Education Reform and Students at Risk.* Washington, DC: U.S. Department of Education.

25. Vaughn, S., Bos, C. S., and Schumm, J. S. (1997). *Teaching Mainstreamed, Diverse, and At-risk Students in the General Education Classroom.* Boston: Allyn and Bacon.

26. Walling, D. R. (Ed.). (1996). *Open Lives, Safe Schools.* Bloomington, IN: Phi Delta Kappa Educational Foundation.

Appendix 5.3
Family Needs Assessment

Name of person completing form: _____

Relationship to child:_____   Date: _____

   Parents and guardians of children have many different needs. Not all parents need the same kinds of help.
For each of the needs listed below, please check the space that best describes your need or desire for help in that
area. Although we may not be able to help you with all your needs, your answers will help us connect you to
community resources.

	I really need some help in this area	*I'd like some help but my need is not that great.*	*I don't need any help in this area.*
1. Someone who can help me feel better about myself	_____	_____	_____
2. Help with child care or after-school and summer supervised activities	_____	_____	_____
3. More money or financial help	_____	_____	_____
4. Someone who can babysit for a day or evening so I can get away	_____	_____	_____
5. Better medical care for my child or another member of the family	_____	_____	_____
6. More information about child development	_____	_____	_____
7. More information about behavior problems	_____	_____	_____
8. More information about programs that can help my child (educational, health, social)	_____	_____	_____
9. Counseling to help me cope with my situation better	_____	_____	_____
10. Day care so I can get a job	_____	_____	_____
11. Information about adult education opportunities	_____	_____	_____
12. Information about job training and employment opportunities	_____	_____	_____
13. A bigger or better house or apartment	_____	_____	_____
14. More information about how I can help my child with a specific problem	_____	_____	_____
15. More information about nutrition or feeding	_____	_____	_____

Source: Carol Calfee, Frank Wittwer, and Mimi Meredith, *Building a Full-Service School: A Step-by-Step Guide*. San Francisco:
Jossey-Bass Publishers, 1998, pp. 218–219. Used by permission.

	I really need some help in this area	I'd like some help but my need is not that great.	I don't need any help in this area.
16. Learning how to handle my other children's jealousy of their brother or sister	_____	_____	_____
17. Help with how to deal with problems with in-laws or other relatives	_____	_____	_____
18. Help with how to deal with problems with friends or neighbors	_____	_____	_____
19. Special equipment to meet my child's needs	_____	_____	_____
20. More friends who have a child like mine	_____	_____	_____
21. Someone to talk to about my problems	_____	_____	_____
22. Problems with my spouse	_____	_____	_____
23. A car or other form of transportation	_____	_____	_____
24. More time for myself	_____	_____	_____
25. More time to be with my child	_____	_____	_____

Please list any needs we have forgotten:

26. _____

27. _____

28. _____

6

Teacher Leaders and the Professionalization of Teaching

The conventional image of the accomplished teacher as solo performer working independently with students is narrow and outdated. Committed career teachers assume responsibility in cooperation with their administrators for the character of the school's instructional program.

—National Board for Professional Teaching Standards

It is near the end of your third year of teaching at a school in a working-class neighborhood in a city of about 300,000. Approximately 35 percent of the students are ethnic minorities, and the school has the largest American Indian enrollment in the state. Fifty percent of the students are on free and reduced lunch. According to a needs assessment conducted by a teacher, approximately 30 percent of students are "at risk" (i.e., they possess two or more at-risk characteristics such as "erratic attendance," "signs of abuse/neglect," "assignments not turned in or incomplete," or "chronic behavior problems").

The school serves the diverse needs of its students well and is generally acknowledged as one of the most innovative in the district. Three years ago, for example, the local newspaper did a two-page feature on the role that teachers were playing in restructuring the school. The article also highlighted the school's partnership with a university and described how two professors were facilitating the change effort and how their students were helping teachers with curriculum development.

You and five other teachers (one of whom is the school's representative on the teachers' union) sit on the Site-Based Council (SBC) that also includes the principal, two assistant principals, and two parents. It is two weeks before the end of school, and the SBC is meeting to discuss the composition of next year's SBC and how it will function.

You enter the conference room and take a seat just as the principal says, "So, today, we've got to decide who's responsible, and ultimately accountable, for what."

The teachers' union representative nods her head in agreement and says, "We need to remember that other teachers, most of whom belong to the union, want the membership of the new SBC to represent their interests vigorously. As professionals, we play a key role in providing leadership for change."

"I agree," adds another teacher. "We've worked extremely hard at restructuring for three years—developing an entirely new curriculum, a mentoring program for new teachers, a peer coaching program, and so on."

The teacher next to you adds, "What we're saying is that next year's SBC has got to continue to place teachers at the center of this change effort. Regardless of how the SBC functions, teacher leadership is essential."

As several members of the group, including you, nod in agreement, you reflect on what you've just heard. What does it really mean to be a professional? What are the characteristics of a profession, and to what extent does teaching reflect those characteristics? What new leadership roles for teachers are emerging? What leadership roles will you play in educational reform?

Guiding Questions

1. To what extent is teaching a full profession?

2. What is professionalism in teaching?

3. To what professional organizations do teachers belong?

4. What new leadership roles for teachers are emerging?

5. How do teachers contribute to educational research?

6. How are teachers providing leadership for school restructuring and curriculum reform?

7. How will teachers shape the future of teaching?

School reform efforts, as the preceding scenario illustrates, are continuing to change dramatically what it means to be a teacher. Steadily, the **professionalization of teaching** is taking place in the United States. National board certification, state-sponsored teacher networks, shared decision making, peer review, and mentor teacher programs are just a few of the changes that are providing unprecedented opportunities for teachers to assume new leadership roles beyond the classroom. Along with these new opportunities for leadership, teaching as a profession is developing greater political influence and acquiring higher status in the public's eye.

In addition, school administration is becoming more collaborative and participatory, and teachers are playing a key role in school governance. As Joseph Murphy (April 1999) points out In "Reconnecting Teaching and School Administration: A Call for a Unified Profession,"

> The hierarchical, bureaucratic organizational structures that have defined schools over the past 80 years are giving way to more decentralized and more professionally controlled systems that create new designs for school management. In these new postindustrial educational organizations, there are important shifts in roles, relationships, and responsibilities: traditional patterns of relationships are altered, authority flows are less hierarchical, role definitions are both more general and flexible, leadership is connected to competence for needed tasks rather than to formal position, and independence and isolation are replaced by cooperative work.

Throughout this book, teaching is referred to as a **profession**; however, if we compare teaching with other "elite" professions—law and medicine, for example—we find some significant differences. As a result of these differences, current opinion is divided as to whether teaching actually is a full profession. Some have labeled teaching a *semi*-profession (Etzioni 1969), a *classless* profession (Mattingly 1975), an *emerging* profession (Howsam et al. 1976), an *uncertain* profession (Powell 1980), an *imperiled* profession (Duke 1984; Sykes 1983; Freedman, Jackson, and Botes 1983; Boyer 1990), an *endangered* profession (Goodlad 1983), and a *not-quite* profession (Goodlad 1990)!

To What Extent Is Teaching a Full Profession?

People use the terms *professional* and *profession* quite frequently, usually without thinking about their meanings. We may refer to those who play "professional" sports, the "professional" truck driver, the "professional" exterminator we must call if we want our home or apartment treated for an invasion of insects, or the "professional" who cares for our lawns and shrubs. In one sense, then, *professional* refers to anyone who does his or her job with skill and understanding. A person attempting that same job without a high degree of competence we would call an *amateur*. In addition, a professional is paid for the work he or she does, and an amateur is not.

The preceding view of what it is to be a professional is rather limited, however. The differences between professionals and other workers are more extensive. Professionals "possess a high degree of specialized *theoretical knowledge*, along with methods and techniques for applying this knowledge in their day-to-day work. . . . [And they] are united by a high degree of in-group solidarity, stemming from their common training and common adherence to certain doctrines and methods" (Abrahamsson 1971, 11–12).

From several sociologists and educators who have studied teaching come additional characteristics of occupations that are highly professionalized. These characteristics are summarized in Figure 6.1. Before reading further, reflect on each characteristic and decide whether it applies to teaching. Then, continue reading about the extent to which teaching satisfies each of these commonly agreed-upon characteristics of full professions. Do the characteristics in Figure 6.1 agree with yours? Most likely, you will conclude that teaching meets some, but not all, of the criteria.

Institutional Monopoly of Services

On one hand, teachers do have a monopoly of services. As a rule, only those who are certified members of the profession may teach in public schools. On the other hand, varied requirements for certification and for teaching in private schools weaken this monopoly. (Although state certification and teacher education courses are generally not required to teach in private schools, a college degree is a minimum requirement.)

Any claim teachers might have as exclusive providers of a service is further eroded by the practice of many state systems to approve temporary, or emergency, certification measures to deal with teacher shortages or the widespread practice of

Figure 6.1   Does teaching meet the criteria for a profession?

Yes	Uncertain	No	
○	○	○	1. Professionals are allowed to institutionalize a monopoly of essential knowledge and services. For example, only lawyers may practice law; only physicians may practice medicine.
○	○	○	2. Professionals are able to practice their occupation with a high degree of autonomy. They are not closely supervised, and they have frequent opportunities to make their own decisions about important aspects of their work. Professional autonomy also implies an obligation to perform responsibly, to self-supervise, and to be dedicated to providing a service rather than meeting minimum requirements of the job.
○	○	○	3. Professionals must typically undergo a lengthy period of education and/or training before they may enter professional practice. Furthermore, professionals usually must undergo a lengthy induction period following their formal education or training.
○	○	○	4. Professionals perform an essential service for their clients and are devoted to continuous development of their ability to deliver this service. This service emphasizes intellectual rather than physical techniques.
○	○	○	5. Professionals have control over their governance, their socialization into the occupation, and research connected with their occupation.
○	○	○	6. Members of a profession form their own vocational associations, which have control over admissions to the profession, educational standards, examinations and licensing, career development, ethical and performance standards, and professional discipline.
○	○	○	7. The knowledge and skills held by professionals are not usually available to nonprofessionals.
○	○	○	8. Professionals enjoy a high level of public trust and are able to deliver services that are clearly superior to those available elsewhere.
○	○	○	9. Professionals are granted a high level of prestige and higher-than-average financial rewards.

"out-of-field teaching." For example, according to an Education Trust (2002) report, about one out of four teachers instructing in grades 7–12 lack even a college minor in the subject being taught. In high-poverty schools, the rate of out-of-field teachers is 34 percent compared to about 19 percent in low-poverty schools. Thus, teaching is the only profession that allows noncertified individuals to practice the profession. Furthermore, a decline of inadequately licensed teachers seems unlikely, given the U.S. Department of Education's projection that more than two million teachers would be needed between 1999 and 2009.

Perhaps the most significant argument against teachers claiming to be the exclusive providers of a service, however, is the fact that a great deal of teaching occurs in informal, nonschool settings and is done by people who are not teachers. Every day, thousands of people teach various kinds of how-to skills: how to water-ski, how to make dogs more obedient, how to make pasta from scratch, how to tune a car's engine, and how to meditate. In addition, young people learn a great deal from their parents and/or guardians, so much so that it is no exaggeration to refer to the "curriculum" of the home and parents and/or guardians as the child's first "teachers."

Despite the fact that young people learn many different things from many different people, teachers are the experts charged with teaching people how to read, write, and compute—the essential skills upon which all later learning depends.

Teacher Autonomy

In one sense teachers have considerable autonomy. Teaching, in large measure, is "a private, individual practice" (Becker April 2001). Teachers usually work behind a closed classroom door, and only seldom is their work observed by another adult. In fact, one of the norms among teachers is that the classroom is a castle of sorts, and teacher privacy a closely guarded right. Although the performance of new teachers may be observed and evaluated on a regular basis by supervisors, veteran teachers are observed much less frequently, and they usually enjoy a high degree of autonomy.

Teachers also have extensive freedom regarding how they structure the classroom environment. They may emphasize discussions as opposed to lectures. They may set certain requirements for some students and not for others. They may delegate responsibilities to one class and not another. And, within the guidelines set by local and state authorities, teachers may determine much of the content they teach.

There are, however, constraints placed on teachers and their work. Teachers, unlike doctors and lawyers, must accept all the "clients" who are sent to them. Only infrequently does a teacher actually "reject" a student assigned to him or her. Moreover, students, unless they choose to attend private schools, must usually accept their assignment to schools and teachers without having much choice. When choosing the services of a physician or lawyer, however, a person has much more freedom.

Teachers must also agree to teach what state and local officials say they must. Moreover, the work of teachers is subject to a higher level of public scrutiny than that found in other professions. Because the public provides "clients" (students) and pays for schools, it has a significant say regarding the work of teachers. Citizens may judge the quality of services delivered by teachers more readily than that of lawyers, physicians, or members of the ministry.

Teaching also differs from other professions in that teachers are usually evaluated by persons who, typically, are not presently teachers—principals and other supervisors appointed by the school districts, for example. In reality, the degree of supervision that teachers actually experience varies greatly, with most teachers having considerable autonomy as long as they continue to perform at a reasonable level of effectiveness.

Currently, all professions in the United States are experiencing some "leveling." "More of the work of the traditional high-status professions, particularly medicine, will occur in bureaucratic or large organizational settings under the watchful eye of managers. [While] doctors are accepting more and more regulation, school teachers . . . will slowly break out of long-established bureaucratic hierarchies and share more of the autonomy previously enjoyed by members of the high-status professions" (Grant and Murray 1999, 231–232).

Years of Education and Training

As sociologist Amitai Etzioni (1969) points out in his classic discussion of the "semi-professions," the training of teachers is less lengthy than that required for other professionals—lawyers and physicians, for example. The professional component of teacher education programs is the shortest of all the professions—only 15 percent of the average bachelor's degree program for a high school teacher is devoted to professional courses. However, several colleges and universities have extended the time it takes to become a teacher by launching five-year teacher education programs. Similarly, in its comprehensive report, *What Matters Most: Teaching for America's Future*, the National Commission on Teaching and America's Future (1996) recommended that teacher education be moved to the graduate level. If the trend toward five-year and graduate-level teacher education programs continues, the professional status of teaching will definitely be enhanced.

In addition, many school districts require that teachers complete a certain number of hours of graduate study within a specified time period as a condition of employment. Still other districts require their teachers to obtain a master's degree within a specified time limit. Steadily, the trend has been for teachers to attain higher levels of education.

Entry into the Profession   In most professions, new members must undergo a prescribed induction period. Physicians, for example, must serve an internship or residency before beginning practice, and most lawyers begin as clerks in law firms. Sociologists have termed this process of gradually moving from simple to more complex tasks, small to greater responsibility, as "mediated entry" into a profession. In contrast, teachers do not go through a formal induction period before assuming full responsibility for their work. Practice teaching comes closest to serving as an induction period, but it is often relatively short, informal, and lacking in uniformity. In reality, entry into teaching is abrupt, and, as the National Commission on Teaching and America's Future (1996) noted, "Our society can no longer accept the [s]ink-or-swim induction [of teachers]."

Until recently, induction into the profession teaching has been minimal. Due to the "flat" career paths of teachers (a veteran of thirty years has essentially the same status as a beginner), experienced teachers may devote little effort to induct beginning teachers into a professional culture or way of life. Though new teachers may certainly expect veteran teachers to help them "learn the ropes," little is done to help beginning teachers identify with the profession. "Assisting occupational identity formation, encouraging collegial patterns of behavior, fostering generational trust, and enhancing self-esteem" (Lortie 1975, 160–61) are forms of assistance that experienced teachers tend not to provide to neophytes.

In spite of the extensive knowledge and skills teachers must possess, teaching has been characterized as an "easy entry" profession (Lortie 1975). Moreover, the training teachers undergo tends not to be valued by teachers themselves, as sociologist Dan Lortie (1975, 160) points out: "Teachers are inclined to talk about their training as easy ('Mickey Mouse'); I have yet to hear a teacher complain that education courses were too difficult or demanded too much effort. Teachers do not perceive their preparation as conveying something special—as setting them apart from others. . . . Teachers do not consider training the key to their legitimation as teachers. That rests in experience."

Provision of Essential Service

Although it is generally acknowledged that teachers provide a service that is vital to the well-being of individuals and groups, the public does need to be reminded of this fact from time to time. This importance was driven home on a large scale during the early 1980s when several reports calling for school reform linked the strength of our country to the quality of its schools. In a sense, it is no exaggeration to say that teaching is a matter of life and death:

> Every moment in the lives of teachers and pupils brings critical decisions of motivation, reinforcement, reward, ego enhancement and goal direction. Proper professional decisions enhance learning and life; improper decisions send the learner towards incremental death in openness to experience and in ability to learn and contribute. Doctors and lawyers probably have neither more nor less to do with life, death, and freedom than do teachers (Howsam et al. 1976, 15).

The ability to function as the spark that stimulates young people to learn and grow can give teachers a sense of meaning and fulfillment they might not be able to find in other professions. A foreign language teacher, who immigrated to this country, summed up during an interview with the author what many teachers feel about their choice of professions: "I feel that I get satisfaction . . . that I am a useful member of the society. I feel this is the field in which . . . I can contribute more to society than in any other field. . . . I am doing a job which is good [for] the American society" (Parkay 1983, 114–115).

Degree of Self-Governance

The limited freedom of teachers to govern themselves has detracted from the overall status of the profession. In many states, licensing guidelines are set by government officials who may or may not be educators. At the local level, decision-making power usually resides with local boards of education, largely made up of people who have never taught. As a result, teachers have had little or no say over what they teach, when they teach, whom they teach, and, in extreme instances, *how* they teach.

In other professions, it is members of the profession, not laypersons, who make decisions about practice. Nonmembers are seen as not having sufficient understanding to participate in professional governance. In fact, these professions (most notably law and medicine) have shown their ability to move swiftly and decisively to squelch any suspected movement toward lay control.

Traditionally, teachers have allowed other parties to make major decisions regarding significant aspects of their work. Occasionally, a teacher, with or without the support of other teachers, will refuse to follow the dictates of a principal or board of education. Such a maverick teacher often faces the prospect of not having a contract renewed, being fired outright, being transferred, or being given an undesirable teaching assignment.

However, recent efforts to empower teachers and to professionalize teaching are creating new roles for teachers. Teachers have expanded opportunities to govern important aspects of their work. Throughout the country, teachers are having a greater voice in decisions related to curriculum development, staffing, budget, and the day-to-day operation of schools. Figure 6.2, for example, compares public and private school teachers' perceptions of teacher influence or control over curricula, student performance standards, discipline policies, in-service training, teacher evaluation, teacher hiring, and budget. Although public school teachers differ significantly in the amount of influence or control they believe teachers have, public school teachers should experience greater degrees of self-governance as principals respond to increasing pressure to become more effective at facilitating collaborative, emergent approaches to leadership (Parkay, Shindler, and Oaks 1997). As Ger-

Figure 6.2 Percentage of teachers who thought they had a lot of influence on various school policies, by sector: 1999–2000.

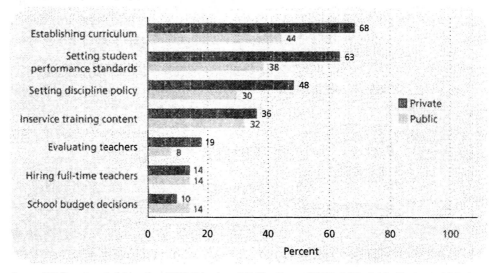

Source: U.S. Department of Education, NCES. Schools and Staffing Survey (SASS), Public, Public Charter, and Private School Teacher Surveys, 1999–2000. Taken from National Center for Education Statistics, *Special Analysis 2002–Private Schools: A Brief Portrait,* Figure 5. Washington, DC: Author.

ald Grant and Christine Murray point out in *Teaching in America: The Slow Revolution* (1999, 217), "schoolteachers can assert that they have genuine expertise in their subject matter and that there is a body of pedagogical content knowledge that is specific to their work. Most important, they are no longer willing to let the administrators define themselves as the exclusive class of experts controlling either the content of the curriculum or decisions about who is fit to teach it."

Professional Associations

Teachers, like other professionals, have formed vocational associations that are vitally concerned with issues such as admission to the profession, educational standards, examinations and licensing, career development, ethical and performance standards, and professional discipline. It is clear, though, that the more than five hundred national teacher organizations have not progressed as far as other professions have in gaining control of these areas.

Professional Knowledge and Skills

Professionals are granted a certain status because they possess knowledge and skills not normally held by the general public. If a person talks with a surgeon about a surgical procedure, for example, it is with the understanding that the physician, by virtue of professional membership, possesses the necessary knowledge and skills. Moreover, for the surgeon, the outcomes of practice are specific and easily determined—the patient recovers from the operation and resumes normal daily activities.

What characteristics distinguish teaching as a profession? What characteristics might distinguish this teacher as a professional?

Within the profession of teaching, however, the requirements for membership are less precise. Despite ongoing efforts of educational researchers, there is less than unanimous agreement on the knowledge and skills considered necessary to teach. This lack of agreement is reflected in the varied programs at the 1,300 or so colleges and universities that train teachers. In addition, as pointed out in Chapter 2, the outcomes of teaching are unpredictable; therefore, it is more difficult to develop a stable knowledge base to guide teachers' practice.

During the last ten years, the National Board for Professional Teaching Standards (NBPTS) has made significant progress toward clarifying the knowledge base for teaching. As you also learned in Chapter 2, the NBPTS (the majority of whose members are teachers) offers board certification to teachers who possess a high level of NBPTS-identified knowledge and skills. At the beginning of 2004, the NBPTS had granted national certification to about more than 32,000 teachers, and the board planned to certify 100,000 teachers by 2006.

Level of Public Trust

The level of trust the public extends to teachers as professionals varies greatly. On the one hand, the public appears to have great confidence in the work that teachers do. Because of its faith in the teaching profession, the public invests teachers with considerable power over its children. For the most part, parents willingly allow their children to be molded and influenced by teachers, and this willingness must be based on a high degree of trust. In addition, most parents expect their children to obey and respect teachers.

At various times during our nation's history, the public's confidence in teachers has been uncertain. During the first half of the 1980s, the profession received considerable "bad press." Teachers were portrayed as incompetent, greedy, unprofessional, unintelligent, immoral, and generally unable to live up to the public's expectations. Just about all of our country's problems—from declining achievement test scores, to our difficulty in meeting economic challenges from abroad, to the lack of respect for authority among youth—were blamed on teachers.

Though all professions have some members who might be described as unprofessional, teaching is especially vulnerable to such charges. The sheer size of the teaching force makes it difficult to maintain consistently high professional standards. Moreover, teaching is subject to a level of public scrutiny and control that other, more established, professions traditionally have not tolerated. However, the era of widespread public trust may be running out for these other professions as well. Mushrooming malpractice suits against doctors, for example, may be a sign that here, too, public confidence has significantly eroded.

Prestige, Benefits, and Pay

While "many teachers and school administrators . . . are thought to be of a more elite social class than the majority of the population in the United States" (Parker and Shapiro 1993, 42) this higher status is based on level of education attained rather than wealth. Thus teachers have not received salaries in keeping with other professions requiring approximately the same amount of schooling. Nevertheless, there is significant support for reducing the salary gap—as mentioned in Chapter 2, 83 percent of the public surveyed for the 2002 poll, *A National Priority: Americans Speak on Teacher Quality*, favor increased salaries for teachers even if it means paying higher taxes (Hart and Teeter 2002).

What Is Professionalism in Teaching?

The current goal among teachers, teacher educators, policymakers, and the general public is to make teaching a full profession. Toward this end, teachers are willing to take risks and learn new roles as they press for greater self-governance, better working conditions, and increased financial rewards. In addition, teachers are acquiring the analytical skills needed to understand and provide leadership for the complex processes of educational reform. The following sections look at the three key dimensions of professionalism in teaching presented in Figure 6.3: professional behavior, lifelong learning, and involvement in the profession.

Professional Behavior

The professional teacher is guided by a specific set of values. He or she has made a deep and lasting commitment to professional practice. He or she has adopted a

Figure 6.3   Professionalism in teaching.

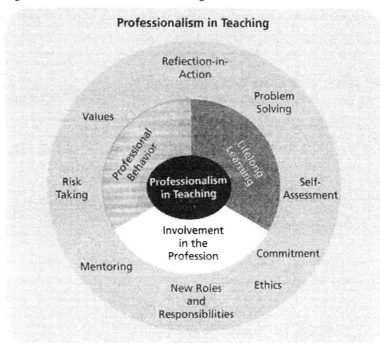

high standard of professional ethics and models behaviors that are in accord with that code of ethics. The professional teacher also engages in serious, reflective thought about how to teach more effectively. Moreover, he or she does this while teaching, continually examining experiences to improve practice.

Reflection-in-Action Donald Schön (1987, 1991, and 2000) has described this professional behavior as **reflection-in-action**, and he describes how a teacher might use it to solve a problem in the classroom:

> An artful teacher sees a child's difficulty in learning to read not as a defect in the child but as a defect "of his own instruction." And because the child's difficulties may be unique, the teacher cannot assume that his repertoire of explanations will suffice, even though they are "at the tongue's end." He must be ready to invent new methods and must "endeavor to develop in himself the ability of discovering them" (2000, 66).

The professional teacher Schön describes makes careful, sensitive observations of classroom events, reflects on the meaning of those observations, and then decides to act in a certain way. A former public school teacher in low-income urban neighborhoods explains professional reflection further: "Reflection is not (educational) reflection unless it is linked to teaching action. Reflection involves conflicting thoughts and questions. It is hard work and it can be painful. . . . Acting professionally on reflection requires true grit" (Freppon 2001, 2).

Becoming a Mentor Because of their positions and their encounters with young people, teachers may find opportunities to become mentors to some of their students. Accepting this responsibility is another example of professional behavior. The role of **mentor** is unique in several ways. First, mentorship develops naturally and is not an automatic part of teaching, nor can it be assigned to anyone. True mentorships grow from teaching relationships and cannot be artificially promoted. Second, the role of mentor is a *comprehensive* one: mentors express broad interest in those whom they mentor. Third, the role of mentor is *mutually* recognized by student and teacher; both realize that their relationship has a special "depth." Fourth, the role of mentor is significant and has the potential to change the quality and direction of students' lives. And fifth, the opportunity to work with a mentor is free, what Gehrke (1988) terms the mentor's "gift of care."

The longer you teach, the more you will encounter opportunities for mentorships to develop. You will also realize that you can mentor less experienced teachers and student teachers as well as students. The rewards that come from the unique role of mentor are among the most satisfying.

Lifelong Learning

The professional teacher is dedicated to continuous learning—both about the teaching-learning process and about the subject taught. No longer is it sufficient for career teachers to obtain only a bachelor's degree and a teaching certificate.

A good mentor can make an incredible difference in the professional life of a new teacher. What qualities make someone a good mentor?

Rather, they see themselves as both teachers and learners. They are lifelong members of learning communities, as this chapter's Relevant Standards feature suggests.

Several states have mandated continuing education for teachers. The content of the curriculum as well as methods and materials for teaching that content are changing so rapidly that teachers must be involved in continuous learning to maintain their professional effectiveness. Continuous learning also enables teachers to "practice what they preach." A teacher who is not continuously learning raises serious questions for students: If it's not important for our teachers to learn, why should we? The attitude toward learning that teachers model for students may be as important as the content they teach.

Many opportunities are available for teachers to learn new knowledge and skills. Nearly every school district makes provisions for in-service training or staff development. Topics can range from classroom-focused issues such as authentic assessment, using the Internet, classroom management, integrated curricula, or learning styles to schoolwide management issues such as restructuring, shared governance, or school–community partnerships. Beyond these in-service opportunities, professional teachers actively seek additional avenues for growth, as a teacher of children from low-income homes in Appalachia observes:

> *My journey toward becoming an effective teacher and a person who is proud of his work has not been easy. However, it has been necessary—I don't think one can be an effective teacher without being proud of one's teaching. For me professional development (being in a constant learning state and networking with other teachers) is the key in maintaining my commitment and building my expertise (Freppon 2001, 50).*

Relevant Standards

Continuous Professional Growth

The following professional standards stress the need for teachers to be committed to continuous professional growth. Teachers seek professional growth through activities such as mentoring other teachers, providing leadership for school improvement, and designing and delivering staff development programs for other teachers.

- "[Teacher candidates] reflect on and continually evaluate the effects of choices and actions on others and actively seek out opportunities to grow professionally." (National Council for Accreditation of Teacher Education [NCATE], 2002, 18. Standard 1: Candidate Knowledge, Skills, and Dispositions.)

- "Teachers think systematically about their practice and learn from experience (Core Proposition #4). "Because they work in a field marked by many unsolved puzzles and an expanding research base, teachers have a professional obligation to be lifelong students of their craft, seeking to expand their repertoire, deepen their knowledge and skill, and become wiser in rendering judgments." (National Board for Professional Teaching Standards [NBPTS], 2002, 16.)

- "The teacher seeks out professional literature, colleagues, and other resources to support his/her own development as a learner and a teacher." (Interstate New Teacher Assessment and Support Consortium [INTASC], 1992, 32. "Performance" statement for Principle #9: "The teacher is a reflective practitioner who continually evaluates the effects of his/her choices and actions on others [students, parents, and other professionals in the learning community] and who actively seeks out opportunities to grow professionally.")

- "Teacher seeks out opportunities for professional development and makes a systematic attempt to conduct action research in his (or her) classroom." (Praxis Series, Domain 4: Professional Responsibilities, Component 4e: Growing and Developing Professionally.) (From Danielson 1996, 117)

One of the most challenging ways to become a more effective professional is to enroll in a graduate program at a nearby college or university. Class schedules are usually developed with teachers in mind, with most courses offered in the evenings, on Saturdays, and during the summer. If you pursue graduate study, not only will you find the professional dialogue with instructors and fellow students stimulating, you'll acquire theories and practical approaches that you can implement in your classroom the following day. Also, you might find some other area of education—administration and supervision, guidance and counseling, special education, or curriculum development—that you want to pursue in your long-term career development.

As mentioned earlier, thousands of teachers have attained National Board Certification, a professional growth experience several board-certified teachers describe this way:

"One of the best professional development experiences—it gave me lots of self-confidence."

"The certification process was a real eye-opener. I realized I've done an awful lot—the process helps document your accomplishments."

"It was like the final stages of a major graduate course or a cumulative comprehensive exam or thesis."

"The certification process far exceeds everything I've ever done, including my M.A."

"The certification process was more focused than a master's program and more valuable because it was what I was really doing in the classroom" (Rotberg, Futrell, and Lieberman 1998, 463).

Learning to Become a Leader   For professional teachers, an important goal of lifelong learning is to acquire leadership skills. Successful educational reform in the twenty-first century will require teacher participation in leadership, as data presented in Table 6.1 imply. The data suggest that public school teachers believe principals do not provide sufficient leadership in many areas of instruction and school management. Only 11 percent of teachers report that the "principal often discusses instructional practices," and less than half believe "school goals are communicated clearly" by their principals. Teachers who have a leadership orientation, however, understand that *they*, as well as the principal, have an obligation to initiate school-wide discussions of instructional practices or school goals. They also understand, as John Gardner (1990) pointed out in his best-selling book *On Leadership*, that "no individual has all the skills—and certainly not the time—to carry out all the complex tasks of contemporary leadership."

Table 6.1   Percentage of teachers who strongly agreed with various statements about the school's principal and management, by sector and private school type: 1999–2000

Sector and type	Principal enforces school rules	School goals are communicated clearly	Administration is supportive and encouraging	Necessary materials are available	Principal expresses expectations for staff	Staff are recognized for good work	Principal often discusses instructional practice
Public	47.4	48.1	41.8	37.2	49.7	25.7	11.0
Private	62.7	61.3	59.9	60.2	56.5	39.8	15.4
Private school type							
Catholic	59.2	59.1	56.1	53.2	55.9	36.5	14.1
Other religious	68.3	66.4	67.3	64.0	60.5	45.7	18.1
Nonsectarian	59.4	56.5	53.6	64.5	51.1	35.7	12.9

Source: U.S. Department of Education, National Center for Education Statistics. Schools and Staffing Survey (SASS), "Public, Public Charter, and Private School Teacher Survey," 1999–2000. Taken from National Center for Education Statistics, *Special Analysis 2002–Private Schools: A Brief Portrait,* Table 10. Washington, DC: Author.

As teachers assume broader leadership roles, collaborative decision making will become more common in schools (Parkay, Shindler, and Oaks 1997). One such school is Anzar High School in San Juan Bautista, California, whose teachers are "committed to collaborative decision making regarding teaching and learning, devoting faculty meetings and professional development time to discussing student progress, curriculum, and assessment" (Davidson 2002). The success of the collaborative leadership model is the result of teachers' commitment to the "Anzar Communication Guidelines" comprised of ten "individual guidelines" and twelve "group guidelines." The following are included among the guidelines:

- I commit to practice these guidelines.
- I listen to the message and not the messenger.
- We are all part of the same team; we collectively own problems, and we collectively solve them.
- We help and support others.
- We allow conflict and differing ideas to exist, and we recognize that tension may be normal (Horace 2002).

Involvement in the Profession

Today's teachers realize that they have the most important role in the educational enterprise and that, previously, they have not had the power they needed to improve the profession. Therefore, they are taking an increasingly broader view of the decisions that, as professionals, they have the right to make.

Across the country, professional teachers are deeply involved with their colleagues, professional organizations, teacher educators, legislators, policymakers, and others in a push to make teaching more fully a profession. Through their behaviors and accomplishments, they are demonstrating that they are professionals, that the professional identity of teachers is becoming stronger. During the last decade, for example, teachers have become more involved in teacher education reform, teacher certification, and professional governance. And, through the efforts of scores of teacher organizations, teachers have also made gains in working conditions, salaries, and benefits.

To What Professional Organizations Do Teachers Belong?

The expanding leadership role of teachers has been supported through the activities of more than five hundred national teacher organizations (*Directory of National Trade and Professional Associations of the United States* 2002). These organizations and the scores of hardworking teachers who run them support a variety of activities to improve teaching and schools. Through lobbying in Washington and at state capitols, for example, teacher associations acquaint legislators, policymakers, and politicians with critical issues and problems in the teaching profession. Many associations have staffs of teachers, researchers, and consultants who produce professional publications, hold conferences, prepare grant proposals, engage in school improvement activities, and promote a positive image of teaching to the public. In the quest to improve the professional lives of all teachers, two national organizations have led the way: the National Education Association (NEA) and the American Federation of Teachers (AFT). These two groups have had a long history of competition for the allegiance of teachers.

The National Education Association

Membership in the **National Education Association (NEA)**, the oldest and largest of the two organizations, includes both teachers and administrators. Originally called the National Teachers Association when it was founded in 1857, the group was started by forty-three educators from a dozen states and the District of Columbia (West 1980, 1).

The NEA has affiliates in every state plus Puerto Rico and the District of Columbia, and its local affiliates number more than 15,000. About two-thirds of the teachers in this country belong to the NEA. More than 78 percent of NEA's 2.7 million members are teachers; about 12 percent are guidance counselors, librarians, and administrators; almost 3 percent are university professors; about 2 percent are college and university students; about 3 percent are support staff (teacher aides, secretaries, cafeteria workers, bus drivers, and custodians); and about 2 percent are retired members.

To improve education in this country, the NEA has standing committees in the following areas: affiliate relationships, higher education, human relations, political action, teacher benefits, and teacher rights. These committees engage in a wide range of activities, among them preparing reports on important educational issues, disseminating the results of educational research, conducting conferences, working with federal agencies on behalf of children, pressing for more rigorous standards for the teaching profession, helping school districts resolve salary disputes, developing ways to improve personnel practices, and enhancing the relationship between the profession and the public.

The Unionization Movement   Prior to World War II, the NEA was more concerned with improving the quality of instruction than with the bread-and-butter issues of teachers' salaries and benefits. Moreover, up until the 1940s it was commonly felt that teaching was a calling similar to the ministry, and that it was therefore inappropriate for teachers to press for higher salaries and better working conditions.

Following World War II, the NEA began to take a more productive stance regarding issues related to teacher welfare. By 1950 the organization had grown to over 400,000 members, and it was capable of making its views widely known. Postwar inflation had caused large numbers of teachers to leave the profession for jobs that kept better pace with rising prices. By the late 1940s, the nation was faced with a critical teacher shortage. The plight of teachers was made known through publications put out by the NEA, the American Federation of Teachers, and other teacher organizations. During this period, some teachers banded together and began using the strike as a means of securing their demands. Initially, the NEA was staunchly opposed to the use of strikes. It stressed the fact that teachers were professionals, and professionals should not resort to the use of a labor union strategy.

Instead of supporting teacher strikes, the NEA worked to obtain more federal monies for education, part of which would be used to improve teachers' salaries and working conditions. If teacher strikes became more widespread, the NEA leadership reasoned, Congress would be reluctant to provide significant aid to education. Federal aid to education was not significantly increased until after the launching of Sputnik by the Russians in 1957. However, most of the federal money poured into education was used to develop new curricula for mathematics, sciences, and languages. Only a small amount was used to increase teachers' salaries.

Though it was not until the late 1960s that the NEA acknowledged the strike as a legitimate weapon for teachers to use, it did use other means to press for improvements. In 1946, at its annual meeting, the NEA established the National Commission on Teacher Education and Professional Standards (TEPS). The TEPS Commission worked from 1946 until its demise in 1971 to improve teachers' working conditions and to develop a "continuing program of teacher recruitment, selection, preparation, certification, and the advancement of professional standards, including standards for institutions that prepare teachers" (West 1980, 211).

Gains in Teachers' Rights   By the late 1960s and early 1970s, the NEA recognized that it had to become increasingly militant in order to secure much needed improvements in teachers' working conditions. In fact, the NEA entered the 1974 congressional elections with the campaign theme, "Get mad: it matters."

Many teachers had been treated unfairly in the United States because they lacked the resources to obtain legal redress through the courts. One particular case, in 1943, marked the start of NEA-funded legal assistance for teachers. Three teachers in Muskogee, Oklahoma, learned through the local newspaper that they had not been reappointed for the following school year. They were given no written or oral notice. No hearing had been held, and no charges had been made. The Executive Committee of the NEA decided to devote $10,000 to support the teachers in their case against the Muskogee school board. The NEA's Committee on Tenure charged the board with dismissal without just cause, failure to state the charges against the teachers, and failure to exercise due process. Following the NEA's successful support of the teachers' case, the $984.39 unspent on legal fees was used to begin the Dushane Fund for Teacher Rights. Since the fund's establishment in 1944, the number of legal cases the NEA has supported has mushroomed. In 1957, the NEA spent $82,620 supporting teachers' rights. During 1978–79, expenditures were $2.6 million, not including state and local funds. The number of cases handled has also increased dramatically. From 1975 to 1979, for example, the number of cases increased from 1,743 to 15,614 (West 1980). The increase reflects issues related to collective bargaining, civil rights, pupil violence, the increased exercise of constitutional rights by NEA members, and the increasing trend toward using legal action to resolve disputes.

Currently, more than two-thirds of states have passed some type of collective bargaining laws that apply to teachers. There is little uniformity among these laws, with most of the thirty-one states permitting strikes only if certain conditions have been met. The NEA has gone on record as supporting a federal statute that would set up uniform procedures for teachers to bargain with their employers.

The NEA continues today to focus on issues of concern to teachers, primarily in the area of professional governance. Efforts are being made to broaden teachers' decision-making powers related to curriculum, extracurricular responsibilities, staff development, and supervision. To promote the status of the profession, the NEA conducts annual research studies and opinion surveys in various areas. The NEA also publishes *NEA Today* and *Tomorrow's Teachers*, an annual magazine for NEA student members that covers job searches, tips for surviving the first year in the classroom, and strategies for parental and community outreach.

The American Federation of Teachers

The **American Federation of Teachers (AFT)** was founded in 1916. Three teachers' unions in Chicago issued a call for teachers to form a national organization affiliated with organized labor. Teacher unions in Gary, Indiana; New York City; Oklahoma; Scranton, Pennsylvania; and Washington, D.C., joined the three Chicago unions to form the AFT. The newly formed AFT had four objectives:

1. to bring associations of teachers into relations of mutual assistance and cooperation,
2. to obtain for them all the rights to which they are entitled,
3. to raise the standards of the teaching profession by securing the conditions essential to the best professional service, and
4. to promote such a democratization of the schools as will enable them better to equip their pupils to take their places in the industrial, social, and political life of the community (The Commission on Educational Reconstruction 1955, 28, 60–61).

The AFT differs from the NEA in that it is open only to teachers and nonsupervisory school personnel. The AFT is active today in organizing teachers, collective bargaining, public relations, and developing policies related to various educational issues. In addition, the organization conducts research in areas such as educational reform, bilingual education, teacher certification, and evaluation, and also represents members' concerns through legislative action and technical assistance.

The AFT has more than 1.2 million members who are organized through 2,265 local affiliates. The AFT is affiliated with the American Federation of Labor–Congress of Industrial Organizations (AFL–CIO), which has over thirteen million members. To promote the idea that teachers should have the right to speak for themselves on important issues, the AFT does not allow superintendents, principals, and other administrators to join. As an informational brochure on the AFT states, "Because the AFT believes in action—in 'getting things done' rather than issuing reports, letting someone else do the 'doing'—a powerful, cohesive structure is necessary."

Unlike the NEA, the AFT has been steadfastly involved throughout its history in securing economic gains and improving working conditions for teachers. Though the AFT has been criticized for being unprofessional and too concerned with bread-and-butter issues, none other than the great educator and philosopher John Dewey took out the first AFT membership card in 1916. After twelve years as a union member, Dewey made his stance on economic issues and teachers clear:

> It is said that the Teachers Union, as distinct from the more academic organizations, overemphasizes the economic aspect of teaching. Well, I never had that contempt for the economic aspect of teaching, especially not on the first of the month when I get my salary check. I find that teachers have to pay their grocery and meat bills and house rent just the same as everybody else (1955, 60–61).

Traditionally, the AFT has been strongest in urban areas. Today, the AFT represents teachers not only in Chicago and New York but in Philadelphia, Washington, D.C., Kansas City, Detroit, Boston, Cleveland, and Pittsburgh. NEA membership has tended to be suburban and rural. The NEA has always been the larger of the two organizations, and it is presently more than twice the size of its rival.

The NEAFT Partnership

For decades, many people within both the NEA and the AFT believed that the interests of teachers and students could best be served through a merger of the two organizations. One national teachers' union with enormous political strength, they believed, could do more to advance the teaching profession than two independent, often competing, organizations. However, until the turn of the century, differences between the two organizations thwarted periodic efforts to merge.

By the end of the 1990s, differences between the NEA and the AFT had become less apparent. Collective bargaining and the use of strikes, long opposed by the NEA, were now used by both organizations. Eventually, a "conceptual agreement" to merge the organizations was announced in 1998 by the presidents of the NEA and the AFT. The presidents cited an "assault" on public education in the form of voucher plans, charter schools, and other approaches to school privatization as a primary reason to merge (Bradley 1998). In 2001, NEA and AFT Unity Discussion Teams and Advisory Committees forged the **NEAFT Partnership** and endorsed the following goals:

- **Building Relationships** to increase knowledge, promote trust and collaboration and involve leaders and affiliates in both our unions at the national, state and local levels.

- **Making Collaboration Work** to more effectively use our combined resources to focus on promoting the welfare of children, public education and our members.

- **Creating Value** from the power of our collaboration to strengthen our ability to resist the challenges by the enemies of public education and collective bargaining.

- **Demonstrating Visibly** our united strength and ability to improve the institutions in which our members work and further signal our commitment to public education and unionism (NEAFT Partnership 2002).

The NEA and AFT have found additional common ground in their opposition to the No Child Left Behind (NCLB) legislation (see discussion of NCLB in Chapter 1). Both organizations maintain that the law is seriously flawed. In particular, NEAFT believes that the NCLB's requirement that schools make Adequate Yearly Progress (AYP) is extremely harmful to public schools. NEAFT believes that NCLB does not give enough credit for schools that make academic progress but fail to reach the legislation's AYP standards. NEAFT is also working with other education associations to develop alternatives to punitive high-stakes testing programs. NEAFT supports high-stakes tests aligned with standards as one, but not the only tool, in student and school assessment.

Other Professional Organizations

In addition to the NEA and AFT, teachers' professional interests are represented by more than 500 other national organizations. Several of these are concerned with improving the quality of education at all levels and in all subject areas. **Phi Delta Kappa (PDK)**, for example, is an international professional and honorary fraternity of educators concerned with enhancing quality education through research and leadership activities.

Founded in 1906, Phi Delta Kappa has a membership of more than 90,000. Members, who are graduate students, teachers, and administrators, belong to one of more than 666 chapters. To be initiated into Phi Delta Kappa, one must have demonstrated high academic achievement, have completed at least fifteen semester hours of graduate work in education, and have made a commitment to a career of educational service. Phi Delta Kappa members receive *Phi Delta Kappan*, a journal of education published ten times a year.

Another example is the **Association for Supervision and Curriculum Development (ASCD)**, a professional organization of teachers, supervisors, curriculum coordinators, education professors, administrators, and others. The ASCD is interested in school improvement at all levels of education. Founded in 1943, the association has a membership of 160,000. ASCD provides professional development experiences in curriculum and supervision, disseminates information on educational issues, and encourages research, evaluation, and theory development. ASCD also conducts several National Curriculum Study Institutes around the country each year and provides a free research information service to members. Members receive *Educational Leadership*, a well-respected journal printed eight times a year. ASCD also publishes a yearbook, each one devoted to a particular educational issue, and occasional books in the area of curriculum and supervision.

In addition, as you will see in Appendix 6.1 many professional associations exist for teachers of specific subject areas, such as mathematics, English, social studies, music, physical education, and so on, as well as for teachers of specific student

Case for Reflection

To Strike or Not to Strike

You are near the end of your first month of teaching at an urban school. The board of education has just announced that it is unable to provide the salary increases promised to teachers last year. According to the board, the school system is faced with tremendous financial problems.

Teachers at your school, most of whom belong to the teachers' unions, are very angry about the board's failure to live up to its promise. Many teachers believe that the board can find the money if it really wants to. Your school's union representative has just called a meeting of teachers to discuss the situation and to consider a possible strike. The day before the meeting he stops by your classroom to urge you to attend.

"This is an important meeting," he says. "As a new teacher, you need to find out how the board of education has treated teachers."

"Well," you begin, "I'm not sure. I'd like to make more money like anyone else, but if we go on strike, what about the kids? We have a responsibility to them."

"Just a minute," he says. "This is not just about money. The board has a history of failing to live up to its promises. We're actually doing this for the kids. If the board gets away with this, a lot of good teachers are going to transfer out of the district. And that's going to hurt the kids."

You agree to attend the meeting, but you're still not sure how you feel about teacher unions in general. Prior to the meeting, several questions keep coming to mind. If teachers are professionals, should they belong to unions? If teachers decide to go on strike, will I honor the strike? Would I cross the picket line in order to teach?

Questions

1. What is your position regarding teacher strikes?
2. Other than going on strike, what other actions could teachers in the preceding case take?
3. Imagine that teachers in the preceding case met with a group of parents whose children attend the school. How might teachers justify going on strike? What concerns might parents express?

populations, such as exceptional learners, young children, and students with limited English proficiency.

What New Leadership Roles for Teachers Are Emerging?

Teachers' roles are changing in fundamental and positive ways at the beginning of the twenty-first century. Greater autonomy and an expanded role in educational policymaking have led to unprecedented opportunities for today's teachers to extend their leadership roles beyond the classroom. To prepare for this future, today's teachers will need to develop leadership skills to a degree not needed in the past.

Teacher Involvement in Teacher Education, Certification, and Staff Development

Teacher input into key decisions about teacher preparation, certification, and staff development is on the rise. Through their involvement with professional development schools and the National Board for Professional Teaching Standards, state professional standards boards, and scores of local, state, and national education committees, teachers are changing the character of pre- and in-service education. For example, the National Board for Professional Teaching Standards (NBPTS) established a network designed to allow nearly 7 percent of the nation's 2.5 million teachers to participate in field-testing various components of the NBPTS certification system. The NBPTS allocated $1 million to teachers, in the form of honoraria, for helping to field-test the NBPTS assessment materials. One participant in the field test reflects on how teacher participation in the NBPTS can positively influence the profession of teaching:

> I am proud to say I was one of the first teachers in the country to participate in NBPTS. At its best, NBPTS can help us validate our skills as teachers; it can help us focus on areas of needed improvement; it can encourage a core of committed teacher-thinkers. . . . As more and more teachers participate and are certified, we will find our voices. We will be able to speak in an articulate fashion about what is important for us and our students. We will be heard (Hletko 1995, 36).

Teachers who have received National Board Certification are recognized as professionals not only in their schools, but also in their districts and beyond. For example, after receiving Board Certification, these teachers had the following professional opportunities:

- Helene Alolouf (Early Adolescence/English Language Arts certificate) of Yonkers, New York, was invited to teach at the Manhattanville Graduate School of Education as an adjunct professor.
- Sandra Blackman (Early Adolescence/English Language Arts certificate) of San Diego, California, was promoted to resource teacher for the Humanities Departments for fifty-five schools, where she provides staff development for a standards-based system.
- Edward William Clark Jr. (Early Childhood/Generalist certificate) of Valley, Alabama, helped the State Department of Education and the Alabama Education Association develop National Board Certification training modules to assist Alabama teachers with National Board Certification.
- Linda Lilja (Middle Childhood/Generalist certificate) of Scranton, Kansas, was invited to serve as a member of the task force for the National Teachers Hall of Fame.
- Donna W. Parrish (Early Adolescence/Generalist certificate) of Shelby, North Carolina, was appointed curriculum specialist at a middle school.

Technology in Teaching

Teacher leadership and the development and dissemination of multimedia software

A key to the effective use of technology to enhance students' learning is the availability of high-quality educational software. Since computer-enhanced instruction (CEI) first began to be used widely in the schools during the early 1990s, there has been a consistent call for higher-quality educational software and a realization that teachers, with their deep understanding of students' learning needs, would need to play a central role in the development of that software. As a software publisher stated in the U.S. Department of Education's publication *Getting America's Students Ready for the 21st Century: Meeting the Technology Literacy Challenge* (1996): "We definitely need teachers to help identify good software—to put some models out there that producers can emulate. Teachers need to be involved in separating the wheat from the chaff."

In response to that call, scores of teachers have become directly involved in developing and disseminating innovative, cutting-edge educational software. Perhaps the best known teacher-developed software is Roger Wagner's HyperStudio®,* with more than two million users in the United States alone. As a science and mathematics teacher in California, Wagner launched HyperStudio® in 1978. According to Wagner, "We wanted to make multimedia authoring a reality for students on the humble Apple IIGS. [The] world at large sets the stage for what is happening in classrooms now. As students increasingly use electronic sources of information for their research, and see the pervasion of multimedia around them, they expect to create their own projects in the same manner" (Davitt, 1997). Currently, dozens of teachers provide Wagner with input as he continues to develop newer versions of HyperStudio®.

Many other teachers around the country are working with instructional technology laboratories to develop and field-test multimedia software. For example, scores of teachers have collaborated with researchers at Wheeling Jesuit University's Center for Educational Technologies (CET), also home of NASA's Classroom of the Future program, to develop Astronomy Village and Investigating the Solar System, two of the most innovative computer simulations currently available.

Still other teachers are providing leadership for the integration of technology into teaching and learning environments. For example, dozens of teachers have attended the CET's Teacher-Leader Institutes, where they acquire strategies for integrating technology into education. Similarly, other teachers have completed the Teacher2Teacher Technology Leadership programs in San Jose, California, where they can earn Teacher Technology Integration Certification (TTIC), Train the Trainer Certification (TTC), or Technology Leadership (TL) Certification.

Clearly, teachers will play three vital leadership roles in the development of multimedia software for classrooms of the twenty-first century:

1. Developing and disseminating increasingly powerful versions of multimedia software
2. Developing strategies for the most effective ways to use that software in the classroom
3. Training other teachers to use that software

---

*© 1993–1999 Roger Wagner Publishing, Inc. and its licensors. All rights reserved. HyperStudio and the HyperStudio logo are registered trademarks of Roger Wagner Publishing, Inc.

Teacher-Leaders

As the titles of the following books suggest, the term **teacher-leader** has become part of the vocabulary of educational reform:

- *Reframing the Path to School Leadership: A Guide for Teachers and Principals* (Bolman and Deal 2002).
- *Leadership Strategies for Teachers* (Merideth 2000).
- *Reflective Action Planning for Teachers: A Guide to Teacher-Led School and Professional Development* (Frost 1997).
- *Teacher Leaders: Making a Difference in Schools* (Gehrke and Romerdahl 1997).
- *Who Will Save Our Schools? Teachers as Constructivist Leaders* (Lambert et al. 1997).
- *Deciding to Lead: The English Teacher as Reformer* (Wolfe and Antinarella 1997).
- *Every Teacher as a Leader: Realizing the Potential of Teacher Leadership* (Ackerman, Moller, and Katzenmeyer 1996).
- *Awakening the Sleeping Giant: Leadership Development for Teachers* (Katzenmeyer and Moller 1996).
- *Collaborative Leadership and Shared Decision Making: Teachers, Principals, and University Professors* (Clift et al. 1995).
- *Educating Teachers for Leadership and Change: Teacher Education Yearbook III* (O'Hair and Odell 1995).
- *A Handbook for Teacher Leaders* (Pellicer and Anderson 1995).
- *Becoming a Teacher Leader: From Isolation to Collaboration* (Boleman and Deal 1994).
- *Classroom Crusaders: Eleven Teachers Who Are Trying to Change the System* (Wolk and Rodman 1994).
- *Teachers as Leaders: Perspectives on the Professional Development of Teachers* (Walling 1994).
- *When Teachers Lead* (Astuto 1993).
- *Teachers as Leaders: Evolving Roles* (Livingston 1992).

"In their new leadership roles, teachers are being called upon to form new partnerships with business and industry; institutions of higher education; social service agencies; professional associations; and local, state, and federal governmental agencies. In this new role, teachers will be the key to promoting widespread improvement of our educational system" (Gmelch and Parkay 1995, 50–51).

A brief look at the professional activities of Sandra MacQuinn, a teacher-leader who worked with the author and a colleague on a major restructuring effort at Rogers High School in Spokane, Washington, illustrates the wide-ranging roles of a teacher-leader. In addition to teaching, here are just a few of MacQuinn's

Professional teachers participate in school governance at the local, state, and national levels. In addition to working to enhance the status of teaching as a profession, teachers are active in advocacy groups and reform lobbies calling for educational excellence and equity in education funding.

leadership activities while serving as liaison and onsite coordinator of a school–university partnership between Rogers High School and Washington State University's College of Education:

- Writing grant proposals for teacher-developed projects
- Helping other teachers write grant proposals
- Facilitating the development of an integrated school-to-work curriculum
- Preparing newsletters to keep faculty up to date on restructuring
- Organizing and facilitating staff development training
- Developing connections with area businesses and arranging "job shadowing" sites for students
- Working with a community college to create an alternative school for Rogers High students at the college
- Scheduling substitute teachers to provide Rogers teachers with release-time to work on restructuring
- Making presentations on the Rogers High restructuring at state and regional conferences
- Arranging for Rogers students to visit Washington State University (WSU)
- Meeting with the principal, assistant principals, WSU professors, and others to develop short- and long-range plans for implementing site-based management;

chairing meetings of the site-based council, the restructuring steering committee, and other restructuring-related committees

Three hundred sixty teachers will participate in the Teacher Leaders in Research-Based Science Education (TLRBSE) between 2002 and 2007. Funded by the National Science Foundation, TLRBSE enables experienced teacher-leaders to mentor teachers new to the profession, participate in a year-round online course, and implement research-based science education in the classroom. The teacher-leaders also participate in a combination of in-residence workshops at Kitt Peak National Observatory and the National Solar Observatory. Participants also receive a stipend, airfare, room and board, and support to attend a meeting of the National Science Teachers Association (Rector, Jacoby, Lockwood, and McCarthy 2002).

Dimensions of Teacher Leadership beyond the Classroom

The National Board for Professional Teaching Standards (NBPTS) observed that "accomplished teachers have a range of duties and tasks outside the direct instruction of students that contribute importantly to the quality of the school and to student learning" (National Board for Professional Teaching Standards 2002, 12). Figure 6.4 illustrates eleven dimensions of teacher leadership beyond the classroom. The many teachers whom the author has assisted on school restructuring

Figure 6.4   Eleven dimensions of teacher leadership beyond the classroom.

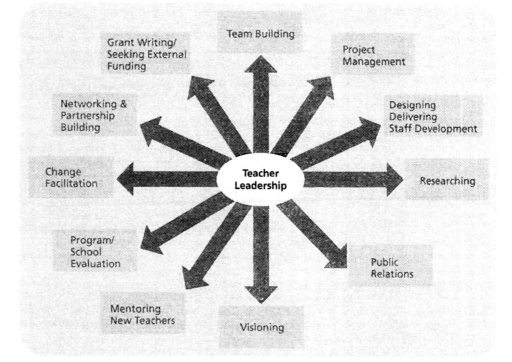

Figure 6.5 Five principles that guide the actions of teacher-leaders.

Five Principles That Guide the Actions of Teacher-Leaders

PRINCIPLE 1

Teacher-leaders accept their responsibility to increase the degree and quality of daily interactions with other teachers, administrators, and staff members. They know that "even if done on a small scale regularly, this can make a very significant difference for other individual teachers and for oneself."

PRINCIPLE 2

Teacher-leaders recognize that they have a responsibility to understand and to improve the culture of the school. "Every teacher must be concerned about the health of the school as an organization. This does not mean getting obsessively involved in every aspect of school life, but it does mean taking some responsibility for the welfare of one's colleagues and the wider life of the school."

PRINCIPLE 3

Teacher-leaders recognize that every teacher is a leader, and that a teacher's leadership role will vary according to the stage of the teacher's life and career. However, "all teachers have a leadership contribution to make beyond their own classrooms and should take action accordingly."

PRINCIPLE 4

Teacher-leaders recognize that they have a responsibility to become informed about the development of educational policies as well as professional and research issues. "This does not mean having a second career as an academic. But it does mean connecting with the knowlege base for improving teaching and schools. The more knowledgeable a teacher is about global educational and professional issues, the more resourceful he or she will be for students as well as for other teachers."

PRINCIPLE 5

Teacher-leaders recognize that all teachers have a responsibility for helping to shape the quality of the next generation of teachers. Teachers can make a contribution by working with student teachers, mentoring new teachers, and supporting and praising other teachers who assume those roles.

Source: Adapted from Michael Fullan and Andy Hargreaves, *What's Worth Fighting for in Your School?* New York: Teachers College Press, 1996.

projects during the last few years have used these skills to reach an array of educational goals. Teacher-leaders "view their responsibilities as extending beyond classroom teaching to include participation in the larger community of educators and administrators" (Becker April 2001).

At schools around the country, teachers and principals are using a "collaborative, emergent" approach to leadership; that is, the person who provides leadership for a particular schoolwide project or activity may or may not be the principal or a member of the administrative team (Parkay, Schindler, and Oaks 1997). Teachers who accept the challenge of becoming teacher-leaders and redefining their roles to include responsibilities beyond the classroom recognize the importance of five principles Michael Fullan and Andy Hargreaves present in their book, *What's Worth Fighting for in Your School?* (1996); they use these principles to guide their professional actions (see Figure 6.5).

As teachers continue to respond to calls for leadership, it is becoming more apparent that the knowledge and skills teachers must possess are very similar to those traditionally required for school administrators. On the other hand, administrators are realizing that, to lead effectively, they must be collaborative and share power with teachers. School administration is no longer seen as a top-down enterprise that places primary emphasis on *management*; instead, administrators are moving from being "manager[s] in charge to facilitator[s] on call" (Bredeson 1993).

To understand how the roles of teachers and administrators are merging in today's complex educational settings, consider the five standards for school leaders presented in Figure 6.6. The standards were developed by the Council of Chief State School Officers and have been adopted or adapted by 35 states. As you continue through your teacher education program, you should realize that *all* of these

Figure 6.6   Five standards for school leaders.

Standard 1: A school administrator [*as well as a teacher*] is an educational leader who promotes the success of all students by **facilitating the development, articulation, implementation, and stewardship of a vision of learning that is shared and supported by the school community.**

Standard 2: A school administrator [*as well as a teacher*] is an educational leader who promotes the success of all students by **advocating, nurturing, and sustaining a school culture and instructional program conducive to student learning and staff professional growth.**

Standard 3: A school administrator [*as well as a teacher*] is an educational leader who promotes the success of all students by **ensuring management of the organization, operations, and resources for a safe, efficient, and effective learning environment.**

Standard 4: A school administrator [*as well as a teacher*] is an educational leader who promotes the success of all students by **collaborating with families and community members, responding to diverse community interests and needs, and mobilizing community resources.**

Standard 5: A school administrator [*as well as a teacher*] is an educational leader who promotes the success of all students by **acting with integrity, fairness, and in an ethical manner.**

Source: Adapted from the Council of Chief State School Officers (1996). *Interstate School Leaders Licensure Consortium (ISLLC)* Washington, DC: Author.

standards should also apply to your preparation as a teacher. Professional teachers realize that they are members of learning communities, and they, as well as school administrators, have a responsibility to provide leadership to promote student learning.

How Do Teachers Contribute to Educational Research?

Most research on teaching is done by persons in higher education or at centers for research and development. Classroom teachers—those most intimately involved in professional practice—are only minimally involved in research efforts aimed at generating a deeper understanding of effective teaching.

However, today's teachers play an increasingly important role in educational research. By applying research to solve practical, classroom-based problems, teachers validate the accuracy and usefulness of educational research and help researchers identify additional areas to investigate. As consumers of educational research, teachers improve their teaching, contribute to educational reform, and enhance the professional status of teaching.

In addition, increasing numbers of teachers are becoming competent researchers in their own right and making important contributions to our understanding of teaching and learning. Prior to the mid 1980s, teachers were the missing "voice" in educational research. However, as teachers and staff developers Holly and McLoughlin (1989, 309) noted more than a decade ago, "We've moved from research on teachers to research with teachers and lately to research by teachers." Since their observation, we have seen the emergence of the **teacher-researcher**, the professional teacher who conducts classroom research to improve his or her teaching.

Part of being a professional is the ability to decide *how* and *when* to use research to guide one's actions. For example, Emmerich Koller, a teacher of German at a suburban high school, describes in an article he wrote for the book *Teachers Doing Research: Practical Possibilities* (Burnaford, Fischer, and Hobson 2001) how he used new teaching methods based on findings from brain research and "accelerated learning." (Accelerated learning is a strategy for optimizing learning by integrating conscious and unconscious mental processes.) After determining how and when to put that research into practice, he commented, "At age 50, after 27 years of teaching, I have found something that has made teaching very exciting again" (Koller 1996, 180).

Sources of Educational Research

Research findings are reported in scores of educational research journals. In addition, there are several excellent reviews of research with which you should become familiar during your professional preparation, such as the fourth edition of the *Handbook of Research on Teaching* (published by the American Educational Research Association, 2001). Its more than 1,200 pages synthesize research in several areas, including research on teaching at various grade levels and in various subject areas. Other comprehensive, authoritative reviews of research you might wish to consult include the following:

- *Encyclopedia of Educational Research*, 6th ed., four volumes (Macmillan, 1992)
- *Handbook of Research in Middle Level Education* (Information Age Publishing, 2001)
- *Handbook of Research on the Education of Young Children* (Macmillan, 1993)
- *Handbook of Research on Improving Student Achievement* (Educational Research Service, 1999)
- *Handbook of Research on Mathematics Teaching and Learning* (Macmillan, 1992), sponsored by the National Council of Teachers of Mathematics
- *Handbook of Research on Multicultural Education* (Macmillan, 1995)
- *Handbook of Research on Music Teaching and Learning* (Macmillan, 1992), sponsored by the Music Educators National Conference
- *Handbook of Research on Science Teaching and Learning* (Macmillan, 1994), sponsored by the National Science Teachers Association
- *Handbook of Research on Social Studies Teaching and Learning* (Macmillan, 1991), sponsored by the National Council for the Social Studies
- *Handbook of Research on Teaching the English Language Arts* (Macmillan, 1991), sponsored by the International Reading Association and the National Council of Teachers of English
- *Handbook of Research on Teaching Literacy through the Communicative and Visual Arts* (Macmillan, 1997)
- *Research Ideas for the Classroom: Early Childhood Mathematics, Middle School Mathematics, and High School Mathematics* (Macmillan, 1993), three volumes sponsored by the National Council of Teachers of Mathematics

Government Resources for Research Application

The federal government supports several efforts designed to help teachers improve their practice through the application of research findings. In 1966, three agencies were created to support and disseminate research: **Educational Resources Information Center (ERIC)**, **Research and Development Centers**, and **Regional Educational Laboratories**.

ERIC was a national information system made up of sixteen **ERIC Clearinghouses** and several adjunct clearinghouses—all coordinated by the central ERIC agency in Washington, D.C. At the start of 2004, the U.S. Department of Education closed all ERIC Clearinghouses and began to "reengineer" ERIC. As part of its new mission, ERIC will continue to provide a centralized database of journal articles and other published and unpublished education materials.

The ERIC database, which continues to be accessible in most college and university libraries, contains descriptions of exemplary programs, the results of research and development efforts, and related information that can be used by teachers, administrators, and the public to improve education. Each clearinghouse specialized in one area of education and sought out relevant documents or journal articles that were screened according to ERIC selection criteria, abstracted, and indexed.

Within the **Office of Educational Research and Improvement (OERI)** in Washington, D.C., the Office of Research (formerly the National Institute of Education) maintains twelve research centers at universities around the country. The centers are devoted to high-quality, fundamental research at every level of education, with most of the research done by scholars at the host university. Among the areas these centers focus on are the processes of teaching and learning, school organization and improvement, the content of education, and factors that contribute to (or detract from) excellence in education.

OERI also maintains ten regional educational laboratories and sponsors a number of Assistance Centers. Each laboratory serves a geographic region and is a nonprofit corporation not affiliated with a university. Laboratory staff work directly with school systems, state educational agencies, and other organizations to improve education through the application of research findings.

Scientifically Based Research   In 2002, the U.S. Department of Education's Institute of Education Sciences created the **What Works Clearinghouse (WWC)**. The Clearinghouse provides educators, policymakers, researchers, and the public with a central, independent source of scientific evidence of what works in education.

This teacher is conducting classroom action research on how students come to understand a problem and to apply appropriate problem-solving skills. What are several ways the teacher might use this research as a professional?

The No Child Left Behind Act (NCLB) requires that all federally funded education programs must be based on research studies that meet scientific standards. The primary goal of **scientifically based research (SBR)** is to ensure that programs for children are based on methods that have been proven effective and are therefore more likely to benefit other children. According to NCLB legislation, educational research should be similar to medical research—that is, medical practice is based on experimental studies (i.e., studies in which participants are randomly assigned to treatment and control groups). According to NCLB legislation, the following principles define scientific quality:

- Use of the scientific method with an emphasis on experimental control (or comparison) groups
- Replication of results, using multiple studies by different investigators
- Ability to generalize results from one sample to other children in the general population
- Fulfillment of rigorous standards with an emphasis on peer review
- Consistency of results among studies

Conducting Classroom Action Research

Almost four decades ago, Robert Schaefer (1967, 5) posed the following questions in *The School as the Center of Inquiry*:

> Why should our schools not be staffed, gradually if you will, by scholar-teachers in command of the conceptual tools and methods of inquiry requisite to investigating the learning process as it operates in their own classroom? Why should our schools not nurture the continuing wisdom and power of such scholar-teachers?

Schaefer's vision for teaching has become a reality. Today, thousands of teachers are involved in action research to improve their teaching. Using their classrooms as "laboratories," these teacher-researchers are systematically studying the outcomes of their teaching through the application of various research methods. In addition, they are disseminating the results of their research at professional conferences and through publications, including *Networks: An On-line Journal for Teacher Research*.

Simply put, **action research** is the classroom-based study by teachers, individually or collaboratively, of how to improve instruction. As in the *reflection-in-action* approach described earlier in this chapter, action research begins with a teacher-identified question, issue, or problem. For example, Laura Jordan, a middle school teacher, explains how she designed an action research study (published in *Networks*) in response to her students' lack of involvement in class activities:

> The students enrolled in my sixth grade advanced language arts class are particularly difficult to engage in discussions and frequently do not put forth their best efforts in completing assignments. [As] a result of my reflections, I discovered that I spend the majority of instructional time lecturing and directing students, as well as giving too few assignments that allow students to express their creativity and individual learning styles.

In light of this realization, I came to the conclusion that I needed to seek a way to engage my students, making learning experiences meaningful and creating in students a spark of excitement for learning. [As] I began this project my goal was to determine whether students would take more ownership of their learning and produce higher quality work if they were allowed to choose responsive activities that reflected their individual learning styles (Jordan and Hendricks 2002).

Action research is also "a natural part of teaching. [T]o be a teacher means to observe students and study classroom interactions, to explore a variety of effective ways of teaching and learning, and to build conceptual frameworks that can guide one's work. This is a personal as well as a professional quest, a journey toward making sense out of and finding satisfaction in one's teaching. It is the work of teacher-researchers" (Fischer 1996, 33). Figure 6.7 presents five steps in the classroom-focused action research cycle.

Not surprisingly, becoming a teacher-researcher is hard work, given the daily demands of teaching itself. However, more schools are redefining the teacher's role to include doing action research. These schools realize that action research can provide data on the effectiveness of educational programs, enhance student learning, and energize teachers for professional growth. Four teachers who are members of the Action Research Laboratory at Highland Park High School near Chicago comment on the benefits of action research:

By far the most rewarding part of working on an action research team was the opportunity to learn and grow with a small group of teacher colleagues. This experience of

Figure 6.7   A classroom-focused action research cycle.

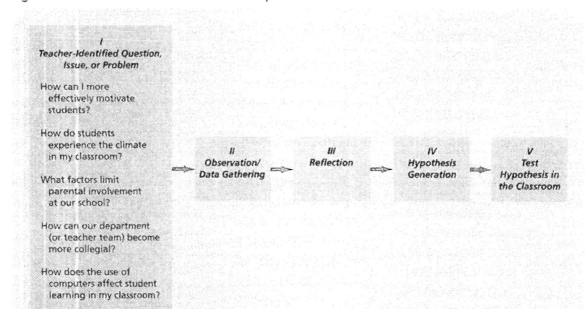

Teachers' *Voices*   Putting Research and Theory into Practice

The Early Literacy Club: Building Excellence through Collaboration

Jane Ching Fung

Every year, California hires thousands of brand-new teachers to its teaching positions. Many of those newly hired teachers enter the classroom with little or no training in the field of education. My concern, as a mentor teacher and former emergency credential teacher, is that these new educators receive adequate support and are provided with professional development opportunities to help them become effective members of our profession.

I teach in an urban primary school located near downtown Los Angeles. Approximately 85 percent of our school population consists of limited-English-speaking students. Almost all of our students receive free or reduced-price meal tickets. Over 60 percent of the teachers at my school are on emergency credentials and have taught less than three years. Although these new teachers are eager to learn and develop their craft, there are few opportunities in our district and at the school site to meet and collaborate on an ongoing basis.

[A] group of new teachers and I created the Early Literacy Club (ELC), a teacher network at our school. Initially, the goal of the ELC was to provide much-needed instructional and emotional support for the overwhelmed new teacher.

Teachers need to discuss their teaching and have ongoing professional discussions with peers, not just read or hear about best practices. New teachers must be given opportunities to "see" what quality teaching looks like in action and be given feedback on their own teaching. [Teachers] and schools involved in these forms of professional development have frequently shown increased student achievement.

The more knowledgeable and successful we are as educators, the more our students will achieve. My study shows the importance of ongoing support and collaboration in the training and retention of new teachers. Networks are one way to improve our teaching practices and train new teachers in a comfortable, risk-free environment.

The network is now a cross-school network and has increased its membership to fourteen. Membership includes: National Board Certified teachers, mentor teachers, literacy and math facilitators, and teacher leaders. The network continues to meet regularly with members' teaching experience ranging from three weeks to fourteen years. The current focus of the network is individual teacher action research. The network's motto remains: *The Early Literacy Club: Building Excellence through Collaboration.*

Questions

1. In what ways might a teacher network support new teachers during their induction into the profession?
2. Why is it important for teachers to "discuss their teaching and have ongoing professional discussions with peers"?
3. Fung started an in-school teacher network focusing on action research and providing support for new teachers. On what other areas might an in-school teacher network focus?

Jane Ching Fung is in her fifteenth year of teaching. She is a MetLife Fellow in the Teachers Network Policy Institute. Her article appeared in Ellen Meyers and Frances Rust (Eds.), *Taking Action with Teacher Research* (Portsmouth, NH: Heinemann, 2003), pp. 41–62.

mutual commitment provided a wonderful staff development experience; by working with these colleagues consistently throughout the year, we were able to explore new ideas and take risks in the classroom with a type of "safety net" in place. For that reason alone, as well as our desire to explore the new questions and challenges raised by our research, we will continue to conduct action research into the effectiveness of our teaching and grading practices (Mills 2000, 97).

This chapter's Teachers' Voices is by Jane Ching Fung, a National Board Certified Teacher at a public school in Los Angeles. Fung started the Early Literacy Club, a support network for new teachers at her school. She conducted an action research project on how a teacher network supports new teachers as they implement state standards in the classroom.

How Are Teachers Providing Leadership for School Restructuring and Curriculum Reform?

Today's teachers welcome opportunities to provide leadership for school restructuring and curriculum reform. Although teachers may have played a limited role in school governance in the past, there are currently many opportunities for teachers to become educational leaders beyond the classroom. Figure 6.8 presents five clusters of educational reform, each of which will offer teachers opportunities to shape policies during the twenty-first century.

Leadership and Collaboration for School Reform

The key to successful school restructuring and curriculum reform is teacher leadership and collaboration. At the National Teacher Forum on Leadership, sponsored by the U.S. Department of Education, participating teachers identified the following ways in which teachers can lead and collaborate for school reform. One example from among the thousands of teachers exercising similar leadership is provided for each leadership activity:

Taking part in school decisions—Melisa Hancock, an elementary school teacher in Kansas, became a clinical instructor at Kansas State University and played a key role in engineering a partnership with the university that led to her school becoming a professional development school.

Defining what students need to know and be able to do—Delaware teacher Jan Parsons was one of several teachers who took leadership roles on Delaware commissions that wrote standards for mathematics, science, social studies, and language arts; teachers also wrote and piloted new statewide assessments in line with the new standards.

Sharing ideas with colleagues—Tom Howe and other Wisconsin teachers developed a "Share Net Program" that allows teachers to make formal presentations to their peers on effective instructional practices.

Being a mentor to new teachers—Science teacher Fie Budzinsky serves as a Teacher Mentor for the State of Connecticut; Budzinsky had, in turn, been mentored earlier in her career by Dick Reagan, another science teacher.

Helping to make personnel decisions—North Carolina teacher Mary Ostwalt served on a selection committee formed to replace a teacher who resigned; other teachers in her district serve on selection committees for the hiring of new principals.

Figure 6.8 Opportunities for teacher leadership in school restructuring and curriculum reform.

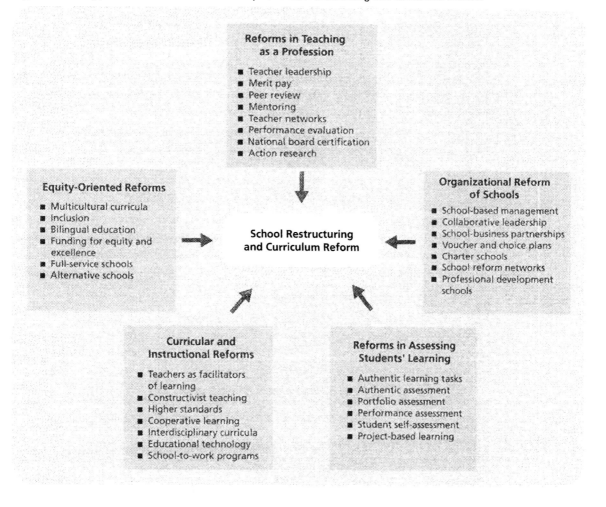

Improving facilities and technology—Ray Hasart and other teachers were the driving force behind the creation of a new $3.5 million technology facility at a Redmond, Oregon, high school; the facility is visited regularly by people throughout the West Coast.

Working with parents—Martina Marquez and a team of colleagues in New Mexico visit Native American villages and surrounding communities to disseminate math and reading activities parents can do with their children.

Creating partnerships with the community—North Carolina teacher Scott Griffin became a member of his community's volunteer fire department and spearheaded the redesign of the fire safety curriculum presented at schools in the community.

Creating partnerships with businesses and organizations—Georgia teacher Stephanie Blakney took the lead in developing a systemwide Partnership with Education program that led to the creation of a food bank and the Atlanta Coca-Cola Bottling Company "adopting" her school.

Creating partnerships with colleges and universities to prepare future teachers—Former Kansas Teacher of the Year Christy McNally and other award-winning teachers organized a partnership with teacher education programs throughout Kansas.

Becoming leaders in the community—Teacher Jacqueline Omland is President of the Legion auxiliary in Aberdeen, South Dakota, and a colleague is Chairman of the Legion.

Becoming politically involved—Washington State teacher Ivy Chan served as treasurer for a person who ran for State Superintendent of Public Instruction.

Leading efforts to make teachers more visible and communicate positive information—High school teacher Larry Torres started a weekly news column in his New Mexico community paper that focuses on positive articles about education; the column has now expanded to a full page.

Collaborative School Reform Networks

Many teachers are involved in restructuring and curriculum change through their schools' participation in collaborative networks for reform. Networks provide teachers with training and resources for restructuring, and they create opportunities for teachers at network schools to help teachers at non-network schools with their restructuring efforts. Among the many collaborative reform networks are the Coalition of Essential Schools, the National Network for Educational Renewal, Accelerated Schools, and state-based networks, such as the League of Professional Schools.

Coalition of Essential Schools   The **Coalition of Essential Schools (CES)**, started in 1984 by Theodore R. Sizer at Brown University, consists of nineteen regional centers that offer direct support to hundreds of schools in the areas of school organization, classroom practice, leadership, and community connections. The regional centers, with the support of CES National, coach schools through a systematic process of change at the school site. No two Coalition schools are alike; each develops an approach to restructuring suited to its students, faculty, and community. However, the efforts of Coalition schools to restructure are guided by ten Common Principles extrapolated from Sizer's (1997a, 1997b, 1997c; Sizer and Sizer 1999) books on redesigning U.S. schools and the beliefs that top-down, standardized solutions to school problems don't work and that teachers must play a key role in the operation of their schools. Recently, the Coalition organized resource centers so teachers at Coalition schools can provide non-Coalition schools with restructuring assistance.

National Network for Educational Renewal   The Center for Educational Renewal at the University of Washington created the **National Network for Educational Renewal (NNER)** to encourage new opportunities for teachers to become involved in school restructuring, curriculum reform, and the preparation of teachers. The NNER consists of nineteen settings in eighteen states, and its members include forty-one colleges and universities, more than one hundred school districts, and over 750 "partner" schools. The NNER is based on nineteen postulates for reforming teacher education that John Goodlad presented in *Educational Renewal: Better Teachers, Better Schools* (1994). For a school to become a member of the NNER, its teachers must demonstrate that they "understand their appropriate role in site-based management and school renewal" (89).

Accelerated Schools   Stanford economist Henry M. Levin has developed a nation-wide network of accelerated schools that provide enriched, rigorous curricula to "speed up" the learning of students at risk. Instead of placing at-risk students into remedial classes, accelerated schools provide students with challenging learning activities traditionally reserved for gifted and talented students. **Accelerated schools** are based on the belief that teachers—in collaboration with administrators, parents, and community members—must be able to make important educational decisions, take responsibility for implementing those decisions, and take responsibility for the outcomes of those decisions. The National Center for the Accelerated Schools Project at Stanford operates eleven regional Accelerated Schools Satellite Centers across the country. The satellite centers provide assistance to teachers and administrators who wish to restructure their schools according to the accelerated schools model.

State-Based Educational Partnerships   Many states have established state-based partnerships between a state university or college and a coalition of public schools. Several of these partnerships are patterned after the League of Professional Schools started by Carl Glickman at the University of Georgia. The overall goal of the League is to improve student learning by using shared governance and action research to focus on instructional and curricular issues. Following guidelines Glickman has outlined in *Holding Sacred Ground: Essays on Leadership, Courage, and Sustaining Great Schools* (2003) and *Revolutionizing America's Schools* (1998), League schools usually begin the restructuring process by developing a *covenant*, a set of mutually agreed on beliefs about how students learn best, and a *charter*, a set of democratically developed guidelines for how shared governance will operate at the school. Presently, nearly one hundred League schools exchange resources and ideas and support one another in their restructuring efforts.

How Will Teachers Shape the Future of Teaching?

Of course, no one really knows how teachers will shape the future of teaching. Nevertheless, it is possible for teachers to create, actively and purposely, a desired future for teaching. In regard to the future, teachers have two choices: (1) to *react* in an unfocused manner to the forces and trends that shape the teaching profession; or, (2) to provide leadership to *create a* desired future for the profession. The aim of this book has been to provide you with an understanding of the social forces and trends that are shaping the future of teaching. That understanding will enable you to become a teacher-leader who contributes to a desired future for teaching as a profession.

A School of the Future

To suggest a vision of what the future of teaching might be like, this book closes with a tour of Eastside School, a hypothetical public school in the year 2030. The conditions under which teachers work at Eastside provide a dramatic contrast to those that teachers experienced during the first decade of the twenty-first century. In short, teachers at this school of the future are well-paid, highly trained, self-governing professionals who have developed specialized areas of expertise.

Eastside is located in a medium-sized city. All of the teachers at Eastside have been certified by the National Board for Professional Teaching Standards (NBPTS). The salaries of these board-certified teachers are on a par with those of other professionals with comparable education and training. About half of the fifty-five teachers at Eastside have also earned the advanced professional certificate now offered by the NBPTS. These teachers are known as *lead teachers*, and their salaries are on a par with physicians, nearly all of whom now work for huge nationwide healthcare providers.

Eastside has no principal; the school is run by an executive committee of five lead teachers elected by all teachers at the school. One of these lead teachers is elected to serve as committee chair for a two-year period. In addition, the school has several paid interns and residents who are assigned to lead teachers as part of their graduate-level teacher-preparation program. Finally, teachers are assisted by a diagnostician; hypermedia specialist; computer specialist; video specialist; social worker; school psychologist; four counselors; special remediation teachers in reading, writing, mathematics, and oral communication; bilingual and ESL teachers; and special-needs teachers.

Eastside operates many programs that illustrate the close ties the school has developed with parents, community agencies, and businesses. The school houses a daycare center that provides after-school employment for several students from the nearby high school. On weekends and on Monday, Wednesday, and Friday evenings the school is used for adult education and for various community group activities. Executives from three local businesses spend one day a month at the school visiting with classes and telling students about their work. Students from a nearby college participate in a tutoring program at Eastside, and the college operates several on-campus summer enrichment programs for Eastside students.

Eastside has a school-based health clinic that offers health care services and a counseling center that provides individual and family counseling. In addition, from time to time Eastside teachers and students participate in service-learning activities in the community. At the present time, for example, a few classes are helping the city develop a new recycling program.

All the facilities at Eastside—classrooms, library, multimedia learning center, gymnasium, the cafeteria, and private offices for teachers—have been designed to create a teaching/learning environment free of all health and safety hazards. The cafeteria, for example, serves meals based on findings from nutrition research about the best foods and methods of cooking. The school is carpeted throughout, and classrooms are soundproofed and well lit. Classroom walls are painted in soft pastels tastefully accented with potted plants, original paintings, wall hangings, and large murals depicting life in different cultures.

The dress, language, and behaviors of teachers, students, and support personnel at Eastside reflect a rich array of cultural backgrounds. In the cafeteria, for example, it is impossible not to hear several languages being spoken and to see at least a few students and teachers wearing non-Western clothing. From the displays of students' work on bulletin boards in hallways and in classrooms, to the international menu offered in the cafeteria, there is ample evidence that Eastside is truly a multicultural school and that gender, race, and class biases have been eliminated.

Each teacher at Eastside is a member of a teaching team and spends at least part of his or her teaching time working with other members of the team. Furthermore, teachers determine their schedules, and every effort is made to assign teachers according to their particular teaching expertise. Students attend Eastside by choice for its excellent teachers; its curricular emphasis on problem solving, human relations, creative thinking, and critical thinking; and its programs for helping at-risk students achieve academic success.

Instruction at Eastside is supplemented by the latest technologies. The school subscribes to several computer databases and cable television services, which teachers and students use regularly. The hypermedia learning center has an extensive collection of CD-ROMs and computer software, much of it authored by Eastside teachers. The center also has virtual-reality interactive videodisc systems, workstations equipped with the latest robotics, and an extensive lab with voice-activated computers.

Every classroom has a video camera, fax machine, hypermedia system, and telephone that, in addition to everyday use, are used frequently during satellite video teleconferences with business executives, artists, scientists, scholars, and students at schools in other states and countries. Eastside's technological capabilities permit students to move their education beyond the classroom walls, as they determine much of how, when, where, and what they learn.

Tomorrow's Teachers

As the preceding scenario suggests, there is a high probability that teaching and the conditions under which teachers work will change in fundamental and positive ways during the next few decades. Teaching will become increasingly professionalized, for example, through such changes as more lengthy and rigorous preprofessional training programs, salary increases that put teaching on a par with other professions requiring similar education, and greater teacher autonomy and an expanded role for teachers in educational policy making. There will be more male teachers who are African Americans, Hispanic and Latino, or members of other minority groups. There will be greater recognition for high-performing teachers and schools through such mechanisms as merit pay plans, master teacher programs, and career ladders. Tomorrow's teachers will achieve new and higher levels of specialization. The traditional teaching job will be divided into parts. Some of the new jobs may be the following:

- Learning diagnostician
- Researcher for software programs
- Courseware writer
- Curriculum designer
- Mental health diagnostician
- Evaluator of learning performances
- Evaluator of social skills
- Small-group learning facilitator
- Large-group learning facilitator
- Media-instruction producer
- Home-based instruction designer
- Home-based instruction monitor

Though the author is unable to hand you an educational crystal ball to foretell the future of teaching, he hopes that this book has provided you with the knowledge and inspiration to help shape a desired future for teaching. Certainly, visions of the future, such as the one of Eastside School, will not become a reality without dedication and hard work. The creation of schools like Eastside will require commitment and vision on the part of professional teachers like you. *Social Foundations for Becoming a Teacher* ends by challenging you to demonstrate the vision and commitment that will move the teaching profession toward such a future.

Summary

To What Extent Is Teaching a Full Profession?

- Teachers are assuming new leadership roles beyond the classroom as educational systems become more decentralized and approaches to school leadership become more collaborative and participatory.

- For an occupation to be considered a profession, it must satisfy several criteria. Of the following nine criteria for a profession, teaching meets some more fully than others: (1) institutional monopoly of services; (2) teacher autonomy; (3) years of education and training; (4) provision of essential service; (5) degree of self-governance; (6) professional associations; (7) professional knowledge and skills; (8) level of public trust; and (9) prestige, benefits, and pay.

- Although teaching does not currently satisfy all criteria for a profession, the collaborative efforts of individuals and groups such as the National Commission on Teaching and America's Future and the National Board for Professional Teaching Standards are rapidly professionalizing teaching.

What Is Professionalism in Teaching?

- The most potent force for enhancing the professional status of teaching is for teachers to see that their actions are professional and to commit themselves to lifelong learning and active involvement in the profession.
- Professional behavior as a teacher is characterized by reflection-in-action (the ability to observe sensitively in classrooms, reflect on those observations, and then act accordingly) and a willingness to serve as a mentor to those entering the profession.
- As lifelong learners, professional teachers actively seek opportunities for growth—from participating in training provided by a school district to arranging one's own "in-service" activities, to acquiring new leadership skills.

To What Professional Organizations Do Teachers Belong?

- Teachers help shape education as a profession through their leadership roles in more than five hundred national teacher organizations.
- As the oldest and largest professional organization for educators, the National Education Association has played a key role in addressing issues of concern to the 78 percent of its members who are teachers.
- Affiliated with organized labor and open only to teachers and nonsupervisory personnel, the American Federation of Teachers has done much to secure greater financial rewards and improved working conditions for teachers.
- After years of competition and conflicting views about collective bargaining, teacher strikes, and affiliation with organized labor, the NEA and AFT formed the NEAFT Partnership to work toward shared goals for improving the profession of teaching.
- Teachers are members of professional associations for specific subject areas and student populations.

What New Leadership Roles for Teachers Are Emerging?

- Through their involvement with professional development schools, the National Board for Professional Teaching Standards, and local, state, and national education committees, teachers participate in making key decisions about teacher preparation, certification, and staff development.
- In their new role as teacher-leaders, many teachers are playing a key role beyond the classroom as they form partnerships that focus on the transformation of schools in the United States.
- Teachers who work collaboratively with principals on school improvement are involved in eleven dimensions of teacher leadership beyond the classroom: team building, project management, designing and delivering staff development, researching, public relations, visioning, program/school evaluation, change facilitation, networking and partnership building, grant writing/seeking external funding, and mentoring new teachers.

How Do Teachers Contribute to Educational Research?

- Teachers validate the accuracy and usefulness of educational research and identify additional areas to research when they put "research into practice."
- When conducting action research, teachers follow a five-step classroom-focused action research cycle to understand the dynamics of their classrooms and to improve their teaching: identify a question, issue, or problem; observe/gather data; reflect; generate a hypothesis; and test hypothesis.

How Are Teachers Providing Leadership for School Restructuring and Curriculum Reform?

- Five "clusters" of educational reform provide teachers with many opportunities to provide leadership for school restructuring and curriculum reform: reforms in teaching as a profession, equity-oriented reforms, organizational reform of schools, reforms in assessing students' learning, and curricular and instructional reforms.
- Through collaborative school reform networks such as the Coalition of Essential Schools, the National

Network for Educational Renewal, Accelerated Schools, and the League of Professional Schools, teachers provide leadership for restructuring their schools and help other teachers promote school reform at non-network schools.

How Will Teachers Shape the Future of Teaching?

○ It is not unrealistic to imagine that teachers in schools of the future will be well-paid, NBPTS-certified, self-governing professionals who have developed specialized areas of expertise. This vision becomes more possible with each teacher who makes a commitment to its realization.

Key Terms and Concepts

accelerated schools, 251
action research, 245
American Federation of Teachers (AFT), 231
Association for Supervision and Curriculum Development (ASCD), 233
Coalition of Essential Schools (CES), 250
Educational Resources Information Center (ERIC), 243
ERIC Clearinghouses, 243

mentor, 224
National Education Association (NEA), 229
National Network for Educational Renewal (NNER), 250
NEAFT Partnership, 232
Office of Educational Research and Improvement (OERI), 244
Phi Delta Kappa (PDK), 233
profession, 214
professionalization of teaching, 214

reflection-in-action, 224
Regional Educational Laboratories, 243
Research and Development Centers, 243
scientifically based research (SBR), 245
teacher-leader, 237
teacher-researcher, 242
What Works Clearinghouse (WWC), 244

Reflective Application Activities

Discussion Questions

1. In your opinion, what accounts for public trust and lack of trust in the teaching profession? What might be the best way to increase that trust?

2. Review several recent issues of the NEA publication, *NEA Today*, and the AFT publication, *American Teacher*. Compare and contrast concerns or issues that each publication addresses. What overall differences do you find between the NEA and AFT publications?

Professional Journal

1. Reflect on your experiences working in two types of groups—one group whose members collaborated successfully, the other whose members did not. In retrospect, what might have accounted for the ability of one group to collaborate and the inability of the other group? Review the "individual" and "group" communication guidelines developed by the Anzar High School teachers (see page 228). What additional "individual"

and "group" guidelines are necessary if members of a group are to collaborate effectively?

2. Imagine what it might be like to teach in the year 2030. Describe a "typical" day in the life of a teacher. How does your hypothetical scenario compare with the one presented at the end of this chapter?

Online Assignments

1. With classmates, join an online discussion on one or more of the following topics or another topic in Chapter 6 of this text.

action research

educational reform

grant writing

mentoring

National Board for Professional Teaching Standards (NBPTS)

school restructuring

teacher leadership

teacher–principal collaboration

teacher strikes

teacher unions

2. Using your favorite search engine, gather online information and resources about school networking and teacher networking. How might online networking contribute to your preparation as a teacher? As a teacher, how might you and your students use networking in connection with your curriculum? What knowledge and skills do you need to start to participate in a school-based networking project?

Observations and Interviews

1. Interview teachers about their involvement in professional associations and the teachers' union. What benefits do teachers obtain from their professional involvement?

2. Collaborate with classmates to study a school that is involved in restructuring and participants' roles in the change process. Compare teachers' activities with the new leadership roles for teachers discussed in this chapter. Are any of the teachers involved in action research in the classroom? How does teacher research contribute to restructuring efforts?

Professional Portfolio

Focusing on the grade level and subject area for which you are preparing to teach, consult several of the sources of educational research listed in this chapter and prepare a set of research findings to guide your teaching. For each entry, include a bibliographic citation and an annotation that briefly describes the research and the results of that research.

Appendix 6.1
Professional Organizations for Teachers

American Alliance for Health, Physical Education, Recreation and Dance (AAHPERD)
1900 Association Drive
Reston, VA 20191
(703) 476-3400
Fax (703) 476-9527
info@aahperd.org
Students and educators in physical education, dance, health, athletics, safety education, recreation, and outdoor education. Purpose is to improve its fields of education at all levels through such services as consultation, periodicals and special publications, leadership development, determination of standards, and research. Publications: *AAHPERD Update; Health Education; American Journal of Physical Education, Recreation and Dance; Leisure Today; News Kit on Programs for the Aging; Research Quarterly.*

American Alliance of Teachers of French (AATF)
57 E. Armory Avenue
Champaign, IL 61820
(217) 333-2842
Fax (217) 333-2842
Teachers of French in public and private elementary and secondary schools, colleges, and universities. Maintains Pedagogical Aids Bureau, conducts annual French contest in elementary and secondary schools, awards scholarships to teachers for study in France, maintains placement bureau and a pen pal agency. Publications: *AATF National Bulletin, French Review.*

American Association of Teachers of German (AATG)
112 Haddontowne Court, No. 104
Cherry Hill, NJ 08034
(609) 795-5553
Fax (609) 795-9398
73740.3231@compuserve.com
Teachers of German at all levels. Offers in-service teacher-training workshops and awards and schol-

arships to outstanding high school students and teachers of German. Publications: *American Association of Teachers of German—Newsletter, Die Unterrichtspraxis: For the Teaching of German, German Quarterly.*

American Association of Teachers of Spanish and Portuguese (Hispanic) (AATSP)
University of Northern Colorado
Gunter Hall
Greeley, CO 80636
(970) 351-1090
lsandste@bentley.univnorthco.edu
Teachers of Spanish and Portuguese languages and literatures and others interested in Hispanic culture. Operates placement bureau and maintains pen pal registry. Sponsors honor society, Sociedad Honoraria Hispanica, and National Spanish Examinations for secondary school students. Publication: *Hispania.*

American Classical League (Language) (ACL)
Miami University
Oxford, OH 45056
(513) 529-7741
Fax (513) 529-7742
americanclassicalleague@muohio.edu
Teachers of classical languages in high schools and colleges. To promote the teaching of Latin and other classical languages. Maintains placement service, teaching materials, and resource center. Publications: *Classical Outlook, Prima* (handbook for elementary school teachers).

American Council on the Teaching of Foreign Languages (ACTEL)
6 Executive Plaza
Yonkers, NY 10701-6801
(914) 963-8830
Fax (914) 963-1275
Individuals interested in the teaching of classical and modern foreign languages in schools and colleges.

Operates materials center, conducts seminars and workshops, and presents awards. Publications: *ACTFL Newsletter, Foreign Language Annals* (professional journal covering teaching methods and educational research).

American Federation of Teachers (AFT)
555 New Jersey Avenue NW
Washington, DC 20001
(202) 879-4400
(800) 242-5465
Works with teachers and other educational employees at the state and local level in organizing, collective bargaining, research, educational issues, and public relations. Conducts research in areas such as educational reform, bilingual education, teacher certification, and evaluation. Represents members' concerns through legislative action; offers technical assistance. Operates Education for Democracy Project. Publications: *American Educator, American Teacher, On Campus, Public Service Reporter*, and others.

Association of American Educators (AAE)
26012 Marguerite Parkway #333
Mission Viejo, CA 92692
(800) 704-7799
(949) 595-7979
A nonpartisan, nonprofit professional association designed to provide an "alternative to the partisan politics and social agendas of the national teacher unions." Membership open to any employee of an educational entity. According to the AAE, "the 'values-neutral' teaching experiment has been a monumental failure and has led to much of the public's negative opinion of our profession. We believe our schools must once again integrate academics, character, and citizenship."

Association for Childhood Education International (ACEI)
11501 Georgia Avenue, Suite 315
Wheaton, MD 20902
(301) 942-2443
(800) 423-3563
aceihq@aol.com
Teachers, parents, and other caregivers in thirty-one countries interested in promoting good educational practices for children from infancy through early adolescence. Conducts workshops and travel/study tours abroad, bestows awards, conducts research and educational programs, maintains speakers bureau. Publications: *ACEI Exchange, Childhood Education, Journal of Research in Childhood Education.*

Association for Supervision and Curriculum Development (ASCD)
1250 N. Pitt Street
Alexandria, VA 22314-1403
(703) 549-9110
Fax (703) 549-3891
member@ascd.org
Professional organization of supervisors, curriculum coordinators and directors, consultants, professors of education, classroom teachers, principals, superintendents, parents, and others interested in school improvement at all levels of education. Provides professional development experiences and training in curriculum and supervision; provides Research Information Service. Publications: *ASCD Update, Curriculum and Supervision.*

Council for Exceptional Children (CEC)
1920 Association Drive
Reston, VA 22091-1589
(703) 620-3660
cec@sped.org
www.cec.sped.org
Teachers, school administrators, teacher educators, and others with a direct or indirect concern for the education of the disabled and gifted. Provides information to teachers, parents, and others concerning the education of exceptional children. Maintains 63,000 volume library. Operates the ERIC Clearinghouse on Handicapped and Gifted Children. Publications: *Exceptional Child Education Resources, Exceptional Children, Teaching Exceptional Children.*

Education International (EI)
Boulevard Emile Jacqmain 155 (8th floor)
1210 Brussels, Belgium
32-2-224-06-80
FAX 32-2-224-06-06
World's largest educators' federation, representing 23 million members in more than 150 countries. EI's 294 member organizations include the NEA.

Foundation for Exceptional Children (FEC)
1920 Association Drive
Reston, VA 22091
(703) 620-1054
Institutions, agencies, educators, parents, and persons concerned with the education and personal welfare of gifted or disabled children. Established to further the educational, vocational, social, and personal needs of the disabled child or youth and the neglected educational needs of the gifted. Publication: *Foundation for Exceptional Children—Focus.*

International Reading Association (IRA)
800 Barksdale Road
P.O. Box 8139
Newark, DE 19714-8139
(302) 731-1600
Fax (302) 731-1057
73314.1411@compuserve.com
Teachers, reading specialists, consultants, administrators, supervisors, researchers, psychologists, librarians, and parents interested in promoting literacy. Seeks to improve the quality of reading instruction at all educational levels; stimulate and promote the lifetime reading habit and an awareness of the impact of reading; encourage the development of every reader's proficiency to the highest possible level. Disseminates information pertaining to research on reading. Publications: *Desktop Reference to the International Reading Association, Journal of Reading Reading Teacher, Reading Today.*

Music Teachers National Association (MTNA)
617 Vine Street, Suite 1432
Cincinnati, OH 45202
(513) 421-1420
Fax (513) 421-2503
mtnaadmin@aol.com
Professional society of music teachers in studios conservatories, music schools, and public and private schools, colleges, and universities; undergraduate and graduate music students. Seeks to raise the level of musical performance, understanding, and instruction. Publications: *American Music Teacher Magazine, Music Teachers National Association— Directory of Nationally Certified Teachers.*

National Art Education Association (Arts) (NAEA)
1916 Association Drive
Reston, VA 22091-1590
(703) 860-8000
Fax (703) 860-2960
naea@dgs.dgsys.com
Teachers of art at elementary, secondary, and college levels; colleges, libraries, museums, and other educational institutions. Studies problems of teaching art; encourages research and experimentation. Serves as clearinghouse for information on art education programs, materials, and methods of instruction. Maintains placement services and library on art education. Publications: *Art Education, Studies in Art Education.*

National Association for Bilingual Education (Bilingualism) (NABE)
1220 L Street NW
Suite 605
Washington, DC 20005-4018
(202) 898-1829
Fax (202) 789-2866
Educators, administrators, paraprofessionals, community and laypeople, and students. Purposes are to recognize, promote, publicize bilingual education. Seeks to increase public understanding of the importance of language and culture. Utilizes and develops student proficiency and ensures equal opportunities in bilingual education for language-minority students. Works to preserve and expand the nation's linguistic resources. Educates language-minority parents in public policy decisions. Promotes research in language education, linguistics, and multicultural education. Coordinates development of professional standards. Publications: *Annual Conference Journal, Journal, Newsletter.*

National Association of Biology Teachers (NABT)
11250 Roger Bacon Drive, No. 19
Reston, VA 22090
(703) 471-1134
nabter@aol.com
Professional society of biology and life science teachers and teacher educators at all educational levels. Works to achieve scientific literacy among citizens. Promotes professional growth and development; fosters regional activities for biology teachers; con-

fronts issues involving biology, society, and the future; provides a national voice for the profession. Publications: *American Biology Teacher, National Association of Biology Teachers—News and Views*, and others.

National Association for the Education of Young Children (NAEYC)
1509 16th Street NW
Washington, DC 20036
(202) 232-8777
(800) 424-2460
Fax (202) 328-1846
naeyc@org/naeyc
Teachers and directors of preschool and primary schools, kindergartens, child care centers, cooperatives, church schools, and groups having similar programs for young children. Open to all individuals interested in serving and acting on behalf of the needs and rights of young children, with primary focus on the provision of educational services and resources. Offers voluntary accreditation for early childhood schools and centers through the National Academy of Early Childhood Programs. Publications: *Early Childhood Research Quarterly, Young Children*.

National Association for Gifted Children (NAGC)
1707 L Street NW
Suite 550
Washington, DC 20036
(202) 785-4268
Teachers, university personnel, administrators, and parents. To advance interest in programs for the gifted. Seeks to further education of the gifted and to enhance their potential creativity. Distributes information to teachers and parents on the development of the gifted child; sponsors annual convention to provide training in curriculum planning, program evaluation, and parenting and guidance relevant to gifted children. Maintains speakers' bureau. Publication: *Gifted Child Quarterly*.

National Association for Trade and Industrial Education (NATIE)
P.O. Box 1665
Leesburg, VA 22075
(703) 777-1740

Educators in trade and industrial education. Works for the promotion, development, and improvement of trade and industrial education. Supports instructional programs for members to prepare for job instruction, apprentice training, adult retraining, and special training for industry. Publications: *NATIE News Notes, State Supervisors/Consultants of Trade and Industrial Education*, and others.

National Business Education Association (NBEA)
1914 Association Drive
Reston, VA 22091
(703) 860-8300
Teachers of business subjects in secondary and post-secondary schools and colleges; administrators and research workers in business education; business-people interested in business education; teachers in educational institutions training business teachers. Publication: *Business Education Forum*.

National Council for the Social Studies (NCSS)
3501 Newark Street, NW
Washington, DC 20016
(202) 966-7840
Fax (202) 966-2061
ncss@ncss.org
Teachers of elementary and secondary social studies, including instructors of civics, geography, history, economics, political science, psychology, sociology, and anthropology. Publications: *Social Education, The Social Studies Professional, Social Studies and the Young Learner, Theory and Research in Social Education*.

National Council of Teachers of English (NCTE)
1111 West Kenyon Road
Urbana, IL 61801
(217) 328-3870
Fax (217) 328-9645
Teachers of English at all school levels. Works to increase the effectiveness of instruction in English language and literature. Presents achievement awards for writing to high school juniors and students in the eighth grade, and awards for high school literary magazines. Provides information and aids for teachers involved in formulating objectives, writing and evaluating curriculum guides, and planning in-service programs for

teacher education. Publications: *English Education, English Journal, Language Arts, Research in the Teaching of English*, and others.

National Council of Teachers of Mathematics (NCTM)
1906 Association Drive
Reston, VA 22091-1593
(703) 620-9840
Fax (703) 476-2970
infocentra@nctm.org
Teachers of mathematics in grades K–12, two-year colleges, and teacher educators. Publications: *Arithmetic Teacher, Journal for Research in Mathematics Education, Mathematics Teacher, National Council of Teachers of Mathematics—Yearbook*, and others.

National Education Association (NEA)
1201 16th Street, NW
Washington, DC 20036
(202) 833-4000
Professional organization and union of elementary and secondary school teachers, college and university professors, administrators, principals, counselors and others concerned with education. Publications: *NEA Today, Thought and Action*, and others.

National Middle School Association (NMSA)
4151 Executive Parkway, Suite 300
Westerville, OH 43081
(800) 528-NMSA (6672)
info@NMSA.org
Professional organization for teachers, administrators, parents, and others interested in the education of young adolescents (ten to fifteen years of age). The only national organization devoted to improving the education of young adolescents, NMSA has more than 20,000 members worldwide. State, provincial, and international affiliates work to provide support for middle-level education at the local level. Publications: *Middle School Journal, Middle Ground*, and others.

National Science Teachers Association (NSTA)
1840 Wilson Blvd.
Arlington, VA 22201-3000
(703) 243-7100
Fax (703) 243-7177

Teachers seeking to foster excellence in science teaching. Studies students and how they learn, the curriculum of science, the teacher and his or her preparation, the procedures used in classroom and laboratory, the facilities for teaching science, and the evaluation procedures used. Affiliated with American Association for the Advancement of Science. Publications: *Journal of College Science Teaching, Quantum, Science and Children, Science Scope, The Science Teacher.*

Phi Delta Kappa
8th and Union
P.O. Box 789
Bloomington, IN 47402-0789
(812) 339-1156
(800) 766-1156
Fax (812) 339-0018
headquarters@pdkintl.org
Professional, honorary, and recognition fraternity—education. To enhance quality education through research and leadership activities. Conducts seminars and workshops. Publications: *Phi Delta Kappan*, and others.

Pi Lambda Theta
4101 E. 3rd Street
P.O. Box 6626
Bloomington, IN 47407-6626
(812) 339-3411
members@pilambda.org
Honor and professional association—education. Presents biennial awards. Sponsors comparative education tours and educational conferences. Publication: *Educational Horizons.*

Reading Is Fundamental (RIF)
600 Maryland Avenue, SW, Suite 800
Washington, DC 20024
(202) 287-3220
Fax (202) 287-3196
Volunteer groups composed of community leaders, educators, librarians, parents, and service club members who sponsor local grassroots reading motivation programs serving three million children nationwide. Purpose is to involve youngsters, preschool to high school age, in reading activities aimed at showing that reading is fun. Provides

services to parents to help them encourage reading in the home. Publication: *RIF Newsletter*.

Speech Communication Association (SCA)
5105 Backlick Road, Bldg. E
Annandale, VA 22003
(703) 750-0533
Fax (703) 914-9471
Elementary, secondary, college, and university teachers, speech clinicians, media specialists, communication consultants, students, theater directors, and others. To promote study, criticism, research, teaching, and application of the artistic, humanistic, and scientific principles of communication, particularly speech communication. Sponsors the publication of scholarly volumes in speech. Conducts international debate tours in the United States and abroad. Maintains placement service. Publications: *Communication Education, Speech Communication Teacher, Text and Per-formance Quarterly*, and others.

Teachers of English to Speakers of Other Languages (TESOL)
1600 Cameron Street, Suite 300
Alexandria, VA 22314-2751
(703) 836-0774
Fax (703) 836-7864
tesol@tesol.edu
School, college, and adult education teachers who teach English as a second or foreign language. Aims to improve the teaching of English as a second or foreign language by promoting research, disseminating information, developing guidelines and promoting certification, and serving as a clearinghouse for the field. Offers placement service. Publications: *Directory of Professional Preparation, TESOL Journal, TESOL Quarterly*, and others.

For complete information on professional organizations, see *Encyclopedia of Associations* (2003), Gale Research, Inc.

Glossary

A

Academies (p. 99): early secondary schools with broader and more practical curricula than those found in grammar schools of the previous era.

Accelerated schools (p. 251): a national network of schools that provide enriched, rigorous curricula to "speed up" the learning of students at risk.

Accountability (p. 116): the practice of holding teachers responsible for adhering to high professional and moral standards and creating effective learning environments for all students.

Action research (p. 245): classroom-based study, by teachers, of how to improve their instruction.

Adequate Yearly Progress (AYP) (p. 9): a provision of the No Child Left Behind Act of 2001 requiring that schools provide evidence each year that students are making "adequate yearly progress."

Afrocentric schools (p. 139): schools that focus on African American history and cultures for African American pupils.

Alternative school (p. 16, 197): a small, highly individualized school separate from a regular school; designed to meet the needs of students at risk.

American Federation of Teachers (AFT) (p. 231): a national professional association for teachers, affiliated with the AFL-CIO.

A Nation at Risk (p. 46): a 1983 national report critical of U.S. education.

Association for Supervision and Curriculum Development (ASCD) (p. 233): a professional organization for educators interested in school improvement at all levels.

B

Bicultural (p. 147): the ability to function effectively in two or more linguistic and cultural groups.

Bilingual education (p. 129): a curriculum for non-English-speaking and English-speaking students in which two languages are used for instruction and biculturalism is emphasized.

Brown v. Board of Education of Topeka (p. 114): a 1954 landmark U.S. Supreme Court case rejecting the "separate but equal" doctrine used to prevent African Americans from attending schools with whites.

C

Classroom culture (p. 26): the "way of life" characteristic of a classroom group; determined by the social dimensions of the group and the physical characteristics of the setting.

Coalition of Essential Schools (p. 250): a national network of public and private high schools that have restructured according to nine Common Principles.

Commission on the Reorganization of Secondary Education (p. 107): an NEA committee that called for a high school curriculum designed to accommodate individual differences in scholastic ability and based on seven educational goals, or "cardinal principles" (1913).

Committee of Fifteen (p. 107): an NEA committee that recommended an academically rigorous curriculum for elementary students (1895).

Committee of Ten (p. 106): an NEA committee that recommended an academically rigorous curriculum for high school students (1893).

Common schools (p. 102): free state-supported schools that provide education for all students.

Comparative education (p. 32): the comparative study of educational practices in different countries.

Compensatory education programs (p. 196): federally funded educational programs designed to meet the needs of low-ability students from low-income families.

Cultural identity (p. 128): an overall sense of oneself, derived from the extent of one's participation in various subcultures within the national macroculture.

Cultural pluralism (p. 127): the preservation of cultural differences among groups of people within one society. This view is in contrast to the melting-pot theory that says that ethnic cultures should melt into one.

Culture (p. 127): the way of life common to a group of people; includes knowledge deemed important, shared meanings, norms, values, attitudes, ideals, and view of the world.

D

Dame schools (p. 94): colonial schools, usually held in the homes of widows or housewives, for teaching children basic reading, writing, and mathematical skills.

Departmentalization (p. 25): an organizational arrangement for schools in which students move from classroom to classroom for instruction in different subject areas.

Desegregation (p. 114): the process of eliminating schooling practices based on the separation of racial groups.

Diversity (p. 126): differences among people in regard to gender, race, ethnicity, culture, and socioeconomic status.

E

Education for All Handicapped Children Act (Public Law 94-142) (p. 117): a 1975 federal act that guarantees a free and appropriate education to all handicapped children (often referred to as the *mainstreaming law* or *Public Law 94-142*).

Educational reform movement (p. 78): a comprehensive effort made during the 1980s and into the 1990s to improve schools and the preparation of teachers.

Educational Resources Information Center (ERIC) (p. 243): a national information system made up of sixteen clearinghouses that formerly disseminated descriptions of exemplary programs, results of research and development efforts, and related information. ERIC clearinghouses were closed in 2004; however, ERIC continues to provide a centralized database of journal articles and other published and unpublished education materials.

Elementary and Secondary Education Act (p. 115): part of President Lyndon B. Johnson's Great Society Program, this act allocated federal funds on the basis of the number of poor children in school districts.

emotional intelligence (12): a level of awareness and understanding of one's emotions that allows the person to achieve personal growth and self-actualization.

ERIC Clearinghouses (p. 243): sixteen Educational Resources Information Clearinghouses that, until their closure in 2004, disseminated descriptions of exemplary education programs, the results of research and development efforts, and related information.

Ethnic group (p. 128): individuals within a larger culture who share a racial or cultural identity and a set of beliefs, values, and attitudes and who consider themselves members of a distinct group or subculture.

Ethnicity (p. 132): a shared feeling of common identity that derives, in part, from a common ancestry, common values, and common experiences.

F

Female seminaries (p. 99): schools established in the early nineteenth century to train women for higher education and public service outside the home.

Freedman's Bureau (p. 98): a federal bureau that created schools for newly freed slaves after the Civil War.

Fringe benefits (p. 56): benefits (i.e., medical insurance, retirement, and tax-deferred investment opportunities) that are given to teachers in addition to base salary.

Full-service schools (p. 193): schools that provide students and their families with medical, social, and human services, in addition to their regular educational programs.

G

Gender bias (p. 160): subtle bias or discrimination on the basis of gender; reduces the likelihood that the target of the bias will develop to the full extent of his or her capabilities.

Gender-fair classroom (p. 160): education that is free of bias or discrimination on the basis of gender.

G.I. Bill of Rights (p. 112): a 1944 federal law that provides veterans with payments for tuition and room and board at colleges and universities and special schools, formally known as the Servicemen's Readjustment Act.

Goals 2000: Educate America Act (8): a comprehensive funding program to help schools achieve a set of eight national goals emphasizing student achievement, effective learning environments, professional development for teachers, and parental involvement.

H

Holmes Group (p. 78): a group of ninety-six colleges of education that prepared *Tomorrow's Teachers*, a 1986 report calling for all teachers to have a bachelor's degree in an academic field and a master's degree in education.

Holmes Partnership (p. 79): a consortium of professional organizations—including the Holmes Group, the National Board for Professional Teaching Standards, the National Education Association, and the American Federation of Teachers—committed to the reform of teacher education.

Horn book (p. 94): a copy of the alphabet covered by a thin transparent sheet made from a cow's horn.

I

Indian Education Act of 1972 and 1974 Amendments (p. 145): a federal law and subsequent amendment designed to provide direct educational assistance to Native American tribes and nations.

Individual racism (p. 135): the prejudicial belief that one's ethnic or racial group is superior to others.

Institution (p. 18): any organization a society establishes to maintain, and improve, its way of life.

Institutional racism (p. 135): institutional policies and practices, intentional or not, that result in racial inequities.

Interactive teaching (p. 74): teaching characterized by face-to-face interactions between teachers and students in contrast to preactive teaching.

Interstate New Teacher Assessment and Support Consortium (INTASC) (p. 14): an organization of states established in 1987 to develop performance-based standards for what beginning teachers should know and be able to do.

K

Kindergarten (p. 106): a school for children before they begin formal schooling at the elementary level; based on the ideas of German educator Friedrick Fröebel, *kindergarten* means "garden where children grow."

L

Latchkey children (p. 181): children who, because of family circumstances, must spend part of each day unsupervised by a parent or guardian.

Latin grammar school (p. 95): colonial schools established to provide male students a precollege education; comparable to today's high schools.

Limited English proficiency (LEP) (p. 129): a designation for students with limited ability to understand, read, or speak English and who have a first language other than English.

M

Magnet school (p. 16): a school offering a curriculum that focuses on a specific area such as the performing arts, mathematics, science, international studies, or technology. Magnet schools, which often draw students from a larger attendance area than regular schools, are frequently developed to promote voluntary desegregation.

Mainstreaming (p. 117): the policy and process of integrating disabled or otherwise exceptional learners into regular classrooms with nonexceptional students.

Massachusetts Act of 1642 (p. 95): a law requiring each town to determine whether its young people could read and write.

Massachusetts Act of 1647 (p. 96): a law mandating the establishment and support of schools; often referred to as the Old Deluder Satan Act because education was seen as the best protection against the wiles of the devil.

McGuffey readers (p. 103): an immensely popular series of reading books for students in grades 1 through 6, written in the 1830s by Reverend William Holmes McGuffey.

McKinney-Vento Act (p. 179): the nation's first law to provide assistance to homeless persons, including free public education for children.

Mentor (p. 224): a wise, knowledgeable individual who provides guidance and encouragement to someone.

Minorities (p. 133): groups of people who share certain characteristics and are smaller in number than the majority of a population.

Monitorial system (p. 92): an instructional method whereby a teacher instructs hundreds of pupils through the use of student monitors—older students selected for their academic abilities; developed by Joseph Lancaster (1778–1838).

Montessori method (p. 110): a method of teaching, developed by Maria Montessori, based on a prescribed set of materials and physical exercises to develop children's knowledge and skills.

Moonlight (p. 56): the practice of holding a second job to increase one's income.

Morrill Land-Grant Act (p. 104): an 1862 act that provided federal land that states could sell or rent to raise funds to establish colleges of agriculture and mechanical arts.

Multicultural curriculum (p. 152): a school curriculum that addresses the needs and backgrounds of all students regardless of their cultural identity and includes the cultural perspectives, or "voices," of people who have previously been silent or marginalized.

Multicultural education (p. 150): education that provides equal educational opportunities to all students—regardless of socioeconomic status; gender; or ethnic, racial, or cultural backgrounds—and is dedicated to reducing prejudice and celebrating the rich diversity of U.S. life.

Multiculturalism (p. 130): a set of beliefs based on the importance of seeing the world from different cultural frames of reference and valuing the diversity of cultures in the global community.

N

National Board for Professional Teaching Standards (NBPTS) (p. 14): a board established in 1987 that began issuing professional certificates in 1994–95 to teachers who possess extensive professional knowledge and the ability to perform at a high level.

National Council for Accreditation of Teacher Education (NCATE) (p. 14): an agency that accredits, on a voluntary basis, almost half of the nation's teacher education programs.

National curriculum (p. 35): a standardized curriculum set at the national level and delivered to students at all schools throughout the country. Usually, countries with national curricula have nationwide testing to assess students' mastery of the curriculum.

National Defense Education Act (p. 113): a 1958 federally sponsored program to promote research and innovation in science, mathematics, modern foreign languages, and guidance.

National Education Association (NEA) (p. 229): the oldest and largest professional association for teachers and administrators.

National Network for Educational Renewal (NNER) (p. 250): a national network of colleges and universities that collaborate with school districts and partner schools to reform education according to nineteen postulates in John Goodlad's *Teachers for Our Nation's Schools* (1990).

NEAFT Partnership (p. 232): an agreement between the National Education Association and the American Federation of Teachers to work collaboratively to attain mutually desired goals for the teaching profession.

No Child Left Behind (NCLB) Act (p. 9): a federal law that mandates statewide testing in reading and mathematics each year in grades 3–8 and holds schools accountable for students' performance on state proficiency tests.

Normal school (p. 103): a school that focuses on the preparation of teachers.

O

Office of Educational Research and Improvement (OERI) (p. 244): a federal agency that promotes educational research and improving schools through the application of research results.

Open-space schools (p. 25): schools that have large instructional areas with movable walls and furniture that can be rearranged easily.

Out-of-school time (OST) activities (p. 198): growth-oriented activities for students that take place beyond the school day; often called "extracurricular activities."

P

Parochial schools (p. 94): schools founded on religious beliefs.

Peer counseling (p. 192): an arrangement whereby students, monitored by a school counselor or teacher, counsel one another in such areas as low achievement, interpersonal problems, substance abuse, and career planning.

Peer mediation (p. 192): experiential activities, such as role playing and simulations, that encourage students to be more accepting of differences and to develop empathy, social skills, and awareness of prejudice.

Phi Delta Kappa (PDK) (p. 233): a professional and honorary fraternity of educators with 650 chapters and 130,000 members.

Praxis Series: Professional Assessments for Beginning Teachers (p. 14): a battery of tests available to states for the initial certification of teachers. Consists of assessments in three areas: academic skills, knowledge of subject, and classroom performance.

Preactive teaching (p. 74): the stage of teaching when a teacher prepares to teach or reflects on previous teaching experiences in contrast with interactive teaching.

Primer (p. 94): a book with very explicit religious and moral messages about the proper conduct of life that colonial children used to learn to read.

Profession (p. 214): an occupation that requires a high level of expertise, including advanced study in a specialized field, adherence to a code of ethics, and the ability to work without close supervision.

Professional development schools (PDS) (p. 78): schools that have formed partnerships with a college or university for the purpose of improving the schools and contributing to the improvement of teacher preparation programs. Activities at a PDS may include collaborative research, team teaching, demonstration lessons by teacher education faculty, and various professional growth opportunities for teachers and teacher educators.

Professional empowerment (p. 65): a trend for teachers to have expanded opportunities to make decisions that affect their professional lives.

Professional standards boards (p. 80): state agencies to regulate and improve the professional practice of teachers, administrators, and other education personnel.

Professionalization of teaching (p. 214): the steadily increasing political influence and status of teaching as a profession; increased political influence and status reflect changes such as expanding leadership opportunities for teachers, national board certification, peer review, shared decision making, and mentor teacher programs.

Progressivism (p. 108): a philosophical orientation based on the belief that life is evolving in a positive direction, that people may be trusted to act in their own best interests, and that education should focus on the needs and interests of students.

R

Race (p. 132): a concept of human variation used to distinguish people on the basis of biological traits and characteristics.

Reading and writing schools (p. 94): colonial schools, supported by public funds and fees paid by parents, that used a religiously oriented curriculum to teach boys reading and writing skills and, to a lesser degree, mathematics.

Reflection-in-action (p. 224): the process of engaging in serious, reflective thought about improving one's professional practice while one is engaged in that practice.

Regional Educational Laboratories (p. 243): nine federally supported, nonprofit agencies that serve a region of the country and work directly with educators to improve schools.

Research and Development Centers (p. 243): fourteen federally supported, university-based centers, each conducting research and development activities in a different area of education.

S

School-based interprofessional case management (p. 195): an approach to education in which professionally trained case managers work directly with teachers, the community, and families to coordinate and deliver appropriate services to at-risk students and their families.

School culture (p. 22): the collective "way of life" characteristic of a school; a set of beliefs, values, traditions, and ways of thinking and behaving that distinguish it from other schools.

School "regularities" (p. 25): the "regular" programmatic and structural features that most schools share—e.g., similar class sizes, 50–60 minute class periods, special programs for students with disabilities, heterogeneous or homogeneous grouping of students, etc.

School traditions (p. 25): those elements of a school's culture that are handed down from year to year.

School-within-a-school (p. 16, 197): an alternative school (within a regular school) designed to meet the needs of students at risk.

Scientific management (p. 105): the application of management principles and techniques to the operation of big business and large school districts.

Scientifically based research (SBR) (p. 245): research that meets the following scientific standards: use of scientific method, replication of results, ability to generalize, rigorous standards and peer review, and consistency of results.

Self-contained classroom (p. 25): an organizational structure for schools in which one teacher instructs a group of students (typically, twenty to thirty) in a single classroom.

Service learning (p. 13): an approach to teaching in which students participate in community-based service activities and then reflect on the meaning of those experiences.

Sex-role socialization (p. 155): socially expected behavior patterns conveyed to individuals on the basis of gender.

Sex-role stereotyping (p. 155): beliefs that subtly encourage males and females to conform to certain behavioral norms regardless of abilities and interests.

Social foundations of education (p. 4): societal trends, issues, and social forces that have shaped (and continue to shape) public and private education in the United States.

Socratic questioning (p. 88): a method of questioning designed to lead students to see errors and inconsistencies in their thinking, based on questioning strategies used by Socrates.

Stereotyping (p. 134): the process of attributing behavioral characteristics to all members of a group; formulated on the basis of limited experiences with and information about the group, coupled with an unwillingness to examine prejudices.

Student diversity (p. 52): differences among students in regard to gender, race, ethnicity, culture, and socioeconomic status.

Student-mobility rates (p. 62): the proportion of students within a school or district who move during an academic year.

Students at risk (p. 173): students whose living conditions and backgrounds place them at risk for dropping out of school.

T

Teach for America (p. 55): a program that enables recent college graduates without a teaching certificate to teach in districts with critical shortages of teachers and, after taking professional development courses and supervision by state and school authorities, earn a teaching certificate.

Teacher accountability (p. 50): society's expectations that teachers will adhere to high professional and moral standards and create effective learning environments for all students.

Teacher-leader (p. 237): a teacher who assumes a key leadership role in the improvement and/or day-to-day operation of a school.

Teacher-researcher (p. 242): a teacher who regularly conducts classroom research to improve his or her teaching.

Teacher–student ratios (p. 62): a ratio that expresses the number of students taught by a teacher.

Teachers' thought processes (p. 75): the thoughts that guide teachers' actions in classrooms. These thoughts typically consist of thoughts related to planning, theories and beliefs, and interactive thoughts and decisions.

Tenure (p. 58): an employment policy in which teachers, after serving a probationary period, retain their positions indefinitely and can be dismissed only on legally defensible grounds.

Third International Mathematics and Science Study (TIMSS) (p. 32): an international assessment of mathematics and science achievement among fourth-, eighth-, and twelfth-grade students in forty-one countries.

Title IX (p. 117): a provision of the 1972 Education Amendments Act prohibiting sex discrimination in educational programs.

U

Uncertainties of teaching (p. 67): the unpredictable, ambiguous dimensions of teaching—predicting outcomes; assessing student learning; influencing student behavior; influencing others by example; responding to rapidly changing, fragmented events; and experiencing the uniqueness of teaching.

W

What Works Clearinghouse (WWC) (p. 244): a central, independent source of scientific evidence of what works in education, operated by the U.S. Department of Education's Institute of Education Sciences.

Women's Educational Equity Act (WEEA) (p. 157): a 1974 federal law that guarantees equal educational opportunity for females.

Z

Zero-tolerance policies (p. 186): school policies that reflect "zero tolerance" for any weapons or drugs on school property.

References

Abrahamsson, B. (1971). *Military professionalization and political power*. Stockholm: Allmanna Forlagret.

Ackerman, R. H., Moller, G., and Katzenmeyer, M. (Eds.). (1996). *Every teacher as a leader: Realizing the potential of teacher leadership*. San Francisco: Jossey-Bass.

Adler, M. (1982). *The paideia proposal: An educational manifesto*. New York: Macmillan.

African American Academy 2003. www.seattleschools. org/schools/aaa/.

Alan Guttmacher Institute. (1999). Teenage pregnancy: Overall trends and state-by-state information. New York: Alan Guttmacher Institute.

Alexander, C. J. (1998). Studying the experiences of gay and lesbian youth. *Journal of Gay and Lesbian Social Services, 8*.

American Association of University Women (AAUW). (1991). *Shortchanging girls, shortchanging America*. Washington, DC: Author.

American Association of University Women (AAUW). (1992). *How schools shortchange girls: The AAUW report*. (Researched by The Wellesley College Center for Research on Women). Washington, DC: The AAUW Educational Foundation.

American Council on Education. (2002). Beyond September 11: A comprehensive national policy on international education. Washington, DC: American Council on Education.

Anderson, J. D. (1997). Supporting the invisible minority. *Educational Leadership, 54*, 65–68.

Anderson, R. J., Keller, C. E., and Karp, J. M. (Eds.). (1998). *Enhancing diversity: Educators with disabilities*. Washington, DC: Gallaudet University Press.

Andrews, S., Sherman, R., and Webb, R. (Winter 1983). Teaching: The isolated profession. *Journal of Thought*.

Annie E. Casey Foundation. (2003). *Kids count data book, 2003*. Baltimore: Author.

Anyon, J. (1996). Social class and the hidden curriculum of work. In E. Hollins (Ed.), *Transforming curriculum for a culturally diverse society* (pp. 179–203). Mahwah, NJ: Lawrence Erlbaum.

Aristotle. (1941). *Politics* (Book VIII). In Richard McKoen (Ed.). *The basic works of Aristotle*. New York: Random House.

Aronson, E., and Gonzalez, A. (1988). Desegregation, jigsaw, and the Mexican-American experience. In P. A. Katz, and D. A. Taylor (Eds.), *Eliminating racism: Profiles in controversy*. New York: Plenum Press.

Artz, S. (1999). *Sex, power, and the violent school girl*. New York: Teachers College Press.

Ashton-Warner, S. (1963). *Teacher*. New York: Simon and Schuster.

Asian Americans/Pacific Islanders in Philanthropy. (1997). *An invisible crisis: The educational needs of Asian Pacific American youth*. New York: Author.

Astuto, T. (Ed.). (1993). *When teachers lead*. University Park, PA: University Council for Educational Administration.

Ayers, W. (2001). *To teach: The journey of a teacher*. New York: Teachers College Press.

Ballantine, J. H. (1997). *The sociology of education: A systematic analysis*, 4th ed. Upper Saddle River, NJ: Prentice Hall.

Baker, K. A. (1991). *Bilingual Education*. Bloomington, IN: Phi Delta Kappa.

Banks, J. A. (1999). *An introduction to multicultural education*, 2nd ed. Boston: Allyn and Bacon.

Banks, J. A. (2001). *Cultural diversity and education: Foundations, curriculum, and teaching*, 4th ed. Boston: Allyn and Bacon.

Banks, J. A. (2002). *An introduction to multicultural education*, 3rd ed. Boston: Allyn and Bacon.

Banks, J. A. (2003). *Teaching strategies for ethnic studies*, 7th ed. Boston: Allyn and Bacon.

Banks, J. A., and Banks, C. A. (Eds.). (1997). *Multicultural education: Issues and perspectives*, 3rd ed. Boston: Allyn and Bacon.

Becker, H. J. (2001, April). *How are teachers using computers in instruction?* Paper presented at the annual meeting of the American Educational Research Association, Seattle, WA.

Bennett, C. I. (2003). *Comprehensive multicultural education: Theory and practice*, 5th ed. Boston: Allyn and Bacon.

Bennett, L. (1997). Break the silence: Gay and straight students in Massachusetts team up to make a difference. *Teaching Tolerance, 6,* 24–31.

Bennett, W. (1987). *James Madison High School: A curriculum for American students.* Washington, DC: U.S. Department of Education.

Berliner, D. C. (November/December 2000). A personal response to those who bash teacher education. *Journal of Teacher Education, 51*(5), 358–371.

Berliner, D. C., and Biddle, B. J. (1995). *The manufactured crisis: Myths, fraud, and the attack on America's public schools.* Reading, MA: Addison-Wesley Publishing Company.

Bernstein, B. B. (1996). *Pedagogy, symbolic control and identity: Theory, research, critique (critical perspectives on literacy and education).* New York: Taylor and Francis.

Besner, H. F., and Spungin, C. I. (1995). *Gay and lesbian students: Understanding their needs.* Washington, DC: Taylor and Francis.

Billig, S. (2000). Research on K–12 school-based service learning: The evidence builds. *Phi Delta Kappan, 81*(9), 658–664.

Bitter, G. G., and Pierson, M. E. (1999). *Using technology in the classroom,* 4th ed. Boston: Allyn and Bacon.

Bitter, G. G., and Pierson, M. E. (2002). *Using technology in the classroom,* 5th ed. Boston: Allyn and Bacon.

Board of Education of Oklahoma City Public Schools v. Dowell, 498 U.S. 237, 249–250 (1991).

Boleman, L. G., and Deal, T. E. (1994). *Becoming a teacher leader: From isolation to collaboration.* Thousand Oaks, CA: Corwin Press.

Boleman, L. G., and Deal, T. E. (2002). *Reframing the path to school leadership: A guide for teachers and principals.* Thousand Oaks, CA: Corwin Press.

Booth, A., and Dunn, J. F. (Eds.). (1996). *Family-school links: How do they affect educational outcomes?* Mahwah, NJ: Lawrence Erlbaum Associates.

Boyer, E. (1983). *High school: A report on secondary education in America.* New York: Harper and Row.

Boyer, E. (1990). Teaching in America. In M. Kysilka (Ed.), *Honor in Teaching: Reflections.* West Lafayette, IN: Kappa Delta Pi.

Boyer, E. (1995). *The basic school: A community for learning.* Princeton, NJ: The Carnegie Foundation for the Advancement of Teaching.

Bracy, G. W. (1996, October). The sixth Bracy report on the condition of public education. *Phi Delta Kappan,* 127–138.

Bradley, A. (1998, February 4). Unions agree on blueprint for merging. *Education Week on the Web.*

Bredeson, P. V. (993) Letting go of outlived professional identities: A study of role transition and role strain for principals in restructured schools. *Educational Administration Quarterly, 29*(1), 34–68.

Brown, F. (May 2002). Changing racial and ethnic demographics in our schools must include a budget plan. *School Business Affairs, 68*(5), 28–30.

Brown, S. (May 7, 2002). Guest viewpoint: The education community can help prevent teen pregnancy by preventing school failure." *School Board News.* www.nsba.org/site/doc_sbn.asp?TrackID=&SID=1&DID=8185&CID=308&VID=58

Brown v. Board of Education of Topeka, Kansas, 347 U.S. 483, 74 S.Ct5. 686 (1954).

Brown v. Unified School District No. 501, 56 F. Supp. 2d 1212 (D. Kan. 1999).

Brunner, C., and Bennett, D. (1997). Technology and gender: Differences in masculine and feminine views. *NASSP Bulletin, 81,* 46–51.

Bucky, P. A. (1992). *The private Albert Einstein.* Kansas City: Andrews and McMeel.

Bureau of Justice Statistics and National Center for Education Statistics. (2003). *Indicators of School Crime and Safety, 2003.* Washington, DC: Author.

Burnaford, G., Fischer, J., and Hobson, D. (2001). *Teachers doing research: The power of action through inquiry.* Mahwah, NJ: Lawrence Erlbaum.

Burns, J. (September 20, 2003). Immersion aims to undo damage of assimilation policies. Associate Press.

Button, H. W., and Provenzo, E. G. (1983). *History of education and culture in America.* Englewood Cliffs, NJ: Prentice Hall.

Button, H. W., and Provenzo, E. G. (1989). *History of education and culture in America,* 2nd ed. Englewood Cliffs, NJ: Prentice Hall.

Buzzell, J. B. (1996). *School and family partnerships: Case studies for regular and special education.* Albany, NY: Delmar Publishers.

Carnegie Council on Adolescent Development. (1989). *Turning points: Preparing American youth for the 21st century.* New York: Author.

Center for Human Resources. (1999). *Summary report: National evaluation of Learn and Serve America.* Waltham, MA: Brandeis University.

Center for Immigration Studies. (2004). (Retrieved from: www.cis.org/topics/currentnumbers.html).

Center for Research on Effective Schooling for Disadvantaged Students. (1992). *Helping students who fall behind*, Report no. 22. Baltimore: Johns Hopkins University.

Centers for Disease Control and Prevention. (1998). *Youth risk behavior surveillance—United States, 1997.* Atlanta: Author.

Clift, R. T., et al. (1995). *Collaborative leadership and shared decision making: Teachers, principals, and university professors.* New York: Teachers College Press.

Cohen, S. (Ed.). (1974). *Massachusetts school law of 1648. Education in the United States.* New York: Random House.

Coleman, J. S., Campbell, E. Q., Hobson, C. J., McPartland, J., Mood, A. L., Weinfeld, F. D., and York, R. L. (1966). *Equality of educational opportunity.* Washington, DC: U.S. Government Printing Office.

Comber, C., et al. (1997). The effects of age, gender and computer experience upon computer attitudes. *Educational Research, 39,* 123–133.

Combs, A. (1979). *Myths in education: Beliefs that hinder progress and their alternatives.* Boston: Allyn and Bacon.

Comer, J. P. (1997). *Waiting for a miracle: Why schools can't solve our problems—and how we can.* New York: Dutton.

Commager, H. S. (1958 October). Noah Webster, 1758–1958. *Saturday Review 41,* 18.

Commager, H. S. (Ed.). (1962). *Noah Websters's American spelling book.* New York: Teachers College Press.

Commission on Educational Reconstruction. (1955). *Organizing the teaching profession: The story of the American Federation of Teachers.* Glencoe, IL: Free Press.

Committee for Economic Development. (1994). *Putting learning first: Governing and managing schools for high achievement.* New York: Research and Policy Committee, Committee for Economic Development.

Costa, A. L. (1984). A reaction to Hunter's knowing, teaching, and supervising. In P. L. Hosford (Ed.), *Using what we know about teaching.* Alexandria, VA: Association for Supervision and Curriculum Development.

Coughlin, E. K. (1993, March 24). Sociologists examine the complexities of racial and ethnic identity in America. *Chronicle of Higher Education.*

Council for Basic Education and Milken Family Foundation. (2002). Teachers' Professional Lives—A View from Nine Industrialized Countries. Santa Monica, CA: Author.

Council of Chief State School Officers. (1996). *Interstate School Leaders Licensure Consortium (ISLLC)*

Standards for School Leaders. Washington, DC: Author.

Counts, G. (1932). *Dare the school build a new social order?* New York: John Day.

Crawford, J. (March 17, 2003). [Online] Language legislation in the United States: Official English and anti-bilingual education bills introduced in 108th Congress, state legislatures. [2003, June 24]. http://ourworld.compuserve.com/homepages/JWCRAWFORD/langleg.htm#108th.

Cremin, L. A. (1961). *The transformation of the school: Progressivism in American education, 1876–1957.* New York: Alfred A. Knopf.

Cunningham, C. (2003). *Trends and issues: Social and economic context.* Eugene, OR: University of Oregon, Clearinghouse on Educational Management.

Cziko, G. A. (1992, March). The evaluation of bilingual education: From necessity and probability to possibility. *Educational Researcher,* 10–15.

Danielewicz, J. (2001). *Teaching selves: Identity, pedagogy, and teacher education.* Albany, NY: State University of New York Press.

Danielson, C. (1996). Enhancing professional practice: A framework for teaching. Alexandria, VA: Association for Supervision and Curriculum Development.

Davidson, J. (2002). Democratic leadership in coalition schools: Why it's necessary, how it works. *Horace, 18*(3).

Davitt, J. (1997, January 3). The ultimate good shepherd. *Times Educational Supplement.*

Deal, T. E., and Peterson, K. D. (1999). Shaping school culture: The heart of leadership. San Francisco: Jossey Bass.

Dewey, J. (1900). *The school and society.* Chicago: University of Chicago Press.

Dewey, J. (1902). *The child and the curriculum.* Chicago: University of Chicago Press.

Dewey, J. (1955). Quoted in *Organizing the teaching profession: The story of the American Federation of Teachers.* Glencoe, IL: The Commission on Educational Reconstruction.

Directory of national trade and professional associations of the United States 2002. (2002). B. Downs (Ed.). New York: Columbia Books.

Doyle, W. (1986). Classroom organization and management. In M. Wittrock (Ed.), *Handbook of research on teaching,* 3rd ed. New York: Macmillan.

Dryfoos, J. G. (1994). *Full-service schools: A revolution in health and social services for children, youth, and families.* San Francisco: Jossey-Bass.

Dryfoos, J. G. (1998). *Safe passage: Making it through adolescence in a risky society*. New York: Oxford University Press.

Dryfoos, J. G., and Maguire, S. (2002). Inside full-service community schools. Thousand Oaks, CA: Corwin Press.

Duffield, B. (2001). The educational rights of homeless children: Policies and practices. *Educational Studies, 32*(3), 323–336.

Duke, D. L. (1984). *Teaching—the imperiled profession*. Albany, NY: State University of New York Press.

Durkheim, E. (1956). *Education and sociology* (trans. by Fox, S. D.). Glencoe, IL: The Free Press.

Durlak, J. A. (1995). *School-based prevention programs for children and adolescents*. Thousand Oaks, CA: Sage Publications.

Edelman, M. W. (1997, November 9). Young families shut out of the American dream. *Seattle Times*, B5.

The Education Trust. (2002). *All talk, putting an end to out-of-field teaching*. Washington, DC: Author.

Education Week. (2000). Quality counts 2000: Who should teach? Retrieved from www.edweek.org/sreports/qc00.

Educational Testing Service. (1995, Spring). Bringing volunteers into teacher education programs. *ETS Policy Notes*, 8–9.

Edwards, A. T. (1997). Let's stop ignoring our gay and lesbian youth. *Educational Leadership, 54*.

Edwards, P., and Young, L. (1992). Beyond parents: family, community, and school involvement. *Phi Delta Kappan, 74*(1), 72, 74, 76, 78, 80.

Eisner, E. W. (1998). *The kind of schools we need: Personal essays*. Portsmouth, NH: Heinemann.

Elias, M. J. (2001). Prepare children for the tests of life, not a life of tests. *Education Week, 21*(4), 40.

Elias, M. J., Arnold, H., and Hussey, C. S. (Eds.). (2003). *EQ + IQ = best leadership practices for caring and successful schools*. Thousand Oaks, CA: Corwin Press.

Epstein, J. L. (2001). *School, family, and community partnerships: Preparing educators and improving schools*. Boulder, CO: Westview Press.

Etzioni, A. (1969). *The semi-professions and their organization: Teachers, nurses, social workers*. New York: The Free Press.

Fashola, O. (1999). Review of extended-day and after-school programs and their effectiveness. Baltimore: Johns Hopkins University, Center for Research on the Education of Students Placed at Risk.

Federal Interagency Forum on Child and Family Statistics. (2003). *America's children: Key national indicators of well-being 2003*. Washington, DC: Author.

Feistritzer, C. E. (1999). *A report on teacher preparation in the U.S.* Washington, DC: National Center for Education Information.

Feller, B. (September 10, 2003). [Online]. Schools focus on America's flaws, report says. *The Washington Times*. www.washingtontimes.com [2003, September 23].

Ferguson, C. (August 30, 2003). Gay high school draws criticism from conservatives and civil libertarians. Associated Press.

Fischer, J. C. (1996). Open to ideas: Developing a framework for your research. In G. Burnaford, J. Fischer, and D. Hobson, *Teachers doing research: Practical possibilities*. Mahwah, NJ: Lawrence Erlbaum.

Franklin, B. (1931). Proposals relating to the education of youth in Pennsylvania, in T. Woody (Ed.), *Educational views of Benjamin Franklin*. New York: McGraw-Hill.

Freedman, S., Jackson, J., and Botes, K. (1983). Teaching: An imperiled profession. In L. Shulman and G. Sykes (Eds.), *Handbook of teaching and policy*. New York: Longman.

Freeman v. Pitts, 503 U.S. 467 (1992).

Freppon, P. A. (2001). *What it takes to be a teacher: The role of personal and professional development*. Portsmouth, NH: Heinemann.

Frost, D. (1997). *Reflective action planning for teachers: A guide to teacher-led school and professional development*. London: D. Fulton.

Fuligni, A. J., and Stevenson, H. W. (1995). Home environment and school learning. In L. W. Anderson (Ed.), *International encyclopedia of teaching and teacher education*, 2nd ed. (pp. 378–382). Oxford: Pergamon.

Fullan, M., and Hargreaves, A. (1996). *What's worth fighting for in your school?* New York: Teachers College Press.

Gandara, P., and Fish, J. (1994, Spring). Year-round schooling as an avenue to major structural reform. *Educational Evaluation and Policy Analysis, 16*.

Garbarino, J. (1999). *Lost boys: Why our sons turn violent and how we can save them*. New York: The Free Press.

Gardner, J. W. (1990). *On leadership*. New York: The Free Press.

Gehrke, N. (1988, Summer). Toward a definition of mentoring. *Theory into Practice*, 190–194.

Gehrke, N. J., and Romerdahl, N. S. (1997). *Teacher leaders: Making a difference in schools*. West Lafayette, IN: Kappa Delta Pi.

George, P. S. (1995). The Japanese secondary school: A closer look. Columbus, OH: National Middle School Association; and Reston, VA: National Association of Secondary School Principals.

Gipp, G. (1979, August–September). Help for Dana Fast Horse and friends. *American Education*, 15.

Glickman, C. (2003). *Holding Sacred Ground: Essays on Leadership, Courage, and Sustaining Great Schools*. San Francisco: Jossey-Bass.

Glickman, C. D. (1998). *Revolutionizing America's schools*. San Francisco: Jossey-Bass.

Glickman, C., Gordon, S. P., and Ross-Gordon, J. M. (2004). *SuperVision and Instructional Leadership: A Developmental Approach*. Boston: Pearson Education.

Gmelch, W. H., and Parkay, F. W. (1995). Changing roles and occupational stress in the teaching profession. In M. J. O'Hair and S. J. Odell, *Educating teachers for leadership and change: Teacher education yearbook III*. (pp. 46–65). Thousand Oaks, CA: Corwin Press.

Goleman, D. (1997). *Emotional intelligence*. New York: Bantam Books.

Goleman, D. (1998). *Working with emotional intelligence*. New York: Bantam Books.

Goodlad, J. (1983, Spring). *Teaching: An endangered profession. Teachers College Record*, pp. 575–578.

Goodlad, J. (1990). *Teachers for our nation's schools*. San Francisco: Jossey-Bass.

Goodlad, J. (1994). *Educational renewal: Better teachers, better schools*. San Francisco: Jossey-Bass.

Goodlad, J. (1998). *Educational renewal: Better teachers, better schools*. New York: John Wiley and Sons.

Graham, P. A. (1967). *Progressive education: From Arcady to academe: A history of the Progressive Education Association, 1919–1955*. New York: Teachers College Press.

Grant, C. A. (1994, Winter). Challenging the myths about multicultural education. *Multicultural Education*, 4–9.

Grant, G., and Murray, C. E. (1999). *Teaching in America: The slow revolution*. Cambridge, MA: Harvard University Press.

Grimes, G. F. (2000). What teacher salary averages don't show. Atlanta: Southern Regional Education Board.

Griego-Jones, T. (1996). Reconstructing bilingual education from a multicultural perspective. In C. A. Grant and M. L. Gomez, *Making schooling multicultural: Campus and classroom*. Englewood Cliffs, NJ: Merrill.

Grossman, D., and Siddle, P. (1999). Combat. In L. Kurtz (Ed.), *The encyclopedia of violence, peace, and conflict*. San Diego: Academic Press.

Groves, M. (August 15, 2000). [Online]. English skills still the key in test scores. *Los Angeles Times*. www.onenation.org/article.cfm?ID=683 [2003, May 22].

Hale-Benson, J. E. (1986). *Black children: their roots, culture, and learning styles*. Baltimore: Johns Hopkins University Press.

Hall, L. S. (2001). *Final report: Youth and family center program, 2000–2001. REIS01-172-2*. Approved Report of the Division of Evaluation and Accountability. Dallas, TX: Dallas Independent School District.

Hammett, R. F. (1997). Computers in schools: White boys only? *English Quarterly, 28*, 1.

Hansen, D. T. (1995). *The call to teach*. New York: Teachers College Press.

Hardman, M. L., Drew, C. J., and Egan, M. W. (2002). *Human exceptionality: Society, school, and family*, 7th ed. Boston: Allyn and Bacon.

Harris Interactive, Inc. (2001). *The MetLife survey of the American teacher: Key elements of quality schools*. New York: Author.

Harris Interactive, Inc. (2002). *The MetLife survey of the American teacher: Student Life: School, Home and Community*. New York: Author.

Hart, P., and Teeter, R. (2002). *A national priority: Americans speak on teacher quality*. Princeton, NJ: Educational Testing Service.

Heath, S. B. (1983). *Ways with words*. Cambridge: Cambridge University Press.

Hedges, L. V. (1996). Quoted in Hedges finds boys and girls both disadvantaged in school. *Education News*. The Department of Education, The University of Chicago.

Henry, E., Huntley, J., McKamey, C., and Harper, L. (1995). *To be a teacher: Voices from the classroom*. Thousand Oaks, CA: Corwin Press.

Henry, M. E. (1996). *Parent–school collaboration: Feminist organizational structures and school leadership*. Albany, NY: State University of New York Press.

Henry, M. (1993). *School cultures: Universes of meaning in private schools*. Norwood, NJ: Ablex.

Herndon, J. (1969). *The way it spozed to be*. New York: Bantam Books.

Hiatt-Michael, D. (Ed.). (April, 2001). Promising practices for family involvement in school. Greenwich, CT: Information Age Publishing, Inc.

Hill, P. (May 12, 2003). School reform efforts aren't reaching underserved students. *Spokesman Review*, A11.

Hirshfelder, A. B. (1986). *Happily may I walk: American Indians and Alaska Natives today*. New York: Scribner.

Hletko, J. D. (1995). Reflections on NBPTS. *Voices from the middle, 2*(4), 33–36.

Hobbes Internet Timeline. (2004). (Retrieved from www.zakon.org/robert/internet/timeline/).

Hodgkinson, H. L. (November–December 2002). Demographics of diversity. *Principal 82*, 2, 14–18.

Holloway, J. H. (December 2002/January 2003). Addressing the needs of homeless students. *Educational Leadership 60*(4), 89–90.

Holly, M. L., and McLoughlin, C. (Eds.). (1989). *Perspectives on teacher professional development*. New York: Falmer Press.

Holmes, M., and Weiss, B. J. (1995). *Lives of women public schoolteachers: Scenes from American educational history*. New York: Garland.

Holmes Partnership. (2001). *Origins of the Holmes Partnership (1987–1997)*. Auburn, AL: Author.

Holt, J. (1964). *How children fail*. New York: Delta.

Homes for the Homeless. (1999). Meeting the educational needs of homeless children and families. *Access to Success, 1*(3), 1–9.

Hopson, J. L., Hopson, E., and Hagen, T. (2002, May 8). Take steps to protect latchkey children. Knight Ridder/Tribune News Service.

Horace. (2002, Spring). Anzar High School communication guidelines. *Horace, 18*(3).

Howsam, R. B., Corrigan, D. C., Denemark, G. W., and Nash, R. J. (1976). *Educating a profession*. Washington, DC: American Association of Colleges for Teacher Education.

Idol, L. (1998). *Optional extended year program*, Feedback, Publication No. 97.20. Austin Independent School District, TX, Office of Program Evaluation.

Igoa, C. (1995). *The inner world of the immigrant child*. New York: Lawrence Erlbaum.

Indiana University. (February 1999). *IU school of education programs offer life-changing experiences*. Bloomington, IN: Indiana University, Office of Communication and Marketing.

Inoue, A. (1996, October 10). *Creating schools with special characteristics*. Paper presented at the eighth Washington State University College of Education/Nishinomiya Education Board Education Seminar. Washington State University, Pullman.

Institute for Educational Leadership. (2002). *Community schools: Improving student learning/strengthening schools, families, and communities*. Washington, DC: Author.

Institute for Social Research. (2002). *Monitoring the future: National results on adolescent drug use, Overview of key findings, 2001*. Ann Arbor, MI: The University of Michigan, Institute for Social Research.

International Association for the Evaluation of Educational Achievement. (1997a). *Mathematics achievement in the primary school years: LEA's third international mathematics and science study*. Amsterdam, Netherlands: International Association for the Evaluation of Educational Achievement.

International Association for the Evaluation of Educational Achievement. (1997b). *Science achievement in the primary school years: LEA's third international mathematics and science study*. Amsterdam, Netherlands: Author International Association for the Evaluation of Educational Achievement.

Interstate New Teacher Assessment and Support Consortium. (1992). *Model standards for beginning teacher licensing and development: A Resource for state dialogue*. Washington, DC: Council of Chief State School Officers.

Jackson, P. (1965 November). The way teaching is. *NEA Journal*.

Jackson, P. (1990). *Life in classrooms*. New York: Teachers College Press.

Jencks, C., et al. (1972). *Inequality: A reassessment of the effect of family and schooling in America*. New York: Basic Books.

Jencks, C., and Phillips, M. (Eds.). (1998). *The black–white test score gap*. Washington, DC: Brookings Institution Press.

Johanningmeier, E. V. (1980). *Americans and their schools*. Chicago: Rand McNally.

Jones, R. (1999). "I don't feel safe here anymore": Your legal duty to protect gay kids from harassment. *American School Board Journal, 186*(11), 26–31.

Jordan, K. M., Vaughan, J. S., and Woodworth, K. J. (1997). I will survive: Lesbian, gay, and bisexual youths' experience of high school. *Journal of Gay and Lesbian Social Services, 7*, 17–33.

Jordan, L., and Hendricks, C. (2002, March). Increasing sixth grade students' engagement in literacy learning. *Networks: An on-line journal for teacher research*.

Jorgenson, O. (2001). Supporting a diverse teacher corps. *Educational Leadership, 58*(8), 64–67.

Joyce, B., Weil, M., and Calhoun, E. (2000). *Models of teaching*, 6th ed. Boston: Allyn and Bacon.

Karp, J. M., and Keller, C. E. (1998). Preparation and employment experiences of educators with disabilities. In R. J. Anderson, C. E. Keller, and J. M. Karp (Eds.), *Enhancing diversity: Educators with disabilities*. Washington, DC: Gallaudet University Press.

Katzenmeyer, G. M., and Moller, G. (1996). *Awakening the sleeping giant: Leadership development for teachers*. Thousand Oaks, CA: Corwin Press.

Kavarsky, M. (1994). Salome Urena Middle Academies. *Journal of Emotional and Behavioral Problems, 3*(3), 37–40.

Kleiner, B., Porch, R., and Farris, E. (2002). *Public alternative schools and programs for students at risk of education failure: 2000–01* (NCES 2002-004). Washington, DC: U.S. Department of Education, National Center for Education Statistics.

Kleinfeld, J. (1998). *The myth that schools shortchange girls: Social science in the service of deception.* Washington, DC: The Women's Freedom Network.

Knupfer, N. N. (1998). Gender divisions across technology advertisements and the WWW: Implications for educational equity. *Theory into Practice, 37,* 1, 54–63.

Kohl, H. R. (1967). *36 children.* New York: Signet.

Koller, E. (1996). Overcoming paradigm paralysis: A high school teacher revisits foreign language education. In G. Burnaford, J. Fischer, and D. Hobson (Eds.), *Teachers doing research: Practical possibilities.* Mahwah, NJ: Lawrence Erlbaum.

Kozol, J. (1967). *Death at an early age.* Boston: Houghton Mifflin.

Kozol, J. (1991). *Savage inequalities: Children in America's schools.* New York: Crown.

Lackney, J. (2000). *Thirty-three educational design principles for schools and community learning centers.* Mississippi State University: Educational Design Institute, 31.

Lambert, L., et al. (1997). *Who will save our schools? Teachers as constructivist leaders.* Thousand Oaks, CA: Corwin Press.

Lau v. Nichols, 414 U.S. 563 (1974).

Learning in Deed. (2004). Learning in deed: Service learning in action. New York: National Service-Learning Partnership, Academy for Educational Development. Retrieved January 4, 2004: www.learningindeed.org/tools/examples.html.

Lee, J. (January–February 2002). Racial and ethnic achievement gap trends: Reversing the progress toward equity?" *Educational Researcher, 31*(1), 3–12.

Lee, V. E., Chen, X., and Smerdon, B. A. (1996). *The influence of school climate on gender differences in the achievement and engagement of young adolescents.* Washington, DC: American Association of University Women.

Levine, D. U., and Levine, R. F. (1996). *Society and education,* 9th ed. Boston: Allyn and Bacon.

Levy, F. (1996, October). What General Motors can teach U.S. schools about the proper role of markets in education reform. *Phi Delta Kappan,* 108–114.

Lichter, D. T., and Graefe, D. R. (2001). "Finding a mate? The marital and cohabitation history of unwed mothers." In L. L. Wu, R. Haveman, and B. Wolfe (Eds.), *Out of Wedlock: Trends, Causes, and Consequences of Nonmarital Fertility.* New York: Russell Foundation.

Lightfoot, S. L. (1978). Worlds apart: *Relationships between families and schools.* New York: Basic Books.

Little, P. M. D., and Harris, E. (2003 July). A review of out-of-school time program quasi-experimental and experimental evaluation results. Harvard University: Harvard Family Research Project.

Livingston, C. (Ed.). (1992). *Teachers as leaders: Evolving roles.* Washington, DC: National Education Association.

Lortie, D. (1975). *School teacher: A sociological study.* Chicago: the University of Chicago Press.

Los Angeles Times. [Online]. English skills still the key in test scores. www.onenation.org/article.cfm?ID=683 [2003, May 22].

Louis Harris and Associates, Inc. (1995). *The Metropolitan Life survey of the American teacher, 1984–1995: Old problems, new challenges.* New York: Author.

Louis Harris and Associates, Inc. (1997). *The Metropolitan Life survey of the American teacher, 1997: Examining gender issues in public schools.* New York: Author.

MacLeod, J. (1995). *Ain't no makin' it: Aspirations & attainment in a low-income neighborhood.* Boulder, CO: Westview Press.

Maney, D., Higham-Gardill, D. A., Mahoney, B. S. (April 2002). The alcohol-related psychosocial and behavioral risks of a nationally representative sample of adolescents. *Journal of School Health, 72*(4).

Mann, H. (1868). Annual reports on education. In Mary Mann (Ed.), *The life and works of Horace Mann,* vol. 3. Boston: Horace B. Fuller.

Mann, H. (1957). Twelfth annual report. In Lawrence A. Cremin (Ed.), *The republic and the school: Horace Mann on the education of free men.* New York: Teachers College Press.

Manning, M. L., and Baruth, L. G. (1996). *Multicultural education of children and adolescents.* Boston: Allyn and Bacon.

Mattingly, P. H. (1975). *The classless profession.* New York: New York University Press.

Mayer, F. (1973). *A history of educational thought.* Columbus, OH: Merrill.

Mayhew, K. C., and Edwards, A. C. (1936). *The Dewey School: The University Laboratory School of the University of Chicago, 1896–1903.* New York: D. Appleton-Century.

Merideth, E. M. (2000). *Leadership strategies for teachers.* Arlington Heights, IL: SkyLight Professional Development.

Mills, G. E. (2000). *Action research: A guide for the teacher researcher.* Upper Saddle River, NJ: Merrill.

Missouri v. Jenkins, 515 U.S. 70 (1995).

Molino, F. (1999). My students, my children. In M. K. Rand and S. Shelton-Colangelo, *Voices of student* teachers: *Cases from the field* (pp. 55–56). Upper Saddle River: Merrill.

Montagu, A. (1974). *Man's most dangerous myth: The fallacy of race*, 5th ed. New York: Oxford University Press.

Moore, D. R. (1992). Voice and choice in Chicago. In W. H. Clune and J. F. Witte (Eds.), *Choice and control in American education: Volume II. The practice of choice, decentralization and school restructuring.* Philadelphia: The Falmer Press.

Moore, J. P., and Terrett, C. P. (1999). *Highlights of the 1997 national youth gang survey. Fact sheet.* Washington, DC: U.S. Department of Justice, Office of Justice Programs, Office of Juvenile Justice and Delinquency Prevention.

Moyers, B. D. (1989). *A world of ideas: Conversations with thoughtful men and women.* New York: Doubleday.

Mukhopadhyay, C., and Henze, R. C. (May 2003). How real is race? Using anthropology to make sense of human diversity. *Phi Delta Kappan, 84*(9), 669–678.

Murphy, J. (1999, April). *Reconnecting teaching and school administration: A call for a unified profession.* Paper presented at the annual meeting of the American Educational Research Association, Montreal.

National Association for Year-Round Education. (2003). History of year-round education. San Diego: Author. Retrieved from www.nayre.org.

National Board for Professional Teaching Standards. (2002). *What teachers should know and be able to do.* Arlington, VA: National Board for Professional Teaching Standards.

National Center for Education Statistics. (1980). *High school and beyond study.* Washington, DC: U.S. Department of Education: Author.

National Center for Education Statistics. (1999). *Digest of education statistics 1998.* Washington, DC: U.S. Department of Education, Office of Educational Research and Improvement.

National Center for Education Statistics. (2002). *The condition of education 2002.* Washington, DC: U.S. Department of Education: Author.

National Center for Education Statistics. (2003). *The condition of education 2003.* Washington, DC: U.S. Department of Education: Author.

National Clearinghouse for English Language Acquisition. (2002). *Survey of the states' limited English proficient students and available educational programs and services.* Washington, DC: George Washington University, National Clearinghouse for English Language Acquisition.

National Clearinghouse on Child Abuse and Neglect. (2002). *National child abuse and neglect data system (NCANDS): Summary of key findings from calendar year 2000.* Washington, DC: Author.

National Coalition for the Homeless. (2003). *Homeless families with children.* Washington, DC: Author.

National Commission on Excellence in Education. (1983). A nation at risk: The imperative for educational reform. Washington, DC: U.S. Government Printing Office.

National Commission on Teaching and America's Future. (1996). *What matters most: Teaching for America's future.* New York: National Commission on Teaching and America's Future.

National Council for Accreditation of Teacher Education. (2002). *Professional standards for the accreditation of schools, colleges, and departments of education—2002 edition.* Washington, DC: National Council for Accreditation of Teacher Education.

National Education Association. (2002). *Results of poll on potential teachers: Answering the call . . . for all the right reasons.* Washington, DC: Author.

National Education Association. (2003). *Status of the American public school teacher.* Washington, DC: Author.

National Education Goals Panel. (1999). National Education Goals Panel recommends that goals be renamed "America's Education Goals" and continue beyond the year 2000. Press Release, National Education Goals Panel.

National Governors' Association and NGA Center for Best Practices. (2002). *After-school plus (+) program: Hawaii.* Washington, DC: Author.

National Institute for Mental Health. (1999). *Suicide fact sheet.* Washington, DC: Author.

NEAFT Partnership. (2002, April 23–24). NEAFT Partnership Joint Council Communique. Washington, DC: Author.

Neill, A. S. (1960). *Summerhill: A radical approach to child rearing.* New York: Hart.

Newmann, F. M., and Wehlage, G. G. (1995). *Successful school restructuring: A report to the public and educators by the Center on Organization and Restructuring of Schools.* Madison, WI: University of Wisconsin, Center on Organization and Restructuring of Schools.

Nieto, S. (1992). *Affirming diversity: The sociopolitical context of multicultural education.* White Plains, NY: Longman.

Nieto, S. (2003). *What keeps teachers going?* New York: Teachers College Press.

O'Hair, M. J., and Odell, S. J. (Eds.). (1995). *Educating teachers for leadership and change: Teacher education yearbook III*. Thousand Oaks, CA: Corwin Press.

Orfield, G., and Yun, J. T. (1999). *Resegregation in American schools*. Cambridge, MA: Harvard University, The Civil Rights Project.

Organization for Economic Cooperation and Development (2000). *International Indicators Project, 2000*. Paris: Organization for Economic Cooperation and Development.

Organization for Economic Cooperation and Development (2003). *Reading for Change—Performance and Engagement Across Countries*. Paris: Organization for Economic Cooperation and Development.

Ormrod, J. E. (2003). *Educational psychology: Developing learners*, 4th ed. Upper Saddle River, NJ: Merrill Prentice Hall.

Pang, V. O. (1994, December). Why do we need this class: Multicultural education for teachers. *Phi Delta Kappan*.

Parkay, F. W. (1983). *White teacher, black school: The professional growth of a ghetto teacher*. New York: Praeger.

Parkay, F. W., Potisook, P., Chantharasakul, A., and Chunsakorn, P. (1999). *New roles and responsibilities in educational reform: A study of Thai and U.S. principals' attitudes toward teacher leadership*. Bangkok: Kasetsart University, Center for Research on Teaching and Teacher Education.

Parkay, F. W., Shindler, J., and Oaks, M. M. (1997, January). Creating a climate for collaborative, emergent leadership at an urban high school: Exploring the stressors, role changes, and paradoxes of restructuring. *International Journal of Educational Reform*, 64–74.

Parker, L., and Shapiro, J. P. (1993). The context of educational administration and social class. In C. A. Capper (Ed.), *Educational administration in a pluralistic society* (pp. 36–65). Albany, NY: State University of New York Press.

Paul, J. L., and Colucci, K. (2000). Caring pedagogy. In Paul, J. L., and T. J. Smith (Eds.). *Stories out of school: Memories and reflections on care and cruelty in the classroom*. Stamford, CT: Ablex Publishing Corporation.

Paul, J. L., and Smith, T. J. (Eds.). (2000). *Stories out of school: Memories and reflections on care and cruelty in the classroom*. Stamford, CT: Ablex.

Pawlas, G. E. (1994). Homeless students at the school door. *Educational Leadership*, 55(8), 79–82.

Pellicer, L. O., and Anderson, L. W. (1995). *A handbook for teacher leaders*. Thousand Oaks, CA: Corwin Press.

Potrikus, A. S. (September 28, 2003). Girls surging past boys academically. Knight Ridder Newspapers.

Powell, A. G. (1980). *The uncertain profession: Harvard and the search for educational authority*. Cambridge, MA: Harvard University Press.

Powell, A., Farrar, E., and Cohen, D. K. (1985). The shopping mall high school: Winners and losers in the educational marketplace. Boston: Houghton Mifflin.

Protheroe, N., Lewis, A., and Paik, S. 2002. Promoting quality teaching. *ERS Spectrum* (Winter). www.ers.org/spectrum/win02a.htm.

Rafferty, Y. (1997). Meeting the educational needs of homeless children. *Educational Leadership*, 5(4), 48–52.

Rand, M. K., and Shelton-Colangelo, S. (1999). *Voices of student teachers: Cases from the field*. Upper Saddle River, NJ: Merrill.

Randall, V. R. (2001). *Institutional racism*. Dayton, OH: The University of Dayton School of Law.

Ravitch, D. (1983). *The troubled crusade: American education, 1945–1980*. New York: Basic Books.

Ravitch, D. (1985). *The schools we deserve: Reflections on the education crises of our times*. New York: Basic Books.

Recruiting New Teachers (2001). *The essential profession: American education at the crossroads*. Belmont, MA: Author.

Rector, T. A., Jacoby, S. H., Lockwood, J. F., and McCarthy, D. W. (2002, January 7). *Teacher leaders in research based science education*. Paper presented at the 199th meeting of the American Astronomical Society, Washington, DC.

Rice, R., and Walsh, C. E. (1996). Equity at risk: The problem with state and federal education reform efforts. In C. Walsh (Ed.), *Education reform and social change: Multicultural voices, struggles, and visions*. Mahwah, NJ: Lawrence Erlbaum.

Rickover, H. G. (1959). *Education and freedom*. New York: E. P. Dutton.

Rippa, S. A. (1984). *Education in a free society*. New York: Longman.

Rippa, S. A. (1997). *Education in a free society: An American history*, 8th ed. New York: Longman.

Rithdee, K. (1996, November 3–9). Fighting drugs with faith. *The Bangkok Post Sunday Magazine*.

RMC Research Corporation. (2001). *Washington state readiness to learn: School-linked models for integrated family services, 1999–2001 evaluation report, Volume 1*. Tacoma, WA: Superintendent of Public Instruction.

RMC Research Corporation. (1998). *Time: Critical issues in educational change*. Portsmouth, NH: Author.

Rose, L. C., and Gallup, A. M. (1999, September). The 31st annual Phi Delta Kappa/Gallup poll of the public's attitudes toward the public schools. *Phi Delta Kappan, 81*(1), 41–56.

Rose, L. C., and Gallup, A. M. (2002, September). The 34th annual Phi Delta Kappa/Gallup poll of the public's attitudes toward the public schools. *Phi Delta Kappan, 84*(1), 41–56.

Rossell, C. H. (1990, Winter). The research on bilingual education. *Equity and Choice*, 29–36.

Rossell, C., and Baker, K. (1996). The educational effectiveness of bilingual education. *Research in the Teaching of English, 30*(1), 7–74.

Rotberg, I. C., Futrell, M. H., and Lieberman, J. M. (1998). National board certification: Increasing participation and assessing impacts. *Phi Delta Kappan, 79*(6), 462–466.

Rothstein, R. (1998, May). Bilingual education: The controversy. *Phi Delta Kappan*, 672, 674–678.

Rury, J. L. (2002). *Education and social change: Themes in the history of American schooling*. Mahwah, NJ: Lawrence Erlbaum.

Schaefer, R. (1967). *The school as the center of inquiry*. New York: Harper and Row.

Schmidt, P. (1991, February 20). Three types of bilingual education effective, E. D. study concludes. *Education Week on the Web*.

Schön, D. (1987). *Educating the reflective practitioner: Toward a new design for teaching and learning in the professions*. San Francisco: Jossey-Bass.

Schön, D. (1991). *The reflective turn: Case studies in an educational practice*. New York: Teachers College Press.

Schön, D. (2000). *The reflective practitioner: How professionals think in action*. New York: Basic Books.

Schubert, W. (1986). *Curriculum: Perspective, paradigm, and possibility*. New York: Macmillan.

Sears, J. T. (1991). Educators, homosexuality and homosexual students: Are personal feelings related to professional beliefs? *Journal of Homosexuality, 22*.

Shade, B. J. (1982). Afro-American cognitive style: A variable in school success? *Review of Educational Research 52*(2), 219–238.

Sheuerer, D., and Parkay, F. W. (1992). The new Christian right and the public school curriculum: A Florida report. In J. B. Smith and J. G. Coleman, Jr. (Eds.), *School library media annual: 1992*, vol. 10. Englewood, CO: Libraries Unlimited.

Shulman, L. (1987, August). *Teaching alone, learning together: Needed agendas for the new reform*. Paper presented at the Conference on Restructuring Schooling for Quality Education, San Antonio.

Simpkins, S. (Spring 2003). Does youth participation in out-of-school time activities make a difference? *The evaluation exchange*, Vol. IX, No. 1. Harvard Graduate School of Education, Harvard Family Research Project (HFRP).

Singer, A. (1994, December). Reflections on multiculturalism. *Phi Delta Kappan*, 284–288.

Sizer, T. (1997a). *Horace's compromise: The dilemma of the American high school*, 3rd ed. Boston: Houghton Mifflin.

Sizer, T. (1997a). *Horace's school: Redesigning the American high school*. Boston: Houghton Mifflin.

Sizer, T. (1997b). *Horace's hope: What works for the American high school*. Boston: Houghton Mifflin.

Sizer, T., and Sizer, N. F. (1999). *The students are watching: Schools and the moral contract*. Boston: Beacon Press.

Sommers, C. H. (1994). *Who stole feminism? How women have betrayed women*. New York: Simon and Schuster.

Sommers, C. H. (1996, June 12). Where the boys are. *Education Week on the Web*.

Spring, J. (1990). *The American school 1642–1990*, 2nd ed. New York: Longman.

Spring, J. (1997). *The American school 1642–1996*, 4th ed. New York: McGraw-Hill.

Spring, J. (1998). *Conflict of interests: The politics of American education*, 3rd ed. Boston: McGraw-Hill.

Spring, J. (1999). *American education*, 8th ed. New York: McGraw-Hill.

Stover, D. (1992, March). The at-risk kids schools ignore. *The Executive Educator*, 28–31.

Sricharatchanya, P. (1996, November 5). Education reforms are also crucial. *Bangkok Post*.

Stanford, B. H. (1992). Gender equity in the classroom. In D. A. Byrnes and G. Kiger (Eds.), *Common bonds: Anti-bias teaching in a diverse society*. Wheaton, MD: Association for Childhood Education International.

Sue, D. W., and Sue, D. (1999). *Counseling the culturally different: Theory and practice*, 3rd ed. New York: John Wiley and Sons.

Swisher, K., and Deyhle, D. (1987). Styles of learning and learning styles: Educational conflicts for American Indian/Alaskan Native youth. *Journal of Multilingual and Multicultural Development, 8*, no. 4.

Sykes, G. (1983, October). Contradictions, ironies, and promises unfulfilled: A contemporary account of the status of teaching. *Phi Delta Kappan*, 87–93.

Teach for America. (2003). About us. New York: Author. (Retrieved from www.teachforamerica.org).

Tellijohann, S. K., and Price, J. H. (1993). A qualitative examination of adolescent homosexuals' life experiences: Ramifications for secondary school personnel. *Journal of Homosexuality, 26.*

Toffler, A. (1970). *Future shock.* New York: Random House.

Tozer, S. E., Violas, P. C., and Senese, G. (1993). *School and society: Educational practice as social expression.* New York: McGraw-Hill.

Trueba, H. T., Cheng, L. R. L., and Kenji, I. (1993). *Myth or reality: Adaptive strategies of Asian Americans in California.* Washington, DC: Falmer Press.

Ulich, R. (1950). *History of educational thought.* New York: American Book Company.

United Press International. (1998, November 15). *Teachers may soon make $100,000.*

Urban, W. J., and Wagoner, J. L. (2004). *American education: A history,* 3rd ed. Boston: McGraw-Hill.

Uribe, V., and Harbeck, K. M. (1991). Addressing the needs of lesbian, gay and bisexual youth. *Journal of Homosexuality, 22.*

U.S. Census Bureau. (1998). *Statistical abstract of the United States 1998.* Washington, DC: Author.

U.S. Census Bureau. (1999). *The Asian and Pacific Islander population in the United States: March 1997.* Washington, DC: Author.

U.S. Census Bureau. (2002). *The American Indian and Alaska Native population: 2000.* Washington, DC: U.S. Census Bureau.

U.S. Census Bureau. (2003). *Statistical abstract of the United States 2003.* Washington, DC: Author.

U.S. Department of Commerce, U.S. Census Bureau. (2000). *Current population survey* (CPS). Washington, DC: Author.

U.S. Department of Education. (1996). *Getting America's students ready for the 21st century: Meeting the technology literacy challenge.* Washington, DC: Author.

U.S. Department of Education. (1997). *From students of teaching to teachers of students.* Washington, DC: U.S. Department of Education.

U.S. Department of Education. (2001, July 27). *Ready to read, ready to learn* [news release]. Washington, DC: Author.

U.S. Department of Education. (2002). [Online]. Introduction: *No Child Left Behind.* Washington, DC: U.S. Department of Education. www.nclb.gov/next /overview/index.html [2003, May 22].

U.S. Department of Education and International Institute on Education. (1996). *A splintered vision: An investigation of U.S. science and mathematics education.* Washington, DC.

U.S. Department of Health and Human Services. (2002). *HHS Fact Sheet, February 26, 2002.* Washington, DC: Author.

U.S. Department of Labor. (2003). *Occupational Outlook Handbook, 2002–03 Edition,* Teachers—Preschool, Kindergarten, Elementary, Middle, and Secondary. Washington, DC: Author.

Valenza, J. K. (1997). Girls + technology = turnoff? *Technology Connections, 3.*

Waller, W. (1932). *The sociology of teaching.* New York: John Wiley.

Walling, D. R. (Ed.). (1994). *Teachers as leaders: Perspectives on the professional development of teachers.* Bloomington, IN: Phi Delta Kappa Educational Foundation.

Washington, W. (1998). Optional extended year program feedback. Austin Independent School District, TX, Department of Accountability, Student Services, and Research.

Webb, L. D., Metha, A., and Jordan, K. F. (1999). *Foundations of American education,* 3rd ed. Englewood Cliffs, NJ: Prentice Hall.

West, A. M. (1980). *The National Education Association: The power base for education.* New York: The Free Press.

Westbury, I. (1992). Comparing American and Japanese achievement: Is the United States really a low-achiever? *Educational Researcher, 21*(5).

Whalen, S. P. (2001). Emerging evidence from the evaluation of the Polk Bros. Foundation's full service schools institute. Chicago: University of Chicago Chapin Hall Center for Children at the University of Chicago.

Whitley, B. E. (1997). Gender differences in computer-related attitudes and behavior: A metaanalysis. *Computers in Human Behavior, 13.*

William Randolph Hearst Foundation. (1999). *United States Senate youth program survey.* San Francisco: Author.

Willig, A. C. (1987, Fall). Examining bilingual education research. *Review of Educational Research,* 363–376.

Willingham, W. W., and Cole, N. S. (1997). *Gender and fair assessment.* Mahwah, NJ: Lawrence Erlbaum.

Wilson, B. L., and Corbett, H. D. (2001). *Listening to urban kids: School reform and the teachers they want.* Albany, NY: State University of New York Press.

Wirt, F. M., and Kirst, M. W. (1997). *The political dynamics of American education.* Berkeley: McCutchan.

Wolfe, D. T., and Antinarella, J. (1997). *Deciding to lead: The English teacher as reformer.* Portsmouth, NH: Boynton Cook.

Wolk, R. A., and Rodman, B. H. (1994). *Classroom crusaders: Eleven teachers who are trying to change the system.* San Francisco: Jossey-Bass.

Woolfolk, A. E. (2001). *Educational psychology,* 8th ed. Boston: Allyn and Bacon.

Wray, H. (1999). Japanese and American education: Attitudes and practices. Westport, CT: Bergin and Garvey.

Young, C. (1999). *Ceasefire! Why women and men must join forces to achieve true equality.* New York: The Free Press.

Zehm, S. J., and Kottler, J. A. (1993). *On being a teacher: The human dimension.* Newbury Park, CA: Corwin Press.

Index

A

Academic goals
  defined, 8
  legislative action on, 8–10
Academies, private, historical role of, 99
Accelerated schools, 251
Accountability, of teachers, 46, 48–50
  demands for, 116
Action research, 245
  cycle of, 246
  as part of teaching, 246
Action Research Laboratory (Highland Park High School, IL), 246
Addams, Jane, 107–108
Adequate yearly progress, defined, 9
Adler, Mortimer, 88, 118
Administration, attitudes toward, 227
Affluent professional school, 17
African American Academy (Seattle), 139
African Americans
  in American population, 127
  in Colonial times, 97
  desegregation and resegregation, 136–139
  learning needs of, 139
  socioeconomic forces on, 136
  in teaching profession, 58–59
Afrocentric schools, 139
After-school programs, 203
Age of Reason, 91
Alaskan Natives
  cultural preservation by, 146
  historical, cultural, and socioeconomic forces on, 145
Alolouf, Helene, 235
Alternative schools, 16, 196
  school-within-a-school, 197
American Alliance for Health, Physical Education, Recreation and Dance, 258

American Alliance of Teachers of French, 258
American Association of Teachers of German, 258
American Association of Teachers of Spanish and Portuguese, 258
American Classical League, 258
American Council on the Teaching of Foreign Languages, 258–259
The American Dictionary, 101
American Federation of Teachers (AFT), 106, 229, 259
  focus of, 232
  membership in, 231–232
  objectives of, 231
  relations with NEA, 232–233
American Jewish Committee, 200
American Revolution, 98
American Spelling Book, 101
Ancient Greece, education in, 87–88, 90
Ancient Rome, education in, 90
Anderson, Sue, 189
Anglo-European Americans, 136
Anyon, Jean, 17
Anzar High School (San Juan Bautista, CA), 228
Aristotle, 8, 88, 90
Ashton-Warner, Sylvia, 115
Asian Americans and Pacific Islanders
  in American population, 142
  historical factors affecting, 142
  socioeconomic forces on, 142–143
  stereotypes about, 144
  subpopulations of, 142
  teacher concerns about, 143–144
Assessment
  of basic skills, 28
  international comparisons, 32–35
  of student learning, 70–71
Assimilation, through education, 12

Associated Colleges of the Midwest, multicultural programs at, 132
Association of American Educators, 259
Association for Childhood Education International, 259
Association for Supervision and Curriculum Development, 233–234, 259
At-risk students
  after-school care of, 202–203
  alternative education modalities for, 196–198
  books about, 208–209
  case studies of, 176, 181
  challenges for, 176
  community and family partnerships for, 198–204
  community schools for, 193–195
  compensatory education for, 196
  factors affecting, 172–173
  family needs assessment for, 210–211
  family-based stressors for, 180–182
  life settings of, 175
  mentor programs for, 200–201
  organizations to aid, 208
  out-of-school time activities for, 198
  peer counseling and mediation for, 192–193
  prevention programs for, 198–204
  remediation efforts for, 190–192
  social factors affecting, 176–180
  social services for, 203–204
  substance abuse and, 182–183
  violence and, 183–186
Austin, TX schools, Optional Extended Year programs of, 202
Authentic pedagogy, 30
Autonomy, teacher, 217–218
Ayers, William, 66